Mrs Duberly's War

Roger Fenton: *Henry Duberly Esqr., paymaster, 8th Hussars & Mrs Duberly*
'Henry's beard will astonish you – the old brute knew he was going to have his
picture taken – and stood all no how on purpose to spite me' (14 April 1855).

Mrs Duberly's War

Journal and Letters from the Crimea, 1854-6

FRANCES ISABELLA DUBERLY

Edited with introduction and notes by

CHRISTINE KELLY

OXFORD
UNIVERSITY PRESS

OXFORD

UNIVERSITY PRESS

Great Clarendon Street, Oxford ox2 6DP

Oxford University Press is a department of the University of Oxford.
It furthers the University's objective of excellence in research, scholarship,
and education by publishing worldwide in

Oxford New York

Auckland Cape Town Dar es Salaam Hong Kong Karachi
Kuala Lumpur Madrid Melbourne Mexico City Nairobi
New Delhi Shanghai Taipei Toronto

With offices in

Argentina Austria Brazil Chile Czech Republic France Greece
Guatemala Hungary Italy Japan Poland Portugal Singapore
South Korea Switzerland Thailand Turkey Ukraine Vietnam

Oxford is a registered trade mark of Oxford University Press
in the UK and in certain other countries

Published in the United States
by Oxford University Press Inc., New York

British Library Cataloguing in Publication Data
Data available

Library of Congress Cataloging in Publication Data
Data available

Typeset by RefineCatch Limited, Bungay, Suffolk
Printed in Great Britain
on acid-free paper by
Clays Ltd., St. Ives plc.

ISBN 978-0-19-920861-6

I

Contents

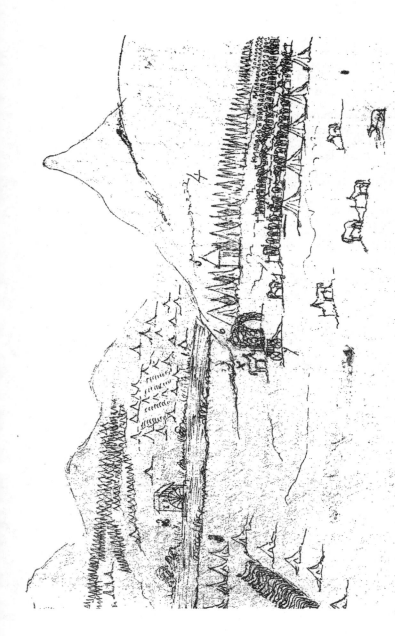

Fanny's sketch of the camp at Devna.

Fanny's sketch of the camp at Devna, sent to Selina on 11 July 1854: 'From it you will be better able to fancy how we live.' The key reads: '1. Infantry camp (7th, 19th, 23rd, 33rd Rifles); 2. River and water mill; 3. Heavy Cavalry camp (15th Dragoons, 1st Royal Enniskillings, Artillery – the tents to the right of Infantry are meant for Artillery and the strokes for the horse pickets; 4. Light Cavalry camp (8th, 11th, 13th, 17th); 5. Our square tent, 8 ft square; 6. My arbor; 7. My araba. The long lines are horses picketed. "Bob" and "Whisker" are behind the square tent out of sight – the araba pony is tied behind my bower, and the line underneath three horses are Henry's big Grey and 2 grey ponies – the office pony is not visible.'

Fanny's sketch of her living quarters in the camp of the Light Cavalry, where she moved in March 1855 after a winter on shipboard. 'My garden is quite gay, with iris and violets.' (See over page)

Fanny's sketch of her living quarters in the camp of the Light Cavalry.

Maps and Illustrations

NOTES ON ENDPAPERS

Charge of the Light Brigade

The Charge of the Light Brigade, showing (red) the direction of the British attack led by Lord Cardigan through the North Valley. The Russians (green) have seized the Fedukine Hills to the north and most of the Woronzov Causeway to the south, where the Redoubts (fortified strongpoints) are marked. Captain Nolan is shown veering towards the south, Lord Lucan less sharply. (From A.W. Kinglake, *The Invasion of the Crimea*, 1863-87)

Fanny Duberly's sketchmap of the Disposition of the armies before Sebastopol

'I sent you a map of the situation of batteries and the position of the forces' (Fanny to Selina, 20 November 1854); she also sent 'a more splendiferous one' to the Queen. Sebastopol is shown with the Round Tower and the Redan, the battlefield of Inkerman on the right. However Fanny's map, which was drawn from her own observations after riding over the ground, is slightly misleading. She places the Sapoune Heights, from where Lord Raglan directed the battle of Balaclava, and the Causeway Heights, with the adjacent north and south valleys, to the east of Balaclava. In addition she draws the two valleys running diagonally from the north-west to the south east. On the ground the Sapoune Heights and Chersonese Uplands are slightly to the west of Balaclava and the valleys with the Causeway Heights between them run from west to east.

The spot where Henry and Fanny watched the two cavalry charges is marked on the map with a cross next to 'Batteries'. From this, and her description of events during the day, it would seem that she was not standing near Raglan and his staff but some distance away, possibly near the uncompleted, unmanned 6th redoubt which was on the western end of the Causeway Heights. On her map, the charge of the Heavy Brigade is marked to the south-west of her vantage point and the position of the Light Brigade, just before their charge, is shown directly north-east from where Henry and she watched.

EDITOR'S INTRODUCTION

I

For the past one hundred and fifty years mingled memories and myths have endured from the Crimean War – the heroic seizing of the Alma heights, the tragic Charge of the Light Brigade, the courage of the soldiers at Inkerman struggling in the fog, the cruel winter when men starved in rags and were issued with left-footed boots only. In among these scenes, the pretty but hard-hearted Fanny Duberly, nicknamed Mrs Jubilee, flirts her way through the army, twisting the susceptible men of influence to her bidding and conducting an affair with Lord Cardigan, while shocking the more serious officers by her outspoken, unwomanly behaviour. This particular myth faded briefly during the early twentieth century, when Henty-like boys' novels such as *Blair of Balaclava* presumed that all English ladies were of unassailable virtue, but was revived in the 1960s in *Flash for Freedom!*, the memoirs of Flashman (Tom Brown's tormentor), 'edited' by George Macdonald Fraser, in which the hero's lascivious flirtation with Fanny is fortuitously cut short when he is expelled from her brother's house for, apparently, cheating at cards. The mythical Fanny Duberly is seen at her most vulgar in the 1968 film *The Charge of the Light Brigade*, where she is portrayed as the raucous, randy mistress of Lord Cardigan, cavorting aboard his yacht while her compliant husband Henry slinks away, but the rumours which led to this entertaining travesty had begun even before the original Charge took place.

Letters home from the Crimea are frequently hostile. Captain Fred Dallas of the 46th regiment was not alone in his views, though more outspoken than many, when he wrote to his family in January 1855,

I am sorry to hear that Mrs Duberly is a friend of Susan's as she is a female of whom I have the greatest horror. . . . Almost the last time I saw her, she was quietly looking through a Lorgnette, at the whole of her regiment being blown to pieces at the dreadful Balaclava affair by the Russian guns, (and if scandal speak truly) a lover of hers being one of the first killed. We were there, sad spectators of it on duty, what she was there for, Heaven knows! What a mistake women make thinking to excite men's admiration by not being womanly.

But Fanny's close circle of male friends certainly thought her womanly. Both her journal and her letters contain numerous instances of young men presenting her with small tokens of their admiration – bunches of wild flowers, exotic feathers to trim her hat – but they also reveal her intense devotion to Henry and show that 'what she was there for' was to ensure Henry's survival. She was convinced he would not survive without her by his side. She was also determined to forward his career and, if possible, to make some money by publishing her journal. But its appearance in December 1855 only added to the antipathy that some had towards her. While many readers admired her courage and appreciated her descriptions of the hardship they or their relatives had been through, others misinterpreted her stoicism as insensitive gloating over the sufferings of the men around her and disapproved of her lack of reticence, whether describing 'strange exultation' at facing death after the explosion on board a powder ship at Balaclava or the relish with which she drank a bottle of beer. The gossip and criticism upset Fanny deeply.

Frances Isabella Duberly was born on 27 September 1829, the youngest, by several years, of the nine children of Wadham Locke, Esq. of Rowdeford House, a large wooded estate near Devizes, Wiltshire. He was the senior partner in the Devizes banking firm of Locke, Hughes & Co. A man of influence, he was deputy-lieutenant and high sheriff of Wiltshire and in 1832 was elected MP for Devizes but died unexpectedly, three years later, at the age of 56. In September 1802 he had married Anna Maria Selina Powell and they had three sons and six daughters. By the time of his death his eldest son, also Wadham, had already married and lived nearby with his family, so for the time being Mrs Locke and her daughters continued to live at Rowdeford. The other two sons had also left home, one to join the East India Company in Bengal.

Fanny's early childhood seems to have been a happy time. As very much the youngest she was probably spoilt by her elder sisters Selina, Elizabeth, Anne, Louisa, and Katherine (known as Katy). At first she was educated at home by governesses – an experience she appears not to have enjoyed, since years later she wrote to Selina, 'I am sorry for you, now you are obliged to admit a governess into your house. I have such dreadful recollections of the vulgarity & ill-temper of many of my own, that I would almost as soon have the small pox in the house.'

Her childhood was brought to an abrupt end with her mother's death in July 1838, when Fanny was only nine. The shock must have been severe, and as late as 1855 she still recorded the anniversary in her journal. Rowdeford House was closed up and Wadham took on the responsibility of his younger sisters' welfare (Selina and Anne were already married). While her elder sisters were engaged in the only employment open to them, the serious task of finding suitable husbands, Fanny was sent to school in Wycombe. It is impossible to tell how extensive her education was but she acquired all the attributes expected of a young lady – she embroidered and sewed, played the piano and sang well, and spoke French so fluently that she later became a favourite with the French generals. She had a lively mind and an interest in her surroundings that meant she read widely about every place she visited, and her letters regularly mention the books she has enjoyed.

After leaving Wycombe, Fanny continued to live with her brother but seems to have been happiest during her visits to

Arle Bury House in Hampshire, the home of her eldest sister Selina, who had been widowed young and was now married to Francis Marx, a young Tory landowner with political and journalistic ambitions. Whenever Fanny was homesick or ill it was to Arle Bury that she longed to return. Meanwhile her brother Wadham's first wife had died and in 1844 he too had remarried. The Locke sisters may well have felt uncomfortable in this new establishment. Two further marriages took place soon after; in 1845 Louisa became Mrs William Colquhoun of Clashick in Perthshire, and a year later the wedding of Katherine Locke and Major George Duberly of the 64th Regiment was celebrated at Cleve. This latter occasion may have been the first time that Fanny, then aged seventeen, met George's youngest brother, Henry, who was twenty-four.

The two brothers were the eldest and youngest of the four children, three sons and a daughter, of Sir James Duberly, knight, and his second wife, Etheldred. Sir James, whose main residence was Gaines Hall in Huntingdon, had also purchased other estates but on his death in 1832 seems to have left them all to James, his only son from his first marriage, bequeathing his other children only a modest annual allowance. The younger James had eight children to support, so that he had little to offer by the time his youngest half-brother needed additional financial help. He had already provided for all his brothers: George had an army commission, the middle brother was Rector of a family living at Wolsingham, and in 1839 James had purchased a commission for Henry as ensign in the 32nd regiment, followed some two years later by a lieutenant's commission in the same regiment.

At this date it was still necessary for an army officer to buy his commission, first to enter a regiment and then to gain promotion. Substantial sums were expended; Lord Cardigan had paid £40,000 some ten years earlier to become colonel of the 11th Hussars, an extremely fashionable cavalry regiment, but most young gentlemen started with a more junior rank and bought their way up to such seniority as and when they had the means. A commission was seen as an investment and was sold on retirement; a smart Guards or Cavalry regiment commission cost a great deal more than a regiment of the line such as the 64th or 32nd. In addition to these costs, an officer needed a private income (estimated at a minimum of £150 a year in the infantry and £700 in the cavalry), not just to buy his expensive uniforms and his horses but also to live in the comfortable style expected in the mess. Promotion through the death or retirement of a senior officer was rare except during active service, which was usually only found in India. For a relatively impoverished young officer like Henry, a posting to India was the only way to make a career, but Indian officers were often sneered at as social inferiors by the rest of the army; they were professionals rather than gentlemen, and their practical experience went unappreciated.

In the spring of 1846, the 32nd were ordered to India. Henry did not regard this as an agreeable prospect; Fanny's letters reveal his nagging worries about his health and, in addition to the hardships and danger of active service in India, there was always the possibility of contracting a fatal or disabling disease. Unable to follow other reluctant officers and exchange his commission for a similar rank in a regiment remaining in England or Ireland, which would have involved a further payment, he left the 32nd on half-pay and began to study for the Paymaster branch of the army. This had several advantages: at every rank he would earn twice as much as the duty officers and he would be promoted to each ensuring seniority without purchase, up to the rank of colonel. The Paymaster of a regiment was a non-combatant who did the bookkeeping and ensured that both men and bills were paid (a peaceful occupation which seems to have suited Henry very well), but it was essential to join a smart regiment since it was regarded as a poor man's job and, as such, often deemed socially inferior. A year after his brother's wedding, in November 1847, Henry became Paymaster to the 8th Royal Irish Hussars, a light-cavalry regiment, thus achieving the respectability so necessary to Fanny's ambitions. His subsequent rise was far from meteoric, and when the warrant for his majority finally arrived in 1860 Fanny wrote:

Poor Henry – he has gone through enough for his bit of promotion, I am sure! & waited long enough for it. ... It is very satisfactory ... Heneage, who always used to try & annoy Henry by addressing him as Paymaster Duberly will have to put 'Major' now. It gives us position. ... I can see that Henry is very pleased – though undemonstrative as usual.

By then they had been married for ten years. The wedding had taken place at Arlesford in the spring of 1850, conducted by the vicar Henry Paddon, Fanny's brother-in-law, who had married her sister Anne ten years earlier. Though in many ways an unlikely couple, Fanny and Henry were clearly devoted to one another and his placidity, which both annoyed and amused her, was probably essential for her restless nature. Theirs was evidently a love match, but one based more on comfort and companionship than great passion and romance. Fanny had grown up within the restricted social life of Wiltshire, with few chances of meeting eligible young men, and from the age of nine she had been an additional rather than integral part of the household she lived in. By the time she was twenty she no doubt yearned for the independence of her own household and Henry, resplendent in his cavalry uniform, must have looked dashing, even if he was not a dashing character. She was certainly amazed by her own audacity and six years later wrote to Selina:

I am the last person in all the world who should give an opinion [on the intended marriage of a friend] as nobody could possibly have married more rashly than I did, and because I happened to make a lucky hit it is no reason everybody else should, or that she should not.

As an exceptionally skilled horsewoman, life as a cavalry officer's wife suited Fanny perfectly. And, as a woman who preferred the company of men, she could remain faithful to Henry while enjoying herself and keeping his interests, both social and professional, in mind. Her plans for Henry's future career, which was the only career open to her, are a constant refrain in her letters. In December 1855, referring once more to her friend's prospects, she extolled the advantages of army life.

Penelope ought to catch one of the Heroes who go home, isn't she in the way of meeting any? In these days of rapid promotion & pay, it is not half a bad spec: marrying into the army. Fancy if I had married James Daubeny with his red hair & freckles & boundless good humour & good heart – I should have been Mrs Colonel now. Not but what I think I shall manoeuvre out of this with gain, & keep half pay, & get a Majority in the Militia at home – & if I do I shall think myself rather a clever card. But it is early days to talk about anything yet . . . .

Three months later, however, the strains of living in a small Turkish town with no European company but that of soldiers had taken its toll. Fanny and Henry considered abandoning army life:

I hardly know what place to try for for Henry. Paymaster of a district is only £350 – and a horse. He would far rather have some civilian appointment – What I don't know, but there must be plenty and with better pay. However at present this is 'counting ones chickens &c.'

She returns to her appraisal of marriage with advice reminiscent of Jane Austen: 'I don't advise a marriage under £1000 a year – Rich in each other's love wants a deal of mutual amiability.'

The search for this elusive £1,000 a year was a constant spur to Fanny's ambitions. When her friend Lord Augustus Vane returned to England in October 1855, he 'asked if there was anything he could execute besides a lot of minor commissions. I told him yes – an Appointment of, or worth, £600 for Henry – you should never turn away a chance you know – and I am heartily sick of all this life.' Between them, Henry and Fanny had private means of approximately £470 a year (£30 of which were Fanny's 'dibs'), so that they depended on his salary, unlike most of the officers she mentions in her letters and journal. It was only during their time in the Crimea that they were on a par with those around them, since expenses were low and everyone suffered similar privation. But Heneage, Portal, Killeen, Chetwode, Poulett Somerset and others all had an income independent of the army and would be going home to inherit, if not a title, then certainly a landed estate. Henry's patrimony was tied up on his commission; they were poor gentry in a regiment that contained many 'swells'.

But for the most part Fanny, with her boundless energy, and Henry, with his placid acceptance of her plans, did not allow these financial problems to weigh them down; they enjoyed themselves and ran into debt when necessary. A letter, written on her return from a house-party on 4 January 1852, describes the pleasures of their life. They had gone to a dinner and danced the New Year in, attended a meet the next morning, 'one of the prettiest I ever remember to have seen' and then

The ball in the evening I enjoyed excessively. ... I danced a good deal with John Piper who is exactly as great a flirt as ever. Bob Pearce very kindly mounted Henry in the morning so I danced twice with him. ... The day after the ball Bob Pearce's harriers met at Haddington at eleven & Penelope & Dora & I went on foot ... *They* [those on horseback] had no sport but I had as we kept up on foot and I had to tuck up my petticoats & run like a Briton to see anything of it ...

A second letter, written in August of the same year, explains why she later felt free to accompany Henry to the east – only two years into her marriage she was certain that she would have no children. There is no hint in any of her letters as to why this was so; whether she had had an earlier miscarriage or a confinement and stillbirth leaving her incapable of conceiving, or whether either Henry or she were infertile, it is impossible to say. The same letter also shows how wearying she found the circumscribed life of the peacetime army.

I called today on Mrs Charlton who was out driving. I saw her only for a moment as she has hardly been confined three weeks. She looks very pale & pretty, & I am so glad I ain't going to have any children as it would kill me first of all & worry me to death afterwards. ... Pray write. What <u>can</u> I have to say? I am working a cushion and generally quarrel with Henry once a day, for my temper is <u>execrable</u>. Henry has a slight attack of Cholera & the cat had a fit yesterday. We thought she was going mad.

By the time war against Russia was declared in March 1854, Fanny was ready for a wider field of action.

II

The Roger Fenton photograph of Mrs Henry Duberly on her horse Bob, with her husband standing nonchalantly beside them, is one of the enduring images of the Crimean War; the only officer's wife to remain for the whole of the conflict, her presence there seems as inevitable as the Highland Brigade or the siege guns. But in fact her situation was precarious; she was there through her own determination and ingenuity and against the express orders of the commander-in-chief Lord Raglan. Disguised in an old feather boa and shawl, and joshing with the sailors, she had smuggled herself on board ship at Varna – slipping past Lord Lucan, the commander of the cavalry division, while he 'scanned every woman, to find traces of a lady; but he searched in vain.' During the voyage to Kalamita Bay Lord Cardigan, who enjoyed the company of a pretty, witty woman and the chance to annoy his brother-in-law Lucan in equal measure, made himself her protector and by the time Fanny arrived at Balaclava she had acquired a coterie of devoted admirers determined to help her. She was to remain reliant on such help throughout the siege.

After the intensity of the first few weeks in the Crimea – the toil of landing the troops and guns, and the battles of the Alma, Balaclava and Inkerman – the army settled into monotonous months of siege work and the struggle to survive the bitter winter. For the officers, a parody of their former sophisticated social life emerged in the midst of these hardships; groups of them huddled together in draughty tents to share their limited supplies of fuel and food or, if they were more fortunate, accepted invitations to dine on board the ships moored at Balaclava. Fanny and Henry's cabin became the centre for a lively crowd.

Men who come down cold, cross and ill go away cheered and refreshed – or when I am <u>savage</u> as I often am – half a dozen noisy men, playing at leapfrog – walking on their hands, up to every imaginable fun – are sure to make me laugh myself into a good humour (p. 131).

In this circumscribed society Fanny met everyone of interest. A young, attractive, married woman, surrounded by men lacking female companionship, had a natural advantage as a popular guest and successful hostess. But there was more to Fanny's success than her flaxen curls: her intelligence, sense of fun and love of word play, apparent in her letters and journal, made her a welcome addition to any gathering. Her lively repartee and engaged intelligence are glimpsed in her description of an evening on board the *Agamemnon* with Sir Edmund Lyons (who, like many others, invited her to dine immediately they were introduced), when she teased Layard about his discoveries at Nineveh (p. 81).

During the winter, while she lived on board ship (where she paid her own way), all was well, but difficulties arose once she wanted to join Henry on shore. No official provision of any kind was available to her and Raglan, understandably, refused her request for a house. She benefited, however, from the collapse of the military administration around her; friends purloined everything required to build her a hut, and Poulett Somerset, one of Raglan's ADCs, even provided coal from headquarters to heat it. In this hut, and the little marquee set up next to it, she gave dinners for many of the important men of the campaign, while her friends came there to relax whenever they could escape from their military duties.

At heart, Fanny was an adventurer and for a brief time she experienced an independence that few Victorian women ever achieved. Despite the hard life and the tragedies around her, which upset her deeply, she revelled in the freedom she had found to 'go where you like, do what you like, say what you like and have such heaps of friends', and in the 'intelligent or quick-witted conversations' she had with them. Although she enjoyed the admiration of these men, repeating their compliments in her letters to Selina, and continuing to pay close attention to her looks and the planning of her wardrobe by sending home detailed requests for skin lotions, dress material and hat trimmings, she avoided the roles of outrageous minx or sultry siren. A flirtatious tomboy, 'fishing for sprats out of my cabin window, or larking over fences with some of the wildest hands in England', she lived a spartan life that startled many of the men in the Crimea and would have shocked most of the women she knew in England. Her courage and endurance were ignored by those who condemned her unconventional ways (particularly her practice of wearing trousers), and misconstrued her easy friendships with men like Nolan or Poulett Somerset; she confessed later that she was driven mad by the lies that were told of her. But appreciative newspaper reports, describing her as the 'Heroine of the Crimea' and a 'Stout-hearted Lady', ensured that she remained an object of romantic fascination to those in England. Sisters wrote eagerly for news of her to their brothers, whose replies were often critical. Solemn young men who had never met her, embarrassed by the sight of her trousers, gave the impression that she went round dressed like a drummer-boy. Fanny was horrified when a family friend wanted 'to know if I ride over the Battlefields (like a ghoul) in <u>man's</u> clothes!!' In fact the trousers, worn under her habit skirt, were the most practical solution to the mud and cold (see her sketch, p. 139) and more modest than a draggle of wet petticoats lifted above the knee.

Despite the hardships and the criticisms, Fanny dreaded returning home. 'I shall be a sort of Bashi-Basouk when I get home – defiant of all laws conventional or fashionable – and then how the women will fall upon me like vultures over a mortally wounded man', and feared she would suffocate in 'all the artificial muslin rags, conventionalities and slanders – the Fashions and the heart-grindings of English sociality.' The formalities of Victorian social life surrounded a lady like a corset, shaping her behaviour and allowing little spontaneity, and Fanny, who continued to lace herself into her stays (specially padded at the ends to prevent chafing) even when wearing the notorious trousers, was unable to ignore these social conventions. Always nervous of her social standing, there was a tension at the centre of her life that made her vulnerable to perceived snubs and criticism. Some years later she wrote to Selina

The <u>great</u> mistake in this world is making hasty or promiscuous acquaintances. ... You, who have an ascertained position can of course afford to a certain extent to know who you like. I, who am a waif & stray, cannot afford to employ any but the best trades people, or to know any but the best people of those among whom I am thrown. For the rest there is no mercy & no appeal (5 April 1860).

Hence her outrage at being invited to join the Commissariat wives, the 'ladies of Kamiesh' as she ironically nicknamed them, and her annoyance at the recently arrived 'dowdy Mrs Forrest', wife of a Major in the 4th Dragoons, whose 'immaculate virtue has not allowed her to return my call!!! Very possibly if she has an opera glass she sees all sorts of swell people in my tent half the day & thinks I keep too good company for my station.' Fanny was well aware that not all this aristocratic company would include her in their intimate social set once they were back in England.

This was emphasised when Lord George Paget's wife Agnes visited him during the summer of 1855, with a glamorous party that included Lord Stratford, the British Ambassador to Turkey. Lord George had been a part of Fanny's select circle (which also included all Raglan's ADCs), joining her picnic parties to the Monastery of St George, and had even promised to find the little dog she wanted to complete her household. Lady Agnes, however, did not accept Fanny into her select circle. The Duberlys were never included in the Pagets' many picnic parties, a palpable snub when there were still so few ladies around, and there is no mention of a meeting in the letters or the journal. Fanny, who dearly loved a Lady, and believed 'it's no good knowing swell men, unless you have the women too', did not openly complain to Selina about these slights. Instead, she made sharp remarks about the tepid state of the Pagets' marriage and Lady Agnes's inability to ride. Her pique was all the greater when two of the most influential men of her acquaintance fell under the newcomer's spell. Raglan, who had been invisible during the earlier months of the siege, spent time squiring Lady Agnes around and frequently invited her to dinner at Headquarters, a compliment that Fanny, in her anomalous situation, had never received. And Roger Fenton (p. 312) described her as the Belle of the Crimea, a role that Fanny surely felt belonged to her. After Agnes had departed, Lord George no longer appeared on Fanny's guest list and she took her revenge by commenting on 'his sour face & boring ways.'

Fanny's resentment was not reserved for Lady Agnes alone. During the summer of 1855 other army wives arrived in the Crimea and Fanny, who had convinced herself she would receive the Crimean medal for being present throughout the campaign, blamed their arrival for the withholding of this honour – she was no longer the only officer's wife in attendance. Even worse, she found no kindred spirit among the newcomers. She decided that her neighbour Mrs Forrest was a 'stupid little ass.' Poor Annie Forrest found camp life difficult and she lacked Fanny's skill in managing those around her. Although their situations were very similar, her failure was in sharp contrast to Fanny's cheerful survival. The Forrests had the sole use of a tent and a marquee together with half of a hut. The other half was occupied fulltime by the colonel of the 4th Dragoons, Edward Hodge, who felt the army was no place for a lady. His diary and letters, which include passing criticisms of Fanny, are a continuous commentary of complaints about Annie's behaviour. 'That horrid Mrs Forrest' sponged on him for her food, living off his rations, and drove him from the hut by her infernal cackle and 'screaming in her vulgar way' at the cook. Worst of all, she had no maid, only a 'great he-dragoon' who was seen 'picking the fleas out of Mrs F's drawers, after which he hung them out to air.' Annie Forrest, meanwhile, was growing thinner and 'was never so hungry' before.

During the heat of the summer, even Fanny temporarily lost her energy and optimism; exhausted and ill after a year of inadequate food and primitive accommodation she pondered, 'If you couldn't cleave your way like a hatchet out here – I wonder where you'd be? Trampled in your grave long enough ago.' And she complained to Selina, 'this world is no place for women – at least for ladies – it is only fit for men – and women who have <u>no</u> self respect' – a failing she observed in most of the women around her. She criticised them every bit as sharply as she had been criticised.

I tell you these soldiers wives from the dirtiest private's wife to the Colonel's wife – are all unlike any other woman. They said that Mrs Handcock didn't care in the least when her husband was killed in the Redan. I don't know – I didn't like her goings on before so did not call on her. ... And once I was in the Piquet house, watching a bombardment – & heard a giggle & found a very merry little lady flirting, & gossiping & jabbering like a cageful of magpies – while her husband was down in the advanced parallel well exposed to a heavy fire and as black as a powder monkey, he was afterwards wounded. These are a few stories by the way. Can you wonder at the abhorrent shrinking that I feel from all women ... [except those few] ... whom I know to be good Xtian women & whom I love & honor as such (6 Feb 1856).

For Fanny the natural order of things was to be both a Christian and a gentlewoman; a lady's behaviour should be based on Christian virtues. Convinced of the benign working of Providence, her belief that 'God never puts people in situations where he doesn't help them through, if they will only trust him' gave her the determination to survive the dangers and hardships that faced her.

Fanny never mentions in her published Journal the other 'Heroines' of the war, Florence Nightingale and Mary Seacole, although she makes sharp comments about the former in her letters and indulged in camp gossip of the kind that made her angry when directed at her. 'I suppose you know that Miss Nightingale is going to marry a pillbox!! A Dr McGregor. Henry used to know him & says he is one of the greatest ruffians in the service. He pretends to have a good turn just now.' Dr Alexander McGregor, who died of cholera the following November, seems to have been the only doctor at Scutari to have welcomed Florence Nightingale and her nurses and make full use of their help, working with her to introduce essential reforms. She reciprocated by ensuring his promotion over more senior colleagues, so provoking the unlikely rumour that they were engaged. In fact she had no time for romance – for herself or for her nurses.

Fanny may have viewed her as a rival for the public's esteem and felt jealous of her achievements even though she genuinely disapproved of ladies nursing, or even visiting the men's wards. She knew from her own experience with the cavalry's overcrowded hospital tents that 'soldiers are never sparing in their indecencies or their remarks.' Although she never set foot in the hospitals, Fanny played her part by writing letters home for sick and wounded officers, or by sending consolation and mementoes to comfort bereaved families. Poignant glimpses of this aspect of her life appear in her letters. On 6 February 1856 she described a husband lying wounded after Inkerman.

Our surgeon attended him (I think his leg was shot away & he wouldn't have it amputated), but at any rate, our surgeon said he must die anyhow – [he] wouldn't believe it – and I remember waiting outside his tent doors to know if he would like me to write to his wife, or if I could do anything for him. He said – No – he would write himself tomorrow – as a strange handwriting might alarm his wife unnecessarily – he didn't see tomorrow – he died in the night.

Although she willingly took on these duties, she must have felt overshadowed by Florence Nightingale's fame, unaware that she was comparing herself to one of the greatest social reformers of her generation. Her irritation is apparent in her response to a letter of praise after the publication of her journal:

Francie's letter ... makes me feel so sincerely ashamed of myself. If Francie knew me as well as I know myself he would think that much praise – given to me – was preposterous. If I had been the whole of Miss Nightingale's staff condensed I could not have had higher praise. They deserve it – I do not.

Miss N. has had her full share of praises. The nurses who had all the drudgery and hard work & especially the Catholic Sisters of Mercy have not had anything approaching to their share. When I think how almost absolutely useless I have been as far as relieving and comforting go – I am astonished at a Providence that allows such praise as I have had to Shower down upon me. It is a subject on which I feel I cannot write much. It forces one, not into words, but into self examination, deprecation, & a silent wonder. For many reasons I was prevented any personal attendance on the sick. Almost all the good, if I have done any, has been by indirect means, & by endeavouring by example, to keep up the courage in men's hearts when they were all suffering sorely (26 March 1856).

Originally the hospital conditions at Balaclava were worse even than those at Scutari. Florence Nightingale would not allow her nurses to enter the undisciplined regimental hospitals and she grew alarmed when some of them moved to the Balaclava hospital. However, when in May 1855 she visited Balaclava to check on their progress, the situation had improved and she was fêted by grateful soldiers who followed her around, cheering. But even this triumph could not save her from breakdown and within a few days, exhausted from months of overwork, she fell ill with fever and spent two weeks recuperating before returning to Scutari. One of the consequences of this was that when Fanny called on her she was too ill to see her, so history is deprived of what would have been a fascinating meeting of two strong-willed but very different women.

There was never any possibility that Fanny and Mary Seacole could have met socially. Yet they had interests in common – though Fanny would have been horrified at such a suggestion and Mary Seacole would probably have laughed at the idea. Both were interested in homeopathic medicine and both provided a place of comfort and refuge from the horrors of war for the homesick men around them. Mary's establishment at Spring Hill, the British Hotel, sold food and drink as well as providing medical care (p. 323). And during the desperate, early months of 1855, when the quayside at Balaclava was covered with wounded men waiting to be transported to Scutari, each in their own way attempted to alleviate the hardships of the men around them – Mary with her practical help to the wounded, Fanny by writing scathing descriptions of the scene and sending them home to be published anonymously in the newspapers (p. 290, note 40).

However, even before Mary Seacole arrived, Fanny also did what she could to help in a practical way. At the end of January she wrote to Selina – 'If there is another row, I shan't go up to it without my little keg of brandy that lord Geo. Paulet gave me – last time I had none – & it is very useful for fainting and wounded men. It slings over my shoulder with a strap'. Fanny was prevented from meeting Mary through social rather than racial prejudice; she later dined happily with the Pasha's wife in the harem in Ismid and was the guest of a Maharajah's mother in India. The men she knew might visit the British Hotel at any time but, despite the fact that neither 'drunkenness among the men, nor gambling among the officers' was permitted, it was impossible for Fanny to enter what was in effect a tavern or to consort with the owner.

If occasionally Fanny felt despondent and 'conscious of having done so little good in any way out here, that it is a matter of more shame than praise' her natural optimism soon revived and she enjoyed her unconventional life – 'if I do have to make my own bed & wash my own clothes and scrub my floor in the morning – in the afternoon I can ride any one of four horses or anybody elses I please, & be as free as the winds of heaven'.

III

A Journal kept during the Russian War – From the Departure of the Army from England in April 1854, *to the Fall of Sebastopol* by Mrs Henry Duberly was first published in December 1855 and sold so successfully that a second edition appeared the following spring. It has not been republished since, although a few entries have been quoted so frequently that they are part of the general knowledge of anyone who has read anything on what is now known as the Crimean War. Fanny's Journal, ending as it does with the fall of Sebastopol, makes a well-shaped narrative. It also contributed to the popular view of the Crimean War – the three hard-fought battles of Alma, Balaclava and Inkerman (after which many a street and pub are named), a long siege through a harsh winter and the surrender of Sebastopol after the disastrous British losses in the Redan. The remaining seven months of stalemate and boredom in the Crimea, while the final defeat of Russia took place in the Baltic and on the further fringes of the Black Sea, have slipped from the national memory.

Throughout the war there was a stream of reports from the Crimea by William Howard Russell to the *Times* (pp. 321) and, less frequently, by other newspaper correspondents. These were reinforced by the hundreds of uncensored private letters sent home by combatants of all ranks describing, and often complaining about, the events as they unfolded. Many of these were published in local and national newspapers. Very little was reported back from the Baltic on the naval blockade of Russia that had such a terrible effect on her economy and morale; after the initial success at Bomarsund there was little of drama to report. But even before the war had ended both Russell and Fanny Duberly had published their accounts of events in the Crimea up to the fall of Sebastopol. This localised view was further reinforced by A. W. Kinglake's eight-volume work *The Invasion of the Crimea*, published between 1863 and 1887. More recent works, written during the last fifteen years, have begun to redress the misconception that the theatre of war was centred entirely on Sebastopol.

The text of this new edition of Fanny Duberly's Journal is taken from the first, 1855, edition – the only omissions being short mottos at the start of each chapter which were not chosen by Fanny, and most of which she did not see until the Journal was finally published. Interwoven with the original text are extracts from the many letters she wrote home to her sister Selina and brother-in-law Francis Marx. For the sake of clarity, these are printed in italics to differentiate them from the Journal.

Fanny's statement in her Preface, 'When this Journal was first commenced I had no intention whatever of publishing it', is disingenuous – she mentions her plans to do so in a letter of 28 August 1854, well before the army arrived in the Crimea. She had already had a letter published in the *Observer* and now hoped to make some money in the only way she could. It was a genuine journal, reflecting her moods and the current gossip of the camp, but the knowledge that she intended to publish it meant that she did not include everything she would have liked to report.

The first part of her Journal, which eventually became the first five chapters (six in this edition), was sent to Selina on 2 July 1855 in the care of a friend because so many letters home had gone astray. Francie, her brother–in–law Francis Marx, undertook to be her editor and Fanny deferred to his taste and opinions throughout the whole editorial process. Without reference to the original manuscript, which has vanished, it is impossible to tell how far he reworked the Journal. Fanny certainly trusted him completely – 'I am troublesome I know. But I have no hope but in you. Scratch out or put in whatever you like – & don't leave my poor book in the lurch.' She was by this time very ill, unable to leave her bed for days at a time, which would partly account for her unusual meekness. She was also very nervous about her skills as an author and at times she lost confidence. Referring to 'that detestable Journal' she scrawled a note to Francis, 'do just as you please, I don't care a jot what becomes of it'; but at heart she cared deeply and confessed 'that I watch the hatching of this chick as anxiously as ever a hen did – and I am most truly grateful to you for your trouble.'

At the end of September, Fanny sent home further pages, which became the final chapter. She believed them to be 'incomparably better written than the first part. I have taken

Selina's hint and made it more like my letters, & taking in two or three days at a time. Lord Raglan & all that set being gone I can express myself more freely & say what I like without fear of forging a thunderbolt for my own head.'

Unfortunately, the change of structure that Selina and Francis had urged on her was not wholly successful, in part perhaps because she had become bored – 'since I knew I was to publish, the book has been a task instead of a pleasure' – but largely because the strong narrative of the earlier sections of the Journal is lost at times in a discursive mode which does not, in practice, have the same energy as her letters. Although it contains some vivid descriptive passages, there is an air of listless confusion about some later sections of this chapter.

This mattered less for her original audience because they would have read the Journal only two or three months after it was written, but for a modern reader it is impossible to know what is going on unless one already has a sure grasp of the sequence of events. The fall of Sebastopol is not mentioned until three or four days after it had happened, leaving the reader floundering. When she wrote these pages Fanny was probably still in shock after the death of her dear childhood friend, John Buckley, two days before the final offensive. This was the culmination of the loss of many of her friends and acquaintances and was followed immediately by the carnage during the storming of the Redan. Fanny's letters provide a comprehensive account of events.

Admirers of Fanny's Journal will find her letters a compelling supplement to her text. Indeed, they have an immediacy and liveliness that is not always apparent in the published Journal (though they may have been present in the original), and are more outspoken, funnier, angrier, and less beset with purple passages. Above all, they are a running conversation with her favourite sister, and, as in any conversation with an intimate friend, mix tragic and serious

moments with inconsequential, selfish matters. Read alongside her Journal they provide an intimate counterpoint to
her public statements, and the extracts published here have
been chosen to amplify the appropriate entries in the
Journal, and to reveal her private character.

Fanny's letters were often written over several days, and she
switches from subject to subject as mood and memory strike
her. She will return to a topic, often just with a brief comment
or aside, several pages, and sometimes days, later so that they
cannot always be placed as an entity within the text of the
Journal. They have therefore been arranged so that her
comments and speculations on one particular idea or event
can be read as a whole, but it is always made clear when this
has been done. Fanny's own spelling, such as 'honor' and
'harbor', is left unchanged but minor corrections in punctua-
tion have been made to aid comprehension and avoid
ambiguity, and her characteristic and enthusiastic use of !!!s
has been retained.

Fanny was determined to obtain permission to dedicate
her Journal to the Queen, which would immediately give it
extra kudos, and writes frequently of this plan. In November
1854 she drew up a map (see end paper) of the area around
Sebastopol, and sent it to the Queen. Early in January
she received a reply, thanking her, 'So that's satisfactory
so far', was her hopeful response. Her hopes rose still further
in July when she heard from her regular correspondent
Hugh Seymour Tremenheere. He had shown Fanny's letters
to the Queen, who returned them 'with many thanks' saying
'she has never read any letters so interesting & curious', and
he now agreed to act as the go-between in Fanny's request
for the dedication. But it was an anxious wait, and when
Russell's book was published she wrote in a panic to Francis
Marx urging him to get her Journal ready – 'And cut in
before anybody else. It must be dedicated to the Queen.'
But in the end her request was refused. Once again, as with

the medal, she had expected too much. A letter from Tremenheere arrived at the end of September regretting that

Her Majesty declines the dedication on the grounds that so many applications of this kind are made to her that she is obliged to draw a line and not to accept a dedication 'except under very particular circumstances. Her Majesty, however, will be most happy to accept a copy when the Volume appears.' Altho' I feel disappointed at this result and I fear you will be too, one cannot but see that it is necessary to draw a line somewhere.

Fanny's first reaction to this polite and encouraging refusal (not everyone was asked to present a copy of their book), was subdued disappointment, probably realising that if Tremenheere had failed it was unlikely that anyone else could have succeeded. As she explained to Selina – 'He is a wondrous diplomatist' – but a few days later she allowed her irritation to show.

I suppose if the Q[ueen] is too stingy to buy a copy she must have one bound in a lot of finery and given to her. 'Les caprices d'une grande dame' did you ever read it? Women are all the same in their nastiness towards each other.

However, she quickly recovered and began to draw up a dedication 'to the Soldiers & Sailors'.

But it would seem that it is on this one petulant outburst that the idea that Victoria snubbed Fanny, first by refusing the dedication and then by ignoring her on her arrival in England, is founded. This charge first appears in the 1963 biography of Fanny, *Mrs Duberly's campaigns: an English-woman's experiences in the Crimean War and Indian Mutiny*, based on her journals and some of her letters, by E. E. P. Tisdall, who believed that because the Queen did not speak to Fanny when she reviewed the 8th Hussars on their arrival in Portsmouth on 12 May 1856, she was cutting her. Fanny's letter to Selina, describing the scene, could, rather, be read as the description of a graceful compliment from a social superior – 'The Queen has just inspected us – she & P[rince]

A[lbert] both made me low bows & the Princess Royal said "Oh – there's Mrs Duberly".' Moreover, it would have been most unlikely that the Queen, when she was reviewing the men of the regiment, would have stopped and talked to a young gentlewoman who had not been presented at court. And while Fanny, exhausted after a stormy sea voyage, repeats her worries about disembarking and travelling, she makes no complaint about her treatment from the Queen. She understood very well the significance of a low bow, having used the compliment herself earlier – 'I admire Canrobert for resigning and made him a lower bow today than I ever did to him as Commander in Chief' (p. 178).

Fanny's flowery dedication, which she sent back to Francis, caused her some difficulties.

Enclosed is an attempt at a Dedication. I suppose I ought to put my name at the bottom, oughtn't I? But I really cannot tell how to drag it in – I have drunk two glasses of sherry without receiving the slightest assistance – and will try a pint of Champagne at dinner – but you can do that if necessary. About which you know best.

Francis refined the dedication to the simple message, including her name as she wished, that now appears in the Journal.

IV

Fanny's Journal ends at the point when many felt that the war should have ended, with the fall of Sebastopol. After months of hardship, the taking of the city had come to be seen as the main objective of the campaign; the long-drawn-out siege was the focus of public attention which overlooked the wider aspects of the war, the blockade of the Baltic ports and the six-month siege of Kars.

The fall of the city provoked very different reactions among the French and British. The French were delighted; the capture of the Mamelon had wiped out the shame of their defeat by the Russians in 1812, and restored their military reputation. France could now claim a leading place at any future peace talks, which many French hoped would soon occur, although the Emperor wanted to fight on. For the British commanders and government there was relief that Sebastopol had fallen but shame and recrimination at the behaviour of the troops in the Redan. Despite a growing desire among the public for a swift end to hostilities, the government determined to continue the war until the Russians were defeated and Britain's honour redeemed.

But the characters of the British and French commanders-in-chief were in direct contrast to their governments. Simpson was a timid man, incapable of initiating a new offensive. He found it impossible to work with the energetic Pelissier, who had assumed virtual command of the allied forces, including the Turks and Sardinians. In late September he resigned and was replaced by General Sir William Codrington, who was believed to have been chosen for his good looks, his good manners and his fluent French. There was some hesitation in announcing his appointment because of his lack of initiative and nerve during the final attack on Sebastopol, and he did not take command until November.

The capture of Sebastopol was soon seen to be an illusion. The Russians (keen to improve their position at any future negotiations by inflicting damage on the Allies whenever possible), continued to bombard the south of the town from their newly strengthened fortifications on the northern shore – forcing the Allies to withdraw. When Fanny hinted to Lyons that the fleet could have prevented this 'he heard me in silence.' Lyons was probably sick of complaints. Thwarted by Simpson's indecision and Pelissier's active opposition to his plan to cut the Russian supply lines to the south-east of Balaclava, he eventually persuaded the French to a joint attack on Kinburn, on the north-western shore of the Black Sea, to threaten the port of Odessa.

Kinburn surrendered on 17 October and although no attempt was made to follow up this achievement (the small holding-force stationed there withdrew a few months later), the victory restored British morale and alarmed the Russians by demonstrating how powerful their enemies were at sea. Only two months earlier the newly reinforced Russian fortress and naval base at Sveaborg in the Baltic had been destroyed, with no Allied casualties, by a ferocious bombardment from the British-led fleet. The Russian ports were effectively blockaded; not one warship left harbour during the entire course of the conflict, and Russian trade suffered. Kronstadt, the fortress guarding St Petersburg, was threatened and rumours of the vast number of steam war-ships being built in British dockyards for a spring offensive reached St Petersburg, stimulating the move towards peace negotiations.

In the Crimea, preparations for winter were well under way. Looking around at the improvements – the huts and roads, the railway, the canteens and shops clustered around Kadikoi – young British officers, wearing their new winter uniforms, wrote home joking that the army was settling in permanently. But they were less enthusiastic about prolonging the conflict – it was known that the Austrians were attempting to broker a peace treaty, and rumours reached them of secret contacts between Paris and St Petersburg. Many officers hoped to survive the winter without further loss of life but still lived in daily expectation of the Russians having 'another go at Inkerman'.

The greater part of the Turkish army left early in October, apparently for Eupatoria, leading to speculation that 'we are to start all over again', as Fanny wearily commented, 'and attack Sebastopol from the north … They report here the fall of Kars & capture of the Turkish force. I don't know if it's true or not.' Although untrue (the Turks had in fact left Balaclava in a belated attempt to relieve Kars), this rumour was plausible – the starving garrison only clung on for a further month before surrendering on 25 November. Treated as heroes by the Russians, the garrison was allowed to march out of the city carrying their arms.

Amidst all the uncertainties around her, Fanny continued to write home with instructions for the publication of her journal and requests for help with her preparations for the winter, in particular her wardrobe. The centrepiece of this was to be a 'riding jacket to be made according to the pattern I sent ... handsomely braided a la militaire on the front pockets & sleeves ... (H says, he doesn't care about the expense of this jacket as he wishes it to be very handsome & well made).' The new wardrobe was much needed since picnics and race meetings had once more become the chief recreations of army life. The first autumn races took place on 5 October and Fanny attended both these and subsequent meetings. Returning from one on 19 October, she reported that at last there was hopeful news.

We shall go down to winter quarters as soon as ever this expected fight is over. ... We are to go to the Ancient Nicomedia to a village called Ismid about 70 miles from Scutari & in Asia Minor of course ... I am so glad ... Beside the classic associations, there are ... lovely country, mild climate, and beautiful shooting.

Despite all the confusions, when the order for embarkation finally came their departure was rapid; on 6 November Fanny sent her last letter from 'the Light Cavalry Camp before Sebastopol':

One line to say we are off to Ismid in the *Jason* at twenty four hours notice and I have no time to write to anybody. If you are writing to any one of my sisters, will you tell them this?

There was a further day's delay stuck aboard ship moored outside the harbour, during which Fanny heard that her long-awaited box had finally arrived in Balaclava, just when she was powerless to collect it.

Her first impression of Ismid was of

a wretched Turkish town, built almost exclusively of wood and with very narrow & crowded streets ... We wish we had been left in the Crimea, instead of coming to this unknown land. ... until some of the regts come down we shall be very lonely. Oh for one's own little garden & one's own cabbages! I'm sick of it ... 'all outdoors' is one long poem, but we are just like so many Robinson Crusoes.

Exhausted, Fanny fell ill and when she was well enough to write again feared for the fate of her box:

A Neapolitan steamer comes huffing & wheezing here once a week but it is not safe to send even letters by her, such ruffians are the crew. ... I want some bootlaces & combs, for my hair is now nearly all fallen off with this last feverish business, and I shall be by the time I arrive in England an astonishing specimen of a washed out old woman.

The box eventually arrived just before Christmas and her letters were full of gratitude and praise. The feather in her hat attracted a crowd 'of about 40 women & children every time I appear in it' and 'the habit exceeds my utmost expectations'. She wore it for the first time on 2 January when she went with the local Pasha 'to pay a visit to his <u>wife,</u> for in compassion to my frankish notions he tried as much as possible to keep the other ladies out of sight'.

The same day she was still 'anxiously looking for the arrival of my copy' of the Journal, which had been published in early December. She had read some of the reviews even before it reached her and was 'as much surprised as I am delighted, at the popularity of what I feel is a very stupid book'. The initial reaction was everything she could have hoped and she was so thrilled that she asked for an extra copy to be sent out so that 'I can give one to the poor fellows in Hospital.' A few weeks later she

was pleased to hear that a group of seven poor sick men in our hospital were sitting round one, appointed as reader, in the day room, and listening with the greatest interest as he read. If it can amuse & alleviate pain, the book has fulfilled its mission.

Her mood changed when she realised *The Examiner* of 29 December had published a full page review mocking both

her and her literary style. She wrote home angry and mortified, her writing sprawling wildly all over the pages.

Never, never, was anything half so sharp – so cruel, so bitter, so
scurrilous – Even all your kindness & that of the *Spectator,
Athenaeum & Press,* for which I am so grateful, has been & ever will
be unable to efface those pages. ... 'The Lady of course upon her
horse Bob went up to the front at the Battle of Balaclava – she had
not been feeling well, and the sight of a Battle she thought would
"freshen her up a bit" .... We cannot suppose that Mrs Duberly
desired to play before the world the part of a "comic Lady Sale" '
&c &c &c &c &c &c. By George it cut one's heart out like a knife.

The barb about being 'a comic Lady Sale' may have hurt
more than all the rest of the review. *A Journal of the Disasters
in Afghanistan, 1841-2* by Florentia Wynch, Lady Sale, had
been a bestseller when it was published in 1843 and Fanny
may well have had this in mind when she decided to publish
her Journal. *The Examiner* concluded 'we believe in the lady
quite sufficiently to regret her literary indiscretion.'

Fanny, however, did not immediately think of the book as
an indiscretion. She received praise from the local soldiers
and wrote in more reconciled mood to Selina:

I am indeed surprised when I look at the book – & think of the
sensation it has made. ... I have had nearly as much newspaper
praise as Windham ... when I feel inclined to get vain, the *Examiner*
pokes his razor under my ribs, and soon takes it out of me. ... For
my opinion of it – I think it too scanty – with too many 'I's & Me's
and hardly enough abuse of everybody. ... Curiosity has sold it, I
suppose.

She was still unaware of the pastiche which had been published in *Punch* (p. xl), on 2 February. When she did see it, it
upset her more than *The Examiner* because it would be more
widely read.

I have been worried fairly ill by that horrid Punch. I can do nothing
but fancy myself lying inside an ammunition wagon and
'bellowing'. In reality it touches me on no point. But I cannot
forget its coarseness, & vulgar [*sic*] oh it is dreadful to be made out
such a woman even in jest – for jest I conclude it is meant for.

THE DIARY OF LADY FIRE-EATER.

OME one—say LADY FIRE-EATER—has just published *The Diary* she kept during the Russian War. She and her horse "Bob," were in the thick of the fight in the Crimea. Of course, she was only there as an amateur. She went to Sebastopol as a lady at home goes out shopping, simply for the amusement of the thing. There was the excitement of the danger, too, that made the shopping all the more delightful. It would be like a military-minded lady, looking at some fifty cachemires at HOLMES's, whilst the shop was in flames. Besides, there was nothing to gain. It was clear that LADY FIRE-EATER could not expect to bring home with her a diamond star, or a jewelled cross, or even as much as a piece of ribbon that might dangle proudly from her sensitive breast. No; it was entirely a disinterested excursion, undertaken as a *passe-temps*, out of pure love for the sport—as something to talk about when the day's adventures were over.

We will endeavour to give a few extracts from LADY FIRE-EATER's *Diary*. It will be seen that LADY SALE's *Journal* was nothing but a bowl of milk and water by the side of her fiery mixture :—

Monday, 5th. Walked to Balaklava. Up to my ancles in mud. Left one of my shoes behind me. The number of dead horses strewed on each side of the road, reminded me forcibly of a knacker's yard.

Wednesday, 7th. Short of hands to-day, such numbers killed yesterday. Had to clean my own boots. GENERAL BOSQUET passing at the time, laughingly exclaimed "*Ah, Madame, quelle main charmante vous avez là pour bien frotter les Russes!*" I touched my hat quietly as he rode by—but on my word, the compliment, whenever I think of it, makes my blood tingle.

Saturday, 10th. Woke up by a loud explosion that made all the glasses in the tent rattle again, like the chandelier-drops during a maddening galopade. Sky burning red, just as on a Vauxhall night. The flames seemed so close that I fancied I could have lit my cigar by them.

Monday, 12th. Walked over the battle-field to collect "charms" for my watch-chain.

Tuesday, 13th. A French trumpeter being killed by my side, I seized his trumpet, and kept up with his regiment during the remainder of the *mêlée*. Played all the tunes every bit as well as VIVIER. CANROBERT sent me the Legion of Honour, which I put round the neck of my dear old "BOBBY."

Thursday, 15th. There being no water, was obliged to wash my face and hands in BASS's Pale Ale.

Wednesday, 21st. Took my album into Sebastopol, and sketched the different ruins. Took a charming sketch of the church of St. Sergius.

Mockery from *Punch*, 2 February 1856.

Saturday, 21th. Rode a steeple-chase with the officers of the 159th. Cleared the walls in grand style. Should have won, if my horse (a villanous screw, only fit for dog's meat) hadn't taken it into his stupid noddle at the last half-mile to drop down dead. Cried with vexation, but soon recovered my usual spirits upon hearing the cry raised " The Cossacks are coming ! " Disappointed, however, as we could not get nearer to them at any time than a couple of miles.

Saturday, 31st. Passed the night in the trenches. Feet very cold. Kept them warm by putting on two of our Grenadiers' schakos. Russians very troublesome. They wouldn't let me sleep. Nearly taken prisoner also—the schakos on my feet impeding my running.

Monday, 2nd. Dog-hunting in the morning—shooting Cossacks in the evening.

Tuesday, 3rd. Not a drop of brandy left !

Wednesday, Nov. 4th. During the whole day kept up by HARRY's side, charging his gun, and handing him my pistols as soon as he had fired off his own. Rather astonished some Zouaves, I think, by singing " *Partant pour la Syrie,*" as they rushed forward to annihilate the Hurrieimoff Invincibles.

Friday, 6th. Passed a quiet afternoon teaching some raw recruits (mere charity-children, that start like rabbits at the crack of a gun) the proper range of the Minié Rifle.

Saturday, 7th. Left my "pocket-pistol" in the Rifle Pits, and sauntered out dauntlessly to fetch it. Thought no more of it than if I had been walking down Regent Street. Brought back two bullet-holes in my hat, and had the tortoise-shell comb in my back hair splintered into pieces—but secured my "pocket-pistol."

Wednesday, 13th. Messed with the Officers of the *Garde Impériale.* Capital fellows ! Glorious amusement ! No salt for dinner—made them laugh by calling for some Saltpetre. Gambling—singing—smoking till a late hour. Being some distance from the English lines, threw myself down in the middle of an open plain, and slept soundly on the hard ground, with my head resting on darling Bobby's. Dreamt I was planting the English Standard in the middle of the Redan. Awoke disappointed.

Thursday, 19th. Tent flooded. Slept inside an ammunition-wagon. So sound asleep that they carried me right into Balaklava before I could make them understand by bellowing there was some one inside. Tucked up my trousers, and walked back through the snow.

Sunday, 22nd. A French *Toulourou,* no higher than a muff, hearing we were short of provisions, gave me half of his *pain bis.* Enchanted with his gallantry, I exchanged ear-rings with *le jeune brave.*

Tuesday, 24th. Surrounded by six Russians—shot three—wounded the fourth—sliced the fifth like a lobster—and took prisoner the sixth, tying his hands with my veil. The coward trembled like a hen-pecked husband about to receive a Curtain Lecture. Carried him into camp amidst the laughter, hurrahs, and exclamations of our soldiers. Serenade in the evening outside my tent by thirty-nine corporals—" She 's a jolly good fellow."

Friday, 27th. Joined the storming party. Met a French colonel whom I had danced with at the Tuileries. " *Charmé de vous revoir, Madame,*" he exclaimed, as he rushed by me like a flash of French lightning; " *autrefois, c'était nous qui allions au Bal—mais ici, c'est la Balle qui vient à nous.*"

The above extracts only form part of a delightful book that has been published by the LONGMANS,—a book in which you meet with all the grace and refinement that a Lady would necessarily acquire by taking her share in military pursuits, and mixing gaily, as in a ball-room, in scenes of bloodshed. Decidedly, there is nothing like gunpowder for preserving the purity of the female mind !

Everyone around her was either anxious to read it, or commiserated with her.

The pious Brigadier [Shewell] who looks upon Punch as he would on the Lady in Red sent up a panting servant to borrow it. ...Mr Wrench our parson sent me up a handful of violets in the afternoon, which last I thought kindest of all.

All this time they had been anxiously waiting for news from Paris where the peace conference was to meet on 25 February. A friend had warned her that the 'English bluster on about continuing the war & the Frogs want to sit down & croak in Peace. Why John Bull should be the only one bellowing for war I can't think. I know I hope he'll be disappointed for I want Peace'. Fanny was not to be disappointed – the day before she wrote this, on 29 February, an armistice lasting until 31 March was signed but it was another month before the news reached Ismid. Every week the soldiers waited on the tiny jetty hoping for the steamer to arrive. On 2 April they were there once more –

O Selina Peace is proclaimed – we knew the boat was due today and every soul, soldiers, officers & natives, were again crowded on the rotten, rocking, creaking wooden pier waiting for the news. ... we saw the big boat in the distance, coming rapidly in, a fleet of caiques put off to her and [on returning] ... One sergeant stood up in the caique & called out 'Peace was proclaimed on Monday in Constantinople & acknowledged by a salute of 101 guns.' The pier rocked again as the men swayed forward & backward – all were glad I think but there was no cheering. We waited for our letters and then came home ... [where] in the quiet we could cry our thankful tears ... Oh how little at one time did Henry or I think we should ever live to see this blessed time. Truly goodness and mercy have followed us both.

As they waited for orders to embark for home, Fanny's happiness was only marred by the realisation that publishing her Journal may indeed have been an 'indiscretion'.

Our punishment for my rashness ... has begun, for the War Office have taken lately to bullying Henry so much ... that even he said the other day, 'If this goes on much longer, I shall know that they are determined to spite and bully me.' However I know that if I have erred it has been on the side of leniency ... so that if we are made losers by it we shall know that it is not we who have done wrong. Fame is certainly not happiness.

She felt that people were avoiding her but fortunately Henry's kindness was greater than ever and he 'has not left me, even to shoot, for a month, and we are perpetual companions, which is a comfort to me quite beyond words'.

On 23 April – 'just two years out' as Fanny noted – they embarked for England and, unexpectedly, they were sorry to leave Ismid. 'I think a sort of weary feeling of tightlacing & constraint came over us all, for we tried to comfort ourselves with the idea that we were going to be "home".' As they approached Spithead at the end of the three week voyage Fanny was very ill and could do nothing but cry for two days; but she revived sufficiently to be fascinated by 'how strange the women look' – it was her first glimpse of a crinoline. She herself had 'no clothes so shall disembark in my habit.' Dressed in this habit ('handsomely braided à la militaire'), she joined the battered remnants of the 8th Hussars on the quayside for the Queen's inspection of the regiment and, as we have seen, received Victoria's gracious acknowledgement and the enthusiastic recognition of the young Princess Vicky.

Four years later Fanny still remembered her homecoming with pleasure. 'I remember how <u>beautiful</u> I thought Arlebury was, the first morning after I arrived from the Crimea & saw the thick tender May foliage hanging over the mowing grass.'

V

After their return from the Crimean campaign the 8th Hussars spent the next seventeen months in Ireland until they were ordered to Bombay in October 1857 to join the British forces already engaged in repressing the Indian Mutiny, which had broken out in May that year. Troopers' wives were forbidden to travel with the regiment and Fanny, undeterred by the reports of massacres, was the only officer's wife who chose to accompany her husband. She had decided to publish a further journal but, once again, her real motive was her desire for adventure and her concern for Henry's welfare.

Her Indian journal, *Campaigning Experiences in Central India and Rajpootana during the Suppression of the Mutiny* (1859), made less impact than her best-selling Crimean Journal but this did not surprise her. 'For myself, I do not expect it to sell well, as India is too far, people do not care or trouble themselves about this war as they did about the Crimea.' And this time she was less at ease with the events she recorded, commenting that 'this Indian warfare is unsatisfactory work, and although it may be true that in this rebellion severity is mercy, there have been cases of ruthless slaughter of which the least said the better.' But the journal remains a testimony to the courage and endurance needed to survive the daily hardships of campaigning life.

During the two-and-a-half month voyage Fanny sketched Henry, leaning against a tree, during their brief stay at Cape Town. After five weeks in Bombay, where Fanny overheard herself described as the 'Crimean heroine' at parties, the regiment embarked once more and sailed north, landing at Mandavee on the Gulf of Kutch. Years later Trooper James Rawlins recalled that he 'carried Lady D. ashore as there was no other conveyance for her.'

The 8th Hussars joined the fighting column that marched through Rajputana in pursuit of two of the most notorious and successful rebel leaders - Tatya Tope, a skilled tactician who retreated slowly before the British troops (forcing them into long marches with men dying from sun-stroke in the exhausting heat), and the Rani of Thansi, who led her troops on horseback dressed as a man. The march began pleasantly during the final weeks of the cool season. On the third day they reached Bhooj, an ancient walled city, where the curiosity aroused in the palace of the Rao by Fanny's arrival resulted in an invitation to visit the Ranees. The Rao's six wives and his daughter-in-law were so delighted with Fanny's conversation (translated by the chaplain of Bhooj's wife), that they exceeded 'ordinary etiquette' and showed her around their sleeping apartments with their handsomely carved swinging cots. It would be six months before she was in such civilised surroundings again.

During 1858 the Rajputana column shifted camp 300 times and marched 2,028 miles, first north-east to Gwalior - where the rebels made their unsuccessful last stand - before turning south to pursue and annihilate the scattered remnants of the rebel army.

Fanny proudly records that she covered 1,800 of these miles on horseback, often at the head of the column to avoid the dust thrown up by hundreds of marching men and horses. A deputation of soldiers later told her that 'many and many a man had been saved from giving way to sickness because he could not give in as long as I was seen daily riding at the front of the column.' Finally however, overcome with the heat and ill with dysentery and blood-poisoning (from an abscess so large that it 'was agony to sit'), she 'fell off one day in a dead faint from sheer pain' and 'the doctor came and cut me very severely until he was obliged to give me chloroform'. For the next seven days she was carried in a dooley (a covered litter), almost unconscious, until, a few miles from Gwalior, they were faced by part of the large rebel army commanded by Tatya Tope. Hearing the preparations for battle, Fanny found that 'Pain was forgotten at such an exciting moment and I got out of my dooley and stood to watch.' During the ensuing conflict the Rani of Thansi was killed, most probably by a trooper of the 8th Hussars. Two days later the British attacked and defeated Tatya Tope's forces on the plain outside Gwalior. At first,

Fanny and Henry merely watched as the Hussars charged and scattered the rebels, but soon the 'impulse to accompany the cavalry was irresistible, and I never shall forget the throbbing excitement of that gallop ... We halted ... underneath the grim walls of the fort ... all was silent and still.' Most of the garrison had slipped away to join the retreating rebels and Gwalior was almost deserted. The Maharajah of Gwalior had opposed Tatya Tope's forces when they marched into his territory and been forced to flee with only his personal bodyguard. Now he returned to repossess his capital and his lands and a few days later he invited Fanny and Henry to stay in the palace as his guests. His mother, who in her youth had fought against the British, particularly wanted to meet 'the Englishwoman who had gone with the armies to make war against the Ruski.' After recuperating amidst the gilded luxury of the palace, Fanny was fit enough to survive the succeeding months of the march, struggling through the monsoon season. She witnessed the column's final battle in November when the rebel force was routed and 'the jungles were filled with wounded.' By February 1859 the Mutiny was collapsing as many of the rebels surrendered or drifted away. Tatya Tope was captured and executed in April.

After the hardship of the campaign Fanny, still only twenty-nine, wrote sadly to Selina: 'my youth is gone and Henry is grievously changed.' It was not until eighteen months later that she recovered. 'My voice has come back - and my color has come back and my good spirits have come back & altogether I have the pleasantest conviction, that I have still got a kick left in me, besides the one I shall have some day to bestow on "the bucket". (That's awful slang, but Francie will tell you what it means).' They remained in India for the next five years. Fanny endeavoured, reluctantly at first, to settle back into the mundane routines of life as a peace-time army wife. She read the latest books from England, rode and sketched and sent long letters home, many complaining of the lack of 'respectable' social life or of their unsuccessful attempts to pay their debts. In 1864 the regiment was ordered home. Fanny obviously intended to cut a dash on her return - among her last letters is a request to Selina for help in finding a good maid to dress her, one who 'understands the business and will take the responsibility of my appearance off my hands.' Whether or not she succeeded is not recorded; with her return to England the letters cease and her personal account of her life with Henry ends.

Henry, a sketch by Fanny enclosed in a letter from the Cape of Good Hope *en route* to Bombay, December 1857.

The 8th Hussars moved frequently from barracks to barracks in England and to Edinburgh before being posted to Dublin in 1869. From there, Henry was seconded as staff paymaster to the 44th Brigade Depot in Essex and after nine years appointed officially to the post. Three years later, in 1881, he retired with the rank of lieutenant-colonel. Fanny and he settled in a villa, St Clair, at Cheltenham (which was then a favourite spot for retired army officers and their families), so that Fanny's wish - 'oh for one's own little garden & one's own cabbages!' - was fulfilled at last. She evidently kept her zest for life until the end - there is one final glimpse of her in a letter from her great-niece as 'an old lady with white hair' with 'red artificial poppies in it.' Henry died in 1891; Fanny remained in Cheltenham and died twelve years later, in January 1903, at the age of 71.

NOTES ON THE TEXT

This is a new edition of *Journal kept during the Russian War* by Mrs Henry Duberly, published in 1855, incorporating a few minor variations from the second edition in 1856. We have omitted the literary quotations placed at the head of each chapter, and the very long chapter entitled 'Balaklava' has been split into two. Otherwise the text is as it originally appeared.

The interpolations in italic type, in square brackets, are passages from the Duberly manuscript correspondence in the British Library, MSS Add. 47218. References for these passages are given in the Notes and Commentary. Unless otherwise indicated all letters are from Fanny Duberly to Selina and Francis Marx, her sister and brother-in-law.

Fanny Duberly's spelling of all proper names has been used throughout this edition.

JOURNAL

KEPT DURING

THE RUSSIAN WAR:

FROM THE DEPARTURE OF THE ARMY FROM ENGLAND IN APRIL 1854, TO THE FALL OF SEBASTOPOL.

BY MRS. HENRY DUBERLY.

"Now all the youth of England are on fire,
And silken dalliance in the wardrobe lies;
Now thrive the armourers, and Honour's thought
Reigns solely in the breast of every man."
SHAKESPEARE.

"Je vais où le vent me mène,
Sans me plaindre ou m'effrayer.
Je vais où va toute chose;
Où va la feuille de Rose,
Et la feuille de Laurier."

LONDON:

LONGMAN, BROWN, GREEN, AND LONGMANS.

1855

TO

THE SOLDIERS AND SAILORS

OF

THE CRIMEAN EXPEDITION

THIS JOURNAL IS DEDICATED

BY AN EYE WITNESS OF THEIR CHIVALROUS VALOUR AND

THEIR HEROIC FORTITUDE,

FRANCIS ISABELLA DUBERLY

EDITOR'S NOTE, 1855

The writer of this Diary accompanied her husband, an officer in the 8th Hussars, who left England, with his regiment, on the breaking out of the war, and she is now with him in the Crimea.

AUTHOR'S PREFACE, 1855

I am aware of many deficiencies in this Journal. It was kept under circumstances of great difficulty. I have always put down information as I received it, as nearly as possible in the words of my informant, in matters which I did not myself witness. I have endeavoured to keep free from comment or remark, thinking it best to allow the facts to speak for themselves. When this Journal was first commenced I had no intention whatever of publishing it; nor should I have done so now, had it not been for the kind interest manifested in it by many of my friends.

CHAPTER I

The Voyage

Even before Britain declared war on Russia on 28 March 1854 (see Appendix I) troops had been posted to Malta in anticipation of their deployment to Turkey. Early in April these regiments, reinforced by others, transferred to Gallipoli ready to defend the Mediterranean should the Russians break through the Turkish defences and reach Constantinople. In all, the initial expeditionary force eventually consisted of one cavalry and five infantry divisions, numbering about 26,000 men. The 8th Royal Irish Hussars, accompanied by Fanny Duberly, were among the last to leave England. By the time they arrived in Turkey both the British and the French armies had been ordered to Varna in Bulgaria to support the Turks who were besieged at Silistria on the Danube. After a few days in Constantinople the Hussars joined them there.

Lord Raglan left England in mid-April, travelling via Paris for a council of war with Marshal St Arnaud, the commander of the French Expeditionary Force (which also numbered around 26,000 men). Unlike his French counterpart, Raglan did not enjoy the total authority suggested by his appointment as 'General Officer Commanding the Forces eastwards of Malta' but presided over a fragmented command system.

The Commissariat and the Purveyors departments, responsible for feeding and clothing the patients in military hospitals and the soldiers in the field, answered to the Treasury in London rather than the commander-in-chief. Both had suffered from years of neglect and cost-cutting, including the disbanding of essential baggage-trains (see p. 267, note 8). And both were administered by inflexible bureaucrats; nothing was issued without a complicated system of requisition forms, and if anything was unavailable, they were powerless to acquire it locally without referring back to London. Even during a crisis the civilian officials were too timid to break the rules. In the Crimea and at Scutari men starved and patients died as a result of their inertia.

The Black Sea naval force, too, was independent of Raglan, under the command of Vice Admiral Sir James Dundas, so that even the transport of troops and supplies by sea had to be negotiated. Within the army, both the Royal Engineers and the Royal Artillery answered to the Master-General of Ordinance and retained a modicum of independence throughout the campaign. Trained professionals, they qualified by examination and were promoted on merit rather than purchase.

The British army had not fought a drawn-out, full-scale land war in Europe since the defeat of Napoleon in 1815. A few of the regiments present in the Crimea had fought overseas but most regimental officers and brigade commanders had had no opportunity to gain any practical knowledge of either fighting or co-ordinated staff-work. Many officers had no desire to learn these skills; they had bought their commissions assuming that they would spend their lives in comfortable circumstances and despised the experienced 'Indian Army' officers as professionals rather than gentlemen. In essence their lives were not very different from those of the country gentlemen, often their brothers or cousins, whose sole military experience was parading as a captain in the local militia.

The navy was an altogether more efficient and professional force, with promotion through examination and merit up to the rank of Captain. Two fleets were employed during the campaign. Part of the Black Sea fleet, *together with ships from the French navy, carried out the first action of the war, destroying the fortifications at Odessa, in mid-May. The whole fleet of sixteen warships later took part in the bombardment of Sebastopol and the equally essential work of ferrying the wounded and sick to the hospitals at Scutari. In early March 1854, amidst great celebrations witnessed by Tennyson among others, the first Baltic fleet of eighteen ships (only six of which relied entirely on sail), left Spithead under the command of Vice Admiral Sir Charles Napier. Though they saw little action that summer, to the disappointment of the government which had expected to hear of the total destruction of the Russian Baltic fleet, they effectively blockaded the Russian ports, thus beginning the slow destruction of her economy which eventually hastened the end of the campaign.*

Monday, April 24th 1854 – Left the New London Inn at Exeter at ten o'clock in the evening, with sad heart and eyes full of tears. The near approach of this long voyage, and the prospect of unknown trials and hardships to be endured for I know not how long, overwhelmed me at the last moment; and the remembrance of dear friends left behind whom I never more might return to see, made me shrink most nervously from the new life on which I was to embark. We reached the Royal Hotel at Plymouth at midnight, after a bitterly cold journey.

Tuesday, 25th – After making a few purchases necessary for our comfort during the voyage, we embarked about three o'clock on board the *Shooting Star*, lying in the Plymouth dockyard; and towards evening, amidst indescribable hurry, confusion, and noise, we weighed our anchor and dropped down the river, where we lay till three o'clock on Wednesday morning; and then, with a fair and gentle breeze, and every prospect of a prosperous voyage, we stood out to sea.

Friday, 28th – The breeze, which had been gradually freshening during yesterday, increased last night. I, sick and almost helpless in my cabin, was told the disastrous news that both the mizen-top and main-top gallant masts were carried away; that fragments of the wreck – masts, ropes, and spars – strewed the deck: one poor fellow was lying seriously injured, having broken his leg, and crushed the bone.

[*As the doctor is unable to amputate because of the motion of the ship he still lies in a fever and a deal of mortification. … If I come back at all I shall be either as hardened as brass or utterly worn down. I have seen so much suffering even now. Our cabin is nearly as large as the Prophet's chamber*[1] *& the men on board appear to wish to do everything to make me as comfortable as they can & show me all the civility in their power … I cannot help telling you how good, careful & kind Henry has been to me since I have been on board. When I was ill he was worth his weight in gold. He begins at times to be down-hearted about having brought me – but I would not have stayed behind. I long <u>heartily</u> to have news from England. The Captain of the ship says we can form no idea how we shall have to rough it out there.*]

Saturday, 29th – Weak and nervous, I staggered up on deck, to see it strewn with ropes, and blocks. During the night the gale had fearfully increased and the morning sun found two of our poor horses dead. The groans of the boy, who was lying in one of the cabins, and the gloom caused by the death of our horses, threw us all into depressed spirits which were not cheered by looking at the ugly, broken mast aloft. I heartily thanked God, who brought us safely through last night's gale.

Although weakened almost to delirium by sea-sickness, and awed by the tremendous force of wind and sea, I could not but exult in the magnificent sailing of our noble ship, which bounded over the huge waves like a wild hunter springing at his fences, and breasted her gallant way at the rate of sixteen knots an hour.

Sunday, 30th – How unlike the quiet Sundays at home! How sadly we thought of them – of pleasant walks to church through sunny fields and shady lanes! After we had read the service, Henry and I went on deck and sat there quietly. The wind had dropped to a dead calm; and our good ship, as though resting after her late effort, dozed lazily along at barely two knots an hour. Towards evening, we saw several whales and porpoises, and phosphorescent lights gleamed like stars on the calm, dark sea.

Monday, May 1st – The wind still very quiet, and our ship hardly making any way.

Tuesday, 2nd – We signalled a vessel which, after much delay, replied that she was the *Blundel*, from Portsmouth, bound to Gallipoli. At ten o'clock tonight we arrived off Gibraltar. For some hours previously we were in sight of the Spanish coast; and, notwithstanding the lateness of the hour, the clear atmosphere and brilliant moon enabled us to discern the town of Gibraltar and the Rock rising behind it. It was a cause of much disappointment to us that we had not passed it earlier, as we hoped to have conveyed to our friends at home the news of our safe arrival thus far. Another horse died from inanition, having eaten nothing since he came on board.

Wednesday, 3rd – An almost entire calm. Our lazy ship scarcely vouchsafed to move at all. Such a glorious day, succeeded by a night which realised all one's dreams of the sweet south! – the Spanish and African coasts still visible, and on the former, mountains capped with snow. We put up an awning on the deck, as the heat was very great. During the night, however, a fresh breeze sprung up, filling our flapping sails, and bearing us on at the rate of fifteen knots an hour.

Thursday, 4th – The breeze continued, and our good ship went cheerily on her course. A fourth horse died last night. They tell me he went absolutely mad, and raved himself to death. The hold where our horses are stowed, although considered large and airy, appears to me horrible beyond words. The slings begin to gall the horses under the shoulder and breastbone; and the heat and bad atmosphere must be felt to be understood. Every effort to alleviate their sufferings is made; their nostrils are spunged with vinegar, which is also scattered in the hold. Our three horses bear it bravely, but they are immediately under a hatchway where they get air.

Friday, 5th – A day of much sorrow and suffering to me as I was awoke by our servant (Connell)[2] coming to our door at seven o'clock, and saying that the Grey Horse – 'Missus's Horse' – my own dear horse, was very ill. Henry ran to him directly, and after examining him, fancied his attack was different from that of the others, and that he might live.

How deeply one becomes attached to a favourite horse! Never was a more perfect creature, with faultless action, faultless mouth and faultless temper.

Saturday, 6th – My horse still lives, and they tell me he is a thought easier; but last night was most unfavourable to him there being a fresh wind and rolling sea. During the forenoon I came on deck, heavy at heart. We passed the island of Galita, of volcanic formation and rocky appearance: it appears to be covered with a rusty brown moss. During the afternoon we exchanged signals with vessels which had been respectively, twenty-eight, seventeen, and fourteen days, at sea. We have been ten.

Sunday, 7th – A lovely morning, and a quiet sea. Although the *Shooting Star* makes but seven knots an hour, we hope to arrive at Malta by dark. Had the wind held, we should have been off the town in time for afternoon service. My letters are ready for S., W. and Mrs F.[3] Would that we could receive news from home! I hear we passed the Island of Pantelaria this morning, but was not on deck in time to see it; indeed, I had no heart for the distractions of outward objects, for my horse, though he still lives, is at the point of death.

Monday, 8th – We were awoke at four o'clock by the sound of a matin bell, and knew by it that we were off Malta.

Looking through the stern windows, we found ourselves at anchor in the harbour; the massive fortifications bristling with guns were close on either side of us, as we lay quiet and motionless on the waveless sea. At eight o'clock Henry went on deck, and soon after returning, put his arms round me, and I knew that my darling horse was out of pain!

Henry went ashore with Captain Fraser, and, amid the sultry heat, sweltered up the 'Nix mangiare' stairs,[4] and through the blinding streets of the town. At ten we received orders to put to sea forthwith: but the wind lay ahead of us, and at five we were barely moving out of port. Shortly after, when the calm evening was dressed in all the gorgeous colours of a southern sunset, and whilst the military calls were sounding those stirring notes he loved to hear, my good horse was lowered to his rest among the nautili and wondrous seaflowers which floated round the ship

A small French brig, containing a detachment of the Chasseurs d'Afrique,[5] lay becalmed close to us. They told us that their vessel was one of 150 tons; that they had twenty-eight horses on board, and had lost none, although they provided no stalls for them, but huddled them into the hold as closely as they could stow them away.

Tuesday, 9th – Our orders are to proceed to Cape Matapan, where, if the wind should be against us, a steamer[6] will tow us to Scutari. Some of our crew, having bought spirits from the bumboats off Malta, became mutinous, and several passed the night in irons.

Friday, 12th – Last night ominous banks of clouds loaded the horizon, and soon proved the truth of my quotation –

> There's tempest in yon hornéd moon,
> And lightning in yon cloud.[7]

A hurricane of wind thundered in our rigging, and a deluge of rain came down. Endeavouring to make head against the gale, Captain Fraser tried our good ship to the utmost, but was at last obliged to let her drive before the storm. It was a fearful night to us who are unaccustomed to the sea; the rolling was very heavy and wearisome. Neither Henry nor I undressed all night.

Today has been a day of as much suffering as I ever wish to experience. Sick incessantly, too weak to turn, I was lying towards night almost unconscious, when I was roused by a most tremendous roll. The ship had heeled over till her deck was under water. Candlesticks, falling from the table, rolled at their leisure into the corners. Captain Fraser rushed on deck, Captain Tomkinson into the hold, where every horse was down, one being pitched half over the manger. I was shot from the stern locker, on which I was lying, to the far corner of my cabin, and every box and portmanteau came crushing over me.

Saturday, 13th – Happily, the violent motion abated during the night, though the thunder and lightning were terrific. And this is the 'Sweet South! whose sky rains roses and violets and whose weary, fragrant heat, combined with gorgeous colours, dazzles the senses so that one feels like a phoenix burning on spice wood.' This is all very fine, but Singleton Fontenoy[8] must have been more fortunate in his time of year. To me, for the last three days, the Mediterranean has been arid and sickly as the first approach of fever – heaving, nauseating, as the deadly approach of plague. Those who are good sailors may linger over it if they will. Give me the smallest house in England, with a greenhouse and a stable, and I will sigh no more for the violet waves of a Mediterranean sea, nor the brilliant stars of a sometimes golden heaven.

Sunday, 14th – Ran on deck to take my first longing look at Greece. We were close under the Arcadian shore, about four miles from the island of Stamphane. The high, bold coast lay hazy and crowned with misty clouds in the early sunlight. I watched for an hour, my mind dreaming poetic fancies: 'I, too, have been in Arcadia.'[9] A brilliant day coloured the *blue* waves once more. We had service for all hands on deck. Mr Coull, the Admiralty agent, officiated; and being somewhat unaccustomed to acting chaplain, he read the prayer for Queen *Adelaide* straight through.[10]

Monday, 15th – Almost a calm. We sighted the *Maryanne*, with Major De Salis and a detachment of 8th Hussars on board. She sailed a week before us, and our having overtaken her is a great triumph to our ship. The Messenian coast lay close to us all day – snow-capped and cloud-wreathed mountains lying in a half indistinct and dreamy haze, a very Eleusinian mystery in themselves.

Tuesday, 16th – After dark we passed the Straits of Cerigo; and all this morning have been gliding amongst the islands of the archipelago, leaving Rock St George upon our left, and the fertile and beautifully cultivated Zea on our right. They lay in beauteous sleep upon the bosom of the ocean, in colouring half intense, half languid, like the tints of the dog-rose and wild violet. Silently and swiftly our good ship held her way. We sighted the *Echinga*, which had sailed ten days before us, but we did not overtake her before night-fall (star-rise would be a better word); but we followed on her track as surely as evil destiny follows a foredoomed soul.

Wednesday, 17th – As I write we are off Mitylene, an apparently uncultivated island, but full of beauty of outline and colour nevertheless; and after coasting for two hours the fertile and well-wooded shores of Asia, we came to the narrow passage between Tenedos and the mainland. This passage is dangerous, from a reef of rocks; but we spanked through it at eleven knots, closely followed by the *Echinga*, while they saluted us from the batteries. Three hours later, our favouring breeze had whispered its own lullaby, and we were lying helpless and becalmed at the mouth of the Dardanelles. A strong current, acting on the ship, swung her round broadside to the forts. The glory of the sunset, the gaily painted little Turkish vessels, with the brilliant fez and long pipes of the sailors, the still water, reflecting every beautiful colour like a lake of mother-of-pearl, made a landscape such as I had never hoped to see save in a picture. The current in the night drifted us twelve miles back, and towards morning we 'let go our anchor, and prayed for' a steamer.[11]

Thursday, 18th – Made up our lost way with infinite diffi-culty, going at the rate of eight knots for five minutes, and then drifting back for ten with the current. We made a triumphant entry into the Dardanelles, in company with the *Maryanne, Echinga*, a man-of-war the name of which we did not know, a French transport, and a steamer. The coast is well wooded and fertile. We saw many Turks assembled on the fort on the left-hand side, and several women, all attracted by the novel sight of so many fine English vessels inside their unknown sea. The current here is so strong that at eight o'clock we cast anchor; and though every eye was strained towards Gallipoli, looking for the steamers, none appeared; and during the night the ship drifted from her moorings, and we were obliged to lower the bower anchor in forty fathoms.

Saturday, 20th – Yesterday we opened the sealed book of the Dardanelles, and what beauties did it not disclose! – a hilly, rocky coast, with interstices of lovely and fertile valleys clothed in rich green, and shaded with luxuriant trees; forts at every point; some of considerable strength, others more picturesque. Numbers of cattle and mules were grazing on the shore; and a string of camels, led by a mule with a bell, reminded one more forcibly than anything else, that we were really in the East. Gallipoli, which was visible from long distance, is a large and apparently good Turkish town, which means an execrable English one, and is finely situated on a high cliff. It is surrounded by a large English and French encampment. Gallipoli has now many French and four English regiments stationed there. We hove to for orders, and were immediately despatched to Scutari, for which place we started with the evening breeze, and, by eight o'clock we were well into the Sea of Marmara. At three o'clock to-day we caught our first sight of Constantinople, and by nine at night were anchored in the harbour. A Maltese pilot, who came on board at five o'clock, told us that the *Echinga*, *Pride of the Ocean*, and *Ganges*, had arrived a few hours before. We hear that there are barracks at Scutari[12] capable of holding 6,000 men, and that 16,000 can be quartered there by being encamped in the enclosure. Towards sunset we watched the Imaum ascend the minaret close to us, and presently the town echoed with the call to prayer. Coming to us across the water, the effect was very musical, and somehow it touched me.

Sunday, 21st – A cold, wet, miserable day, during which we remained at our anchorage. Every one except myself went on shore: Henry tells me that the filth, stenches, and dogs on shore are *indescribable*. The prospect from the deck is not tempting certainly. The captain returned with news of a steamboat tomorrow to disembark the horses, and also a quay for them to land on. I never was more completely *désillusionée* in my life than with my first day in Constantinople.

Tuesday, 22nd [*23rd*] – Disembarked at last! The tug came alongside very early, and towed us to the quay near Kulali. Such a quay, after our dockyard at Plymouth! – a few old rotten planks, supported on some equally rotten-looking timbers, about three feet above the water's edge. However, they must have been stronger than they looked, for they resisted the plunges and kicks of our horses, as they were tumbled out of the ship, without giving way. No accident befell the disembarkation. Our horses were in wonderfully good condition, and appeared fresh and in good heart. I went ashore and went up to Bob but the sight of him, and the memory of his lost companion, completely upset me and I could only lay my head on his neck and cry.[13] A good Greek who, I suppose, fancied the tears and the horse were someway connected, came and stroked the charger's neck, and said, 'Povero Bobo'!

After dinner Mr Philips, Henry, and I rowed up to the barracks in Mr Coull's gig.[14] They appear from the outside to be a very fine building, close to the sea, and with a very handsome facade; but the inside – the dilapidation! the dirt! the rats! the fleas!! These last are really so terrible that several officers have been fairly routed by them, and obliged either to pitch their tents on the common or to sleep on board the ships. No provision whatever has been made for the soldiers; and, if Captain Fraser had not put a basket of provisions in the caïque[15] that took the baggage, neither officers nor men would have broken their fast tonight. The stables into which I went first, of course, are more like the crypt of a church than anything else - dark, unpaved, unstalled, of enormous size, and cool: no straw and no mangers!

Wednesday, 24th – Our orders are to have the ship ready for sea tomorrow, and to re-embark the horses on Friday, to proceed to Varna. We hear that an English frigate has been run on shore by a Greek pilot, and blown up by Russians or Austrians, no one is very clear which.[16] Today, for the first time since I left England, I induced Mrs Williams,[17] the sergeant-major's wife, who came out as my maid, to wash a few of the clothes which had accumulated during our voyage. I mention this, as being the first assistance she has ever thought fit to render me since I left England.

Thursday, 25th – At five this morning a tug came alongside, and took us to the quay at Kulali barracks. Steamers which arrived yesterday evening confirmed the intelligence respecting the *Tiger*. We are under orders to proceed to Varna without delay. A more brilliant morning never smiled upon the earth; and I think I never can forget the *coup d'oeil* that presented itself as I ran up on deck. Behind us on either side lay the beautiful city of Constantinople, embowered in trees, and surmounted by its tall and slender minarets. The gay-coloured houses, painted in every imaginable colour, lit up the already brilliant scene; while the picturesque costumes of the Turkish and Greek boatmen, rowing down the current in their gaudy and well-poised caïques, with the long line of Kulali barracks, with its avenue of shady trees, formed a picture of light and shadow truly fascinating. The horse artillery were ranged on the quay, in marching order, with guns mounted, and several pack horses loaded, waiting the signal to embark on the transport, which was moored alongside. Our horses were being exercised beneath the spreading trees.

Turkish dogs, lazy and dirty, were lying about in all direction; while horribly filthy beggars were hovering everywhere, interspersed with Turkish soldiers and Greeks. The little harbour is filled with cabbages, and refuse of every description – a dead dog floating out, and a dead horse drifting close to the shore, on whose swollen and corrupted flanks three dogs were alternately fighting and tearing off the horrible flesh. Beyond this lay the sea – quiet, blue, serene, and beautiful beyond all words!

We hear that our troopers are to return to their stalls in the hold, and that we are to take government horses on our decks. We *expected* to have to convey an infantry regiment, so we are let off cheaply.

Friday, 26th – Lord Lucan,[18] who commands the Cavalry, sent an order to Major De Salis yesterday, to the effect that, 'unless Mrs Duberly had an order sanctioning her doing so, she was not to re-embark on board the *Shooting Star*, about to proceed to Varna.' Major De Salis returned for answer, that 'Mrs Duberly had not disembarked from the *Shooting Star*, and he had not sufficient authority to order her to do so.'

Up to this time (ten o'clock) I have heard nothing further about it. My dear husband has worried himself into a state of the greatest uneasiness. He looks upon the order as a soldier: I look upon it as a woman, and laugh at it. Uneasy, of course, I am; as should the crew refuse to assist me, I must purchase a pony, and ride 130 miles (up to Varna) through a strange and barbarous country, and over the Balkan. Should I find that

Lord Lucan has taken other steps to annoy me, I have settled with two of the ship's company, who have agreed to put me on shore and bring me off again after dark and allow me to remain either on the main deck or in the hold until we reach Varna; and once landed, and once on horseback, shall be able to smile at this interference, which is in every way unwarrantable, as I left England by permission of the Horse Guards, and with accommodation provided by the Admiralty.

Our horses re-embarked today from a temporary quay made of boats and planking. I spent this lovely day imprisoned in my cabin – thinking it wisest not to appear on deck.

Saturday, 27th – Major De Salis let me out of durance by telling me that Lord Raglan[19] had been applied to by Lord Lucan, and had stated that he had no intention of interfering with me; so, after luncheon, Henry, Mr Coull, and I started in Mr Coull's gig for Pera, and went to Mr Seager's store, where we met Captain Tomkinson and Dr Mackay, and all went together to the Stamboul bazaar. What a walk we had! Alas that the beautiful illusion of this fairy city, as seen from the harbour, should vanish the moment one sets foot in the streets, – paved with small rocks, against which you cut your feet while stumbling over every imaginable abomination!

Ownerless dogs lying and prowling about in all directions, – horses and men heavily laden with enormous weights push through the streets, regardless of your shoulders or your toes.

The bazaar is certainly worth seeing but will be too often and too well described to make it necessary for me to enlarge upon it here. It is *amusing*, if only to listen to the enormous prices asked, and the very small ones taken. I bought some crimson slippers embroidered in gold, and Henry bought a chibouque,[20] and then we all started to walk up to the Hôtel de Bellevue for our dinner. The dinner was a failure, though the walk was not; for it was a scramble up a perpendicular hill, repaid with an exquisite view from a graveyard at the top. The row home at night refreshed me both in body and mind.

Sunday, 28th – Our orders are to be ready tomorrow to sail for Varna.[21] Someone brought a report that, immediately on landing, we were to go three days' march up the country. Nothing is arranged until the last moment; the authorities do not appear to know their own minds. The subject was discussed at grog-time, and the clamour of opinions and tongues – some witty, some discontented, some facetious, and some fuddled – was the most amusing thing possible.

Monday, 29th – King Charles's day![22] And never had King Charles more vexations to encounter on that day than we! At half-past seven came the major, with an order that all extra tents, picket poles, &c., should be landed without delay (they having all been embarked the day before). I, not feeling well, remained in bed until ten o'clock. Although the *Megaera* steam-ship was ordered to be alongside to tow us at nine this morning, she has not made her appearance, and it is now four. Neither the commanding officers afloat or ashore appear to have the least idea of what they are about. The 17th Lancers have had no order to re-embark; while we, who are only part of a regiment, and without our headquarters, are sent up to encamp at Varna, within sixty miles of the Russian force. Fifteen ponies are purchased to carry the baggage of the regiment; and the allowance for Officers is only sufficient to allow Henry and me a bullock-trunk[23] apiece – rather different to our notions of the impedimenta of a regiment! They report the commissariat at Varna as being so ill-arranged that we must not expect to get anything but salt meat for some weeks after our arrival. The *Megaera* has just passed us with the 7th Fusiliers on board. I waved my hand to Colonel Yea as they passed, the decks crammed with soldiers. I find, by the shaking of the ship that we are weighing anchor, and that the *Megaera* is going to take us in tow.

The *Maryanne* and *Echinga* have both passed us on their way up the Bosphorus – transports are coming up fast alongside Kulali barracks, and, in about an hour we too shall have looked our last upon the (outwardly) fair city of Stamboul.

Wednesday, 31st – 'In about an hour!' Why, we began to weigh anchor at four o'clock on Monday and at one o'clock today it is only just out of the water. Our ship, fitted up in such unseemly haste, has not a rope or a cable on board worth sixpence. The anchor, when half out of the water yesterday, slipped, and the cable breaking disabled two of our best men. Our captain, after running through the various courses of rage – swearing and cursing – has become philosophical and smilingly indifferent. Captain Johnson, of the *Megaera*, who began at the other end, is going rapidly mad. We, the *Clipper*, the finest ship afloat, who were the first to receive orders to get under weigh, are the last to leave the harbour. Let me shut up my journal, the subject is too disastrous. Oh, the creaking of that windlass! the convulsive shivering of the ship! the grinding of the hawsers! However, at four o'clock we are off at last; and I think there is not one who does not regret leaving the gay and lovely Bosphorus, and Pera, near which we have been anchored so long, refreshing ourselves with strawberries, oranges, and sherbet,[24] lying lazily on the burning deck, and feeling as though excess of beauty overcame our languid pulses.

Eight o'clock – We have all been on deck, watching the beauties of the coast as they disappeared behind us: Therapia – where is the Hôtel D'Angleterre,[25] the resort of the wives of English naval and military officers, who have 'accompanied their husbands to the seat of war'; the stone bridge and plane trees of seven stems; the noble viaduct overlooking Beikos Bay, and, finally, the broad surface of the Black Sea. The huge engines and filthy smoke of the *Megaera* made our vessel heave and filled us with nausea.

CHAPTER 2

Embarkation and
Encampment at Varna

*The French and British armies arrived at Varna in early
June and set up camp in the countryside around the town,
ready to aid the Turks besieged at Silistria, seventy miles
away (see map, p. 20). After invading Wallachia (modern
Rumania), the Russians had concentrated their attack on
Silistria in an attempt to cross the Danube, march into
Bulgaria and advance on Constantinople. In the event
no troops were sent by the Allies (apart from two young
British officers), and it looked as though the fortress
would fall despite the Turks' determined stand against
increasingly overwhelming odds. But the siege ended
abruptly when the Austrians, who had earlier declared
their neutrality, issued an ultimatum to the Tsar on 18
June: either he withdrew his army from the principalities
north of the Danube or Austria would support Turkey.
Four days later the Russians withdrew. Meanwhile the
Austrians agreed to occupy the principalities for the
duration of the war.*

*The French and the British now faced a dilemma—
whether to return home, or to attack Sebastopol and
destroy the Russian Black Sea fleet and the dockyard in
which it was based. Both governments were keen to
attack, envisaging a short, sharp engagement, but the
commanders in the field, with little information as to the
strength or disposition of the Russian forces and defences
in the Crimea, were less certain of a swift conclusion to
the campaign. Raglan reluctantly agreed to move after
receiving a strongly worded dispatch from Newcastle in*

mid-July. He sent out a naval reconnaissance party and began the slow task of collecting transport ships. The huge fleet of over a hundred vessels finally set sail in early September.

In the interim the troops sweltered in the summer heat during interminable field-day exercises. Men and horses suffered acutely. The infantry spent hours drilling while stifled in their heavy uniforms and high leather stocks (see p. 296, note 27). The cavalry, carrying out manoeuvres in the blazing sun, were ordered to charge and 'Chargeagain'—which became Fanny's nickname for Lord Cardigan—until 'their horses were fit to drop' (see Biographies: Cardigan). The cavalry's troubles culminated in Cardigan's infamous 'sore-back reconnaissance' when they covered some three hundred miles in seventeen days; many of the troopers fell sick and nearly a hundred of their horses died from the harsh conditions (see p. 270, note 23).

The flaws in the Commissariat were apparent from the start. Unable to procure sufficient transport locally, they regularly failed to distribute food and supplies. The first of Fanny's anonymous letters, published in the Observer (see p. 269, note 18), exposed these problems and the over-optimistic view of the press. British troops were amazed at how completely the French had taken over Varna. In every street were cafés and stores selling French goods, emphasising how much more efficient they were at procuring supplies. The fire that destroyed much of Varna in early August also burnt huge quantities of British food and equipment that should have been distributed earlier. The loss delayed the start of the expedition by several weeks.

Already weakened by exhaustion and lack of proper food, men soon succumbed to the epidemic of cholera that swept through the camps from mid-July. Some

*10,000 men died even before the army left Bulgaria. The
soldiers Fanny saw marching into the camp of the Light
Brigade singing the popular marching song of the
campaign 'Cheer, boys, cheer, for the new and happy
land' soon felt very differently about their situation.
These months spent 'rotting at Varna' (as the young
adjutant of the 55th regiment wrote, lying lethargically
on his camp-bed watching the flies crawl up the tent
pole), sapped the morale and health of the British army
and sowed the seeds of future disaster.*

On Thursday, June 1st, our disembarkation commenced. We
came in sight of Varna about nine o'clock. It is a small but
clean-looking town, and certainly, from the harbour, gives
one no idea of the impregnable fortress which resisted the
Russians in 1828-9. Here the disembarkation of the horses
was dangerous and awkward, for they were obliged to lower
them into boats, and row them ashore. All were frightened -
some very restive. One trooper kicked two men, bit a third,
and sent a fourth flying overboard. At half-past four Henry
and I came ashore in Mr Coull's gig. We took leave of
Captain Fraser and the officers of the *Shooting Star* with
great regret, and, as we rowed off, all hands came aft and
cheered. [*I had made friends with nearly all of them.*] It was
kindly and heartily done, and I did not expect it; it overcame
me, and filled my eyes with tears. The landing-place gave me
a greater realisation of the idea of 'war time' than any
description could do. It was shadowing to twilight. The quay
was crowded with Turks, Greeks, infantry, artillery, and
Hussars; piles of cannon balls and shells all around us; rattle
of arms everywhere; horses kicking, screaming, plunging;
and Bob, whom I was to ride, was almost unmanageable
from excitement and flies. At length, horses were accoutred,
and men mounted, and, nearly in the dark, we commenced

The Danube front.

our march, Henry and I riding first. [*Every French soldier I passed took off his cap to me.*] Luckily, our camp was merely about a mile off. I looked at the streets, vilely paved, full of holes, and as slippery as glass, but feeling how useless was any nervousness, now that the die was cast, I gave the dear old horse his head, and he carried me without a trip to the camp. Our tent had to be brought up with the impedimenta. It was pitch dark, and the dew fell like rain. Major De Salis most kindly came to meet me, and, taking me to his tent, gave me some ham, biscuit, and brandy and water, and allowed me to lie down until my own tent was erected.

Friday, 2nd – A broiling day. There is no tree or shelter of any sort near our encampment, which is finely situated on a large plain fronting the lake. Artillery, Turkish cavalry, and eight regiments of infantry compose our camp at present, though, through the dust on my right hand, I can discern French troops marching in fast. Some of our infantry tents are pitched on mounds, which mounds are the graves of those Russians who fell in the campaign of 1828-29.[1]

Saturday, 3rd – About ten o'clock Major De Salis brought us some milk in a bottle, and we broiled a slice of the ham kindly given us by Captain Fraser of the *Shooting Star*, and so over the camp fire we made our breakfast. Our dinner at night consisted of the same, as no other rations than *bread* have been served out; and but for our ham we should have had no meat at all. Later, a welcome sight presented itself in the shape of Captain Fraser and some bottles of beer, one of which I drank like a thirsty horse. The horses are wild with heat and flies, and they scream and kick all day and night.

Lord Cardigan and staff rode into our lines.[2] Henry went into Varna, and bought a very fine grey cob pony, of the British consul, for twenty guineas. Captain Eden, of the *London*, called on me and invited me to church and luncheon tomorrow. Captain Tomkinson, Mr Philips, Dr Mackay, Henry, and I dine on board the *Shooting Star*. Am I *not* hungry?

[*Lady Errol is here with the Rifles. She and I the only ladies. She* *always* *goes about with a brace of loaded revolvers in her belt!! Very* *cocktail and no occasion for it ...* [3] *There are enormous snakes − a* *yard long − lizards in our beds and our tent is on a black ant's nest!* *I am bitten literally all at once − what with Kulali fleas & the ants* *here. The outlying party of Cossacks were seen in the hills about ten* *miles off last night and the R*[ussian] *army is within 60 miles ...* *The Turks are barbarians and dirty to a degree ... I fancy you* *think we are sitting upon divans − drinking sherbet & smoking* *Narghillies − instead of being eaten alive − boiled − & feeding on* *junk. However we are all in good heart and have plenty of pluck.*][4]

Sunday, 4th − We started on horseback at half-past nine to meet the gig, which was waiting for us in the harbour. Lady Erroll, whom I am curious to see, was also asked, but as Lord Erroll was under arrest she could not leave.[5] After service we inspected the ship, a magnificent two-decker of ninety guns, and partook of a most refreshing luncheon. Lord George Paulet, who had written to me in the morning, came and carried us off to the *Bellerophon*, and entertained us most hospitably. When we rode home at night, we found the 17th Lancers disembarking.

Captain Wallace, 7th Fusiliers, who was killed yesterday by a fall from his pony, was buried today − the first-fruits of the sacrifice! We march to-morrow morning at five to Devna, a village about nineteen miles up the country. After I had packed, I sat down outside the tent, and wrapped myself in the novel beauties of the scene − the great plain bordered by the vast lake; the glorious colours of sunset; the warlike confusion of foreground; hussar and artillery horses picketed; infantry encamped; Turkish soldiers galloping here and there on their active little horses; Bashi-Basouks[6] all round us, and the smoke of the camp-fires throwing a blue haze over the whole.

Monday, 5th − Was awoke by the *reveillée* at half-past two; rose, packed our bedding and tent, got a stale egg and a mouthful of brandy, and was in my saddle by half-past five.

I never shall forget that march! It occupied nearly eight
hours. The heat intense, the fatigue overwhelming; but the
country – anything more beautiful I never saw! – vast plains;
verdant hills, covered with shrubs and flowers; a noble lake;
and a road, which was merely a cart track, winding through a
luxuriant woodland country, across plains and through deep
bosquets of brushwood.

A most refreshing river runs near our camp, but we have
no trees, no shelter. Captain Tomkinson made me a bed of
his cloak and sheepskin; and drawing my hat over my eyes,
I lay down under a bush, close to Bob, and slept till far
towards evening.

Tuesday, 6th – The major was busy in arranging and
settling the men; but towards the afternoon, Captain
Tomkinson, Henry, and I rode into the village, to try to
procure some *vin du pays* for our dinner (wherein we failed);
and to the hills, to try for some green forage for our horses,
as the straw brought by the natives is little else than old bed
stuffing, and full of fleas. We met one of the commanders of
the Turkish army going with an escort to Schumla. His belt
and holsters were most magnificently chased. He was on the
small horse of the country, and had just mounted a fresh
relay. His escort looked like a collection of beggars on
horseback; but the little active horses sprang into a gallop at
once, and kept it up over tracks that would puzzle many a
clever English hunter. After our horses had fed on long grass
and flowers, we came home to our dinner. A French colonel
in the Turkish service, Colonel Du Puy, called on us in the
evening, and interested us much by his account of his last
winter's campaigning in this comfortless country.

Wednesday, 7th – Captain Tomkinson and Mr Clutterbuck,
each with eight men, went out to patrol: they went about ten
miles, in different directions, but saw no Cossacks.

Lord Cardigan joined this detachment of the brigade
today.[7] Part of the 17th Lancers also marched in.

Saturday, 10th – The headquarters and Captain Lockwood's troop have arrived at Varna, and were expected up today; but as they had no baggage ponies, nor any means of conveyance for the baggage, they were detained until we could send down our ponies to bring them up.[8] This does not strike me as well arranged. Whose fault is it? The infantry of the Light Division were also ordered up to Devna today, to form a large camp in conjunction with us; but as it poured with rain they could not march. Captain Tomkinson, with a sergeant and nine men, has been away on patrol these three days, but is expected back tonight. Lord Cardigan forbids them to take their cloaks to wrap round them at night, as he considers it 'effeminate'. Luckily it is summer, though the dews fall like rain. Our camp is most picturesque, in the midst of a large and fertile plain, near a sparkling river, and carpeted with brilliant flowers – burrage, roses, larkspurs, heather, and a lovely flower the name of which I do not know. Henry and I wandered among the hills this afternoon; and Bob sped over the long grass and delicate convolvuli, neighing with delight at being loose from his picket rope, where he has been rained and blown upon incessantly for two days and nights.

Monday, 12th – Captain Tomkinson returned to-day from Basardchick, bringing me a handful of roses from the ruined village observing, as he gave them to me, that I now possessed roses from nearer the enemy than any one else.

Thursday, 15th – A mail came up today, brought up by an orderly from Varna. I received letters from S., F., and E.[9] I also got a Devizes paper, which pleased me much. The morning wet and chilly; the noon hot and sultry.

Friday, 16th – A report was rife in camp that 57,000 Austrians were marching to our assistance against the Russians; also that the whole force, English and French, will be under immediate marching orders for Silistria, as 90,000 Russians are investing the town.

Saturday, 17th – Weather intensely hot – no shade, no breeze. Headquarters marched up today from Varna. Mr Philips left today for Tirnova, where he was sent to purchase 500 horses. They inform us today that the Austrian force is 300,000, and it is uncertain upon which side they will fight. What a comfort we find in our double marquee tent! The lining excludes the heat more effectually than anything else, and it is so much more easy of ventilation than a bell tent. The Bulgarian pony Whisker, proving too active with his heels, was obliged to be picketed by himself; and not liking it, amused himself, and bothered us, by untying the knot with his teeth, and scampering all over the country. The Light Division are *really* expected up on Monday, when it is supposed we shall begin our march in earnest. Such an expectation fills all minds with excitement and hope: I pity the Russian army which encounters our men as they are now. We hear wonders of the valour of the Turks. Every day the Russians make breaches in the walls, and rushing on to the attack, are beaten off every day by these dauntless men at the point of the bayonet. The Russians, a few days since, sent in a flag of truce to bury their dead: the Turks not only agreed, but sent a party to assist.

[*Lady Erroll fights on very well, Sir G. Brown*[10] *puts every obstacle he can in her way but (Lord Erroll) has got out of his scrape and they say she has nothing but a baggage pony to ride & she tried to ride on top of the baggage when they marched from Varna. So they all fell down together and she had to pick up her boxes and lead the pony and <u>walk</u>. One poor soldier's wife walked that burning day nine miles & was within an ace of her confinement.*]

Wednesday, 21st – The 5th Dragoon Guards and two troops of the 13th Light Dragoons marched to join our encampment today. The former took up a position nearer the river, but the 13th came up on our right, between the 17th Lancers and ourselves. Yesterday we performed a 'grand march': we shifted our ground, and went about 200 yards further up the valley. This movement occupied us from six a.m. to three p.m. The ground, which had not been previously marked out, took some time to choose, and Lord Cardigan and aides-de-camp were a wearisome time in arranging it; and when it *was arranged,* we were put more than a mile from the water; whereas, by a different disposition of the troops, all might have been equally near to the river bank.

Thursday, 22nd – Henry and I started at half-past twelve to ride over to the Infantry Camp; Captain Lockwood mounted me on his roan horse, and Henry rode the grey. We missed our track, and made thirteen miles out of seven. We wandered through most exquisite woodlands, through sunny glades and banks of sweet spring flowers, passed trees through whose green leaves the golden sunlight fell dropping in a shower, and through deep shadows and thickets, beneath which our horses could hardly force their way. Arrived at the camp, we inquired for about a dozen of our friends, and found they had, everyone, without a single exception, 'gone into Varna'; so there was nothing for it but to turn our horses' heads homewards through the weary heat. Hurrying home to be in time for dinner (we had had nothing but a piece of bread and a glass of water, kindly given me by a good commissary), we found only dis-appointment, for the bottom of the pot had come out, and all the stew was in the fire.

Friday, 23rd – The 17th Lancers got up some pony races today, over a tolerable course of a mile. Captain Morgan won gallantly, on a pony for which he had paid 50s.

Sunday, 25th – Was awoke at four o'clock from a profound sleep, by the words, 'A general order for the regiment to be prepared as soon as possible to march thirty miles.' All the camp was alive. No tents were to be struck, but every one was to move. We could make nothing of the order, until we

heard that a courier had arrived to say that the Russians had
abandoned the siege of Silistria, and had crossed the
Danube. We still dressed in haste, wondering at the order,
when an aide-de-camp came up to say that only a squadron
of the 8th and a squadron of the 13th were to go; and that
they were to march toward Silistria to make a reconnaissance of the Russian army. The order to 'bridle and
saddle' was given, and all was ready for a start, when a
counter-order arrived – 'The squadrons are to wait until
three days' provisions are cooked'; so that of the whole
regiment roused at four, two troops went away at half-past
ten. If it takes six hours and a half to get two squadrons
under weigh, how long will it take to move the whole British
force?

[*At last we had the satisfaction of seeing the poor old creature
(pitiable old Cardigan) ride away at the head of a squadron of
8th & a squadron of 13th without having, as I believe, the smallest
idea of where he was going or what he was going for. Cardigan,
who commands us, Lord Lucan, who commands the whole
cavalry,*[11] *& Sir Geo(rge) Brown, who commands the Lt.
Division are three of the greatest fidgets and most pitiable old
women you ever heard of. The very privates scoff at them and they
drive the officers wild.*]

At six o'clock Henry, Major de Salis, and I rode over to
the Turkish camp to dine with Colonel Du Puy.

[*We shall dine in his tent and take our forks and plates. ... The
French are all delighted at my coming out and the Turks wonder
as much as such nil admirable people can at a woman galloping
about on a big English horse instead of being bundled in a veil &
huddled out of sight.*]

We met Mr G[odkin],[12] the correspondent of the *Daily
News,* also M. Henri, and another officer, aides-de-camp to
Maréchal St Arnaud.[13] These two last were returning from
Schumla, whither they had conveyed a fine Turkish horse, as
a gift from the Maréchal to Omar Pasha.[14] I saw the little

horse. He was about fourteen hands, black, with the exception of two white marks and a white foot. Omar Pasha returned him, as a Turkish superstition prevents the soldiers from riding horses not entirely of a colour. He who rides a black, bay, or chestnut horse with white marks, or a white foot behind, will assuredly be slain in battle. A Turkish officer joined our party during the evening; and after sitting, for some time in silence, smoking his chibouque, he informed me, through his interpreter (he had been staring at me for half an hour previously) that it was only permitted him to sit in my presence during war-time; under any other circumstances he could not sit down with a woman who was unveiled.

[*Does it not seem wonderful that we have been disembarked nearly a month and have made no attempt to get near the Russians in any way? Everything seems to be done to delay and clog. No conveyance, no food, and the Army arriving up by driblets as slowly as it can. Should we march to Silistria, of which I suppose there is no chance now, we shall have to go 40 miles without water in one day's march at the rate of about 3 miles an hour – about 16 or 17 hours in the saddle.*]

Monday, 26th – Henry rode into Varna to procure money from the commissariat chest. I went out to meet him in the afternoon, and Captain Chetwode rode with me. We went as far as the Infantry camp at Aladyn, and on our way passed the headquarters of the 13th, marching up to join our camp. The lovely evening and clear sky induced us to prolong our ride so far, and we found Henry among the officers of the 23rd Welsh Fusiliers, who most hospitably pressed us to stay and partake of their excellent dinner, which we did. On our way home, in the almost impenetrable twilight, we passed close by Captain Tomkinson's poor horse, which fell under him last night as he was returning from Varna. There he lay stark and stiff, a white mass amid the dark shadows – as fine a fencer as ever strained upon the bit on a hunting morning;

and, hark! the gallop and baying of the wild dogs, even now trooping over the hills to feed upon his almost palpitating heart! Ah! mournful sight, that he should lie there, so ghastly and so still.

Thursday, 29th – Two troops of the 11th Hussars joined us today. We had no news of Lord Cardigan's patrol until after dinner, when Bowen rode into the lines on Captain Lockwood's roan horse, who bore him feebly to the picket ropes, and then fell down. For many minutes he appeared dying of exhaustion, but eventually we revived him with brandy and water. Bowen tells us that the squadrons will not return for some days; that their fatigue has been excessive, and their hardships very great. They appear to have been marching incessantly, for which hard work neither men nor horses are fit.

A French colonel on his way to Silistria dined with us this afternoon, and interested us much by his accounts of the Turkish army. He told us no army cost so much to maintain, with such infamous results. The soldiers are neither fed nor clothed. All the money which passes through the hands of the pashas sticks to their fingers. Often, when halting after a long march, they inquire whether any meat is to be served out to them. 'No!' 'Any bread?' 'No!' They shrug their shoulders and betake themselves to cold water and a pipe. A more wretched appearance, than that which they present cannot be imagined; but at Silistria they have proved their courage.

Friday, 30th – Part of the Light Division marched up this morning, and encamped on the opposite side of the valley. The Rifles [15] marched in first; next followed the 33rd playing 'Cheer, boys, cheer;' and cheerily enough the music sounded across our silent valley, helping many a 'willing, strong right hand', ready to faint with heat and fatigue. The 88th Connaught Rangers gave a wild Irish screech (I know no better word) as they saw their fellow countrymen, the 8th

Royal Irish Hussars, and they played 'Garry Owen' with all their might; while the 77th followed with 'The British Grenadier'. A troop of R[oyal] H[orse] A[rtillery] also came up to Devna. The accession of 7,000 men will be like a plague of locusts: they will eat up our substance. We can get little else but stale eggs, tough chickens, and sour milk, and now we shall not get even that; and the cries of 'Yak-mak Johnny!', 'Sud Johnny', 'Eur mooytath Johnny' will be transferred from the cavalry to the 'opposition lines'.

[*When you read beautiful stories in* The Times *of the comforts of the British Army, its groceries, porter, and patés de foie gras, don't believe a word of it. It's all humbug and sham invented I believe by that cunning old dodger Aberdeen,*[16]*as never was an army worse provided; we had one cask of porter at Varna, but never any since often as it has been applied for; the Guards when at Scutari ate up all the stores, while we poor devils of the Light Division far ahead of them can get nothing but black bread and buffalo beef. The puffs in the paper have prevented speculators &> sutlers* [17] *from coming out &> doubtless when they know the truth many will come out. Our men grumble dreadfully, as well they may, as they are paid in English gold for which until lately they only got 16/- a sovereign. ... Our horses have eaten all the barley here now, very nearly. We can only buy eggs and tough chickens! Tough as old shoes &> milk which is always sour before we can get it. This and poor, sour wine is all the men have to live on with their hard stable work, patrols, field days and the intense heat.*][18]

Sunday, July 2nd – Captain Tomkinson returned today from Silistria, whither he had been sent to ascertain the best road for marching troops. He described the whole Russian force, although they have lately raised the siege of Silistria, as being still in sight of the town, and speaks much of their numerous field pieces [guns]. He brought back a Russian round shot,[19] and told me he had seen two of the enemy, but lying cold and still. I hear the Turks are hardly to be restrained from mutilating their dead foes. If they can do so unseen, they will cut off three or four heads, and, stringing them together through the lips and cheeks, carry them over their shoulders, like a rope of onions.*[20] The Turks inform us that the Russians say they will treat the Turks whom they make prisoners, as prisoners of war, but the French and English will be treated as felons, and sent to Siberia; and really, if the Russians are as uncleanly, smell as strong, and eat as much garlic, as the Turks, it will be the best thing that can happen to us under the circumstances. We have had a hurricane all day, filling our tents, eyes, dinners, hair, beds, and boxes with intolerable dust. Our chicken for dinner was so tough that not even our daily onions could get it down. We were forced to shake our heads at our plates, and relinquish the dinner. The black bread, which is kneaded on the ground, is a happy mixture of sand, ants, and barley – and it is besides so sour that it makes my eyes water.

Monday, 3rd – At three o'clock we were ordered to turn out as quickly as possible in light marching order, to receive Omar Pasha, who wished to inspect the troops, and was on his road from Schumla to Varna, where he was to hold a council of war. In ten minutes the cavalry were mounted, and Henry and I started upon Bob and the Great Grey, to see the man whom war had made so famous. His appearance struck me as military and dignified. He complimented all our troops, and insisted on heading the Light Cavalry charge, which made me laugh, for he was on a small Turkish horse, and had to scramble, with the spurs well in, to get out of the way of our long-striding English horses. He was loudly cheered; appeared highly gratified; made me a bow and paid me a compliment, and proceeded to his carriage to continue his journey.

---

* Although this may have been true of some of the irregular troops in the Turkish army, such a practice is utterly abhorrent to the Turks themselves, who know how to combine the highest degree of bravery with the most chivalrous humanity (1855 Editor).

Thursday, 6th – Reports of a more peaceful nature reach us. We hear that Omar Pasha is the only counsellor for war. The Russian force is retreating daily. Now the 'shave' [rumour] is, that Austria is beginning to be afraid lest the English and French armies should decline to leave this fertile land, and all the powers, inimical or neutral, appear desirous to hush the matter up.[21] The party which returned today from Silistria inform us of the good feeling shown by the Turks to their Russian prisoners. They feed them with their meat and rice, and treat them with every mark of kindness and consideration. The peaceful reports which reach us give dissatisfaction. We are all for one good fight, to see which is the better man; all for one blow, struck so effectually as to crush all warlike propensities against us forever. We hear today of the terrible fate of the *Europa*.[22] Report at present speaks so vaguely that we know not what to believe. At first we were told that every soul had perished, and afterwards that only Colonel Willoughby Moore and the veterinary surgeon fell victims to this terrible catastrophe. A more frightful tragedy could scarcely occur than the burning of a transport ship – soldiers ignorant of seafaring, and horses crammed in the hold! Omar Pasha returned again today, and on his way inspected the Heavy Cavalry and Artillery. Lord Raglan also came up, and the staff made a brilliant display. Omar Pasha again expressed himself in the most complimentary manner; and after it was all over, Henry and I turned our horses' heads and went for a ride.

[(*Omar Pasha*) *is quite a famous man and one I am proud to have seen. He is grey – small – clean & gentlemanly. A Croatian – talking indifferent French. Went away into Varna, after inspecting us, to hold a Council of War, and would not begin till he had been told who 'the beautiful English Lady with the long flaxen curls' was – at least Lord Raglan told me – when he came up with him on Thursday. Lord Raglan came up immediately to be introduced . . . (Omar Pasha) was astonished by the rapidity of* *our charge. ... He wanted to give <u>us all medals</u> but Raglan chaffed him out of it ... Bob looked remarkably well both days and O.P. admired him and asked if I was not afraid of so big a horse. I have sent for a Turkish bridle to Constantinople, a crimson one – all over tassels & silver crescents.*

Meantime our unfortunate squadron which went out on 25th June under Lord Cardigan ... have never turned up. Cardigan started the morning after the news reached us that the Russians had raised the siege of Silistria & taking two squadrons went to 'try & discover the movement of the enemy', the wildest goose chase that ever was undertaken. Lord Raglan sent after him to stop him – and we heard yesterday that the aide-de-camp had traced them to Schumla by the dead horses on the route! I hope and trust Cardigan will get his head into such a jolly bag that he will never get it out again. They of course have seen nothing of the Russians who are far enough away from Silistria by this time.

Poor Lady Erroll is sick of campaigning – tho' she has a ladys-maid and a foreign servant to cook &c. <u>We</u> engaged a servant yesterday, after immense trouble, for we found <u>seven</u> horses & <u>valeting</u> rather too much for Connell's weak mind – but we could get no one until yesterday, when we took an English coachman, whose wife is at Malta and who tempted by the enormous rate of wages has come out here ... He has £7 a month, and laughs at the idea of less. He could get 8 or 9 if he tried but we are lucky to have got him.]

Tuesday, 11th – The reconnaissance, under Lord Cardigan, came in this morning, at eight, having marched all night.[23] They have been to Rassova, seen the Russian force, lived five days on water and salt pork; have shot five horses, which dropped from exhaustion on the road, brought back an araba full of disabled men, and seventy-five horses, which will be, as Mr Grey says, unfit for work for many months, and some of them will never work again. I was out riding in the evening when the stragglers came in; and a piteous sight it was – men on foot, driving and goading on their wretched,

wretched horses, three or four of which could hardly stir. There seems to have been much unnecessary suffering, a cruel parade of death, more pain inflicted than good derived; but I suppose these sad sights are merely the casualties of war, and we must bear them with what courage and fortitude we may. One of these unfortunate horses was lucky enough to have his leg broken by a kick, as soon as he came in, and was shot. There is an order that no horse is to be destroyed unless for glanders or a broken leg.[24]

[*I will not disgust you by detailing reports just sent in by Cardigan saying that the 90 horses will be reported to Hd Quarters as fit to work in 3 days tho' most of them have the whole surface of the saddle raw – flyblown & green.*

I must have thick boots. Today I have made myself a drab jean habit skirt! Cut it out, made it, all myself!

You ask me what I wear – Brown holland or cotton gowns – things that will wash. A drab jean habit embroidered (the body) with dark blue – and a white felt hat with a quantity of white muslin bound round it. ... I have been obliged to discard all extra petticoats, and have only a gown tail and some linen drawers – and of course no bonnet.]

Thursday, 13th – A long morning was spent in investigating the state of the horses by Colonel Shewell, Lord Cardigan, and Mr Grey. I despatched letters to Captain Fraser of the *Shooting Star*, and Lady Duberly. A sad event closed this day. One of our sergeants, who had been ill for some days previously, left the hospital tent about three o'clock a.m., and, when our watering parade went down to the river, they found his body in the stream: he was quite dead. He was a steady and most respectable man: could he have had a fore-boding of the lingering deaths of so many of his comrades, and so rashly have chosen his own time to appear before God? The band of the Connaught Rangers came at seven o'clock to play him to a quieter resting-place than the bed of the sparkling, babbling stream – a solitary grave dug just in front of our lines and near enough for us, during our stay, to protect him from the dogs.

Three more of the reconnoitring party's horses are lying in the shadow of death. I had been pained by all this, and Henry and I, ordering our horses, rode out, in the cloudless summer evening, to a quiet little village nestled among the hills, where the storks build their nests on the old tree-tops that shade the trickling fountain where the cattle drink. Colonel Shewell met us as we rode into camp, with a radiant face, telling us that all the transports are ordered up from Varna, and that we are to embark immediately for *Vienna*, as the Russians are so enraged with Austria for taking part against us that they have determined on besieging that place.

Saturday, 15th – The Vienna 'shave' turned out false; instead, came an order desiring that all our *heavy baggage* should be sent to Varna, to be forwarded to Scutari. Heavy baggage! when we are already stript of everything but absolute necessaries, and are allowed barely sufficient ponies to transport what we have!

[*We have nothing for transport but <u>baggage</u> ponies. Sir G. Brown will not allow <u>a single</u> bullock cart for regimental baggage. These small ponies are cut down to as small a number as possible and are most cruelly overloaded. ... <u>We</u> have baggage ponies and <u>I</u> have an araba, or light cart with a good sturdy pony, which said araba <u>I mean to keep</u>, and drive though all the regulations in the world.*]

Letters arrived last night, but were not delivered till today. Yesterday evening Henry and I took a lovely ride to Kosludsche, a small town about eight miles from the camp. The pastoral scenes, in this land of herds and flocks, speak in flute-like tones of serenity and repose – the calm, unruffled lives of the simple people, the absence of all excitement, emulation, traffic, or noise; valley and hillside sending home each night its lowing herds, and strings of horses, flocks of sheep and goats. The lives of the inhabitants are little removed above the cattle which they tend; but to one who has 'forgotten more life than most people ever knew', the absence of turmoil and all the 'stale and unprofitable uses of the world,' the calm aspect of the steadfast hills, the quietude of the plains, and the still small voices of the flowers, all tell me, that however worn the mind may be, however bruised the heart, nature is a consoler still; and we who have fretted away our lives in vain effort and vainer show, find her large heart still open to us, and in the shadow of the eternal hills a repose for which earth has no name.

Sunday, 16th – Henry and I took a new ride this evening. We turned into the gorge to the left of our camp; but leaving the araba track, we struck into a narrow footpath embowered with trees, and frowned over by stern and perpendicular rocks, at whose foot ran the narrow fissure along which we rode slowly. Emerging at last, we came on an open plain; covered with heavy crops of barley; crossing this for a short distance, we came presently into another thick copse of underwood, down which we had to ride over precipitous and rocky ground, where the horses could barely keep their footing, and where a false step must have been fatal. The stars lighted our track, and we descended safely. We found ourselves on the road to Devna, and, waking up our horses, we cantered over the plain to our camp.

Wednesday, 19th – I have mentioned nothing that has happened since Sunday; as, except the usual routine of parades and camp-life, and perpetual fresh reports as to our eventual destination, nothing has occurred. But today we lost one of the poor fellows who had returned ill from the reconnoitring expedition. He came back with low fever; and, after being two days insensible, expired this afternoon. Henry and I, accompanied by Captains Hall Dare and Evans of the 23rd, rode today to Pravadi. We started at one o'clock, and returned soon after eight. Next to Silistria,

Pravadi is the strongest fortified town in Bulgaria. The town lies in what (approaching from the Devna side) appears to be an abyss. High, perpendicular rocks, like the boundaries of a stern sea-coast, enclose it, east and west. Fortifications protect it on the south, and a fortification and broad lake on the north. We rode to it through lovely home scenery, softened by the blue range of the Balkan in the distance. We saw almost to Varna. In the town we found shops, and purchased damson-cheese and some Turkish scarfs. My pony, Whisker, cast a shoe in going, and Captain Hall Dare started without one; so we stopped at a farrier's and had them shod. My saddle excited immense curiosity. They touched and examined it all over; and several men tried to sit in it, but Henry prevented them. We went to a café where we got a cup of first-rate coffee; and at about half-past four, we started to ride home. Oh, the heat! We made a ride of about twenty-two miles, but its beauty well repaid us for our trouble.

The Turks have a unique way of shoeing horses. One man fastens a cord round the horse's fetlock, and so holds up his leg; a second man holds aside the animal's tail, and with a horse-hair flapper keeps away the flies; a third man holds his head and talks to him; while the fourth, squatting on the ground with his head on a level with the horse's foot, hammers away with all his might at eight nails, four on each side.

Friday, 21st – News came that Sir G. Brown had gone to the Crimea, to discover the best place for landing troops, and that we should follow him before long – at which we were glad.

Sunday, 23rd – The cholera[25] is come amongst us! It is not in *our* camp, but is in that of the Light Division, and sixteen men have died of it this day in the Rifles.

We hear the whole camp is to be broken up; the Light Division are to march to Monastir, and *we* are under orders to march to Issyteppe tomorrow. I regret this move very

much, as it will separate me from Lady Erroll, whose
acquaintance has been the greatest comfort and pleasure to
me; but I trust we shall soon be quartered together again, as
no one but myself can tell the advantage I have derived from
the friendship of such a woman.

Monday, 24th – The march is postponed, owing to the
difficulty of finding sufficient water at Jeni-bazaar, which is
to be our destination. Captain Lockwood volunteered to
ascertain for Lord Cardigan what were the supplies of water,
and started for that purpose this afternoon. I, acting on Lady
Erroll's suggestion, rode down to the 11th lines this evening
to call on Mrs Cresswell, who has arrived with her husband,
Captain Cresswell, of the 11th Hussars. I could not but pity
the unnecessary discomforts in which the poor lady was
living, and congratulated myself and Henry, as we rode
away, on our pretty marquee and green bower.

*[A new importation has arrived at the 11th Hussars in the
shape of a Mrs Cresswell, wife of Capt. C. She was a Miss Gordon
Cummings & we heard wonderful stories of her before she arrived
– such as that she was a 'tremendous woman', a dead shot, a
brilliant rider & very fast. Poor Lady Erroll (who is so kind to
me) & I were frightened out of our wits, especially as they put in
an Irish paper that 'when her husband was killed she would lead
the troop into action!' At last we determined to put on our most
feminine get-up, and go and call. Lady E. went on Wednesday &
did not find her at home. I went last night (Saturday) and was
unfortunate enough to find her in. We expected something rather
fashionable & brilliant – but after waiting some time a woman
came from among the troop horses – so dirty – with such
uncombed scurfy hair – such black nails – such a dirty cotton
gown, open at the neck without a sign of habit shirt or collar – or
linen sleeve – Oh you never had a kitchen maid so dreadful. She
calls the officers 'the boys' & addresses them as 'Bill' & 'Jack' –
talks of nothing but her horses – and found fault with my saddle –
which happens to be a particularly good one – says she hasn't*

*ridden for nine years – and cries with fear if the horse does
anything. Told me I was 'a fool' to have a marquee, a bell was quite
good enough for anyone – that my husband would vote me 'a bore'
if I didn't cook his dinner – that I was foolish to wear collar &
sleeves, as they were unnecessary - & that if I wished my husband
to like me I should always, the night before a march, strike my tent
& sleep either wrapped in a cloak or 'anywhere'. I should like to
see Henry sleeping out! In fact she took my breath away so
completely that I doubt if I shall not be broken-winded all my life.
I do not exaggerate when I say that her neck and bare arms were
earth-colour with dirt. They eat with three pronged steel forks with
black handles and among the plates laid for dinner was a very
old hair brush with the handle broken off. Lady Errol is charming
– she is an innate lady and is very kind to me – we are great
friends. She can ride a bit but I never hear her mention her horse.
Mrs Cresswell allows no woman near her tent, so who empties the
slops or how she manages about &c &c I can't divine – I suppose
the soldier servant does it.*

*It is very agreeable having so many men that one knows & we
know two or three in almost every regiment out.*

*Our English servant is a great comfort and Connell works
better for his help. Lynch who we have out of the troops is also a
useful man. And I find the officers & Colonel all ready & willing
to do anything for me. I take it as easy as I can for I find that even
this foolish work is hard & tough & the food is so uncertain & the
exposure to the weather is trying. I have not been under a roof for
these three months. Yesterday in the midst of the heat we had a
dust storm. The wind suddenly sprung up & volumes of dust
covered us – the dust subsided in an hour but the wind raged all
night blowing down several of the tents.]*

Present orders say we do not march till Wednesday. Lord
Cardigan has been searching unsuccessfully for another
camping-ground.

[*We remain here until our sagacious brigadier Lord Cardigan
has discovered a place where we can move. ... He has been*

worrying and harassing the men and destroying the horses by having incessant field days, parades, & marching orders every day since we have been here, each of which has occupied about five hours. Now five hours on horseback is known to take as much out of man & horse as a twenty mile march, consequently all the hospitals are now full, and there is hardly a horse, except here and there an officer's second or third charger who is fit to be taken from the picket lines.

Things being in this state Cardigan began to fear he should get a second reprimand so this morning he rode into the lines, assembled the Colonels and said, 'I have been given to understand that the illness of the men & inefficiency of the horses arises from overwork & not from the insalubrity of the air. I desire <u>all Colonels not to overwork</u> their men!! & Colonel Shewell I particularly request you will not allow your men to be worked!!'

Poor Col. Shewell who has been almost weeping every day over the way Cardigan overworks his men is now nearly frantic.]

Mr Macnaghten, who rode into Varna, tells me that the transports are all being ordered up, but that the *Shooting Star* had been cast on account of defective rigging. Henry rode into Varna. Towards evening I started on horseback with Captain Chetwode to meet him, and we rode to Aladyn. The infantry of our division moved today eight miles over the hills. They move in the hope of averting that fearful malady which has crept among them. We hear it is raging at Varna, and that a quarantine is established between that place and Constantinople. For ourselves, we have had a solitary case of small-pox; but the poor fellow has been taken to the hospital at Varna today.

Tuesday, 25th – Orders to march tomorrow morning to Issyteppe.

Two o'clock, p.m. – Captain Lockwood having returned, and reported an insufficiency of water, he was ordered to repair again to the place to endeavour to discover water in the neighbourhood.

Three o'clock – March postponed till tomorrow night at soonest, Lord Cardigan having taken a fancy to a night march. There is no moon just now.

Five o'clock – March definitely settled for tomorrow morning at six.

Thursday, 27th – The cavalry of the Light Division, with Captain Maude's troop of Horse Artillery, marched this morning to Issyteppe, a wretched village situated in a large plain about twelve miles from Devna.

[*The staff doctors all told Lord Cardigan that a move of three miles, just to leave the foul ground and cross to the other side of the river, was all that was necessary – but – My Lord being fond of flourishing about the country, and there being no water or any conveniences for the troops at Jeni-basar he resolved to remove us there instantly, though at a distance of nearly 30 miles up the country ... we began our march – at six o'clock* <u>*without*</u> *watering the horses though we crossed our river that runs thro' Devna. The 8th went first, Mrs H. Duberly riding at the head of the column.*]
A most uninteresting country led to it – flat and bare, destitute of trees or water, except one half-dried fountain, with a rotting carcass lying beside it. When we attempted to water our thirsty horses, only few could drink; the rest had to hold on, as best they could, till they reached their journey's end. A now dry, boggy ditch which runs through the village brought a plague of frogs to our camp; and a heavy thunderstorm, rattling on our heads as we sat on the sward at dinner, drove us, drenched and uncomfortable, to our tents, and wetted our boxes. Captain Lockwood and I walked down to the village before sunset, to endeavour to procure an araba wheel (ours had come off), also a chicken for tomorrow's breakfast; but we failed in both; there was nothing but old women, cats, and onions in the place.

Friday, 28th – My husband's birthday! and he is likely to be, for today at least, miserable enough. We were roused, wet and dreary, at three o'clock. At six we were in our saddles; and a very distressing march I found it, though it did not exceed fourteen miles. The heat was intolerable, the sun blinding. The horses again started without water; nor was there any between Issyteppe and Jeni-bazaar. We reached the latter place about half-past eleven; and immediately after the piquet poles were put down, there was a simultaneous rush to the fountains of the town to water the horses. Poor wretches, how they rushed to the water! Poor old Hatchet (Captain Lockwood's horse) nearly went head foremost down the well, while others upset bucket after bucket, by thrusting their heads into them before they reached the ground. There was a fine group of trees near a fountain opposite our lines and under their refreshing shade the brigadier pitched his tent. A feeling of great dissatisfaction was caused by the troops being forbidden either to water their horses or to obtain water for the use of the officers from the fountain in question, although the other fountains are so far off. The fountain, being so little drained, overflowed in the night and a fatigue party were put in requisition to make a drain. If Æsop were alive, I wonder if this would inspire him with another fable? Tonight I am thoroughly exhausted with fatigue.

[*Immediately on arriving at our camping ground, which is a high plain, as bare as your hand and as ugly as heart can desire, we descried two solitary trees and a fountain trickling beneath them within 100 yards of where our regt stands. H and I cantered off to it at once and when the horses had drank we stayed for five minutes in the pleasant shade while they were marking out the ground for our tent. We had not been there five minutes hot, tired and grateful for the shade when my Lord Cardigan sent his aide de camp to deliver the following message 'Lord Cardigan desires I will say you must not pitch your tent under these trees, as he is going to put his there.' ... Of course, I told the story and it spread all over the camp. ... one man when he heard it, was silent for a moment & then said slowly, 'I wish a great, d—d, wind would come & blow down those d—d trees upon his d—d, d-a-m-d-d old head.' They built me a bower*

*before evening & Cardigan saw it. The fountain Cardigan desired
might be left for his own use – & no horses but his go there –
consequently it overflowed in the night & ran into his tent.*

*The confusion of the people at Jeni-bazaar when these 1,200
unbelieving soldiers came tumbling down upon their fountains &
shops was indescribable. The great horses scrambling for water,
some nearly plunging into the well, & the clamour for eggs, chickens,
curds, milk & barley terrified them so that they shut up their
shops & popped their turbans out of windows crying out 'Yok',
'yok' meaning that they had nothing to sell tho' we had seen just
before that 'their granaries were stored well'.*]

Sunday, 30th – Lord Cardigan tells us today that we
shall remain here until we go into winter quarters at
Adrianople.

Tuesday, August 1st – Our tents not being pitched on the
right (our place as senior regiment out), Lord Cardigan
changed us today causing us to change places with the 13th
Light Dragoons. Our tents when changed were not quite in a
line, though I confess it was barely perceptible; but at evening we had to strike and move all our tents about a foot and
a half further back. We hear today that the Light Division
have lost 100 men and 4 officers.

Friday, 4th – I regret to say that poor Captain Levinge of
the R. H. A. is dead. The report is, that having been suffering
from incipient cholera, he took an overdose of laudanum.
He is much regretted. An artilleryman of Captain Maude's
troop died of cholera, and was buried yesterday. This is our
first case of cholera. Captain Stevenson, 17th Lancers, took
me for a ride this evening to a wondrous gorge, about three
miles from our camp. We passed suddenly from a sunny
landscape, laden with grain, into Arabia Petraea. It was as
though the hills had been rifted asunder, so high, so narrow,
sombre, and stern were the gloomy walls that almost
threatened to close over our heads. A small torrent ran at the
foot, tumbling over huge masses of rock, which had fallen

from the grim heights above. I felt oppressed; and reaching
the open fields once more, put Bob into a canter, which he
seemed as willing to enjoy as myself.

Saturday, 6th – 'I never watched upon a wilder night.'
At evening-tide it was hot and sultry, but at midnight up
came the wind, sweeping broadly and grandly over the plain.
We feared for our tent, although well secured; and presently
across the hurricane came booming the great guns of
the thunder. The lightning seemed to pierce our eyelids.
By morning every trace of storm had vanished, and day
looked out smiling as before, though her lashes were gemmed
with heavy tear-drops, and the deep trees near us at intervals
shivered out a sigh. The adjutant-general came to camp
today. He says the Infantry are under orders to embark on the
16th for the Crimea. Are we to go too? or are we to be left out
here, to constitute a travelling Phoenix Park for Lord. ... ?[26]

Thursday, 10th – Rose at half-past three, and by five,
Henry, Captain Tomkinson, Captain Chetwode, Mr
Mussenden, and I were starting for Schumla. We broke into
a canter after leaving the village of Jeni-bazaar, and in
two hours and five minutes reached Schumla, a distance
of fifteen miles. Here we met Captain Saltmarshe, Mr
Trevelyan, and Mr Palmer, of the 11th, and Mr Learmouth
of the 17th, and had a joint breakfast, and a very nasty one, at
the Locanda, kept by Hungarians. That over, we walked
about the town. It is very picturesque; the houses are nestled
in trees, but are irregular, dirty, and mean. In the Greek
shops we succeeded in making a few purchases, such as a
glass tumbler, five china plates, a soup ladle (tin), and some
Turkish towels. I tried hard to procure some tea, lemons, or
arrowroot for our sick in hospital, but I might as well have
asked for a new-fashioned French bonnet. They did not
know what I wanted. I bought a fine crimson Turkish bridle,
and we returned to the Locanda, where I lay down on the
boards (oh, how hard they were!) to try to sleep for an hour.

It was impossible. The bugs took a lease of me, and the fleas, in innumerable hosts, disputed possession. A bright-eyed little mouse sat demurely in the corner watching me, and twinkling his little black eyes as I stormed at my foes. Our dinner was tough meat and excellent champagne, which we did not spare; and after admiring the sunset tints on the fine forts of the town, we again got into our saddles; and a great moon, with a face as broad, red, round, and honest as a milkmaid's, shed her hearty beams over us and lighted us home, and afterwards to bed.

Poor Major Willett lies sick in the village of Jeni-bazaar, where he has been moved for the sake of quiet.

Friday, 11th – Illinsky (or some such name), the Hungarian commandant, came over and dined with us. Two or three funerals today. The 5th Dragoon Guards are suffering terribly from cholera. Two days ago eleven men died. The report of the great fire in Varna, which reached us two days since, proves to be quite correct. It seems to have ravaged the town. Various rumours are afloat concerning its origin; some suppose it was set on fire by the Greeks, at Russian instigation. Many shops, and much of the commissariat stores, are burnt; and the plunder during the fire was said to be enormous.[27]

Our supplies must in future be drawn from Schumla. Why has there been no branch commissariat at Schumla? Varna is a two days' march from us. It is also a fact, that the commissariat chest in Varna was guarded by one slovenly Turkish sentry. Our sad sickness increases. Our hospital tents are full. Poor Mr Philips is now attacked with fever and the sun sets daily on many new-made graves. A second hospital marquee arrived for our regiment today.

Wednesday, 16th – Today's mail brought us the sad news of the death of Miss D., Henry's step-sister – loved and regretted by us all.[28]   This took away the pleasure we felt in the arrival of our letters.

Thursday, 17th – Henry and I took a ride, to endeavour to shake off the depression which this perpetual sickness forces upon one. We had never before seen suffering that we could not alleviate; but here there are no comforts but scanty medical stores, and the burning, blistering sun glares upon heads already delirious with fever. I am sure that nervous apprehension has much to do with illness; and, indeed, if the mind abandons itself to the actual contemplation of our position, it is enough to make it quail.

[*Private & Confidential*

I have nothing more to tell you this (letter), than of sickness & death. The moans of a poor wretch now dying in the hospital marquee not twenty yards from me stab my ear at this moment. Three more men died last night & Lord Fitzgibbon's private servant. Our araba is now conveying two of our sick officers to a hovel in the town where at least they will be out of trumpet call. One poor young fellow will never see his mother again I fear.

You ask how I _really_ endure what I go thro' – By never thinking of it for one moment. If anyone abandons themselves to the _contemplation_ of actualities they either fall ill or die. Nothing but the most reckless determination carries you thro'. I never, if I can avoid it, have an idle moment. Work – wash – write – all the morning – ride from four till seven _every_ day and then dinner & rum & water till bed time, or the very strongest Turkish coffee. I am very thankful for their sakes that no other women have come out – it is no place for women. You must have just as much pluck as the rest of the men – or you are trodden down. Men are so eager for their own health & their own lives – their own sports & amusements that if you cloy them – they leave you behind, if you go _with_ them it's all very well. For myself I thank God that since I put my foot on board the Shooting Star *I have never known what fear was – have never been flurried or nervous. I have ridden down steep gorges after dark with only Henry & no pistol, where men have been shot, & been just as happy as at home. My own horses fall sick, anyone who will mount me lends me a horse – none here ever had on a* *side-saddle – I ride without fear. This is to me a proof that God never puts people in situations where he doesn't help them through, if they will only trust him. I have never been absolutely ill. Out of health of course I am ... but I can't expect to be well on the food. You <u>can't</u> get arrowroot, lemons, good tea, sago, or any groceries except rice, simply because they are not in the country.*

Henry & I still have an arbor close to our tent, a table, (very rough) & a wheelwright of the Artillery has made me a camp stool. For breakfast we have bread & a <u>little</u> tea & lots of milk. We have a couple of pack-saddles in the arbor & make very comfortable divans of cloaks & wrappers, lying on the ground and leaning on the saddles. I was amused at reading one of my own letters in Galignani *the other day, who has copied it from the* Observer. *It looked deuce well in print. I wrote it to Mr Butt, MP for Weymouth. It was from Devna, June 24.*[29] *We take wonderful rides sometime with Lord Cardigan, but not often as I detest him, then we dine about seven and go into one of the officers' tents, generally Capt. Tomkinson's till bedtime. There we sit on the ground just like the 'interior of a tent' in the* Illustrated [London News] *and they smoke while I surreptitiously drink their rum and water and coffee. (see p. 262)*

This paper made at <u>Bath</u> was bought at <u>Schumla</u>.]

Friday, 18th – Poor Mrs Blaydes (my servant), after recover-   S
ing from an attack of fever, brought on a relapse today from
over-anxiety to attend to my comforts. She endeavoured to
work till her health absolutely forbad it; and a great assistance
she was to me. Poor woman! she has been insensible since
morning. A woman of the 13th died today. Hospital marquees
were shifted to fresh ground, as it was observed that men put
into them almost invariably died. Henry and I rode to where
Captain Chetwode and Mr Clutterbuck were shooting, and
on our return we met Lord Cardigan, who tells me all the talk
is of Sebastopol; and he thinks the Light Cavalry will be under
orders before long. Another mail laden with heavy news. Poor
little W.! F.'s only son![30] I have so many feelings my heart; and

yet they must all be absorbed in sympathy for the sorrowing father and mourning mother!

Saturday, 19th – Rode with Henry to a village on the left of our camp, about six miles off, the name of which I do not know. What a ride that was!

> What a day it was that day!
> Hills and vales did openly
> Seem to heave and throb away
> At the sight of the great sky
> And the silence, as it stood
> In the glory's golden flood,
> Audibly did bud and bud.[31]

After climbing up the sides of an interminable hill, we reached the table land – oaks, walnuts, filberts, a very wilderness of trees. We plunged down into a deep and leafy gorge, stopped at the wayside fountain, and finally emerged into the broad plain of the camp.

Sunday, 20th – Poor Mrs Blaydes expired this morning! Truly, we are in God's hands and far enough from the help of man! Insufficient medical attendance (many of the doctors are ill), scanty stores, and no sick diet – we must feed our dying on rations and rum! As far as I am concerned, I feel calm and filled with a tranquil faith: I have the strongest trust in the wise providence of God.

Monday, 21st – Went out with Henry over the stubble to shoot quail: Captain Chetwode had the gun, and killed several brace.

Tuesday, 22nd – Henry made a 'salmi' [32] of the quail for breakfast that was truly delicious: I could be a gourmet, if I could always feed on such salmis. Mr Clowes, Henry, and I went out today: Henry shooting, Mr Clowes and I beating from our ponies with long whips.

Wednesday 23rd – Mr Maxse, aide-de-camp to Lord Cardigan, who has returned today from Varna [sick leave], says the troops are embarking fast; that siege guns are being put on board, and every preparation making for an expedition to the Crimea. We are reanimated! The sickness decreases; cooler weather is coming on; things look cheerily now. We rode today with Captain Tomkinson – such a pretty ride! Going south for five miles, we turned to our right on smooth, long turf, by a little stream whose course was only marked by the flowers along its banks. Then came large trees bowed down with foliage, and hill sides matted with creeping plants, clematis and vine. Turning homeward, we saw fields of tobacco and Indian corn. We were a long way from home; so waking up our ponies, we left the Turkish camp and conical hill on our left and galloped over the turf to Jeni-bazaar and then uphill to our lines.

Thursday, 24th – Returning from among the filbert trees – how the nuts fell in our hands and laps! – we met Mr Maxse riding at a gallop. He bore orders for our immediate embarkation at Varna for Sebastopol. The artillery and 11th Hussars are to march tomorrow; we, and the 13th and 17th, follow on Saturday. The order was heard silently, not a single cheer: we have waited in inaction too long. Sickness and death are uppermost in our thoughts just now. I also am not well – the hard food tells on me; and to become well, rest and change of diet are necessary: but I don't see much chance of getting either.

Saturday, 26th – We started at ten on our first day's march. We left our poor colonel on the ground, too ill to be moved. Mr Philips and Mr Somers were also left behind in the village, to follow as they best could. We halted at Issyteppe, where we had also stopped on our way up. Here the 13th and 17th remained until Monday; and we fondly hoped to do the same, but are ordered to march on tomorrow to Gottuby. Both our servants, Connell and Hopkins, are ill; and I am very suffering, so much so as to doubt my ability to march to-morrow.

[*Cardigan and the Major had a row which ended in Cardigan's saying 'Major de Sawlis you are the most troublesome officer I ever met with & you shall march at six o'clock tomorrow morning.'*]

Sunday, 27th – Marched to Gottuby, and encamped on the cholera-stricken ground just vacated by the Heavies. We had appalling evidence of their deaths! Here and there a heap of loose earth, with a protruding hand or foot, showed where the inhabitants had desecrated the dead, and dug them up to possess themselves of the blankets in which they were buried. Nevertheless, we gladly halted, for the heat was very distressing; though it would have been better if the sick had gone on to Devna, as they will now have no halt in their march to-morrow. The 13th, who remained at Issyteppe, lost a man of cholera. He was taken ill at four, and buried at six o'clock. We do not start before nine o'clock tomorrow. I *hope* to be able to ride.

Monday, 28th – A cold, showery morning refreshed us all, and made the horses' coats stare. Oh, how much have I, though only slightly ill, felt the miseries attendant on sickness out here! It depresses one to know that every remedy is out of one's power. Come rain, come heat, on you must go: were it not for my trust in the Great Strength my heart would fail. We reached Devna about eleven, glad to see the old place again. And the river! how we walked the horses up and down in it, and how they thrust their parched heads into the stream, than which no stream ever seemed so limpid or so sweet!

[*Here the mail arrived … I shuddered as Mrs Butt said 'She hoped soon to see me in Eaton Square & laugh over my adventures with me.' Why – not far from me was … Connell moaning with pain, I ditto & nothing for dinner but onion soup & beer & champagne for the water was not fit to drink. No wonder men die in such a desert land. … They expect half the horses to die from inflammation after being in the cold and then put into hot steamers for 6 days. I think I can get on board very well & if the worst comes to the worst I can borrow little Glyn's frockcoat & be*

as right as possible.[33] *They do say that if we don't make a mess of*
Sebastopol, which they seem to fear, we shall get home this winter.
– Oh! If we do! I see in the Morning Post *they have put down*
heaps of women as being out <u>with</u> the troops. I don't expect many
of 'em would stay long or live longer either if they weren't half
tigress & half She Bears.

Caricatures of this life are all very well so long as I don't have
to see 'em. Depend on it there is nothing to caricature or laugh at,
except one or two little <u>private</u> stories that I can tell but they don't
know. It grieves me that people can be so careless of brave men's
hardships & sorrow. The poor man who buried his wife & had to
march three days after (she was buried without coffin & <u>I believe</u>
<u>without service</u>) felt it <u>cruelly.</u>

If we don't go back this winter I shall send my journal to
England for publication. Oh the flys, they are getting torpid. ... I
am not feeling well so must leave off as I have 21 miles march
tomorrow, about 9 hours.

Connell is sent into hospital. Sea air will do us all good. They
expect to lose 9,000 men in this battle. We shall land under fire of
the fleet. Oh what a glorious sight.]

Tuesday, 29th – 'March at half-past six to Varna.' March
delayed till half-past seven, at which time we started (I with
an aether bottle) over the hills to Aladyn, and so to Varna by
the upper road. The colonel was unable to leave his bed, and
followed in an araba. The ride was beautiful. We passed a
singular geological formation of large rock, resembling the
ruins of a huge temple with many towers. We reached our
camping ground (the middle of a stubble field) at twelve
o'clock. We passed two camps on the road – one Sir De L.
Evans's; the other a part of the Light Division, consisting of
the 19th, 77th, and 88th. The 88th seemed in sad spirits: they
lost their surgeon yesterday of cholera, and the major was
then supposed to be dying. All round us are camped the
various regiments – French and English Cavalry, Infantry,
and Artillery, and Turkish Infantry and Cavalry. The Rifles

embarked today. I heard that Lady Erroll was seen riding into Varna, to embark with them. Colonel Yea (7th Fusiliers) called on me, and told me that his regiment was to embark tomorrow in the *Emperor*; he also said his regiment was to be the first to land. At five o'clock we saw no chance of getting anything to eat (we had had nothing since six in the morning), and I could not bear it any longer; so we saddled the ponies, and cantered into Varna. Here of course we found all the shops closed, but at length discovered a small restaurateur in a back street, who gave us some excellent soup, vile cutlets, and good macaroni. In the almost pitchy darkness, we felt for our ponies, and were groping our way home, when we passed the hospital in which Dr Mackay, who came out with us in the *Shooting Star*, and who was appointed to the staff from the 12th regiment, resides. We ran upstairs, and found him, with one or two brother medicos, drinking rum-and-water, and 'smoking a weed'. He made us most welcome; and from his account of his patients, appears to be working hard and most self-sacrificingly in the good work of trying to alleviate pain. We soon left him to continue our way home. Lord Cardigan, immediately on my arriving at Varna, went to headquarters to ask Lord Raglan's permission for me to accompany the troops to the Crimea.[34] Lord Cardigan was at the trouble of bringing me Lord Raglan's answer himself. It was a decided negative. 'But,' added Lord Cardigan (touched perhaps by my sudden burst of tears, for I was so worn and weak!), 'should you think proper to disregard the prohibition, I will not offer any opposition to your doing so.'

Wednesday, 30th – Too weak to rise. I thank God we remain here today, and perhaps tomorrow, as the *Himalaya* has not yet come in. Captain George and Major Eman called on me, but I was not able to see them. Two men who marched in with us yesterday are dead of cholera today. 'Oh God, in whose hands are the issues of life and death!'

Thursday 31st – I was congratulating myself on the chance of another quiet day, when an aide-de-camp galloped up to say that the *Himalaya* had arrived in harbour, and we were to turn out immediately to embark. It was then one o'clock. I tried to rise, but at first could hardly stand, and gave up all hope of packing. As soon as they could be got under weight, the bullock wagons started for the quay. Wrapped in an old hat and shawl, Henry lifted me on my dear, gentle pony's back, and we crept down to Varna. But no embarkation for us that night. Till ten o'clock I waited before our arabas arrived, and our tent was pitched; a kind-hearted woman of the regiment gave me a boa, and at half-past ten we got a little dinner, and turned into bed.

[*Accordingly we did not embark – we had to pitch our tents and strange to say our private arabas & three extra horses did not appear – it got darker & colder – no tent – no dinner – I fainting with weakness hunger & excitement. At last our carts were found stuck in the mud with the £6 a month servant lying drunk as ten Lords & roaring like Bedlam possessed. A good thick stick well laid in battered him to his senses & at last we got our bed & some dinner.*]

CHAPTER 3

The Expedition to the Crimea

The embarkation for the Crimea took the British army six days, to the annoyance of the French, who loaded swiftly with no cavalry horses to winch on board but then had to wait idly for days in their overcrowded ships while cholera continued to decimate their ranks. The British transports were so crowded that each man was allowed only one horse and one piece of baggage. With so many men and horses emaciated and ailing, the lack of extra horses to carry equipment and transport the sick and wounded created problems from the moment they landed. The entire Heavy Brigade was also left behind, hampering the cavalry's effectiveness during the battle of Alma. And with so little space on board, hundreds of desperate soldiers' wives were abandoned on the quayside to fend for themselves. The subsequent history of most of these unfortunate women is unknown, although some 250 found their way back to Scutari where they were discovered months later in the cellars, lice-ridden and starving, by Florence Nightingale (see Biographies, p. 315).

Even as the fleet cast off, no final decision had been made about their landing place. Only after Raglan had personally carried out a further reconnaissance in his steamer the Caradoc, together with the French general Canrobert, was it decided to land at Kalamita Bay some thirty miles north of Sebastopol. Early on the morning of 14 September some 26,000 British, 30,000 French and 6,000 Turks, with a combined total of 128 guns, began to disembark. No tents were landed the first night for the British and they slept, 'nesting like pigs', in the pouring rain. The heavy, eight-men bell-tents were later briefly taken on shore but put back on board once it was realised they were too heavy to carry without horse-transport. (The French, with their light two-man tents, slept under cover throughout the campaign; the British tents eventually arrived at Balaclava in mid-October.) Anticipating a lightning raid Raglan ordered the men to leave their knapsacks and kit behind and carry only a shirt, a forage cap and a spare pair of boots and socks, all rolled up in a blanket. The officers were allowed no more than they could personally carry. They lived in these clothes for the next two months and many never saw their other possessions again.

Five days later the three armies marched south to meet the Russian force that waited on the newly fortified heights above the river Alma, blocking their way to Sebastopol (see map, p. 57). That evening the cavalry engaged in a brief and indecisive skirmish at the Bulganek river. The next day, 20 September, with great courage and much loss of life, the Allied armies stormed the heights of Alma, driving the Russians from a position that their commander Menshikov had boasted he could hold for three weeks. So confident was he that he had invited several aristocratic ladies to picnic with him and watch the battle below. In the event, they joined the Russian army in their ignominious flight back to Sebastopol, one leaving her petticoat behind in her panic (see pp. 273 and 274, notes 10 and 14 for Bulganek and Alma).

Although a magnificent victory, Raglan's perceived failure to follow it up (again, see p. 274, note 14) frustrated many regimental and staff officers and critical comments on his leadership, later picked up in newspaper reports, began to run like a leitmotiv through their letters home. They felt that if he had used the cavalry to harass the stricken enemy and then pressed on to take the ill-defended northern defences around Sebastopol, he might have achieved the original objective of the 'grand raid'—to destroy the dockyards and city with a bombardment from the heights. All this depended on rapid action. But Raglan acceded to the wishes of the French and St Arnaud, the commander-in-chief, was dying from cancer. Decisions were largely made by Canrobert, who replaced him a few days later, and was thereafter known as 'Bob can't' by the British troops because of this refusal to pursue the Russians. Instead the victorious armies spent two days on the battlefield while the Russians fortified the city and Menshikov's army regrouped outside Sebastopol ready for future action.

————◦◦◦————

Friday, September 1st – The embarkation began at six o'clock. Whilst the troops were filing down, Captain Lockwood, one of Lord Cardigan's aides-de-camp, rode up with an order from Lord Lucan that no officer was to embark more than one horse; those who had embarked more were to send them ashore again. Pleasant news this for me! However, I had no time to grumble, but hoisting myself into an araba full of baggage, and disguised as much as possible, I went down to the shore. Lord Lucan, who was there, scanned every woman, to find traces of a lady; but he searched in vain, and I, choking with laughter, hurried past his horse into the boat. Here the crew received me very hospitably, gave me some water, and a compliment on the clearness of my cheeks, which 'did not look as though I had done much hard work in the sun,' and finally put me safely on board the *Himalaya*, where I was immediately handed down to my cabin.[1]

[*When the baggage boat was loaded Mrs Sergeant Cammell & I got into it & I think the sailors fell in love with me for I got no end of chaff – 'Your cheeks seems to stand the sun right well' – 'You're aware there's a widow's pension all regulated I s'pose young*

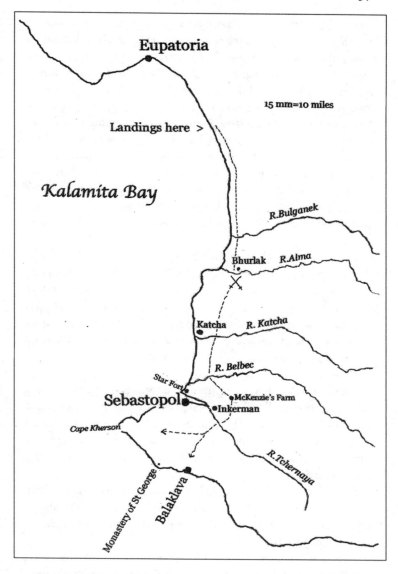

The landing in the Crimea, showing the march to the south
of Sebastopol.

*'ooman' &c &c. Henry standing on the quay with the rest of the
regiment not daring to come near me, but looking like a hen with a
young duck. I laughing heartily. The worst was having to get up the
ship's side by myself, not being 'Quality' I received no assistance.
However the Col. & Major received me right kindly at the top &
took me into a cabin where I have been shut up ever since for
fear anyone from shore should know I am on board & tell that
old brute Lord Lucan. ... I have passed all day in my cabin peeping
out of the window like a little prisoner. Now the band of the
42nd Highlanders moored close to us on board the* Emer *are
playing delightfully to me – little thinking I who have danced
with every officer of them am looking out & listening ... More than
20 officers, when the Sebastopol order came out, sent in their papers
to sell.*[2]

*I wish I could keep quiet. I am so nervous & weak & excitable.
We have a piano on board this magnificent ship. Alas! My hands
are too brown & my voice too unused to singing for me to venture
to open it. I look at it from a distance like a shrine. If I pass safe
thro' the landing & the long shots (we land under fire) & rockets
&c – I'll write to you about the siege. Lord C is on board now &
the shore birds who will take this are all going.*]

Monday, 4th – We hoped to sail today.

Tuesday, 5th – I have remained in my cabin ever since I
came on board. Well may we pray for 'all prisoners and
captives.'[3] After my free life under the 'sweet heavens,' to be
hermetically sealed up in the narrow cabin of a ship – I
cannot breathe, even though head and shoulders are thrust
out of window.

Since I have been here death has been amongst us. Poor
Captain Longmore, who on Friday helped me up the ship's
side, was dead on Sunday morning, 'stretch'd no longer on
the rack of this rough world'.[4]

Death with such inexorable gripe appears in his most
appalling shape. He was seized but on Friday with diarrhoea,
which turned to cholera on Saturday, and on Sunday the

body was left in its silent and solemn desolation. During his death struggle the party dined in the saloon, separated from the ghastly wrangle only by a screen. With few exceptions, the dinner was a silent one; but presently the champagne corks flew, and – but I grow sick, I cannot draw so vivid a picture of life and death. God save my dear husband and me from dying in the midst of the din of life! The very angels must stand aloof. God is our hope and strength, and without Him we should *utterly* fail.

Today the signal came to proceed to Balchick Bay; and having hooked ourselves to No. 78, with the Connaught Rangers on board, we steamed to join the flight of ships sailing from Varna. About two hours brought us to Balchick; and the appearance of the bay, crowded with every species of ship, from the three-decker man-of-war down to the smallest river steam-tug, filled the mind with admiration at the magnificent naval resources of England. [5]

Delay prevails here as everywhere. The fleet are all collected and awaiting the order to proceed. Sebastopol is within thirty-six hours' sail, and apparently there is no impediment: but not a vessel has weighed anchor.

Wednesday, 6th – Some say we are waiting for the wind to change, or lull; others that we are to wait until the *Banshee* arrives with despatches from England. Many more are betting that peace is proclaimed, and that we shall be met at Sebastopol by a flag of truce. I incline to the opinion that we are waiting for the *Banshee*. The weather continues lovely. The master of the *Echinga* came on board tonight, and tells me that Lady Erroll is in his ship, and that she intends remaining on board during the siege. I had fully made up my mind to land until this unhappy order of 'Only one horse' threw over all my plans. My husband, too, seems to think that I *could not* encounter the fatigue on foot, so I fear I must (*most* reluctantly) consent to follow him by sea to Sebastopol. Our sick list increases frightfully.

Thursday, 7th – We sailed in company of the fleet, a truly wonderful sight! News arrived last night of the taking of Bomarsund, which put us all in spirits;[6] and as no accident occurred beyond the snapping of a hawser, we made a successful start.

Friday, 8th – No motion is perceptible in this magnificent ship, though her mighty heart throbs night and day, and there is sufficient sea to make the transport behind us pitch disagreeably. Were it not for the rush of water beneath the saloon windows, I should fancy myself on land. Walking on the deck, between the lines of horses, I cannot fail to have made friends with two or three – one in particular, a fine large Norman-headed chestnut, with a long flowing mane, and such kindly eyes.

Saturday, 9th – At a signal from the flagship, we pulled up to anchor, in order to concentrate the fleet and allow the laggards to come up. Ignorance concerning our movements prevails everywhere, and conjectures are rife. Many absolutely doubt whether Sebastopol is to be our destination or not. Henry has been very far from well these last few days, and is laid up with an attack of lumbago, particularly unwelcome just now. Dr Evans, who has been appointed to the regiment, shows very humane feeling; and I trust, under his kind care, my dear husband will soon recover. Poor Connell, our soldier-servant, still lies sick, and suffering; but I hear from Sergeant Lynch that he is, if anything, better.

Sunday, 10th – Still at anchor, 160 miles from Sebastopol. Yesterday, when we stopped our engines, we were nearly meeting with a serious accident. The transport ship behind us, having too short a hawser, and too much way on her, ran into us, smashing our jollyboat, and crashing through our bulwarks and taffrail like so much brown paper.

[*I write in the middle of the sea & of the Fleet. We are 150 miles from Sebastopol. In sight of us are 760 ships: Men of War, English, French & Turkish steamers & transports to match. Each steamer*

tows one or two transports ... The most entire ignorance prevails
thro' the fleet. We conclude Lord Raglan knows what he is about
but none share his counsels – not even the Duke of Cambridge[7] *or*
James Thomas E. of Cardigan ... we have no chance of losing
him (Cardigan). Indeed nothing but Death would ever make him
resign his commission and Death like every one else has been
afraid to meddle with him as yet. He has been very kind to me
about getting me on board. Unless he had been my friend I must
have been left behind at Varna, or had to slink away to the
woman's colony at Therapia. I mention this injustice to him.
Henry is down with an attack of rheumatism & lumbago.
Cardigan insists on him landing with the troops. But I don't
intend him to do so. For the first week after the army lands they
will have no tents, no baggage horses & nothing to eat, but what
they can carry with them. Consequently I have determined on
going from the Himalaya *on board the* Shooting Star *until the*
tents arrive when I shall disembark and join the army. I intend to
take H. on board with me, if he don't get right, as he has nothing
to do, can't fight & there is no occasion for his landing. The
weather is as cold as November & it's folly my landing without a
horse or a tent. And the siege is expected to take a month, so that
besides seeing the whole from the harbor for a week, I shall be in
amongst it for three more. I am annoyed at seeing in the U[nited]
Services Gazette *that my name (Jubilee) is put down as being*
with the women & Lady Erroll as being with the troops.[8] *The*
infantry have not been half the distance or had half the hardships
we have had.]

Monday, 11th – The *Caradoc* and *Agamemnon* have
returned. Signals fly from the mast-head of the flag-ship:
'Prepare to get under weigh.' Discussion of our unknown
destination; some say Odessa – some Sebastopol.

Sunshine above, and smooth water below. On board not
half-a-dozen men feel 'as if they were on the eve of fighting.'

[*Monday Sept 11th, 11 o'clock. I find to my great disgust that*
a post goes out in an hour so that the letter in which I had

*intended to have bombarded Sebastapol must go before we leave
our anchorage. At any rate the next mail will bring you some
news. We must do something now. ... Lady Erroll is on board the*
Echinga. *Mrs Cresswell on board the* War Cloud. *I hear the latter
lady proposed being carried on board in a beer barrel, breathing
thro' the bung hole! Her husband is on board the* Trent *& has
never been to see her yet! How scandalous people are, even with
only three ladies, the gossip is intolerable ... All our soldier*
<u>servants are to be mounted</u> *& go into action. There are only 9 out
of the lot who are out of Hospital & these 9 are to be mounted so
that there will not be a single servant to use. Thank goodness our
two men are safe in hospital. Cardigan is getting wild with
ferocious excitement already and he has been making himself as
disagreeable <u>as possible</u> all day. Beginning with taking away the
servants ... Lockwood is appointed A.D.C. and the way he
toadies Cardigan is <u>disgusting</u>.*]

Tuesday, 12th – At 9 a.m. we came in sight of the Crimea.[9]
We have been on board twelve days today. Twelve days
accomplishing 300 miles! The delay puzzles as much as it
grieves and disgusts. Lord Cardigan, too, is growing very
impatient of it. Towards evening the ships drew up closer
together. Magnificent two- and three-deckers sailed on each
side of the transport fleet. A forest of masts thrust their
spear-like heads into the sunset clouds. Birnam Wood is
come to Dunsinane! At even-fall, the *Brenda*, a little Danube
boat, drawing four feet of water, was ordered off to Sebastopol to reconnoitre. An answering pendant was run up to
her peak: a puff of smoke, a turn of her paddle-wheels, and
away flew the little craft, shaking out her white wings like a
bird.

[*We are within 18 miles of Sebastopol. 1 o'clock signal 'Prepare
for disembarkation.' No sign of a Russian vessel, no sound of a shot.
All peace & tranquility and best of all nobody cares about fighting
except Cardigan who paces up & down like a soldier in a country
theatre. Everyone else's excitement has evaporated in the long term.*

… Our Major, although the harbor is on the right, still maintains stoutly that we are not going there at all! Henry still seedy.]

Wednesday, 13th – The entrance to the harbour of Sebastopol is distinctly visible. Every one is roused up and full of energy, except my dear husband, who lies sick and full of pain in his cabin. I much fear he will not be able to land. A signal at twelve o'clock to 'Keep in your station.' We are near enough to the shore to see houses, corn, cattle, and a horse and covered cart.

Not a shot has been fired; all is tranquillity in the serene sky above, and the unrippled waters beneath. All are quiet except Lord Cardigan, who is still full of eagerness. Poor Connell is not nearly so well. There is a soldier's wife on board, too, suffering severely from fever. What will become of her when the troops disembark!

Thursday, 14th – Leaving Eupatoria behind us, we hauled close in shore, about nine o'clock, about thirty miles from Sebastopol. The French began to disembark forthwith, and by ten o'clock the tricolor was planted on the beach. I have a painful record to make. During last night our poor servant Connell, after struggling long with fever, succumbed to it, and closed his eyes, I trust, in peace. I did not know of his danger till I heard of his death. Today he was committed to the keeping of the restless sea, until the day when it shall give up its dead.

[*Henry is <u>determined </u>to land <u>at all risks</u>. I hope to join him in a day or two. Poor, poor Connell died last night. He died of fever, I am indeed grieved. We anchored in Eupatoria Bay last night – 26 sick men are to be sent back to Scutari, I mean 26 of ours! This and about 30 dead make a hole in a regt of 240 strong!! The expedition appears ill-managed – why have such a long march with them all so seedy? & horses ditto.*]

Friday, 15th – English troops disembarking in a heavy surf. The landing of the horses is difficult and dangerous. Such men as were disembarked yesterday were lying all exposed to the torrents of rain which fell during the night. How it did rain! In consequence an order has been issued to disembark *the tents*. The beach is a vast and crowded camp, covered with men, horses, fires, tents, general officers, staff officers, boats landing men and horses, which latter are flung overboard and swim ashore. Eleven were drowned today. I am glad to say we lost none. Lord Cardigan begins to be eager for the fray, and will be doing something or other directly he has landed, I fancy. He landed today at five.

Saturday, 16th – All our horses were ashore by half past ten, and started immediately on outpost-duty, for which they tell me Lord Cardigan has taken a force of Rifles and Artillery as well. At ten o'clock today, with failing heart, I parted from my dear husband, and watched him go ashore; whilst I, alas! having no horse, cannot follow him, but must go on board the *Shooting Star*, and go round by sea. How I hate it! How much rather I would endure any hardship than be separated from him at this time! But my reason and strength both tell me it is impracticable, and so I must make up my mind to it. Captain Fraser received me with his usual most considerate kindness, and tried by every means to make me forget my wretched position.

[*My heart begins to fail me now I am left alone tho' H & I are only a few miles apart & only for a few days. God Bless you all F.I.D.*]

Sunday, 17th – Artillery disembarking all day from the *Shooting Star*. One poor fellow caught his foot in a block, and tore it terribly.

Monday, 18th – Today I set my foot in the Crimea.

A lovely day tempted me to disembark and try to see my dear husband on shore. Captain Fraser and I started at twelve o'clock. On landing amongst the Artillery, we first inquired for the poor fellow who was hurt yesterday, and then for the Light Cavalry. 'They are seven miles inland!!' I never can forget, or be sufficiently grateful to the officers of

Artillery for the kindness they showed me this day. After looking about for a quiet horse to carry me, they decided on stopping a party of Horse Artillery, and getting them to give us seats on the gun-carriage. Mr Grylls, who had charge of the party, most courteously assented, and by his kindness I was able to reach the outposts. Here I surprised my husband, who shares a tent with five officers and who was delighted to see me. Whilst I remained there, a patrol of the 13th Light Dragoons came in, commanded by Colonel Doherty. They had seen a body of about six hundred Cossacks, who had fired at them, but without effect. These same Cossacks, a few minutes later, had set two of the neighbouring villages, and all the corn, on fire.

After about an hour spent in camp, Henry put his regimental saddle on his horse, and I mounted him, Henry and Captain Fraser walking by my side, and we returned to shore. Our road was lurid with the red of the vast fires. This country is as fertile as Bulgaria, and has all the advantages of cultivation. In the village close to the outposts, of which the Rifles had possession, were found comfortable and well-furnished houses, with grand pianofortes, pictures, books, and everything evincing comfort and civilisation. Several of our riflemen have been killed by the Cossacks, who hover round the army like a flying cloud. We reached the beach at dusk; and again taking leave of my husband, with a heavy heart I stepped into the boat and was rowed on board.

Tuesday, 19th – The troops have all advanced today; and about half-past three we heard the heavy sound of the guns booming across the water, as we lay quietly at anchor. What can those guns mean?[10] I wonder if, among the annals of a war, the sickening anxieties of mother, wife, and sister ever find a place. Let us hope the angel of compassion makes record of their tears.

[*The troops are nearly all disembarked – 8th Hussars were all ashore Saturday (16th) and marched 5 miles up the country with some rifles & Artillery to cut off a Russian force which were defending the river. Henry is gone with them and will be in the thick of everything. None but those who feel it can have an idea of the anxiety & horror that fills one's heart. ... I trust to get round to Sebastopol in a few days – but no one knows whether transports go there or whether they go to Scutari or Eupatoria. I never felt so adrift in my life – but I shall get to Sebastopol somehow. No troops have begun to march yet, the shore is still covered with tents & armies. The French are pillaging & behaving badly – the people are well disposed – & will sell anything & be very friendly. All the sick & women are put aboard the* Kangaroo [11] *steamer & going to Scutari. The steamer is <u>crammed</u> with them & yesterday hoisted signals of distress. She refuses to take more women & when Lt Maxse went on board he found even her upper decks crowded with sick & dying & <u>seven</u> corpses kicking about with no hands to bury them. ... Lord Raglan has drowned one horse & another of his was swimming about <u>all night</u> & picked up & hauled aboard the* Ag(amemnon) *at 5 next morning. He is doing well ...*

Pray for us both. How I do pray for Henry now he's out there under fire.]

Wednesday, 20th – Left Kalamita Bay, and, with several other ships, joined the rest of the fleet off Eupatoria.

Thursday, 21st – Captain Tatham, of the *Simoom*, took me ashore in his boat. It was a lovely day. We walked about Eupatoria; and Captain Tatham introduced me to the governor, Captain Brock, who showed me great kindness and attention. In his house (a very comfortable one, with polished oak floors and large windows) he had safely secured in 'durance vile' two prisoners, the land steward and shepherd of Prince Woronzov. [12] After leaving Captain Brock, we met a Russian *propriétaire* – one of the very few who remained in the town. He conversed with us in French for some time, and showed us over the Greek church. Nearly all the inhabitants, terrified at the apparition of an enemy's fleet, had fled. Captain Brock, in the hope of procuring prompt supplies, has fixed a tariff regulating the price of all kinds of stock; the Tartar population, delighted at the ready and large circulation of money, bring in provisions freely and willingly. Eupatoria is rather a pretty town, interspersed with trees, with large, low, comfortable-looking, detached houses.

Friday, 22nd – Was awoke from a restless sleep by the entrance of my maid [13] – a soldier's wife – with her apron over her eyes. I naturally asked what was the matter. 'Oh, ma,am! Captain Tatham has sent to say he has received despatches, which will oblige him to leave Eupatoria today. And there has been a dreadful battle – 500 English killed and 5,000 Russians; and all our poor cavalry fellows are all killed; and, the Lord be good to us, we're all widows.'

God, and he only, knows how the next hour was passed until the blessed words, 'O thou of little faith,' rang in my heart.

At breakfast I asked Captain Fraser for the particulars of the message; but he, from a feeling of kindly wishing to save me anxiety, assured me he had heard nothing about the battle, and did not believe a word of it. However, at two o'clock, I went ashore to see the Governor and ascertain the words of the despatch. He told me that there had been a severe battle at the river Alma, but no official particulars had yet reached him.

Saturday, 23rd – I heard more particulars of this great fight,[14] though very few: 2,090 English killed and wounded; the 7th and 23rd Fusiliers almost destroyed, and, thank God! the Cavalry not engaged. How can timorous, nervous women live through a time like this?

The guns which we heard as we were breasting our swift way from Kalamita to Eupatoria, were merely messengers to us of the heavy firing inland, causing wounds, blood, and sudden death – lives, for which we would gladly give our own, extinguished in a moment; hands flung out in agony, faces calm and still in death; all our prayers unavailing now: no more speech, no more life, no more love.

Sunday, 24th – Again awoke by the guns. Captain Fraser assured me they were the guns of the fleet. The Cossacks, last night, made a descent upon Eupatoria, and having secured some plunder, fired on our soldiers. Their fire was returned with such interest that they were soon glad to retire.

The *Danube* steamboat went this afternoon to Katcha, laden with sheep, and taking with her a Russian prisoner – a gentleman – and supposed to be a spy. I met him directly after he was taken, as he was walking from the guard to the shore.

Monday, 25th – A steamboat came in this morning, and Captain Fraser immediately sent off a boat to the *Simoom* (which had not left, as she threatened, on Friday) to ascertain the news.

Until as late as six o'clock we had been listening to the guns, but were little prepared for such news as Captain Tatham sent back to us.

The fleet are at the Katcha, and the army also. The fleet stood in yesterday, and fired about twenty shots. The Russians sunk five line-of-battle ships and two frigates across the harbour. Three remain, which cannot get out nor can we get in. A prisoner reports that all is consternation – Menschikov in tears. At Eupatoria news flies from mouth to mouth. They say that, at Alma, the charge of Highlanders was most magnificent; that they swept over the Russian entrenchments like a sea. Our Cavalry being so weak we were unable to follow up our advantage, or we might have cut off the enemy in their retreat. It is said that the whole garrison of Sebastopol was engaged at Alma – 50,000 Russians to about 45,000 English and French. I hear the English bore the brunt of the fight.

Went ashore this afternoon, and rode with Captain Brock, who most kindly provides me with both horse and saddle.

After we had finished our ride, we went to one of the deserted houses, where we found a grand pianoforte – the first I had played on for so long! It was like meeting a dear and long absent friend.

The house and garden were soon filled, and echoing to the magnificent chords of 'Rule Britannia'; whilst Tennyson's sweet words, 'Break, Break, Break', and the 'Northern Star' fitted both the occasion and the place.

One more song and I must hasten back, to be on board my ship by twilight. Heavy guns are pouring their dull, broadsides on our straining ears. What shall the song be, sad and low, or a wild outburst of desperate courage? I have it:

> Non curiamo l'incerto domani:
> Se quest' oggi n' e dato goder. [15]

Tuesday, nine o'clock – The day rose foggy and gloomy, and my heart, notwithstanding its elation yesterday at the brilliant conduct of our troops, was dull, anxious, and sad. I am engaged to ride with Captain Brock, and am restless to go ashore, in the hope of hearing news. Oh this suspense! How could I be so weak as to allow myself to be separated from my husband? A lifetime of anxiety has been crowded into these ten days.

Eight o'clock found me on board the *Danube* steaming, trembling, rushing through the water towards the fleet at Katcha. A note from Captain Tatham, brought up by the *Danube* at three o'clock, induced me to go and see whether I could not get on board the *Star of the South*, and so go down to Balaklava with the siege train. I had one hour to decide, and, packing up a few things in a carpet bag, and taking my saddle, I went on board at four o'clock.

September 27th – Mr Cator having duly reported my arrival to Admiral Dundas,[16] the admiral did two things: first, he sent on board some excellent white bread, milk, eggs, &c. &c., for breakfast; and, secondly, he proposed

either that I should go down to Balaklava in the *Simoom*, and
so be passed to the *Star of the South*; or else, if, as was most
probable, this latter ship had been sent to Scutari with
wounded, that I should return to Eupatoria, and be sent
down by the earliest opportunity. I decided, therefore, on
availing myself of Mr Cator's kind offer to take me back to
Eupatoria, and we started at eleven o'clock. To-day we stood
close in shore, on the coast of ALMA. On our right stood
heights occupied by the Russian army; on our left the place
where our army bivouacked. Huge volumes of thick,
smouldering smoke still rolled heavily over the plain. The
Albion, close in shore, was occupied in removing wounded.
Here and there dark masses lay about, war's silent evidence;
and over all was the serene heaven, smiling on a lovely
landscape, sunny and bright. And I too,

Smiled to think God's greatness shone around our incompleteness,
And round our restlessness – His rest. [17]

The cabin of the *Danube* was full of trophies of the fight
– helmets pierced with shot and dabbled in blood, little
amulets of brass, all blood-stained and soiled, muskets,
bayonets, and swords stained with the red rust of blood. We
hear that our army have taken Balaklava, after a slight
resistance. Balaklava is a small harbour to the southward of
Sebastopol, affording, from its depth and shelter, a wonderful anchorage for ships. This we suppose will be the
base of operations; here all our ammunition stores, troops,
&c., will be disembarked. They compute the number of
men inside Sebastopol at about 16,000. On arriving at
Eupatoria I heard, with feelings of great sorrow, that
Colonel Chester and Captain Evans, of the 23rd, are both
killed; that Lord Erroll is wounded; and that poor Mrs
Cresswell is a widow. God help and support her under a
blow that would crush me to my grave! The last tidings
heard of Mrs Cresswell were that she had gone down to

Varna in the *War Cloud*. I conclude by this time she has gone home, as Captain Cresswell died of cholera on the Monday of the march.[18] Major Wellesley also died about that time, on board the *Danube*; and his boxes, sword, hat, &c., were lying in the cabin – a melancholy sight! How full of anxiety I am!

About two o'clock we were safely at anchor off Eupatoria. We went ashore. Captain Brock very kindly mounted Mr Cator and me, and we three rode round the fortifications. Captain Brock received information, last evening, of 800 Cossacks within a few miles of the town. We, too, shall have to record the Battle of Eupatoria. The ride over, I adjourned to the *Shooting Star*; but during the afternoon I met, and was introduced to, Captain King, of the *Leander*, who very kindly asked me to dine to-morrow. Thus ends my birthday! – day ever to be remembered, as on it I saw my first battlefield. How many more shall I see ere I am a year older? Shall I ever live to see another year? Look on into the winter, with its foreboding of suffering, cold, privation, and gloom!

> What wilt thou become
> Through yon drear stretch of dismal wandering? [19]

September 28th – The *Leander*'s boat came for me at two o'clock, and. I had a very rough and wet passage on board. I met the captain of the *Jena*, a French man-of-war, Colonel D'Osman, in command of the French troops, Captain Brock, &c.; a very agreeable party, at which we were most hospitably entertained.

Friday, 29th – I take a letter to Henry ashore with me to-day, as I trust to find some means of forwarding it, and I cannot bear the suspense any longer.

Today I am all unnerved; an indefinable dread is on me. Captain Fraser caught a magnificent Death's Head moth, and gave it to me. I shivered as I accepted it. This life of absence and suspense becomes at times intolerable. Oh, when shall I rejoin the army, from which I never ought to have been separated! Any hardship, any action, is better than passive anxiety.

A friend of Captain Fraser's, who came on board, tells me that none have had the courage to acquaint Mrs Cresswell with her loss; and she is actually coming up to Balaklava with troops. Cruel kindness!

Saturday, 30th – Oh that my grief were thoroughly weighed, and my heaviness laid in the balances together, for the sorrows of the Almighty are within me, and terror sets itself in array before me. [20]

Sunday, 1st October – The *Shooting Star* is under orders for Katcha; and I am engaged to ride with Captain Brock ashore. Not a ripple stirred the water; so, trusting to Captain Fraser's assurance that the ship would not move today, I went ashore after breakfast. It was indeed a heavenly day! Our horses sauntered along, and my heart involuntarily looked up, through the radiant sky, to the universal God of peace and war, sunshine and storm!

We saw an immense cloud of locusts, making for the sea. The air was quite obscured by them. Returning about one o'clock what was my dismay to see the *Shooting Star* spreading her white wings, and dropping quietly out to sea! Fortunately, *Danube* was going down at two o'clock, I did not lose a moment, but after taking a most regretful leave of pleasant, cordial Eupatoria, I went once more on board the *Danube*, and started in pursuit of the *Star*. The breeze had got up considerably, and favouring her, we found her at anchor at Katcha when we arrived.

Monday, 2nd – Today my adventures have been more amusing still. Not liking a dull day alone on board, I wrote a note to Lord George Paulet, who called on me immediately after breakfast, and took me away to the *Bellerophon*. Here I was in the midst of a most agreeable, lazy morning looking out on the sparkling sea, and listening to the wondrous harmonies of a most perfect band,[21] when Admiral Dundas sent on board to say, that if I wished to go down to Bala-klava, 'the *Pride of the Ocean* was then passing with troops, and he would order her to be hove to; but Mrs Duberly must not keep her waiting a moment longer than necessary.' My transit from the *Bellerophon* (through one of the lower ports), laden with a ham, some miraculous port wine, and all sorts of good things provided by Lord George's kind hospitality, was accomplished in a very short space. [*Lord George bundling after me laden with two bottle of Old Port, a bottle of brandy, a cake, a ham, & a little keg of whisky we pulled to the* S(hooting) S(tar) *where he & I scuttled some things into a carpet bag.*] The admiral, however, was impatient, and Captain Christie more so. Mr Cator was sent in the *Britannia*'s galley to take me on board; and after accomplishing my packing in ten minutes and taking my desk and carpet bag, I started in the galley and had some difficulty in overtaking the *Pride of the Ocean* [*after she was under weigh and climbed up her like a monkey*].

Tuesday, 3rd – We expected a three hours' sail; but the wind dropped, and we were becalmed for four-and-twenty. By three o'clock we were lying almost stationary before the forts of Sebastopol, and within range of the guns. It was a moment not altogether free from nervousness; but no guns molested us, and we passed unharmed. [*They were so busy throwing shot & shell from the other side into the camp that by great luck they let us alone or we should have come off badly.*] Presently we passed the light off Khersonese. We lay off the point beyond the Monastery of St George all night; and at morning, the *Simla* came to tow us to our anchorage just outside Balaklava harbour. This anchorage is a wonderful place; the water is extremely deep, and the rocks which bound the coast exceed in ruggedness and boldness of outline any that I ever saw before. The harbour appears completely land-locked. Through a fissure in the cliffs you can just see a number of masts; but how they got in, or will get out, appears a mystery; they have the appearance of having been hoisted over the cliffs, and dropped into a lake on the other side.

At three o'clock, tugs came alongside the *Pride of the Ocean*, to disembark her troops, the 1st Royals, who, horses and all, were landed before dark.

At dinner, whilst I was quietly eating my soup, I heard some one enter the cabin, and looking up saw Henry, who had heard of my arrival, and had come on board. I need not say that the evening passed happily enough! He brought me a handful of letters, which occupied me till late at night.

CHAPTER 4

Balaklava
October–November 1854

After two days on the battlefield at Alma, burying the dead and embarking the sick and wounded for hospitals in Scutari and Constantinople, the Allies continued their advance on Sebastopol. After a flank march around the city they encamped on the Uplands to the south. Raglan's immediate priority was a safe harbour to land men and equipment for the short siege he now envisaged. He chose Balaclava (which had surrendered on 26 September after firing a few token shots), on the advice of Rear Admiral Lyons the naval second in command (see p. 277, note 1). To the fury of his own second in command, General Cathcart, Raglan had refused to make an immediate attack from the south on the unprepared city. Instead he deferred once more to Canrobert and General Burgoyne, the senior British military engineer, with his long-held assumption that Sebastopol would only fall after a heavy bombardment. While the British hacked out trenches in the rocky ground and brought their guns ashore, painfully dragging them into position—the terrain was more rugged and impassable than at first thought—the Russians swiftly raised a sophisticated defence system (see p. 278, note 4). In the British camp the numbers of sick and dead increased daily; the cholera epidemic continued while the harsh living conditions and poor diet of salt meat and no fresh vegetables meant that scurvy, dysentery and diarrhoea were rife. By 17 October, the date chosen for the bombardment and storming of Sebastopol, only some 16,000 men were fit for action.

This attack was planned as a combined operation by the Allied naval and land forces but their lack of co-ordination ensured confusion and failure. All parties initially agreed to commence firing at dawn but the warships only opened fire some seven hours later; they had little effect on the harbour forts but were themselves severely damaged. Meanwhile the French batteries were silenced when a huge magazine exploded mid-morning, hit by Russian counter-fire. The British guns damaged the Malakoff and Great Redan, key Russian fortifications, but Raglan had insufficient men to attack unaided and was unable to contact the French to request extra infantry. The assault was abandoned and by the next morning the Russians had rebuilt their defences. The bombardment continued sporadically for several days but it made no permanent damage to the Russian fortifications, which were reconstructed and even improved every night. No further attempt was made to storm the city. The scene was now set for a protracted siege, the very scenario that Raglan had dreaded when first ordered to invade the Crimea. Raglan neglected the defences on his vulnerable right flank even though Menshikov's army was hovering ominously in the rear. During the next two months Menshikov made two determined attempts to dislodge the besieging forces before reinforcements arrived. The British bore the brunt of these attacks and the ensuing engagements—Balaclava and Inkerman—sapped their strength and prevented any further attack on Sebastopol until the following year.

On 25 October the Russians attacked the small force defending Balaclava, intending to seize the harbour and break the British supply lines (see Appendix II for details of the battle). Although driven back from Balaclava, the Russians captured the partially completed British redoubts which guarded the metalled Woronzov road, the final part of the supply route from the harbour to the British right flank on the Uplands. Without access to this road, all supplies now had to be carried some seven miles along a rough unmade track and up the sharp Sapoune escarpment to the Uplands via the Col, a steep and narrow pass. This track had previously been used mainly to supply the troops on the left of the British line. With the winter weather and the increased, continual traffic, it soon degenerated into a muddy morass often taking more than six hours to traverse, causing further suffering and loss of life.

Ten days later, 5 November, Menshikov threw all his forces against the thinly defended sector of the British lines on the Inkerman heights in a desperate bid to drive the army into the sea. Despite superiority in numbers the Russians failed to break through, and the British, supported at the crucial moment by French troops, held their ground. The battle of Inkerman was won by the bravery of individual groups and regiments, already worn down by illness and excessive hours on piquet duty or in the trenches (see p. 282, notes 29 and 30). For many the exertion was too much; they survived the battle but succumbed in the coming weeks to dysentery and cholera. It became apparent that Sebastopol would not be taken without reinforcements. But few preparations had been made for a winter campaign. Matters were made worse by the great storm of 14 November when tents and belongings were scattered far and wide and ships, carrying vital provisions, were sunk in the harbour (see p. 283, note 34).

In mid-October Florence Nightingale, with a group of nurses, set off for Scutari (see Biographies, p. 315).

Wednesday, October 4th – This morning I landed at Balaklava, having left the *Pride of the Ocean* with regret, after endeavouring to express to Captain Kyle my deep sense of the great consideration and kindness he showed me whilst on board his ship.

Mr Cunningham, the admiralty agent, was going on shore, and I availed myself of a seat in his boat, notwithstanding the day was a rough one; and then I learned the entrance to this wonderful harbour,[1] where the ships lay side by side, moored to the shore as thickly as they could be packed.

In the afternoon, Henry came down to see me; and scrambling into his regimental saddle – for I had left my own on board the *Shooting Star* – we rode up to see the Cavalry camp. Here I was obliged to confess, though *sorely* against my will, that it was *impossible* I could live in the camp. Henry shares his tent with three men. The cold – the impossibility of getting a separate tent, has made me resolve to remain on board ship, and go daily to the camp.

[*I think the last time I wrote to you was from Eupatoria. Since then I have been lurching about a good deal endeavoring to join Henry ... Balaclava is close to the army – it is about seven miles from Sebastopol and between Balaclava & Sebastopol the entire ground is occupied with troops. Artillery, & sailors, camp on the shore, Light Cavalry Brigade two miles in – also Heavy Cavalry & Infantry & Artillery close to Sebastopol. The siege guns are all landed. The ships are (many of them) landing their guns. The amount of shell now moving up to Sebastopol is incredible. General opinion says it will fall in 24 hours. We cannot but think Lord Raglan dilatory but at the same time 'slow and sure'. The preparations appear solid enough to take London. There is no doubt Sebastopol is a deal stronger place than is generally thought. The maritime defences are very strong.*]

Thursday, 5th – I rode all over the camp; went on to the Light Division, to the 63rd and 68th; took my first look at Sebastopol from the land as it lay in a hollow about two miles from us. It is a much finer town as seen from the land. The fortifications appear of great strength and number, and the buildings struck me as being large and handsome. They were busy throwing shell into our lines, but the range was too long to do us any harm. The shells fell into a hollow at our feet; and all that I saw exploded harmlessly; though two days before one had burst in a tent of the 68th, killing one man, and wounding two. We returned through the French lines. The French soldiers seemed astonished at the apparition of a *lady* in their lines, and made various but very flattering remarks thereon. Late at night Mr Cator arrived in Balaklava, and came on board the *Star of the South* to see me.

[*When they open the fire of the siege I shall be close to the Lancaster guns, which range at 5,000 yards.*[2] *It will be a magnificent sight. I think I described to you the field of Alma. I could not look at it long - & the glance I had gave me lurid dreams for a week. I think I told you Mrs Cresswell is a widow. He has been dead three weeks & no one has had the courage to tell her! & she is expected in here daily. Lord Erroll is gone home, he has lost two fingers & is much pulled down. Lord Chewton is a mass of wounds, two in the shoulder, a smashed thigh, a contused rib & when he was rescued a Russian was smashing in the back of his head.*[3] *However he behaved with the greatest pluck – & won't die because of his pluck. ...*

We Cavalry have hardly been engaged as yet. I read the letter about Lord C. I hope my name won't appear – I am sorry it has made such a ferment tho' it is all perfectly true. He has been exceedingly kind to me lately, to make up I suppose. He lends me horses – and tells me all his troubles and quarrels with Lord Lucan. They fight like cat and dog.

The camp is a wonderful sight. The sailors are all landed & employed a hundred at a time hauling up the heavy guns. The largest requires 18 or 20 horses. I was at the Lancasters when they were put in position. They are placed so as to command the fort but be out of range of the Russians. I mean to go up there on the day of the storming which we hope will be tomorrow or next day. I could see yesterday the Russian soldiers employed inside the town. They tell me they have been seen being urged to work hard by the point of the bayonet.[4] *The* Tyrone *came in last eve. All her horses are saved so I shall see my dear Bob & Whisker come tumbling out this afternoon. The ship I am now in is being fitted as a Powder Magazine.*

This morning at sunrise 1,500 Russian cavalry surprised our cavalry & had a scrimmage but not much I believe. I shall go up to the camp by & by to find out. But I forgot to bring my saddle & have only Henry's or Cardigan's to ride on, so it tires me a good deal. Don't publish this letter for goodness' sake. Cardigan read me my own letter from the Advertiser *yesterday!!!* [5] *I thought I should have died of suppressed laughter. When the siege storm opens we shall be in Sebastopol in 3 days. We have 75,000 shell!! Cholera still very bad.*]

Friday, 6th – The *Shooting Star* arrived outside Balaklava last evening. Mr Cator sent off a gig to her for my saddle, which came ashore about twelve, and will save me much fatigue, as I find the big grey and the regimental saddle very tiring, especially in trotting.

I hear today of poor Dr Mackay's death with great regret. He died from the effects of over-exertion in the zealous discharge of his arduous duties amongst the sick.

Sunday, 8th – Lord Cardigan very kindly lent me a horse, and Mr Cator and I rode up to the front. Here we saw Captain Hillyar of the Naval Brigade, who is working hard to get his guns into position.[6]

These seamen appear to work with the greatest energy and good-will. One meets a gang of them harnessed to a gun, and drawing with all their might and main; or digging at entrenchments, singing, laughing, and working heartily and cheerily. But their experience of camp-life is short indeed in comparison with that of our poor soldiers, with whom they contrast so gaily.

Returning home, we met Sir Edmund Lyons, to whom I was introduced, and who asked me to dine with him tonight on board the *Agamemnon*, where I met a very old and valued friend, Captain Drummond, of the *Retribution*.

[*Sir Edmund Lyons* [7] *is very kind to me. I met Layard.* [8] *I talked to him some time without thinking that he was the Nineveh man, & when he told me so, I answered him by saying he ought to have a head like a Sphinx so as to be recognisable. Sir Edmund has lent me Demidov's* Russia. [9] *Old Dundas has not been particularly civil – for which I hate him.*]

Today an affair took place which was severely canvassed at dinner. Some Russian Cavalry drove in our out-lying piquet in the morning, and in consequence all the Cavalry and Captain Maude's troop of H[orse] A[rtillery] turned out under Lord Lucan. By judicious generalship, they say, the whole force might have been taken, or severely punished; but a hesitation at the wrong moment allowed them all to retire out of range, after having killed two or three of our men, while they escaped unhurt. [10]

Monday, 9th – Walked up to camp with Mr Bosanquet. Found Henry, who accompanied us part of the way back, and then went on board the *Danube* to luncheon. Henry and I dined there at six o'clock. In the afternoon I walked along the ridge of the stupendous rocks overlooking the sea. The spray dashed into my face – the sea foamed far beneath my feet. There was something in the strong wind, the beetling cliffs, the churning sea, and the boundless view that filled me with glorious admiration and delight. Last night our dear horses Bob and Whisker arrived from Varna, and were taken to the camp this afternoon. I look forward to tomorrow, when I shall see them again.

Tuesday, 10th – Henry brought down the grey horse and Whisker. The day was *intensely* cold, a bitter wind swept through us, chilling every pulse. When we reached the camp, we found poor Bob half dead with cold; so, shifting the saddles, Henry got on his back, and we stretched away at a rapid canter for the front.

Here we met Major Lowe, of the 4th Light Dragoons, and Captain Portal, [11] who asked us to dine. We gladly accepted;

and while dinner was preparing, he rode with us to the extreme right, to show us Sebastopol from a fresh point of view.

Close to us, hid in brushwood, was our own piquet; about 1,000 yards from us was the Russian piquet. From the forts of Sebastopol the shot and shell came hissing every two minutes.

I could not but feel a high degree of excitement, and I think it was not unnatural. We were standing on the brow of a hill, backed by our magnificent troops, and fronting the enemy; the doomed city beneath our feet, and the pale moon above: it was indeed a moment worth a hundred years of everyday existence. I have often prayed that I might '*wear* out my life, and not rust it out,'[12] and it may be that my dreams and aspirations will be realised.

[*The shells were coming in about one every two minutes. We heard them whizzing by, or saw them (generally) burst in the air, but before dinner was over we got so used to them we did not hear them. They fired 1,000 shells during the night at one of our breastworks but they only killed one officer, one private & wounded two more & a horse.*

This life is full of charm for me. You have an adventure, a danger, an excitement, every hour. Either you are impaled on the horns of a couple of bullocks in an araba, with which the streets [of Balaclava] are crammed, <u>locked</u> and blocked or bitten by a vicious camel – so that to save myself being crushed by a gun-wheel I had yesterday to jump the pony over a bullock which was lying down in the shafts of an araba right across the road.]

Wednesday, 11th – A French transport got aground yesterday before Sebastopol. The Russians fired at her, and carried away her bowsprit. The crew deserted her, but endeavoured to get her off during the night. The garrison made a sortie this morning with the bayonet, but retreated as soon as our men turned out.

Friday, 13th – A report was current that the fire of the siege was to open today, but hardly a shot disturbed the warm serenity of the air. What a variable climate! Three days ago the cold was intense, today the sun is oppressive. Captain Lockwood rode down to call on me. He told me with a melancholy face, that the Russians had made a successful descent on Eupatoria, and had wrested the place from us; but a lieutenant in the navy who came in shortly after declared this information was false, as, although driven back, the force had returned, and effectually driven out the enemy.

The arrival of ships from Eupatoria laden with supplies, would seem to say that at any rate the *Russians* had not possession of it. The *Cambria* and *Medway* arrived today, each with a regiment of 1,300 Turks.

[*We have been daily expecting an attack on the town of Balaclava but it has not come on yet. The inhabitants were all driven out yesterday. I am in the camp all day long but dine & sleep on board ship. The horses Bob & Whisker are well & safe – but the cold was yesterday equal to January & 14 horses died of it in the night. We ride up to the Front everyday. … Poor young Thynne [13] of the Rifles was brought on board ship yesterday in a state of Cholera collapse. He is alive at present. Lord Raglan & I helped to get him in the boat. Lord Raglan was as anxious & tender with him as possible. I love Lord R's private character though I can't but think him a dilatory general. …*

You can imagine what the climate is when I tell you that two days ago it was so intensely cold that 300 sick men came down from the camp in consequence of the cold – & yesterday it was so hot that it was almost too much trouble to move. Cholera is still bad.]

Saturday, 14th – Since last night two yachts have come into harbour, the *Dryad* (Lord Cardigan's) and the *Maraquita* (Mr Carew's). What a satire is the appearance of these fairy ships amidst all the rough work of war! They seem as out of place as a London belle would be; and yet there is something very touching in their pretty gracefulness.

Henry, Captain Fane, Mr Goss, R.N., and I started on horseback for the camp. We lunched at our own tent. Our ride took in nearly the whole front line of the camp, commencing on the right, at the ground lately occupied by the 4th Light Dragoons, passing the Rifles and the 23rd, and then returning by the French.

The entrenching work progresses rapidly, under a heavy and continuous fire. I hear that Lord Raglan was in the foremost trench last night till one o'clock. A rifleman standing near him had his head taken off by a round shot.

Either today, or yesterday, a rifleman, seeing a shell light in the entrenchment, knocked out the fuse with his rifle. He was mentioned in general orders. I cannot but think it a pity that our service provides no decoration, no distinctive reward of bravery, for such acts as this. If it were only a bit of red rag, the man should have it, and wear it immediately, as an honourable distinction, instead of waiting for a medal he may never live to obtain, or may only obtain years hence, when it shall have lost half its value.[14]

Guns are run into position tonight; the wheels were being muffled in sheepskin when I was in camp. I heard of a sortie on the French this morning, but no particulars.

Sunday, 15th – Awoke exhausted.

What an exhaustion! It seemed to me as though my life was ebbing away, my sands running quietly down; so I lay for a long time, becalmed in soul and body. I cannot account for this at all. I remained in this state all the morning; and did not get up till twelve o'clock; at which time Captain Nolan[15] came in, and we had a long and interesting conversation. After discussing my afternoon's amusement, I determined on accepting his horse and saddle, with a tiger-skin over the holsters; while he borrowed a pony, and we rode together to see Henry at the camp. After spending an hour in his tent Henry and I walked down to the *Star of the South* to dinner, Henry returning on foot at night.

Monday, 16th – For three days the firing has been continuous. Captain Nolan told me yesterday that the siege would open in earnest on Tuesday. A party of us sat till late on deck, watching the flashes of the guns.

All night they kept it up, but now, 11 a.m., are quiet. The *Agamemnon* steamed out yesterday from Balaklava to join the fleet. The French are at this moment landing a fresh regiment of Cavalry, and the *Medway* is being cleared of her cargo of Turks. We wait, with some little excitement, for tomorrow. I have ordered my horse at eight o'clock in the morning.

Tuesday, 17th, 10 p.m. – At half past six o'clock began that fearful rain of shot and shell, which poured incessantly on the forts and batteries of Sebastopol, until night befriended the city, and threw her shade over it. At a quarter past seven the Round Tower was silenced, though the battery at its foot still kept up a fire from two guns, which we could not enfilade. Soon after ten Henry and I had arrived, and took our place opposite the Fourth Division.

At ten o'clock a French powder magazine exploded, which dismounted fifteen guns, and killed about forty of their men.

At half-past one, the French and English fleets, with the *Mahmoudie*, brought in their fire. The *Agamemnon*, with Sir E. Lyons on board, went close in, followed by the *Sanspareil*. The *London, Albion, Bellerophon, Retribution,* were all more or less severely mauled, as they poured in broadside after broadside, with incredible and incessant noise. I merely mention the names of such ships as I know something of. There were many others, amongst them the *Rodney, Arethusa, Trafalgar,* and the *Tribune.* The *London* was twice on fire. The *Albion* had a shell which, by unlucky chance, pitched into Captain Lushington's stores, destroying his cellar and his clothes. The *Bellerophon* had a shell through Lord George's cabin; the *Retribution* lost her main mast.

[*The firing all day from the united Fleet has been 'incredible'. And with the following result ... all their shot has no effect on the superb forts of the Town. <u>On dit</u> that Old Dundas in the* Britannia *was never within range! I wish I could just put the poor old woman to the sufficiently slow torture he merits.*][16]

At ten minutes past three a magnificent sight presented itself – a huge explosion in the Mud Fort (Redan), the smoke of which ascended to the eye of heaven, and then gathering, fell slowly and mournfully down to earth. I thought of torture and sudden death, and was softened to tears, while round me cheers burst from every throat – 'All down the line one deafening shout.'

Officers and men were carried away with enthusiasm, and I felt myself half cheering too.

[*My God, I never shall forget it! 27 guns one moment before had been in full play – then came a burst of smoke like the day of judgement & after was silence – one hour after and <u>one</u> gun began to play slowly.*]

Three quarters of an hour after a smaller explosion caught our eye. Again the cheer rang out. 'Men! Men, for God's sake! It is *ours!*' and an ammunition-waggon sent up its contents to form a fierce cloud in the serene sky [*but neither horses nor drivers were hurt!!!*]

We left at dusk, and rode slowly down to Balaklava, our hearts and ears filled with the magnificent din of war. Our casualties have been very few. Poor Captain Rowley and the assistant-surgeon of the 68th are dead. The gathering twilight prevented our seeing much of the damage done to the town. We fancied it greater than it proved. One of our Lancaster guns burst today; the other is doing good work. The shot rushes with such vehement noise through the air that it has been surnamed the 'Express Train'. We fired 170 rounds a gun yesterday (so they say). I was not sorry to find rest on board ship, being tired out with the excitement and exertion of the day.

[*There will be a storming party tonight. I think it's premature. Next time I write will be I think from the ruins of Sebastopol. Don't publish any more about Cardigan, please. If I had my way I would cut old Dundas into little bits & roast him to death. He is a disgrace to the fleet. Our fleet ought to have engaged at 10 o/c & had hardly begun at one. He is hated universely*[sic] *& they go by the name of Mrs Dundas & Lady Emmeline. I am too tired for more. And deaf from the firing. A shell came where we were sitting yesterday but today they left us alone.*]

Wednesday, 18th – Did not intend going out early, but at nine o'clock I saw my horse saddled on the beach. A large Russian force is collected on the plains, at whom, as is evident, we are firing hard. I dressed in all haste, and started to the front. Here I found Cavalry, Artillery, and Turks drawn up beyond our camp, and a Russian force in the valley, at some 1,800 yards distance, standing gazing at them. The firing had all ceased, and the greater part of the Russians had retired under shelter of a hill. As soon as we were tired of looking at them, and tired of waiting for them to advance, we left the field battery, behind which we had taken our places, and went slowly on to the front.

The French batteries were unable to reopen fire. The ships were a great deal too much mauled yesterday to be able to go in again for some time. The English guns were firing, and we had some red-hot shot, in the hopes of setting fire to the town; but the town appears built of incombustible materials, as, although it was twice slightly on fire yesterday, the flames were almost immediately extinguished. I am told that the men of Captain Lushington's battery last night refused to be relieved, though they had been at work all day. They said they had 'got their range, and were doing good work, and would not go away – all they wanted was something to eat, and some grog.'

Sir George Cathcart sent them down immediately all the food and grog he could muster. 'Ah!' exclaimed one of the riflemen who had been firing at the gunners in the Mud Fort before the explosion took place, 'When it blew up, in the confusion, there was beautiful shooting!'

We had luncheon in Major Wynne's tent, of the 68th, and left again about three o'clock to ride back to Balaklava. Passing the fortifications between the front and rear, we found the French mustered in rather a strong force in the battery overlooking the Russian army. No movement had been made by the Russians. They will probably remain in the shelter of the hill until they are *drawn*. Artillery and Cavalry were coming slowly home as we approached our lines. The heavy guns of the siege still follow us with their ceaseless sound.

Colonel Hood, of the Guards, was killed today, and the ambulance corps brought down forty sick, to be embarked on board ship at Balaklava. Today, with the aid of glasses, I saw a loose horse going with a strange halting gait before the batteries of the Russian forts. He was thought to be an English Artillery horse wounded yesterday; strange that, among all that thunder of shot and shell, not one bullet could be spared for him.

Thursday, 19th – We thought Sebastopol was to stand, *perhaps*, a three days' siege – more likely a single day's while some, more arrogant still, allowed it eight hours to resist the fury of the allies!

Now there are orders that no shot is to be fired into the town for fear of destroying the houses. Is this because Lord Raglan is confident of the speedy possession of the town, or from the estimable amiability of his private character, which makes him shrink from inflicting wanton damage or death? This order to spare the town is much commented on.

[*The Russians fire away in front and take in fresh supplies & reinforcements behind. Unless we storm it Sebastopol will never be taken. The lying* Times *with its 'Fall of Sebastopol'*[17] *grieves and disgusts us, many a brave man must fall and many alike be sacrificed before Sebastopol will fall – And will it fall then? – If*

*you could see the anxious faces. Everyone regards Lord Raglan
with affection but his best friends sigh over his wondrous levity.*]

However commendable the greatest humanity may be, we
cannot but remember that the blood of 2,090 men, lying on
the field of Alma, calls to us from the ground. Were *we*
besieged, the Russians would not show the like consideration to us.

Today we moved our camp, so as to be out of the way of
the batteries we have erected on the heights round
Balaklava.

I did not go to the front today. I got sick with anxiety, and
deaf with the guns.

Friday, 20th – Today the French siege-guns are in good
play, and firing with good aim. They commenced their
rocket-practice about two o'clock, and created a fire in the
direction of the harbour. The battery at the foot of the
Round Tower is still working away, though the Round Tower
itself has been silenced since seven o'clock in the morning of
the siege.

The French silenced a square fort on the left early today.
As we rode home, we found the Russian Army had moved
out again, and all our forces were outposted in the batteries
and at the top of the hills. However, I was too hungry to stay
and watch them, and left them to look at each other at their
leisure.

There is a *talk* of storming the town tomorrow. I fancy, if
it was intended, it would not be talked about beforehand. A
deserter reports that the troops inside are in fear and dis-
heartened; if so, an assault may not be necessary. Major
Norcott, of the Rifles, to whom I was talking today, gave me
a most affecting account of the death of his favourite horse at
Alma. He spoke with his eyes filled with tears; and, indeed,
he could hardly have found a more sympathising auditor, for
I never think of my own dear grey without a sharp and cruel
pain. A sailor in one of the naval batteries was wounded

yesterday. But 'he wasn't going to be carried about as long as he could walk'; and he actually crawled to the 68th camp, and asked for a 'drink of water.' Individual instances of courage are too many for me to record separately.

[*Mrs Creswell arrived at Balaclava today, and rode up to the camp. I understand she intends remaining in Colonel Douglas' tent. I have not seen her. Lord Raglan's aide-de-camp, whom in his kindness he sent immediately to her, reports her 'very cheery'. Fancy the sympathy, tears & prayers I've wasted, vexatious to think of!*]

Saturday, 21st – Hearing that nothing more than the usual fire was going on at the front, I did not hurry forward today, but reached my usual ground of observation in time to see an explosion behind the Round Tower, followed by a heavy fire from the two unsilenceable guns, which they kept up viciously for some time. The Russian fire was slack, and principally directed on the French lines. The French batteries are firing well. Sir George Cathcart, with whom I was in conversation for some time, tells me that no attempt must be made to storm the town *now*, until the French are ready to act in concert with us.[18] All appear to concur in thinking that the Crimea will be our winter quarters. A very promising officer, Mr Greathed, was killed in the naval battery today.

[*Lord Lucan persisted in turning out <u>all</u> the Cavalry at 5 <u>o'clock</u> having every camp fire & light put out at 5 p.m. & keeping men & horses out till seven next morning not 500 yards in advance of their tents. Some had cloaks, some hadn't. The night was very dewy & cold ... I believe Lord Lucan's incapability will be officially notified to Lord Raglan.*

... We all dread the winter here. I fear the 'snow will be the winding sheet' of many a gallant heart. I wonder if I shall live through it? I often doubt it. I <u>pray</u> I may die in England and not be buried here. ... My great wish is to see an English drawing room & breakfast table again. With milk & butter which we]

never see. Only fancy cream!! We think we shall be in, in about four days. I am sick of the siege & the noise of the guns.]

Sunday, 22nd – Guns as usual.

Monday, 23rd – Rode up to the battery on the left; I do not know which it was. Last night the men were making a new parallel, 500 yards in advance of the present ones. At what an enormous range (it appears to me) we have placed our guns! Will this long range answer? I think the siege progresses very slowly. They ran the Lancaster in and pointed it on the dockyards.

A sortie was made this morning on the French. Their first intimation of it was from a party of soldiers appearing on the embrasures, crying out, 'Ne tirez pas! nous sommes Anglais!' Before the French discovered their mistake they had spiked three guns. A sortie was also made on our piquets, led on *most gallantly* by a Russian officer. He was shot in the mouth, and taken prisoner. Captain Brown, of the 44th, lost his right arm and two fingers of his left hand.

Tuesday, 24th – Awful confusion, hurry, and noise in the harbour of Balaklava, facilitating (?) the disembarkation of twenty-four pound shot and powder.

Some Artillery officers, who lunched on board the *Star of the South*, speak much of the fatigue consequent on the work in the trenches. Our batteries succeeded in setting fire to a part of the town at half-past three p.m., which burnt fiercely for a short time, but was eventually extinguished. A flag of truce was sent to our headquarters today, to say that the sick and wounded were distributed in various houses in Sebastopol, which should be distinguished by a yellow flag, and to request that they might be exempt from fire; but Lord Raglan, fancying this merely a scheme to make magazines of such houses, refused to comply with the proposal.

[*Wednesday, 25th* – *I have a letter of disastrous news – not so much perhaps for our* army *or our story eventually – but one that affects us all nearly & deeply. I mentioned in my last that the*

*Russians had a force advancing towards Balaclava - to attack us
in [the] rear and endeavour both to regain Balaclava & make us
raise the siege of Sebastopol. Well we knew that they had been
hanging about among the hills for some days but we fancied in our
folly that they would not attack us.*]

Feeling very far from well, I decided on remaining quietly
on board ship today; but on looking through my stern cabin
windows, at eight o'clock, I saw my horse saddled and waiting
on the beach, in charge of our soldier-servant on the pony. A
note was put into my hands from Henry, a moment after. It
ran thus: 'The battle of Balaklava has begun, and promises to
be a hot one. I send you the horse. Lose no time, but come up
as quickly as you can: do not wait for breakfast.'[19]

Words full of meaning! I dressed in all haste, went ashore
without delay, and, mounting my horse, Bob, started as fast
as the narrow and crowded streets would permit. I was
hardly clear of the town, before I met a commissariat officer,
who told me that the Turks had abandoned all their
batteries, and were running towards the town. He begged
me to keep as much to the *left* as possible, and, of all things,
to lose no time in getting amongst our own men, as the
Russian force was pouring on us; adding, 'For God's sake,
ride fast, or you may not reach the camp alive.' Captain
Howard, whom I met a moment after, assured me that I
might proceed; but added, 'Lose no time.'

Turning off into a short cut of grass, and stretching into
his stride, the old horse laid himself out to his work, and
soon reaching the main road, we clattered on towards the
camp. The road was almost blocked up with flying Turks,
some running hard, vociferating, 'Ship Johnny! Ship
Johnny!' while others came along laden with pots, kettles,
arms, and plunder of every description, chiefly old bottles,
for which the Turks appear to have a great appreciation. The
Russians were by this time in possession of three batteries,
from which the Turks had fled.

[*Had I known more of their* <u>*Brutal*</u> *cowardice I would have ridden over them all ... the moment the Russians advanced upon the three Turkish batteries – every Turk turned tail &* <u>*ran*</u> *like rabbits.*[20]]

The 93rd and 42nd were drawn up on an eminence before the village of Balaklava. Our Cavalry were all retiring when I arrived, to take up a position in rear of their own lines.

Looking on the crest of the nearest hill, I saw it covered with running Turks, pursued by mounted Cossacks, who were all making straight for where I stood, superintending the striking of our tent and the packing of our valuables. Henry flung me on the old horse; and seizing a pair of laden saddle-bags, a great coat, and a few other loose packages, I made the best of my way over a ditch into a vineyard, and awaited the event. For a moment I lost sight of our pony, Whisker, who was being loaded; but Henry joined me just in time to ride a little to the left, to get clear of the shots, which now began to fly towards us. Presently came the Russian Cavalry charging, over the hill-side and across the valley, right against the little line of Highlanders. Ah, what a moment! Charging and surging onward, what could that little wall of men do against such numbers and such speed? There they stood. Sir Colin did not even form them into square.[21] They waited until the horsemen were within range, and then poured a volley which for a moment hid everything in smoke. The Scots Greys and Inniskillens then left the ranks of our Cavalry, and charged with all their weight and force upon them, cutting and hewing right and left.

[*Not a man stirred, they stood like rocks till the Russian horses came within about thirty yards - Then one terrific volley – a sudden wheel – a piece of ground strewed with men and horses – when the Scots Gs & Royals bounding from the ranks dashed with their heavy horses on the mounted foe & hewed them down. Ten minutes more and not a live Russian was seen on that side the hill. I cannot pain you with a description of the sights I saw that hour.*]

A few minutes – moments as it seemed to me - and all that occupied that lately crowded spot were men and horses, lying strewn upon the ground. One poor horse galloped up to where we stood; a round shot had taken him in the haunch, and a gaping wound it made. Another, struck by a shell in the nostrils, staggered feebly up to Bob, suffocating from inability to breathe. He soon fell down. About this time reinforcements of Infantry, French Cavalry, and Infantry and Artillery, came down from the front, and proceeded to form in the valley on the other side of the hill over which the Russian Cavalry had come.

[*Such a goodly army as they were lying beneath us in the sunshine – with the Russian force half hidden behind the hill. Some wounded French soldiers came to us – Henry helped one poor fellow from his horse who was shot in the arm and another thro the thigh.*]

Now came the disaster of the day – our glorious and fatal charge. But so sick at heart am I that I can barely write of it even now. It has become a matter of world history, deeply as at the time it was involved in mystery. I only know that I saw Captain Nolan galloping; that presently the Light Brigade, leaving their position, advanced by themselves, although in the face of the whole Russian force, and under a fire that seemed pouring from all sides, as though every bush was a musket, every stone in the hillside a gun. Faster and faster they rode. How we watched them! They are out of sight; but presently come a few horsemen, straggling, galloping back. 'What can those *skirmishers* be doing? See, they form up together again. Good God! it is the Light Brigade!'

At five o'clock that evening Henry and I turned, and rode up to where these men had formed up in the rear [*& shook hands with them – poor fellows our hearts were all too full for many words.*]

I rode up trembling, for now the excitement was over. My nerves began to shake, and I had been, although almost unconsciously, very ill myself all day. Past the scene of the morning we rode slowly; round us were dead and dying horses, numberless; and near me lay a Russian soldier, very still, upon his face. In a vineyard a little to my right a Turkish soldier was also stretched out dead. The horses, mostly dead, were all unsaddled, and the attitudes of some betokened extreme pain. One poor cream-colour, with a bullet through his flank, lay dying, so patiently!

Colonel Shewell came up to me, looking flushed, and conscious of having fought like a brave and gallant soldier, and of having earned his laurels well.[22] Many had a sad tale to tell. All had been struck with the exception of Colonel Shewell, either themselves or their horses. Poor Lord Fitzgibbon was dead. Of Captain Lockwood no tidings had been heard; none had seen him fall, and none had seen him since the action.[23] Mr Clutterbuck was wounded in the foot; Mr Seager in the hand. Captain Tomkinson's horse had been shot under him; Major De Salis's horse wounded. Mr Mussenden showed me a grape-shot which had 'killed my poor mare.' Mr Clowes was a prisoner. Poor Captain Goad, of the 13th, is dead. Ah, what a catalogue!

[*My poor woman who waits on me has lost her husband. He was seen to fall over his horse.*]

And then the wounded soldiers crawling to the hills! One French soldier, of the Chasseurs d'Afrique, wounded slightly in the temple, but whose face was crimson with blood, which had dripped from his head to his shoulder, and splashed over his white horse's quarters, was regardless of the pain, but rode to find a medical officer for two of his 'camarades,' one shot through the arm, the other through the thigh.

Evening was closing in. I was faint and weary, so we turned our horses, and rode slowly to Balaklava. We passed Mr Prendergast, of the Scots' Greys, *riding* down to the harbour, wounded in the foot; the pluck with which an Englishman puts pain out of the question is as wonderful as it is admirable. Time would fail me to enumerate even the names of those whose gallantry reached my ears. Captain Morris, Captain Maude, both cut and shot to pieces, and who have earned for themselves an imperishable name!

[*And after all came the dreary ride back to the ship. ... I felt no horror, no fear, no pain, until after I reached the ship & then the reaction was like what I should fancy occurs after suspended animation.*]

What a lurid night I passed. Overcome with bodily pain and fatigue, I slept, but even my closed eyelids were filled with the ruddy glare of blood.

Thursday, 26th – They are sending as many ships as possible out of harbour. On board the ship in which I live are 400 tons of gunpowder, and she is to be gradually filled up.

The Russians, to the number of 5,000, made a sortie on the French lines this morning, but were repulsed with loss.

[*Until late last night it was determined to abandon Balaclava but gallant Sir E. Lyons has come amongst us again & all are re-inspired with courage. As to Mrs Dundas [i.e. the Admiral] I believe she is to be 'sat upon' as soon as Parliament meets.*[24]]

Two Russian officers, wounded yesterday, were brought down and embarked today from Balaklava. No tidings of Captain Lockwood. They tell me that there is a chance that Captain Morris may survive, and that poor Maude, though seriously, is not mortally wounded. I wrote to his wife to-day, to endeavour to break to her, as best I could, the fact that he was *only* wounded!

My poor servant, whose husband was in the 8th, has been in deep anxiety and distress, as, when I left last night, her husband had not been seen. One man told me he thought he saw him fall; but, of course, I would give her no information but *facts*. Today, hearing that he had returned wounded, and was in hospital, she started to see if it was true. Alas, poor woman! all she heard was tidings of his death.

[*It is a novel office for me to be comforter to the poor broken-hearted little woman who is with me. She will not leave me for a moment 'Oh ma'am it's my heart that's bad you seem to give me strength.' Fancy me – from my weakness dealing out strength. ... my first battle, I hope it may be the last tho' I don't think it will.*]

Mr Cator walked over from Khersonese tonight, and arrived about nine o'clock.

Saturday, 28th –What an anxious night. Guns firing incessantly from the batteries round Balaklava! and occasional volleys of musketry seemed to say that the enemy were having another *try* for it. I lay awake, a little anxious and doubtful. The harbour was astir – steamers getting up their steam, anchors being weighed, and all made ready for departure. If they should be able to shell the harbour!

The *Star of the South* is full of powder, and every ship has more or less on board.

Daylight brought news that upwards of 200 horses had escaped from the Russian lines, and galloped towards our entrenchments and those of the French. The marines, thinking, in the dark, that it was a charge of Cavalry, fired right and left; the affrighted horses, turning off, dashed over the plain towards the French, who opened on them immediately. Many were killed, but many more, rushing over everything, were caught in the camp, and distributed – a welcome windfall after the 25th.

A flag of truce went into Sebastopol today, to enquire the number of officers taken, and their fate and names. The answer was, that eleven officers were captured, of whom only two survive. Who may those two be? We are to send again tomorrow to learn their names. Lord Cardigan tells me, that the loss of the Light Brigade in the charge was 300 men, 24 officers, and 354 horses. Twenty-seven wounded horses have since been shot. Lord Cardigan received a slight lance wound in the side; he distinguished himself by the rapidity with which he rode.[25]

Shifted camp today to be out of the way of the French guns.

Sunday, 29th – Tremendous gale of wind all last night. Fortunately it blew off shore, or it might have caused serious damage among the ships lying outside.

Why are the ships allowed to lie outside? All the transport masters object to the anchorage. Why are they kept there against their judgments and their will?

Saw Colonel Lake and Mr Grylls yesterday, for the first time since they so kindly assisted me in my search for Henry at Kalamita.

The flag of truce went in again today, and returned answer that Mr Clowes, 8th Hussars, and Mr Chadwick, 17th Lancers, were the only survivors. Poor Lockwood!

Wednesday, November 1st – A bright, cheery day in harbour tempted me to ride to the camp. Oh, false valley of Balaklava, to conceal amongst thy many surrounding hills the bitter cold of the higher lands! Auctions of deceased officers' effects occupied almost everyone today. The prices were fabulous.[26] An old forage cap fetched £5. 5s. 0d.; an old pair of warm gloves, £1. 7s. 0d.; a couple of cotton night-caps, £1. 1s. 0d.; whilst horses sold as absurdly cheap - one fetched £12. 0s. 0d. and another, £9. A common clasp knife fetched £1. 10s. 0d.

Reinforcements of French troops, Guards, and High-landers, to the amount of 2,000, arrived to-day. Osten Sacken,[27] with a force of 20,000 men, has come to the relief of the besieged city. We are doing nothing particular today beyond firing red-hot shot. All are in expectation of the storming, and all, meanwhile, shivering with cold. Henry succeeded in purchasing a very large waterproof wrapper for Bob, which makes me much easier on his account; but, Oh! how anxious do I feel as often as I look at that dear old friend, and think of the hardships he has to undergo.

[*I have not sat by a fire since we left England. This is a powder ship – so no fires are allowed.*]

Sunday, 5th – I heard very heavy and continuous firing, which lasted all the morning; but as I saw no one from the front, and Henry was there with his regiment, I could learn nothing about it before twelve o'clock. Then, indeed, news came in fast. At five o'clock this morning, in the middle of a dense fog, our outlying piquets suddenly found themselves surrounded and fired at from all sides – heavy guns, of large calibre, with shell and musketry, ploughing in every direction.

How can I describe the horrors and glories of that day? It was a hand-to-hand battle, wherein every man fought for his life. Stunned, and confused for a moment, our troops rallied with inconceivable energy and courage. From five a.m., till three in the afternoon they fought with all the *acharnement* of wild beasts—

> Groom fought like noble, squire like knight,
> As dauntlessly and well.[28]

But I! – I only knew that Henry was there; and begging Captain Buckley, of the Fusilier Guards, who was recovering from his wound at Alma, and on board the *Star of the South*, to accompany me, we started on foot for the front.

With such work going on, reports were not likely to be slack.

I had barely left the town before I was told of the utter destruction of the Cavalry, which had 'remained the whole day passive under a galling fire.' But I had learnt experience, and this did not trouble me much. We pushed on, and met a cart coming down slowly: in it was Sir George Brown, wounded in the arm. A melancholy train of ambulance was winding slowly down to Balaklava. Alas! I well knew its ghastly freight. An hour later, and Henry was giving me himself an account of the terrible casualties of the day. He spoke with grief of Sir George Cathcart, who bravely met with a soldier's highest honour – a death won with such impetuous courage that the memory of it must last through-out all time. The brigade of Guards has suffered cruelly.

General Strangways is dead; poor Major Wynne, of the 68th; Major Dalton, of the 49th, who leaves a young widow and children alone at Constantinople.

But who is not among the list of dead? Poor young Cleveland, with his fair, boyish face. Ah me! how ruthless is the sword!

I cannot hope to glean full and correct particulars of this day, wondrous in the world's history, until time has allowed the feeling of excitement a little to subside.[29]

Monday, 6th – Henry and I rode up to our camp, which is situated near the windmill at the front. Here we met le Baron de Noe, who, with Henry, rode on to inspect the battlefield.

I could not go. The thought of it made me shudder and turn sick. On his return, Henry told me that the field of Alma was child's play to this! Compressed into a space not much exceeding a square half-mile, lay about 5,000 Russians, some say 6,000; above 2,000 of our own men, exclusive of French, of whom, I believe, there were near 3,000; lines upon lines of Artillery horses, heaps upon heaps of slain, lying in every attitude, and congregated in masses – some on their sides, others with hands stiffening on the triggers of their muskets; some rolled up as if they died in mortal pain, others smiling placidly, as though still dreaming of home: while round the batteries, man and horse piled in heaps, wounds and blood – a ghastly and horrible sight!

We were taken by surprise, attacked where we had no intrenchment or fortification of any kind.[30] We fought as all know Englishmen will fight; and our loss was in proportion to the carelessness that permitted the attack, rather than to the magnificent courage that repelled it.

Wednesday, 8th – The 46th, under Colonel Garrett, arrived in Balaklava today, and disembarked this afternoon. They are a particularly fine looking regiment; two companies are already here. They landed, 750 strong.

Thursday, 9th – Rode up to the front to-day with Captain Sayer and Mr Rochfort, who took up their quarters yesterday on board the *Star of the South*; the former having come out to see his brother, who was wounded at Alma, and the latter as an amateur.[31] They went to inspect the horrors of the battlefield; Henry and I went to Sir George Cathcart's grave – fit resting-place for the heart of such a soldier. In the centre of what has been a ruined fortification, in front of the division he led so gallantly, almost within range of the guns of Sebastopol, surrounded by those officers of his division who fell by his side, he sleeps until the *reveillée* of the Great Day. A cross, rudely built of rough stones, stands at the head of his grave. [*(Cathcart) was a friend of mine and strange to say three days before he met his gallant death, he & I were talking within ten feet of the spot since chosen for his grave. He lies in a grave meet for such a man. He was one of our best generals ... next to Sir Geo. lies Major Wynne ... whose head was taken off by a round shot. We lunched with him two days before.*]

Friday, 10th – A heavy gale of wind made terrible disturbance among the shipping, both inside and outside the harbour, so much so that several ships' masters outside protested at not being admitted to the shelter of the harbour.*[32] Owing to the heavy rain, the roads were nearly impassable on Wednesday and today I hear that several of the poor, starved, worn-out Artillery horses died on the road, vainly endeavouring to drag up guns to the front.

Saturday, 11th – The 62nd regiment landed today at Kamiesh Bay. The severe weather affects both men and horses terribly; of the latter, I fear, few will survive to feel the warm breath of spring. These horses have no clothing, and

---

*It would have been well indeed had this warning and remonstrance been attended to. Not only the crews who perished on the 14th, but many brave soldiers, who afterwards died of cold and hunger, might still have survived, had the stores in the *Prince* and other vessels been saved. No inquiry has been made public, but the officer who appears to have been responsible for this catastrophe has been rewarded. (1855 Editor)

very insufficient food; and the *men* live in a state that few of our paupers in England would endure.

[*We are now living in immediate expectation of an attack on Balaclava. It has been threatened these two days but as it is blowing a hurricane tonight & raining into the bargain we think it probable they will come … When we first came there was not an eagle or vulture in the Crimea and now they abound. … They say if Lord Raglan does not withdraw his army he will lose them nearly all. Upon my word I don't believe there ever was a campaign of such continuous hardship & so little prospect of success.*]

Monday, 13th – The *Jura* arrived today. It is still blowing as if it never blew before, and raining in torrents. The Russians made a sortie last night on the French, and were repulsed – with what loss, on either side, I am unable to learn.

[*I am sorry poor dear Wadham fusses about me. I* can't *come home. It is impossible. I cannot leave Henry alone out here, where he may be ill or die any day - & I wouldn't if I could – as I believe I am his only comfort. I believe we are to be* hutted *this winter. …*

I have heard of Florence Nightingale.[33] *The first thing her principal assistant did – was to elope with a doctor. She will have a nice job to keep the staff in order; but I dare say some of them, if steady &* respectable, *which no soldier's wife out here even dreams of being, may do good. And if she keeps them from drinking. The* transport *service are much to be blamed for inattention & rough usage to the wounded, they contrast in this way with the navy. The men-of-war's men are as gentle & tender with the wounded – whom they slip on board the transports – as if they were their mothers – English, Russian, & all. In this censure I don't include all transports but a great many. They hate having them on board.*]

Tuesday, 14th – The most terrific gale commenced blowing at about five o'clock this morning. By seven o'clock, when I looked through the stern-cabin windows, the harbour was seething and covered with foam, and the ships swinging terribly. By nine it had increased to a frightful extent, and I could hardly, even when clinging to the ship, keep my footing on deck. The spray, dashing over the cliffs many hundred feet, fell like heavy rain into the harbour. Ships were crushing and crowding together, all adrift, all breaking and grinding each other to pieces. The stern-work of the *Star of the South* was being ground away by the huge sides of the *Medway*, which was perpetually heaving against her.

By ten o'clock we heard that the most fearful wrack was going on outside amongst the ships at anchor, and some of the party – Captain Sayer, Mr Rochfort, and Captain Frain – started for the rocks to try if by any means they could save life.

The next tidings were, that the *Prince* [34] and the *Resolute*, the *Rip van Winkle*, the *Wanderer*, the *Progress*, and a foreign barque, had all gone down, and, out of the whole, not a dozen people saved. At two o'clock, in spite of wind and weather, I managed to scramble from ship to ship, and went ashore to see this most disastrous sight. Ah me! such a sight, once seen, who can forget!

At the moment after my arrival, the devoted and beautiful little clipper ship *Wild Wave* was riding to her death. Her captain and crew – all but three small boys – had deserted her at nine o'clock; and she was now, with all her masts standing, and her helpless freight on board, drifting with her graceful outlines and her heart of oak, straightway to her doom. She is under our feet. God have mercy on those children now!

Captain Frain, Captain Liddell, and some seamen heave a rope downwards, at which one boy springs, but the huge wave is rolling backwards, and he is never seen again.

A second time they hurl it down to the boy standing on the stern frame, but the ship surging down upon the ruthless rocks, the deck parts beneath his feet, and he is torn, mangled, and helpless; but clinging still, until a wave springs towards him eagerly, and claims him for the sea.

The third and last survivor catches at the friendly rope, and swooning with exhaustion and fear, he is laid upon the rock; while in a moment, with one single bound, the little ship springs upwards, as though she, too, was imploring aid, and falls back a scattered mass, covering the sea with splinters, masts, cargo, hay, bread, and ropes.

Meantime the *Retribution*, the *Lady Valiant*, the *Melbourne*, the *Pride of the Ocean*, the *Medora*, the *Mercia*, and several more, are all more or less damaged; and most of them entirely dismasted, riding it out as best they may. The greatest praise is due to the crew of the *Avon*'s life-boat, who went out fearlessly to endeavour to render aid, but were unable, owing to the heavy sea, to get near the ships. Let me shut up my book, for the more I contemplate it, the more terrible the disaster appears.

Captain Jennings, who came on board ill today, talks of beds and clothing carried bodily into the air, and of tents being split to ribbons, or torn from the ground, and hurled away.

This is nine o'clock p.m. The *Medway*, *Marmion*, *Brenda*, and *Harbinger* are hard at work on the sides of our unlucky ship; and I much fear the figurehead of the *Medway* will be into my cabin tonight.

[*Wind and darkness increasing – and all might have been saved if we had marched straight into Sebastopol after Alma.*[35] ... *No help was practicable from the shore. Henry & Bob Sayer ran to the rocks to try to help but the hurricane forced them to throw themselves down repeatedly. No boats either could live. It is now 2 o'clock, the harbour is filling fast with masts, spars, dead bodies, rum casks, dead cattle, hay, vegetables & every item of wreck. ... The* Medway *as I tell you is gradually boring into my cabin. They say she will be in before morning. She has wounded on board – wounded on the 5th & this is the 15th. There are twelve men dead on the deck. She has shown great negligence towards the wounded and deserves reporting - but they say the stench on board from dead men and wounds & close atmosphere &c is absolutely* *intolerable. In camp they have been 24 hours exposed to fearful rain, hail and this awful hurricane which has split their tents to ribbons & carried them away & <u>blown down horses & men.</u> To give you an idea – Our ship's long boat, lying on the beach, was taken up by the wind, pitched on her bows, & carried along the beach, some yards head over heels till <u>she rose & went over</u> two men's heads on the beach. You can believe it as I saw it – & this, if you realize it – will give you as good an idea as any of the awful force of the wind. She wants six hands to row her at all. Of course when she fell – she crushed up like a bit of paper.*

I wonder if this will <u>spur Lord Raglan</u>? ... I think he is a good & feeling-hearted man – but if he doesn't make a decided movement now – What can become of us? No Powder, – no ships – & one small force? I have bet that he will go on just in the same dawdle that he has done all along – & that his army will be annihilated before spring – the answer I get is – he <u>must</u> go in – it is the only chance.

<u>Don't publish it</u>, and I will tell you an anecdote of Cardigan. He ordered that in consequence of the horses being so cold double stable hours must be observed in order to keep them in circulation. It was objected that all unnecessary exposure of the men was apt to be fatal: 'Ah – we can replace the men – but we cannot replace the horses'!]

Wednesday, 15th – The sky is serene and blue, and nature, weary of her hurricane of tears, has sobbed herself into quietness. Captain Kyle, of the *Pride of the Ocean*, came into harbour this morning, having, together with his crew, abandoned his ship. How beautifully she rode through yesterday's gale! All her masts cut away, and her long black hull, with its graceful lines, sitting on the troubled water like a bird. The *Retribution* rode out the gale safely, though holding by only one cable.

Thursday, 16th – Report mentions twelve ships lost at Katcha, and thirteen at Eupatoria, but as yet this wants confirmation.

Today one of the crew of the *Star of the South*, Welsh by name, has been indefatigable in endeavouring to save the lives of some poor fellows who had been cast on the lower rocks, where they were scarcely to be got at from the heights above. About twelve o'clock, we heard that this fine fellow, in endeavouring to reach a sailor below him, lost his balance, and was lying with a broken leg close to the man he had risked his life to save. A party went to fetch him in, and found him suffering only from contusion, and not from a broken limb. The man appears to have behaved with wonderful courage and good feeling, and is deserving of unqualified praise.

Saturday, 18th – A day like the renewal of youth – cloudless, warm, and so bright. Captain Howard, of the 44th, took pity on me, a prisoner on board ship, and sent down a white Spanish horse for me to ride. I went to the camp, and found them all spreading themselves out to dry in the sunshine like so many torpid flies. Henry applied to be allowed an office in Balaklava, so as to secure a stable for Bob, who is half starved and as rough as a terrier. The grey horse was stolen two days ago, and is not yet recovered.

Sunday, 19th – A mail has arrived. I thirst for letters from England, as a feverish man thirsts for a draught of water. On Friday the Cavalry horses had *one handful of barley* as their day's food.

Yesterday they had the same.

Monday, 20th – Heavy rain. The 97th landed today. They look fresh and well; but I should fancy few will be so tomorrow morning, if this is to be their inauguration day in camp.

[*31 ships are lost & disabled. Two or three days ago we were in very gloomy spirits as the Commissariat said that in consequence of the loss of stores they could not feed either army or horses. And the roads were so bad and all our horses & mules so exhausted that they were unable to bring up stores – even at the rate of 8 horses to a cart and two trusses of hay. ...*

I sent you a map [36] of the situation of batteries and the positions of the forces – I hope it will reach you – I did a much more splendiferous one & have sent it to – whom do you suppose? – no less a person than the Queen. I think it was not a bad hook to throw into the water – it may catch a little fish, and if it doesn't there's no harm done. People begin to get more in spirits, we have reinforcements coming out. ...

Captain Dawson Damer dining on board last night and he says they hope to have sufficient reinforcements to storm in about three weeks. One of those jolly rascally Zouaves[37] has been in already. <u>He crept into the sewer</u> & wrote his name inside with chalk. Jean – somebody, I forget who.

I see by yesterday's mail, which was many days late, that news of the cavalry affair at Balaclava has been received in England but is doubted. Alas it is but too true. Also the frightful loss on the 5th Nov. The guns at the front are going very fast now but I cannot tell whether there is an attack or not – we shall know this afternoon.]

Wednesday, 22nd – Yesterday the *Queen of the South* disembarked draughts of Guards, &c., to the amount of 800 men. They were hardly disembarked before nightfall, and as we were returning at dusk from a ride to camp, we met them marching up.

Henry and I had an adventure today, exciting though harmless. We were riding slowly across the plain, under the French batteries but in full view of the Russian force, when I saw a fragment of shell lying on the ground, and forgetting all about the Russian Artillery, requested Henry to pick it up; he dismounted for the purpose, when luckily I turned round in time to see the smoke of a piece of field artillery. I need hardly say we lost no time in taking ourselves out of range! We were both on white horses, and afforded a conspicuous mark. Lord George Paget is gone home. Thirty-eight other officers, profiting by his example, have sent in their papers.[38]

[*I see by your letter & Katy's ... that those men who have sold out & gone to England are held very cheap & <u>cut</u>. Now it is but fair to say that these men all fought well when there was any fighting – that the prospect of the winter is not cheerful – that it is a great chance if <u>any one</u> will get thro' the winter & live – that they have all been under fire – some have large properties – others are only sons – & altho' I for one cannot understand their leaving especially until Sebastopol is ours – yet I can understand enough of the hardship & trial to health & strength. And also their want of confidence in the expedition – they all say the war is a <u>personal</u> matter, every man fights his own way for his own life – he has no general.* [39]

Oh, about the Lady nurses – I'm afraid they will find it different to what they expect – they have got the name of 'The New Matrimony-at-any-Price Association.' One lady was present in England at the amputation of a finger & is classed as 'experienced in amputation'. <u>I</u> think they may do good sometimes. But <u>your linen</u> that you & Lady Rodney[40] *sent out is far more judicious for the men are crowded into hospitals & really where there are many together it is not <u>decent</u> to go amongst them as I know by our hospital tents & soldiers are never sparing in their indecencies or their remarks. Still the intention is good. But they should all be <u>married</u> women. Now such people as fine young ladies of 26 or 28 is all bosh.*][41]

Thursday, 23rd – Perpetual sounds of heavy firing during the night told us that something was on hand; and next morning we heard that the Rifles had attacked a battery of twenty guns, but owing to insufficient numbers, they were three times driven back, until a French reinforcement enabled them to hold it. A very intelligent French soldier of the *20 ième de la Ligne* came into our tent today, when we were up in camp. He had read part of 'Byron', and the *Vicar of Wakefield*! He told us that on the 5th several of our men, in the confusion, lost their regiments, and placing themselves in the French ranks, fought side by side with their neighbours and allies. Poor Colonel Shewell, overcome at last by the rough life, has been obliged to make up his mind to remain for some days on board ship. The appearance of the officers very much resembles that of the horses; they all look equally thin, worn, ragged, and out of condition in every way.

Sunday, 26th – A brilliant morning induced us to try and attend church on board the *Sanspareil*. Arrived there, we were told there was no service, all the men being employed ashore. We stayed for some time in the wardroom, looking at the many scars left in the good ship's timbers by the shells on the 17th of October, when she followed the *Agamemnon* so closely into action.

In late afternoon Captain Anderson, Mr Goss, and I went to service in the chaplain's room in Balaklava, – an interesting congregation enough, composed entirely of soldiers who had come fresh from the noise of war. The quiet voice of the chaplain was inexpressibly soothing, and the words he chose peculiarly applicable to the excited and half-tired state of my mind – 'There remaineth therefore a rest.' He spoke for ten minutes, though at times his voice was barely audible amidst all the din and noise on the quay, the flogging of jaded and dying horses, and the voices of the soldiers, cursing with every imaginable oath their exhausted cattle.

The grey horse, Job, died this evening of sheer starvation: his tail had been gnawed to a stump by his hungry neighbours at piquet. Misfortune appears to haunt us, as this is the third horse we have lost since leaving England: but we will 'live misfortune down', with that dreary and desperate courage that the terrible scenes of this terrible life impart. Poor Job! he earned his name from his exhaustless patience under innumerable afflictions: he was an enormous, powerful, and hungry horse, and he sold his life by inches. There was no help for it: had it been myself instead of him, I must have died.

[*November 27th. Now for the letter which you may publish or not as you please but if you do I hope you'll put it in the* Daily

News *or* Herald *as well as any other papers you please. Our Big Grey Horse died last night of attenuation and want. When he left England (H. gave 55 for him three days before) he was a fine slashing horse – but now he has thank god ceased to suffer hunger anymore. … Our cavalry camp is a knacker's yard.*

Lord Raglan is never seen. One never meets him riding round the camp inspecting his positions or his works. Canrobert [42] *& his staff I often meet riding round the fortifications. Lord Raglan has not been down to Balaclava for many weeks. If he came down he would see the daily embarkation of the sick – which is conducted in this wise. They come down in ambulance wagons to Balaclava harbour and stepping out of them they go over their ankles in mud, before they can get into the* <u>boat</u> *they have to step over the margin of the bay where I am assured it is not less than a foot deep. Thus perfectly soaking with wet & mud these poor creatures are towed alongside the transports where they may be embarked immediately or left waiting for an hour or so according to the pleasure or convenience of those who are to receive them. Across on the other side of the harbour is a perfectly dry and convenient place for embarking sick & wounded (but Dr Lawson the medic in charge says it is too far from his house, he can't go all that way – tho' doubtless he has a pony – & if not – it is* <u>not</u> *half a mile) … This is true but Mr Goss says if it is published it may get him into a scrape. The* <u>Master</u> *eye is wanting here. I have been almost tempted to endeavour to see Lord Raglan myself on this subject, but I might not do myself or them any good by my interference. So we must imitate the wolves and 'die in silence'.*

The drivers of the ambulance too are anything but careful in some instances. One poor fellow whose arm had been amputated said they had driven fast down hill, & over rough ground, & had jolted him so that all his bandages had slipped & his arm had burst out bleeding again. The roads are such that a cart going at the gentlest walk must be far too rough. The French ambulance mules are far better. [43] *Oh how far superior are the French to us in every way! Where are our huts? Where are our stables? All lying at* <u>Constantinople</u>. *The French*

are hutting themselves in all directions ... while we lie in mud and
horses and men alike die of an exposure which might oh so easily be
prevented. It is all alike – the same utter neglect & mismanagement
runs throughout and really could you hear the many discontented &
complaining voices that I hear all day long you would think I took a
very cheery view of it on the whole. I earnestly pray that my dear
husband & I may live to come back to some quiet corner in England.

Our private servant left at a day's notice the day after the
shells came into our lines. ('He warn't going to stay to be
frightened to death.')

Oddly enough the two men who are lunching on board have just
said: 'It is so odd we <u>never</u> have seen Lord Raglan ... I wish to
goodness some one would burn his fine house down & make him
live in a tent like another man.' Old Dundas walks about with a
stick now.]

Tuesday, 28th – Captain Dawson Damer came down this
afternoon; and I rode back with him to Kadikoi, where the
officers of the Guards have a house, and dined there, Henry
joining us from the camp. The excellent dinner and kindly
hospitality put us quite in spirits, after the ship food and our
long fit of depression. Major Hamilton lent me his white
pony. Oh, dainty pony! with black lustrous eyes, and little
prancing feet, and long white tail dyed red with henna, like
the finger-tips of the most delicate lady in Stamboul! We
rode home at dark, along the rotten, deep, almost impracticable track. The dead horses lying right across the road, as
they fell, and the dead and dying bullocks, filled me with
horror, and the white pony with spasms of fear. Now we trod
upon the muddy carcass of a horse; now we passed a fallen
mule, and a huge bullock, sitting up, with long ghastly horns
pointing upwards in the moonlight, awaiting his death.

No horse is permitted to be destroyed without a special
order from Lord Lucan, except in case of glanders, and, I
believe, a broken leg. Some horses in our lines have been lying
steeped in mud, and in their death agony, for three days!

Thursday, 30th – Tempted by the sunshine, I left my work, and walked over the cliffs with Captain Damer. My work (what will the young ladies at home say to my fingers?) is an enormous canvass sheet and breastplate, which I have made to cover up Bob, and which I must take tomorrow to the *Sanspareil* to have waterproofed. I was scarcely over the ship's side, when the boat drifted – oh, horror! – against a dead body, one of the many that were floating in from the wrecks outside. It was the first I had happened to see. The *Times* of the 13th is in harbour, and somebody, I forget who, tells me that my name appears in it.[44] I wish they could put in that I had left the ship, and was established on shore, if only in a single room. Of this, however, I fear there is but little chance, as I hear Balaklava is to be given up to the sick. The place stinks already with the number of sick Turks, who have turned it into a half-putrid hospital.[45] I never saw people die with such a dreary perseverance as these Turks. Two hundred of them were buried in one day a short time since.

I am happy to hear that it is at last arranged to bring the Light Cavalry down from the front, and quarter them near Balaklava, it being found impossible to convey forage up to them at the front.[†] Fifteen of our horses died last night.

[†] How inconceivable it seems to us at home that our commanders should have suffered the surviving horses of our Light Cavalry Brigade to die of starvation and cold on the heights, when they could have moved them to Balaklava, where they would have found both forage and shelter. – 1855 Ed.

CHAPTER 5

Balaklava
December 1854– March 1855

From late November to February action at the front consisted of little more than a desultory exchange of artillery fire and occasional sorties from the opposing trenches. Both sides concentrated on surviving the harsh winter. The Russians, hampered by the naval blockade of Black Sea ports, were forced to transport their supplies (in primitive ox-carts) over hundreds of miles of rough tracks. The French, with a tradition of self-sufficiency from their overseas campaigns, lived comparatively well and were the envy of their allies (see p. 289, note 33).

In the British camp officers and men lived amid scenes of squalor. Still sleeping in tents and wearing the remnants of their summer uniforms, they spent long hours in the trenches exposed to wet and cold day after day. There was no system of communal cooking; unlike the French army or the Royal Navy, every man had to fend for himself, even finding his own water and firewood in an area stripped bare of every twig. With no latrines the areas around the camps became filthy quagmires. Rats and lice abounded, spreading disease. By the end of November the Commissariat had virtually collapsed and Airey, the Quartermaster-General, lacked the initiative to over-rule the local hide-bound officials, who still refused to release supplies without the completion of numerous forms (see p. 283, note 32, and Biographies: Airey and Boxer).

The uncensored reports of Russell, the Times *correspondent, had alerted the public to this confusion and incompetence, but it was his colleague Chenery's horrific description of the sick and wounded from Alma arriving at the squalid barracks at Scutari (dated 25 September, published 12 October; see p. 273, note 11), that shocked the nation into action. The government responded immediately—Herbert, the Secretary at War, arranged for his friend Miss Nightingale to take thirty-eight nurses to Scutari. Meanwhile Delane, editor of the* Times, *initiated the CrimeanWar Fund to provide comforts for the men (see p. 296, note 28, and Biographies: Nightingale and Russell). Contributions of money, food and clothing flooded in. Even the Queen knitted mittens for the troops. Many of those who answered the appeal already knew of the army's sufferings. Week after week uncensored letters poured back from the Crimea—during 1855 alone over 1,200,000 reached home—and many appeared in newspapers, some forwarded by anxious or angry recipients, others sent directly by anonymous soldiers. Fanny herself continued to send anonymous letters to the press throughout her time in the Crimea (see p. 290, note 40).*

The growing criticism of the General Staff's ineptitude soon engulfed the government, since it was quickly realised that the problems were not due solely to mere military mismanagement. During December Delane thundered dramatically in editorials while the government was attacked in a series of Parliamentary debates. In January, after what was effectively a vote of no confidence, they resigned and it was widely believed that the leaders, reports and letters in the press had brought about their downfall. On 4 February the Queen invited Lord Palmerston to form a government. A couple of weeks later General Simpson was sent out as Chief of Staff to the army to report on conditions and, in effect, to select scapegoats. This he refused to do, although Burgoyne was recalled (see p. 287, note 20; p. 290, note 38; Biographies: Simpson).

Despite the arrival of raw young recruits, many of whom sickened and died within weeks, the effective British fighting strength had fallen to little more than 12,000 by the end of February. The French, with superior numbers, took over the extreme right of the line leaving their allies to concentrate on the Great Redan. But the situation gradually improved as the first huts finally arrived and measures were taken to organise distribution and sanitation. The engineering firm of Peto & Brassey undertook the construction of a railway line (including supplying the navvies) from Balaclava to the camps. In early March the government Sanitary Commission arrived in Scutari and installed a new drainage system before moving on to Balaclava and overseeing the cleaning up of the harbour and the camps. However, by the time the winter uniforms arrived it was so hot that the photographer Roger Fenton had great difficulty persuading men to wear them, even briefly. And the siege work recommenced. The newly dug French tunnels were soon so close to the Sebastopol defences that the sappers could hear the Russian soldiers cursing.

———◦◦◦———

[2nd December 1854. I did not intend writing any more letters as I am quite sure half those I write do not even leave the Crimea[1] ... But this one I will put into Lord Raglan's bag myself if I can get a horse to carry me so far – or do not die of excessive irritation before tomorrow. You are slightly irritable so you will understand the following sketch of what my life has been ever since I have been in Balaclava. I have not mentioned it before but it has begun to affect my health now. ... We are on board ship moored close to the shore in a harbor that often stinks so from the vast numbers of sick & wounded that it makes me retch – dead bodies only recognisable from a thigh bone or an arm floating round the ship, a sight so horrible that it seems to stop the current of one's blood. On the *quay, ankle deep in wet mud ... you stumble over a dirty muddy bundle that looks like a sack, it is a dead Turk in a blanket put down in the mud. All the time the rain goes on, hard & ceaseless. Out of the town in the middle of the road, throwing up the mud like a fountain spurt, is an Artillery horse, kicking in his death struggle. When I have had sufficient <u>fresh</u> air and <u>exercise</u> & refreshment I return to the ship.*

The master of the ship is a man whom I should fancy few housekeepers would admit into their housekeeper's rooms. Vulgar? You can form an idea of vulgarity, but of this man you form <u>none</u>. He claps his hands till the cabin rings – he sucks his teeth – he picks them with a fork, he cleans his nails over his plate at dinner, <u>whistling incessantly</u>: he eats with his knife, spits upon his hands & rubs them together, leans over me almost when I am writing (I wish to goodness he'd come now. Instead of making noises in imitation of animals at the other end of the table.) <u>Whenever</u> he has a chance of speaking to me in public it is so familiar, so patronizing, that I tremble with passion, as it must give an idea that we are on the best possible terms. He caught me up the other day and lifted me out of the boat, while I was like a baby in his arms, for he is an immensely strong man, and I was held up, dangling, frantic with rage and utterly helpless till he was pleased to put me down. At once a ludicrous and (to me) disgusting position. Henry been obliged to be away all day in camp and I am only very rarely able to go with him & though every one who has a spare moment, soldier or sailor, always comes to me, yet when H. goes away I shut myself up in my cabin – occasionally <u>in the dark</u>, as they perpetually shut down my ports then for no earthly reason I can see but to annoy me. Then the steward is so insolent – so dirty! He never even blacks my boots or Henry's. ...

Colonel Lake who is gone home says the moment he reaches England he will go away to the very heart of it & shut himself up in a dark room & never see a soul, or hear a sound, and that's what I will do you may depend on it. Darkness, solitude & profound quiet.

Lord Cardigan is invalided and goes home in a day or two. I was discoursing him yesterday and he said 'My health is broken down, I have no brigade, my brigade is gone, if I had a brigade I am not allowed to command it, my heart & health are broken I must go home.' Ever since he has been in the Crimea he has behaved very well & upon my word I'm sincerely sorry for him.

The siege goes on as usual. Everybody is bored with it and nobody thinks of attending it now ... I am delighted at seeing myself described in the Illustrated News *as a 'Stout-hearted lady'* [2] *... only fancy how great a heroine coming into this mess has made one. ...*

P.S. Tell Charles today a sailor & our corporal stole a sack of oats for Bob & I gave them 5/- each & they've been dead drunk ever since but the old boy ate till he couldn't hold anymore – he has a bit of barley today as well.]

Sunday, 3rd – It rained viciously all day. Captain Buckley came down to see me in the afternoon. I hear the sick are dying at an average of eighty per diem. I know that the mortality amongst the newly-arrived regiments is very great; nor can any one wonder at it! We, who are acclimatised, can hardly make head against the hardships of the life, – what, then, must those feel who have just left an English barrack, or even the crowded discomforts of a transport! With some little horror (not much), and a great deal of curiosity, I watched from over the taffrail of the *Star of the South* the embarkation of some Russian prisoners and English soldiers (all wounded) for Scutari. The dignified indifference of the medical officer,[3] who stood with his hands in his pockets, gossiping in the hospital doorway, – the rough and indecent way in which the poor howling wretches were hauled along the quay, and bundled, some with one, and others with both legs amputated, into the bottom of a boat, without a symptom of a stretcher or a bed, was truly an edifying exemplification of the golden rule, 'Do to others as you would be done by.'

On board the steamship *Avon*, I hear the sights and sounds are too dreadful to imagine. An officer, who was sick on board, tells me the wounded men were laid on the deck with nothing but a blanket between them and the boards. Oh, how their wounded limbs must have ached! He said the groans and moans of these poor creatures, on the night he spent on board, were heart-rending; but by the next night the noise had considerably decreased – death had been more merciful to their pain than man. Independently of the wounded soldiers, with whom our hospitals are full, the dreary, weary Turks have got a kind of plague amongst them, which infects the air. If anybody should ever wish to erect a 'Model Balaklava' in England I will tell him the ingredients necessary. Take a village of ruined houses and hovels in the extremest state of all imaginable dirt; allow the rain to pour into and outside them, until the whole place is a swamp of filth ankle-deep; catch about, on an average, 1,000 Turks with the plague, and cram them into the houses indiscriminately; kill about 100 a day, and bury them so as to be scarcely covered with earth, leaving them to rot at leisure–taking care to keep up the supply. Onto one part of the beach drive all the exhausted *bât* ponies[4], dying bullocks, and worn-out camels, and leave them to die of starvation. They will generally do so in about three days, when they will soon begin to rot, and smell accordingly. Collect together from the water of the harbour all the offal of the animals slaughtered for the use of the occupants of above 100 ships, to say nothing of the inhabitants of the town, – which, together with an occasional floating human body, whole or in parts, and the driftwood of the wrecks, pretty well covers the water – and stew them all up together in a narrow harbour, and you will have a tolerable imitation of the real essence of Balaklava. If this is not *piquante* enough, let some men be instructed to sit and smoke on the powder-barrels landing on the quay; which I myself saw two men doing today, on the Ordnance Wharf.

Monday, 4th – The *Europa* steamship came in this afternoon with draughts, and the 97th regiment – *1,100* men in all. Last night the Russians from Kamara made an attempt to get into the town and fire the shipping. They were intercepted – some shot, and some taken prisoners. It was well they were; for had they not been, Balaklava by this time would have existed only in the past tense, as I should also have done most probably myself – an event on which I do not wish to calculate just yet. [*There are 70 sail in Harbor all with more or less hay & powder. Fancy us with our 600 tons of powder!!!*]

There are Russian residents permitted in Balaklava; amongst them a Mr Upton, son of the engineer who constructed the forts of Sebastopol, and who was taken prisoner when we first marched down upon that place.[5]

Thursday, 7th – The *Queen of the South* came in today with Turks on board, but was sent on to Eupatoria to disembark them. The *Sydney* also arrived with part of the 34th on board, and Mr Chenery, the *Times* correspondent at Constantinople.[6]

Several men dined on board, and we had no lack of intelligent conversation for that evening at least, whatever the case may usually be. Captain Hillyar, of the *Agamemnon*, came down from the trenches today and called on me. He tells me the French were repulsed last night in attacking a Russian battery; and also that the Russians made a sortie on our trenches, from which we drove them back. [*He says he has been to Lord Raglan this morning and *told* him that unless something was done everyone of us would be destroyed & Capt Hillyar has just said, 'Mrs Duberly, Lord Raglan doesn't care a pin – he said "Well you know we can't leave, we must remain if we all die".' Lord R. has a capital table and lots of wine and all that. ...*

Our adjutant went up to Hd Qrs yesterday to see one of the ADCs. He found him in a carpeted room with a fireplace, bed, glazed windows & arm chair & yet those fellows will get all the credit of the campaign by & by when they go home. I should like some of the fine young ladies in England to see their smart partners now! Some of them (and in the Guards and Cavalry) covered with lice. Even l'Allegro [7] has not been exempt from them, nor have many of our fellows – but I have lost all of mine now, you may depend on it.]

It appears that the Russians are every day improving their position, as far as new batteries, new trenches, and fresh guns go. A story is current in Balaklava (but people in Balaklava are apt to be scandalous) that one of the Engineers, whose business it indubitably is to watch the various points of attack, being in a battery this morning (whose battery I will not mention), a new mud fort, with sixteen guns mounted and in position, was pointed out to him. 'God bless my soul; so there is! I never knew anything about that!' was his exclamation.

A Maltese man and woman were found murdered on the rocks just outside Balaklava yesterday. I have not heard that anything has been done towards tracing the crime; indeed, such a process would be impossible in such a crowd and confusion of all nations, languages, and peoples.

[*Our Ld Cardigan is now formally reported as 'totally unfit for duty of any kind' & now warm clothing is come out – to dress up the rows of corpses that the eagles haven't quite devoured – 35 sets of rugs were given out to our regiment yesterday so Master Whisker's bones will be wrapped up and until he has eaten it the clothing may keep him warmer...*

I tell you what tho' – few people have any notion into what they send their sons and husbands. If it was all fighting & glory & crash & victory & excitement it would be all very well but it is months of misery, death of cold, starvation, sickness, long days & dreary nights, mud, rheumatism & lumbago to one day of hurry & glory – & what is so fine here, is that thro' all this – there has not been one instance of insubordination or grumbling among all our thousands of men – that's very fine.

You tell me to write of Henry. As far as my experience goes, that man has not got a fault. He is to me like an epitome of the Old Testament, having the meekness of Moses, the patience of Job and the faith of Abraham. His gentleness – temper – and kindness are simply miraculous. I sometimes wish him more energetic – but I feel I have plenty of energy for both. The way he eats tripe, salt horse and boiled missionary (i.e. salt pork and boiled junk) is marvellous, considering his love of a good dinner, & he sits under my petticoat & in my pocket for warmth, poor old cat! – till I am heartily sorry for him.

I have long ago given up all petticoats except a tail gown & wear a pair of man's trousers and thick boots. Petticoats are an impossibility.]

Sunday, 10th – A mild, warm, damp day. I write so seldom in my journal now, because I have nothing to say, except to grieve over the cruel detention of the mail, now four days overdue. [*The mail has been in two days, another is due today & yet we have not received a single letter. Lord Raglan & the fleet have had their letters two days & will not take the trouble to send them round to Balaclava ... this has occurred more than once ... it is likely to promote the affectionate feelings at present subsisting between Lord R. & his deserted troops – deserted is not a badly chosen word by the way. Capt. Pigott was saying yesterday that the only campaign this could be said to resemble is the Retreat from Moscow. Men die nightly in the trenches from cold & wet. They fall asleep & when roused up somehow they do not answer. ...*

Lord Raglan's hall porter has not seen him for 3 weeks, they say he has gone off to Malta. I don't believe it of course but I shouldn't wonder and he would do just as much good there as here. ...

I send this by the naval bag.]

Tuesday, 12th – Heavy firing last night from nine o'clock till twelve – followed this morning by an exquisite specimen of Balaklava reports. They said, 'The Russians had come down last night in force, and had established themselves (or endeavoured to do so, I forget which) between the army in front and the army in the rear; that the Rifles had fired away all their ammunition; and that the Russian loss was (as usual) tremendous!' An Artillery officer, who came down this evening from the trenches, in which he had passed all the previous night, was considerably astonished to hear of this wondrous battle; but said that the Rifles certainly fancied they heard the sound of approaching troops, and blazed away as hard as they could – firing all their ammunition – the result being, I believe, one dead Russian!

Saturday, 16th – Torrents of rain have fallen. The country is more swampy than any words of mine can convey an idea of. Fresh Russian reinforcements have arrived, both to the army in Sebastopol and the army in the field. Today two steamers arrived; one full of Artillery, and the other with the 89th regiment on board. The French have been landing troops very fast, the last few days, at Kherson; and there is a sort of vague idea floating about in the minds of men that a battle is in meditation on the 19th.

The French, who the other day put their admirable walking ambulance at our disposal to bring down our *1,300* sick, have today lent us sixty horses to assist to drag up the *munitions de guerre*. Finding it impossible, by any amount of curses and blows, to get as much strength out of a dying horse as out of one in full vigour, they have at last agreed to give up the attempt; and 400 Turks are to be stationed on the hills to unload the carts at the bottom, and load them again at the top, passing their shot and shell up from hand to hand.

A few Russian prisoners are also employed in assisting the French to mend our roads. Their countenances are wonderfully alike, all with flat noses and short chins; but they seem cheerful and wondrously willing to work. I hear they receive one shilling a day, and a ration of rum.

Sunday, 17th –Went to morning church; afterwards walked with Mr Anderson, and, returning through a deluge of mud, met the 89th and 17th regiments, which had disembarked at an hour's notice, as an attack is expected tomorrow, it being St Nicholas's day, when the Russian soldiers are supposed to have an extra ration of rakee; and as they never fight unless half-drunk, the argument is not so bad after all.

[*I confess to having had enough of battle. I shiver when I think of the horrors I shall most probably have to encounter again. But the old spirit is in me still , and I* must *be with our gallant men and see them fight their way.*]

Monday, 18th – A brilliant, warm day tempted us out; and, at eleven o'clock, Henry, Mr Rochfort, Mr Aspinall, and I,[8] found ourselves on horseback starting for the Monastery of St George. After about three miles of extremely heavy riding, we got upon the downs, and broke our wearisome walking-pace. [*The country is so deep it's like drawing corks at every step, but the Monastery is beautifully situated, half way between this & Kherson & we shall get some luncheon there.*]

The monastery soon came in sight. Built on the edge of a rock, with a precipitous and wooded descent to the sea, it stands quite alone, a solid and rather fine building, surrounded by massive rocks and high cliffs. We tied our horses to the railings of a church outside the precincts, and, guided by a Zouave, penetrated to the gardens within. A few monks were amusing themselves on the terraces, and against the rails, over which we leaned to take in the beauty of the abrupt cliffs, which sloped, laden with trees and foliage even at this time of year, down to the water's edge. Mr Rochfort left us, and presently returned with a handful of Russian stocks in bloom, which he gave to me. Several Russian families have taken refuge here from the lines of the English and French armies. One Englishman interested us all; a Mr Willis, who had been for five-and-thirty years head caulker in the harbour of Sebastopol.[9] He grumbled sorely at the advent of his countrymen, who, as he said, had pulled down his house, and loopholed it, and had destroyed his vineyard -- his 999 trees! General Bosquet[10] and staff rode up as we left, and several English officers were leaving at the same time as ourselves. We had a cheery canter home, during which one of us put up a hare, which, although we had a very speedy greyhound with us, we could not catch. I rode the white Spanish horse.

Tuesday, 19th – Rode my dear old horse today, for the first time since his starvation, and nearly cried with joy as I felt him straining on the bit. A few days ago, when he came down from the front, a mere skinful of bones, and with an expression of human woe and suffering in his large sad eyes, he haunted me night and day; but, remembering former loss, I would neither mention him in this book, nor would I inquire whether he was dead or alive, as each morning came, and today he was able to canter for a couple of dozen yards.

Wednesday, 20th – Rode the white Spanish horse, and hearing that the French were intending to make a reconnaissance, we cantered into the plain and joined them. The Chasseurs d'Afrique, the *6ième Dragons*, and another regiment (which, I do not know) were riding towards Kamara and Canrobert's Hill. As they approached the latter, the enemy showed themselves on the top; mutual skirmishers were sent out; several shots were fired. One *Dragon* was killed, a Chasseur wounded, and a Chasseur horse destroyed; and then, after sitting and looking at each other for some little time, we turned and rode slowly back.

The object of this reconnaissance was to endeavour to ascertain the number of the enemy, and also to try to recover the batteries abandoned by the Turks on the 25th of October. Whether either of these objects was accomplished, I cannot tell, but I think not. It seemed to me cruel enough to leave the one poor fellow in the middle of the great plain, lying on his face, in his gay-coloured uniform, to be either prodded to death with the Cossack lances, or eaten by the eagles and the wild dogs. The scene haunted me for days – aye, even in my dreams.

Friday, 22nd – Incessant rain.

Saturday, 23rd – Ditto, only twice as hard.

Sunday, 24th – The two previous days condensed in one; and this is Christmas eve. How many hearts in our sodden camp must feel sad and lonely today! How many pictures of home, and how many faces (how much loved we never knew till now) rise before our hearts, all beaming with a happiness probably unpossessed by them, but in which our imagination loves to clothe them!

Alas! how many assembled round the blazing fires at home drink no healths, but meet in sorrow to pour out the wassail as a libation to the many honoured dead!

Heavy firing today from the ships. Sir Edmund Lyons has been but three days in command.[11] He is popular, and much is expected of him.

Christmas Day – A brilliant frosty morning. After church Henry and I walked up to the Cavalry camp, and invited Lord Killeen and Colonel De Salis to join our dinner party on board the *Star of the South*, which somehow was prolonged far into the night.[12]

Wednesday, 27th – We started intending to ride up to headquarters, but the roads were so deep and rotten, so full of holes that seemed to have no bottom, the day was so raw, and our progress so slow, that, notwithstanding my endeavours to keep my habit short and temper long, I was too much disgusted and wearied to struggle further than our Cavalry camp.

The cold tonight is intense, and as we have no fire on board this ship our sufferings are very great. But 'there is in every depth a lower still,' and we should be worse off in the trenches. It is when suffering from these minor evils of cold and hunger (for our table is very much neglected), that I feel most how much my patience, endurance, and fortitude are tried. The want of fire, of a carpet, of even a chair, makes itself terribly felt just now.

[*28th December – I can get no warm boots and my feet are* <u>*covered in*</u> *chilblains. Bob Sayer who is staying on board this vile ship, has kindly lent me a pair of his shooting boots, which I can wear with a pair of worsted socks underneath. It is a great kindness to me… . If I had not taken Homerpathy out here, I believe I shouldn't have been alive now. I have never taken allopathic medicine for twelvemonths. I hope your box will turn up all right.*[13]

Would that they [people at home] were more awake to – or acquainted with the shameful mismanagement here.

Any amount of planking for huts lying at Varna. *Ditto on board ships lying in harbour here – some of which have gone out again <u>taking their</u> cargo with them.*	*Not a single private soldier is hutted*
29 Horses of the Heavy cavalry died the night of the first frost. *38th Hussar horses died on the road to picket.* *800 sick embarked since Christmas Day.*	*Lord Raglan said to Capt. Chetwode on Xmas Day:-* *'It is very cold & frosty, but I suppose all the cavalry are snug, you've all been hutted and stabled for some time, haven't you'!!!!!*
Govt: have sent out greatcoats & boots.	*The coats are only big enough for quite undersized men – and the boots are little better than paper.*

If this is not a mockery, what is?

Thursday, 29th [actually 28th]

<u>*We*</u> *live in a perpetual noise. 3,000 French are supplied daily to* <u>*carry*</u> *up shot & shell to the Front. Two men to a shell. Our cavalry are turned into a sort of sick ambulance.*[14] *Oh, by the way Quarter Master General Airey*[15] *riding thro' our lines*

yesterday saw an 11th horse dying in the mud, at his picket rope.
He rode up furious to Col. Douglas & remonstrated on the
horrible sight & the cruelty of allowing a horse to die smothered in
wet mud. Douglas told him if he had come by two days before he
would have seen 29 doing the same thing. – Thus you see, the men
at H.Q. are in absolute ignorance of all that goes on. It was
observed last night at dinner that there has been only one order
given throughout the whole campaign and that was the order for
the Balaklava Charge!!]

Friday, 29th – Lieutenant Ross, of the *Stromboli*, called
on me this afternoon, and joined us in a charming walk
to the ruins of the Genoese Fort, whence we watched the
sparkling sunlight on the sea; and then turning to our left,
we stretched across the hills to the Marine and Rifle camp,
and returned by descending the precipitous cliff into
Balaklava.

Saturday, 30th – The French Cavalry, a regiment of
Zouaves, and some of the Highlanders of Sir Colin Campbell's division, made a reconnaissance today over the ground
supposed to have been occupied by the Russian army under
Liprandi.[16] This force they found had almost entirely
vacated the plain, owing, as we suppose, to the severe
weather cutting off their supplies of provisions. The French
set fire to all the huts they found, and the party returned
about dusk, having met with very few casualties.

I did not go out with the reconnaissance, as our horses
require rest rather than work, and would never have carried
us through the deep mud for so many hours. Instead, we
walked up to the camp, where the sale of the late Major
Oldham's kit was in progress. We were fortunate enough to
find some excellent soup, manufactured by Captain
Jennings, of the 13th Light Dragoons, of which I am afraid
we left him very little.

We hear that Lord George Paget has started on his return
to the Crimea.[17]

Monday, January 1st, 1855 – Day cruelly cold, but very bright. Henry and I walked to the Genoese Fort, and watched the ships sailing harbourwards on the calm and shining sea.

The 39th regiment arrived in the *Golden Fleece*, and Mr Foster shortly after came on board the *Star of the South*; and we discussed the merry old days spent together at Weymouth, until the sound of the old waltzes rang in my ears, and the horn of Mr Farquharson's huntsman came up echoing from far over the sea.

Wednesday, 3rd – The quay covered with French soldiers, whom I watched with the greatest amusement, as they absolutely plundered our shot and shell, so rapidly did it disappear under their hands for conveyance to the front. Before our men can collect their wits for the work, *100, 200, 250* shell are passing from hand to hand into the waggons waiting to receive them.

But, as their officer remarked to me, 'Les Anglais sont de très bons soldats, mais ils ne savent pas faire la guerre. Ils se battent très bien (Allons, mes enfans, vite! vite!), mais ils n'aiment pas travailler. Ils ont peur de se souiller les mains. (Nous voilà prêts pour le départ.) Nous sommes aussi prêts pour aller à Sevastopol; mais les Anglais – c'est eux qui nous font toujours – attendre – attendre. Madame, j'ai l'honneur de vous saluer'; and away went the whole corps, every two men carrying a 10-inch shell. Ah! how have our resources been wasted! – our horses killed! – our men invalided; while over it all broods the most culpable indifference!

[*January 4th – We have got snow and very cold weather. 800 sick are to be embarked today. We have been doing nothing for a fortnight. I believe our batteries have not fired more than three shots a day each, for that length of time and they are not supposed to recommence firing before the 15th. Meantime the French keep up a heavy & continuous fire, mostly with <u>our shot</u> which they come down to Balaclava for, 1,600 at a time & carry off like the magpies do bones. ...*

By the way <u>the box</u> has not turned up yet. Poulett Somerset has given me a stall in Lord Raglan's stable at Balaclava for Bob.[18] *I have had rather a disagreeable business lately – the only women (there have been two) who have come up here are people who nobody knows anything about. One of these delectable Ladies came up with the 39th regt in the* Golden Fleece *on Monday. She belongs to the 9th regt but as the* Golden Fleece *is ordered down to Scutari immediately the Lady actually endeavoured to come on board the ship with me! And produced papers which she said were her marriage certificates!!! There has been a slight shindy as I announced my intention of leaving the ship if she came into it. So instead she is gone into my old cabin on board the* Shooting Star *who is lying close alongside us in the harbour. It is very disagreeable having these women – as, as soon as a gown is seen, all the harbour is alive – & I am perpetually being asked – 'If there isn't another lady in the harbour? Do I know her? &c &c.' – However I hope this amiable weakness will take herself off to Constantinople in a day or two.*

The 39th Regt are to be employed in taking up provisions and forming a depot at Lord Raglan's so that the men in front may not all starve. All their horses are dead, the front is carpeted with dead horses. One soldier who had been 24 hours in the trenches was taken from them & sent down to Balaclava (7 miles) to fetch his food – as he was on his road home the poor man <u>died</u> of exhaustion. But who cares? – Oh what a weight of indolence, neglected responsibilities, carelessness and serious neglect will weigh down that man's soul by & by, who has had the chief ordering of all these things, the chief command, the chief power & who never supervises, never sees, never enquires, never knows, never cares. – Now goodbye ...]

Tuesday, 9th – A day of miraculous escape. Henry and I were writing in the cabin, and I was just finishing a note which a sergeant of the 62nd was waiting to take up to the front – our ship had been engaged for some days previous in taking in powder and ammunition, and she had on board nearly 1,000 tons – when suddenly the sergeant put his head in at the door, and asked if the note were ready. I said 'Not yet; you must wait a moment.' The reply was, 'I cannot wait – for – the ship's on fire!'

A moment after, and the noise and hurry showed us it was too true. The fire was in the lower hold, and burning within six feet of the magazine!

At such a time there was no thought of fear. It had been raining; and Henry and I, unwilling to add to the crowd forward, after getting some galoshes, went on deck. We were then advised to go and stand on shore, and to take my poor maid, who was screaming, and praying to every saint in the calendar, by turns. We were soon overboard, and watching the exertions of the men at the pumps. The hose of the steam-ship *Niagara* was in a few moments at work, as well as our own, and in a short time the alarm was over, and the fire extinguished. Moored next us was the *Earl of Shaftesbury*, also a powder ship; and a little ahead of us lay the *Medora*,[19] likewise with powder on board. All felt that their last moment was come; and yet, a strange exultation possessed my heart in contemplating so magnificent a death – to die with hundreds in so stupendous an explosion, which would not only have destroyed every vessel in harbour, and the very town itself, but would have altered the whole shape of the bay, and the echoes of which would have rung through the world!

[*At the moment, excitement left no room for fear, the thought of the magnificent holocaust, the stupendous death! Ten minutes hard pumping of our own pumps & the steam pumps of the* Niagara *alongside put out the flames which were caused by the boatswain taking a lighted candle into the lower hold, among a quantity of old sacks & dry oakum. Imagine having such things stored in a powder ship, & imagine the carelessness of the whole business.*

I read Layard's & Disraeli's speeches with admiration & delight, also Lord Derby's.[20] *Our papers have miscarried lately (purposely we conclude) as we hear that the Commander in Chief has been shewn up – I am heartily glad he has been – and yet am sorry for him – for he is a naturally good hearted man and as about as much fitted for his work out here as I should be to navigate a ship. I hope if they supersede him they'll send out a man who has made up his mind not to go to bed for a fortnight, to spend the first three days & nights on horseback, inspecting evils, the next three in devising remedies & the next six in seeing them carried out. Ah how many evils are chargeable on his head, and yet I cannot think he is aware of his responsibility.*]

Wednesday, 10th – Not liking the anchorage, after yesterday's experience, I endeavoured to ride up to headquarters, to petition for rooms on shore, but the heavy rain stopped all that.

[*January 12th – The roads yesterday were so rotten, that in riding by the Commissariat road up to the Cavalry camp Bob sunk twice to his shoulders. Today it is all iron bound with the most relentless frost, the snow falls like a fog, and a wind sweeps over the valley which comes from over the boundless steppes, – and is colder & keener than a knife. Poor Capt. Dent of the 9th was frozen to death the night before last – & two officers whose names I forget were asphyxiated with Charcoal, so that between the two one has a choice of evils…*

They are taking levels for our railroad from Balaclava to the Front, which will be a great saving of horse life. The roads are sickening to ride along from the numbers of dead & dying horses. … We are on salt pork on board now, and are likely to be worse off as there is no fresh meat to be had. Oh the luxury of a fresh meat dinner! We have got a stove on board & try to sit nose & knees in it – but cannot get warm. And yet it is a jolly, jolly life. Hard enough but very jolly. You can go where you like, do what you like, say what you like and have such heaps of friends. Men who come down cold, cross and ill go away cheered and refreshed – or when I am <u>savage</u> as I often am – half a dozen noisy men, playing at leapfrog – walking on their hands up to every imaginable fun – are sure to make me laugh myself into a good humour. The 39th

are on the next ship to us. … There is usually a rubber [bridge]
every night and always either intelligent or quick-witted
conversations… Mrs Butt promised me a long political letter from
her husband which I look forward to very much.]

Saturday, 13th – Frost, snow, and bitter cold. This morning
I ran up on deck, for the day was bright and sunny, in spite of
the cold, keen air. It was a wondrous sight! – everything
buried in a foot of snow; rocks, houses, gun-limbers, plants,
and tents, all covered. The ships in harbour were the
prettiest: they were all dressed in purest white; the capstan
tops looking like huge twelfth cakes[21]; the yards and spars
glittering like rods of ice bound together by fairy ropes of
snow; the whole glistening in the sunlight like an
illumination.

I thank God heartily that I can see and appreciate beauty
of every kind. How many have eyes which see not; ears
which hear not; hearts which cannot understand – men who
perpetually remind one of the character described by Wordsworth, of whom he says –

> The primrose by the river's brim
> A yellow primrose was to him,
> And it was nothing more.[22]

Monday, 15th – Took the dear old horse's bridle over my
arm, and walked him up to camp, as he has not been out for
some days, and it is too slippery to ride.

Appreciated most gratefully the kindness of Captain
Naylor, who sent me out, two days ago, a wondrous plaid,
the thickness and warmth of which is of the greatest service
to me. Tried to find a pair of muffetees for poor Lord
Killeen, whose fingers, like mine, are chilled to the bone.

Tuesday, 16th – We changed our anchorage to-day, and
moved to a berth nearer the mouth of the harbour. Ingress
and egress to the ship is now much more difficult, as we are
much further from shore.

Thus we shall lose many of our most frequent visitors, and be made almost prisoners on board the ship, which is a nuisance that we resent in true English fashion, by grumbling all day long.

A large augmentation of the Russian army arrived yesterday near Inkerman. Our (English) force consists now of 11,000 bayonets. The leaders of the *Times* have, I see, taken up the subject warmly enough, and by so doing have cheered and refreshed many a heart that was well nigh tired of 'the trouble and the pain of living.'

Friday, 19th – Captain Sayer, who has been so long a resident on board the *Star of the South*, left us early and suddenly this morning, fearing he should not be able to reach England by the expiration of his leave. When going ashore this afternoon, I discovered that, not satisfied with the ten dead horses and three camels already rotting on the shore, they make a practice of goading all the dying commissariat animals to this corner, to add to the congregation already assembled.

Saturday, 20th – For two days we have had alongside our ship a Turkish steamer, so close as to chafe our ship's side very considerably. She took up a position in the harbour pointed out to her by the authorities; and soon after she had anchored, she began blowing off her steam, and emptying the burning cinders overboard between her own side and ours. Henry and Captain Frain were both on deck; but it was not until after many and frantic efforts that they at last made the captain of the steamer understand that we had powder on board.

Today 360 plague-stricken Turks have been put into her; but one becomes so indifferent and callous that nothing dismays one now. Henry and I tried to go out fishing this morning, but we got the net foul of the rocks, and caught nothing. The band of the 14th regiment was playing on board the *Emeu* all the time. They have just arrived in harbour.

The 39th, on board the *Golden Fleece*, are suffering terribly from sickness, and have lost so many men that a portion of them are to be disembarked and sent ashore today, so as to render her less crowded and more fit for the accommodation of the sick. The *Arabia* steamship, which succeeded the Turkish steamer in the occupation of the berth alongside us, was discovered to be very extensively on fire this morning about five o'clock. I look upon the preservation of our lives, entrusted as they are to such inefficient and unprincipled hands as those who have the management of ships in this harbour, to be a perpetual miracle.

[21st January – My dear Francie – I write on the spur of the moment and while the facts I am going to mention are fresh in my mind and you will do a great service to many out here, who are living in hourly danger of their lives, if you would insert it in any paper or papers you like, and take care that <u>it is</u> laid before the Public.

There is a great crowd of shipping now in Balaclava Harbor – steamships, powder ships, transports for sick and commissariat vessels, and the Sans Pareil *is also moored in the harbor as guard ship. Captain Christie is Principal Agent of Transports, and a man who in his urbanity and kindness has won everybody's good opinion. Captain Heath of the* Sans Pareil *who succeeded Captain Dacres who was invalided nearly two months ago is Harbor master & directs the positions and moorings of every vessel in Harbor. The confusion & negligence attending the disposition of these ships is inconceivable. I may instance the* Star of the South *which is the principal Magazine Ship in harbour & who at the moment I write is placed near the entrance of the harbour, in such a position that owing to the impossibility of mooring her safely astern, should it blow a gale she must infallibly drift. <u>Alongside, touching</u> are six vessels – three on each side. One of these is a <u>Turkish Steamer</u> which grates against her sides all day & when she first came in they blew off their Steam & were emptying their cinders between the sides of their vessel & the*

*powder ship. That was it until after considerable time & difficulty
they could be made to understand that there was Powder in the
deck against the sides of which the red hot cinders fell. Vessels are
moored in every imaginable direction. The harbour is almost
blocked up with hawsers stretching across the harbour. Captain
Heath appears to moor the ships in unsafe places* purposely *so
inconceivably bad are the arrangements. Should one of these ships
take fire, the whole English expedition would be at an end ...*

*A Master of a Transport told me this morning (Capt. Frain of
our own ship) that he considered our lives were not safe from hour
to hour. He has applied twice to Capt. Christie, & once to
Captain Heath & has most fully represented the danger to all in
Balaclava from the present unsafe position of his ship. He meets
with neither attention nor redress and the matter has been today
submitted to Lord Raglan.*[23] *You must be out here – to believe to
the full extent what I write – At this moment lying astern of these
ships: [drawing of little boats]* Charity, Hope, Turkish [steamer],
S. of South, Columba, Harkaway, Pride of Ocean, *within 15
yards are* thirteen *dead horses, 3 dead camels &* two *bullocks, all
in various stages of decomposition – to say nothing of camels
humps, horses legs, parts of sheep & offal floating everywhere.*
This *is the Harbor Master. – Why it is enough to breed the plague
– even if the Turks had not already got it & are being drafted off
by boatloads as I write, to the Turkish steamer.*

*If you can publish or make anything out of this it would be a
good thing to get it in before* Heath's Testimonials *appear.*[24]
Russell of the Times *is living in Balaclava now & is going to give
him a mauling.*[25] *He has crowded all the powder ships together in
an unsafe anchorage, as far from the* Sans Pareil *as possible, – &
appears either not to care what becomes of them or to wish them
destroyed. The fact is, no Powder ought to be on board ship at all.
If those wonderful wooden houses they talk so much about had
come out, they could have made a Magazine in a safe place on
shore – but we've been on fire once, & we've made up our minds
that we don't like it. ...*

[*The Harbor*] *is* <u>*alive*</u> *with dead bullocks and camels floating about. You see the* <u>*Heads*</u> *are weak so villains get undue authority. If the Heads made themselves a terror to evil doers it would all be 'serene' enough. So curious it is, that there is a lady now in harbour whom it is not correct to know anything about. She has been aboard the* Golden Fleece, *but seems to have set her soul on coming on board the same ship with me; and she has talked over the naval men, & it is only the Master of the Transport who refuses to allow her on board. Capt Christie and the Agent would not refuse her for a moment. This would make it very pleasant for me, wouldn't it! But I don't suppose I would get redress anymore than my neighbours so I put my trust in Capt Frain and wait the event. Henry's letter to you is also full of grievances.*[26] *I am really afraid you will think us both croakers; but if I write truth, I must write as I do.*

Tell Selina, Mrs Finnegan thanks her very gratefully for the £1.]

Wednesday, 24th – Riding to the camp today I met Lord Raglan coming down to Balaklava, and I took the opportunity of asking his lordship whether I might not live in any house, however small, on shore. My request was not acceded to.[27]

[*25 January – My dear Selina, I write more from force of habit than from having anything to say – unless indeed I expatiate on the letter I wrote to Lord Raglan respecting the unsafe mooring of the powder ship, and which has drawn down upon my head as many hornets, and as much murder, hatred, malice and all uncharitableness as the biggest nunnery of old women could produce. Captain Heath, Captain Powell, and the clique, meet to abuse me, and were heard today to express the greatest satisfaction at having discovered a separate &* <u>*unsafe*</u> *mooring for the vessel where they can put 'that Mrs Duberly & the whole damned lot of 'em'. So Mrs Duberly, hearing this, put her saddle into the boat & went off to Bob, who carried her into the jaws of Raglan and his staff as he was (actually!) on his way to Balaclava to hold a council with Sir E. Lyons, & I asked him there & then to give me a house in Balaclava, & took him so by surprise, that he said he would see if there was one – so there the matter rests. ...*

We open fire with 3 thirteen inch mortars in a couple of days and also with 5 new guns. The Russians have new batteries every day – they have one of 50 guns not yet opened – they walked into our 'Five Gun Fort' and have knocked it all to pieces. We hear nothing but rumours of peace, counterbalanced by rumours of 'war to the knife'. What it all means we know not, but we do know that the 8th Hussars have 22 horses left, and one of them was dying when I was up there today ...

The Spirits did not wail and lament here on the last night of the year, if they did so, as you say, in England it was because they knew it was no good wailing out here – for there's neither pity nor redress for anybody here. They buried a Turk the other day, and one hour after he got up out of his grave, and stultified everybody by appearing! This shows how deep they bury them, God bless me! Why when the weather gets hot, there won't be a man alive here in three days, the pestilence will be strong enough to reach to, & infect, England.

The little kitten who swam off the ship was begged of me by a sick officer going to Scutari and as the chief delight of the fiends on board this ship was to teaze her, I let her go. I hope God will put down all that I have endured on board this ship – the insults of the Captain, the utter insouciance of my husband, and the salt provisions – as a hedge against my debt book by & by. I have got too <u>hard</u> to cry now for anything but Bob – but sometimes when I think of it I am sick with tears. Whenever I say my prayers I thank God I have no children – at any rate no daughters – for this world is no place for women – at least for ladies – it is only fit for men – and women who have <u>no</u> self respect. I shall be a sort of Bashi-Basouk when I get home – defiant of all laws conventional or fashionable – and then how the women will fall upon me like vultures over a mortally wounded man.

It is a great comfort being able to write to you. I never write so to anyone else – but I must say out sometimes what is in my heart, *or it would burst like a pipe in frost. I cannot imagine what H is about – either he doesn't care twopence for me (which I sincerely <u>do not</u> believe) or else he is growing idiotic – he cannot see that so long as I have food, and a roof, that I can complain of anything else – and as <u>you</u> know – I don't want a roof – I don't want comforts, I don't want to be coddled and cosseted. I would sooner take a gun in a battery every night than be wounded in the only way that a woman feels pain. I daresay I am foolish to write this, & I hope <u>you'll burn it</u> but the act of writing does me good.*]

Saturday, 27th – 250 sick embarked today.

Sunday, 28th – 130 sick embarked today.

Monday, 29th – 295 sick embarked today.

Truly our army is in a lamentable state. I have grieved until I have no power of grieving left. I think that if I knew I was going to die myself, I should merely shrug my shoulders and lie down quietly.

We have no ambulance waggons; they are nearly all broken down, or the mules are dead, or the drivers are dead or dead drunk: as well one as the other, as far as usefulness goes. Our poor Cavalry horses, as we know full well, are all unequal to the task of carrying down the sick; and the French have provided transports for us for some time. They were complaisant enough about it at first, but now (the men I mean) begin to grumble, and to do their work cruelly. One poor fellow, wounded and frostbitten in the hands and feet, was taken roughly from his mule and huddled down in the mud, despite his agonised screams and cries. Another Frenchman drove his empty mule so carelessly past one that was still laden as to cut the poor sufferer's legs with the iron bar, and cause him cruel pain.

Why can we not tend our own sick? Why are we so helpless and so broken down?

Oh, England! England! blot out the lion and the unicorn: let the supporters of your arms henceforth be, Imbecility and Death!

A cargo of 'navvies' came out today in the *Lady Alice Lambton*. Their arrival makes a great sensation. Some of them immediately went ashore, and set out for a walk 'to see if they could see e'er a —— Roosshian.'

The 39th, who have been hitherto employed as working parties on the road, yield their work to the navvies, after having given the greatest satisfaction at it themselves.

Henry and I dined in camp with Captain Portal, of the 4th Light Dragoons, who gave us a dinner that contrasted wonderfully with our hard fare on board ship, and whose hospitable and cheerful welcome we shall always remember with pleasure.

'This is my walking costume.'

[*... it does one good to dine with him, he is so cheery and hearty. He has a very nice tent, paved with flints, and nine hens, and a hen coop, and a regular little establishment. His servant has built a mud kitchen.*

The Oscar *has not spit out my box yet as she cannot disembark it until the Quarter Master General takes out his stupid stores which are sitting like an inquest on my dear little box.*

The underlined is my appearance when dressed. This is my walking costume for going up & down ship's sides – holding on by ropes – tumbling in & out of boats – and waddling through the knee deep mud. I can wear no other – as to a bonnet I can never stand one again. I haven't worn one since 28th April. Petticoats also are an abomination. I have only a gown. Now for business ... I am going to ask you to do some commissions for me. I am afraid I shall be troublesome, but I cannot procure them nearer than England & you are the only person who would execute them all right.]

Tuesday, 30th – Captain Hillyar, who came in last night in the *Malacca*, called on me this morning with his brother, and asked us to dinner tonight.

[*I was dining out last night on board Capt. Hillyar's ship the* Malacca. *We had a very agreeable party and such a good dinner. Iced Punch after the soup and* <u>such</u> *Madeira! Capt. Heath was there – I laughed when I was introduced to him – (but then I have no manners) and we sat up and talked together half the evening. He is rather agreeable – but then I met also a 93rd man, one of the little single line that stood the shock of the Russian cavalry at Balaclava before the Heavies swooped down upon them, and didn't we 'fight the battle o'er again'. I was so glad to be able to express to one of the regiment my great admiration of their magnificent steadiness. He says the last thing he remembers before their volley – was seeing me riding between the Cossacks & our own camp.*]

Wednesday, 31st – Eight nurses, under the direction of a 'Lady Eldress' and Miss Shaw Stewart, came up today from Scutari to the Balaklava hospital.

[*The 'Lady Eldress', and another fine lady & six subalterns, landed but it seems the ladies make the nurses do all the work while the ladies do all the swagger. The more I see of women the more entirely I hate them – No, I don't hate them but I have for them a feeling of infinite and half compassionate scorn. Except for such women as Selina (some years ago) Madame Roland & Becky Sharpe.*[28]]

We lunched on board the *Malacca*, and met Captain Lushington,[29] who engaged us to luncheon on Tuesday next.

The report is that the Grand Dukes are again in Sebastopol.[30]

[*If there is another row, I shan't go up to it without my little keg of brandy that lord Geo. Paulet gave me – last time I had none – & it is very useful for fainting and wounded men. It slings over my shoulder with a strap...*

February 1st – The box was safely put into my own hands by dear little Fred. Foster, who ran all through the mud, down to the Parcels office as soon as he heard it was disembarked and brought it up on his shoulder. What a pleasure it was to open it – the little screwdriver that drew each screw, and then the layer of brown paper on top. I have a pair of the warm stockings on – and most comfortable they are! The mittens are very pretty. Will you thank Mrs Deane very kindly from me for making me such a pretty pair? They are beautifully knitted and very warm. Henry put his head into his fur bag immediately and has hardly taken it out since, a very handsome cap it is. Thanks for the books. I am already deep in Courtship & Wedlock,[31] *it being a title I consider myself competent to criticize. Everything in the box is well thought of and well chosen. Henry's socks too are beautiful. ... The shirt too is a good length &* black *for which kind thought I thank you as I can have an opportunity now of appearing in at least partial mourning, which I have much regretted not being able to do before.*

Tomorrow I dine with Major Peel of the 11th hussars – who has got a big keg of most undeniable brandy sent him by Sir Tatton Sykes.[32]

Feby 2nd. No chance of Peel's dinner for I fainted in the cabin last night & have hardly sat up since... .

Captain Hillyar saw more than 500 waggons loaded with stores come into Sebastopol two days ago & one of his subalterns saw two or three hundred more. When Hillyar went to Lord Raglan to report this, Lord Raglan said, 'It was impossible, impossible they could get in, & impossible that it had not been reported'! 'Well' – says Hillyar – 'I can't say about the impossibility, all I know is – I saw it.' 'Really' says Lord R. 'I cannot believe it – it is very extraordinary that the Navy are always reporting things to me'! I am going on Monday to dine with Peel & on Tuesday to lunch with Capt. Lushington at the Front – when I shall go down into his battery & if it is at work, shall hope to fire one Lancaster at the Rooshians.

One story I must tell you, though I desire you don't tell Francie, or anybody, it comes from Russell the Times *correspondent. Two sailors walking up to camp met a vivandière*[33] *riding down into Balaclava. 'Hullo Jack'. Says one 'is that what they call a "She dragon"?' 'Oh no', says the other 'that's what they call their "hors de combat"'.*]

Monday, 5th – Dined with Major Peel.

Oh! what terrible work it is to ride over these wretched roads! You flounder along in the most helpless manner; and coming back in the dark, I put the reins on the old horse's neck, and exhorted him in this wise: 'Remember, Bob, that any fool of a horse can tumble down here, so pray recollect what a much cleverer horse you are than any other of your species.' I conclude the admonition had the desired effect; at any rate, we got safely home.

[*This bitter weather knits up one's bones, imagine living in a tent, in the same atmosphere as the outer air, without a bedstead, without a stove, without a carpet, with nothing but misery. Take my word for it – it's a* terrible *life – and tho' I live on board ship, I find the wretched food, and the draughts & oaths and vulgarity and all that nearly as much as I can stand ...*

It makes me very angry to see his (Lord Raglan's) staff, A de C.s &c coming down looking so sleek & well fed, so polished & smiling ... when men and horses are dying & dead all round them & thousands are groaning out their miserable lives, each groan being a curse, on the accursed indifference & the accursed mismanagement which has lost England her finest army in the most popular of her wars.]

Tuesday, 6th – A beautiful morning, but blowing very heavily. We started about twelve for the naval camp, and ten minutes after down came the rain! We persevered, and arriving at last like drowned rats, were most hospitably entertained. Captain Lushington appeared sufficiently amused at my determined indifference to the rain. The weather cleared about four; and we had a delightful ride home along the high land, and then down to Kadikoi, by the brook in the valley, and over the dykes. I hardly know whose heart laughed the most, the brave old horse's or mine, as he laid his slender ears back, and, bearing on the bit, flung himself along, as though the starvation and the cruel suffering were all a myth, and he was once more in the merry hunting field at home.

[... *that day, the first I have been to the front for more than two months ... Old Lushington won my heart as we were riding back, as the old boy (Bob!) was straining on his bit, by saying twice – 'What a noble horse', 'How he breasts his way along'. ...*

Poor Lockwood's & Fitzgibbon's[34] *horses & ponies came up from Varna yesterday with one of ours. ... Poor Fitzgibbon's Newfoundland dog is come up too. This is pitiful, she never used to be away from him & now there is nobody to take her. I* can't *or would so gladly but there is one beastly greyhound on board ship now & they won't have two big dogs on board, we haven't food for two. ... I see they have me as being in 'good health' in the* Observer, *as well as 'of a grave aspect' in the* Times *which is a great story – as I always grin – I get letters from all sorts of people whom I don't know or have scarcely seen – one crazy woman told me I was 'the glory &*

envy of every Englishwoman'. A fine squawking there would be, if we had all the Englishwomen out here.

We have just heard that Lord Clare has sent out for poor Lord Fitzgibbon's dog, so she will go back to England to comfort that old man's heart instead of his son.]

Thursday, 8th – Roused in the middle of the night by a report that the Russians were coming down in force, and that the crews of the transports must all turn out armed. What an order! What could such a disorganised rabble do in the midst of regular troops? They would most probably fire away at whatever came first, and cause endless worry and confusion.

[*Admiral Boxer is up here in Balaclava harbour – he is a noisy, vulgar, swearing old ruffian and a man very easily swayed. He has given an order that in case of an attack the transport crews are all to be landed, armed & to fight. … so you see age does not always bring common sense .*[35]]

Saturday, 10th – Exchanged the *Star of the South* for the *Herefordshire*,[36] a fine old East Indiaman, and a most comfortable ship; a most desirable change in every way as far as comfort and good living go.

[*I have changed my ship and am on board the Herefordshire – a fine old East Indiaman where the dinners are wonderful, the wine miraculous, the good manners excessive, the company stupid & the Bore of the whole – extreme. … In fact I have sold myself for a good dinner and a four oared gig – for I feel as if I was in prison. But I've got a tent and shall be up under the 'Sweet Heavens' before long.*]

Monday, 12th – What a soft and pleasant day. The sun was so hot as to make it impossible to walk uphill. We sat in the valley and thoroughly enjoyed the genial day, and, then descending to the shore, watched the varying colours on the rocks and sea.

At night came on a hurricane of wind and rain.

Tuesday, 13th – Blowing terrific squalls. Captain Lushington, however, came on board, at great risk, to call on me.

Some of the sick officers, who are on board the *Herefordshire,* left today for Scutari, and others came in their places. Amongst them Colonel D—, of the 90th, who had wounded himself this morning while playing with a revolver. [*We have sick officers – 5 who are able to appear, 4 who cannot appear & one who shot himself in the hip yesterday whilst playing with a revolver in bed. He is in the next cabin to me – and his groans & Henry's snores kept me awake all night.*]

Friday, 16th – Henry, Mr Foster, Mr Carr, Captain Lushington, and I rode over to the monastery, and I was as much pleased with it the second time of seeing it as the first.[37] They report an attack on Inkerman this morning, but although the firing was very heavy I believe nothing extraordinary occurred.

Lord Lucan sailed for England.

[*I have just been reading a 'ripping' letter of Francie's in the* Spectator *and I think it is very good.*[38] *He ought to be pleased that the ministry have 'hashed it', and he ought to be in a stew lest Palmerston should come in. We are 'kicking up behind & before' as Old Lucan was recalled yesterday and goes down to Constantinople* today*. There was not a man in the camp who did not throw up his cap, having only one they could not kick the crown out. ... Now we want old Raggles to hack it too – and then if they made me Commander in Chief I'll answer for it we would dodge the Ruskies somehow. I have no spite against the Ruskies, the prisoners who are working in Balaclava work very well and are very cheery, always laughing amongst each other.*

Our rail is growing fast. The Turks are aghast at it and squat down opposite it turning up their thumbs & saying Mashallah! Mashallah! Ad lib. – A mile of it is completed, sleepers, rails, trucks, engine & all. The Ruskies sit in clouds on the tops of the hills all round & watch it and I say that as soon as ever our new toy is completed they will swoop down upon it & carry it away hastily.

Did Mr Lane come to you, if he did pray tell me what you thought of him. Did he tell you about his giving me the identical inexpressibles[39] *in which I now sit – It made me laugh a good deal at the time but they are a beautiful pair. I like Mr Lane very much though he made me pay my way on board the* Himalaya *like a princess.*

We have poor Lockwood's private servant, Michael Barbara, a Maltese and a right good servant. He refused to go to anybody but 'Capt. & Mrs Duberly his masters old friends'. Lockwood certainly had the art of attaching people even against their better judgement. ...

The sick officers keep on coming to this ship in shoals – four have left us for hospital & four more are come down. A crowd of men – sick & strangers to each other – all dining together is the most desperate affair – so silent, so stupid, so constrained.

Capt. Lushington is collecting up all the superfluous warm clothing to send back to the poor in England; some regts, Artillery & Naval Brigades have heaps more than they can use. As Lushington says – 'Why don't they send us out more men & horses instead of mistaking us for a parcel of frowsty old women & smothering us in flannel petticoats.']

Tuesday, 20th – A reconnaissance in force started this morning at four o'clock, to endeavour to surprise and take the outlying army over the hills. The snow began to fall immediately that the men were under arms, and presently came down with such hearty good-will as to render it impossible to proceed.

The English Infantry who turned out were the 14th, 17th, 42nd, 71st, 79th, 93rd. The Light Cavalry, also, made a contribution of about thirty-five or thirty-eight men and horses. But after groping about in the intense cold and utter darkness, till every man was saturated and chilled to the bone, they were all ordered to turn in again.

On board our ship, the *Herefordshire*, we have a most painful scene. One of the chaplains (Mr Wyatt), who has long been ill of fever, is now delirious and in the utmost danger. He lies in a cabin separated from us by only a Venetian shutter; his incoherent ravings and frantic efforts to escape intrude themselves above the hushed voices of all who occupy the cabin. Fortunately, we none of us have a dread of infection.

Poor Mr Taylor, too, another chaplain, whose exertions have been most unremitting and most noble, lies also on board another ship in the shadow of death. I know that Mr Taylor has spent day after day in these pestilential hospitals, never giving himself rest or purer air.

[*February 23rd –You are right as to the Authorship of the letter in the (De)Vizes paper.*[40] '*One who has shared the Fortunes of the Men.*' *It puts me so frantically out of patience to read old Simpson's leader praising Lord Raglan*[41] – *and the government (as if it was not a proof of how low they have fallen for the* Devizes Gazette *to be obliged to be their trumpeter!*)

We have been wonderstruck at reading in the Times *of our 'orgies on board the* Star of the South'. *We never had any orgies – we never had the luck! A dinner of salt junk, & preserved tripe & preserved potatoes, followed by the snores of one of the company, the rheumatic complaints of another, the growls of a third smothered in tobacco smoke and the inexorable dowsing of the glim at 10 o'clock are not lovely materials for an orgie. At least if that's an orgie – I shall take orders & look out for a living. ... Especially after my row with Captain Heath, some people were delighted to give the ship a bad name – however nobody cares a fraction about that – besides I had left the ship a fortnight before this appeared and received the intelligence with an innocence of demeanour & compassion for the poor devils in the* Star of the South, *quite edifying to the most mature minds.*

Old Admiral Boxer is up here as busy as the Devil in a gale of wind, making indescribable confusion, interfering with everybody, bullying all round and swearing like a trooper *&* that's *saying something. He bustles all the ships out of harbor before they can discharge their cargoes – and kicks up no end of a hobbery.*[42]

When I get back I mean to kill some rich old buffer and bag his money, and buy half-a-dozen horses and ride like fun. If some old buffer doesn't die and leave his tin to me, I don't know what I <u>shall</u> *do. But as Henry very wisely observes – 'All very fine Miss Pussy, but you've got to get home first.'*]

Saturday, 24th – Lunched in camp with Colonel Doherty, and afterwards went to see one of the women of our regiment, who is suffering from fever. I found her lying on a bed on the wet ground; she had lain there, in cold and rain, wind and snow, for twelve days. By her side, in the wet mud, was a piece of ration biscuit, a piece of salt pork, some cheese, and a tin pot with some rum! Nice fever diet! She, having failed to make herself popular among the women during her health, was left by them when she was sick; and not a soul had offered to assist the poor helpless, half-delirious creature, except her husband, and a former mate of his when he was a sailor.

Thursday, March 1st – It being reported that all the transports are to be ordered out of Balaklava harbour, Captain Lushington rode down from the Naval Brigade, and most kindly, and with great consideration, offered to put up a hut for us in the camp – it being too cold for me to think of living in a tent. Captain Lushington, who is a very old friend of Henry's family, could not have given them a greater proof of friendship: he has offered to furnish men to put up the hut, dig the cooking house, stables, &c.

[*2nd March – Yesterday as I was in great depression & perplexity, Captain Lushington who commands the naval Brigade, rode down & after thundering for some time said – 'You know you'll be stranded on the beach – better let me help you – I've been to the Commissariat and got a hut for you, and I'll send down a gang of men tomorrow to put it up for you, and I'll put a staple and padlock on the door, and dig you out a cooking place & places for your horses and do all I can for you.'!!!! Here was a piece of luck! But the elements conspire against me – on Tuesday it was oppressively hot, now it is snowing hard and we are half frozen, besides I am not very well just now and like the Parsons, I*

*have 'green shrinkings'. It is six weeks at least too early for me to
go up with anything like safety.*

*Oh I do wish we could get home – I think Henry would almost
throw up his commission and get home at any rate – but I will not
agree to it till I am absolutely obliged. Poor Henry is most patient
and good – but it is a life of suffering that kills you by inches – like
the water torture drop by drop. ... I think that the folly of ever
supposing that this war would be over in a trice was the greatest
folly of all. It seems to me, it never will be over, not until it has
ground the hearts & lives out of all of us. We heard that our second
servant, poor Connell's successor, died on the way to Scutari!*

Buckley has given me Sweet Pea for as long as I can keep him.]

Sunday, 4th – The *Herefordshire*, which Admiral Boxer had
long been threatening, was duly turned out of Balaklava
harbour at eight o'clock this morning. We had been cried
'wolf' to so often, that when the order really did arrive it took
us all by surprise. The hurry and confusion was most absurd;
and, after all, we were obliged to go out to sea in her, and
return in the tug. But it was a lovely day, and we enjoyed the
sail. Everyone left the *Herefordshire* with regret; and we took
leave of kind, cordial, hospitable Captain Stevenson with
many expressions of hope that we should soon meet again.
We returned to the *Star of the South*.

Monday, 5th – Started on horseback at one o'clock, to
attend the 'First Spring Meeting', the first race of the season.
Wonderful, that men who have been starved with cold and
hunger, drowned in rain and mud, wounded in action, and
torn with sickness, should on the third warm, balmy day start
into fresh life like butterflies, and be as eager and fresh for the
rare old English sport, as if they were in the ring at New-
market, or watching the colours coming round 'the corner'.

There were four races: the first I was not in time to see.
Just as the riders were going to the starting-post for the
second race, somebody called out, 'The picquets are coming
in; the Russians must be advancing!'

Away we all hurried to the camp, but found out it was a false alarm, caused by two Russian deserters whom our picquet had taken. It did not take long to return to the race-ground: and the transition struck me as equally abrupt – from the racecourse to the battlefield, from the camp to the course. Two pony races were won by sheer good riding, by Captain Thomas, R. H. A.; and after the 'Consolation Stakes', as the sun was still high, the meeting dispersed for a dog-hunt. I rode with them as far as Karani, and then turned back. I could not join in or countenance in any way a sport that appears to me so unsportsmanlike, so cruel, so contrary to all good feeling, as hunting a *dog*.[43]

I must mention that our hut progresses wonderfully; it is nearly finished, and the carpenters are making me a table. We are indebted to the kindness of Captain Franklyn, master of the *Columba*, for a large sheet of plate glass, which makes a magnificent window.

[*My hut is 9 foot 8 ins square built of planks, inside are a stove, a little table, piles of boxes, meat, bread, a canteen, pickles, wine &c and all the accessories of the toilette & the writing table.*]

Tuesday, 6th – The *Canadian* went down to Constantinople today full of sick. What a serene and balmy day!

Wednesday, 7th – In spite of a fog, which hung like a pall over the summits of the hills, I resolved to join a riding party we had made to the Monastery of St George. I thought that I could fight with a Crimean fog, and get the best of it; but I very soon found out my mistake. Oh, the fever, lassitude, aches, and pains of this evening!

[*7th March – I have just had your joint letters but I am not coming home. I could not live at home. I should suffocate. You may say this is all bosh but I assure you it is the truth. I dread going back. Fancy coming from being <u>the only</u> woman back into all the artificial muslin rags, conventionalities and slanders – the Fashions and the heart-grindings of English sociality – after being out here on a fresh horse, free as air, to come & go, & do what you please &*

not a woman near you to remind you of King David's experience, that 'their teeth are spears and arrows – & their tongues, sharp swords.'[44] Beside upon my honor I wouldn't leave Henry, as if I did I believe in my heart he would die and I couldn't not,[45] so that in short I <u>won't</u> leave him – so there's an end of that. And I have a hut put up for me now by Captain Lushington and I go up to camp next week so I shall get out of these cursed ships.

If I die out here, why it's no great matter, and if I don't, the more the luck. Nobody knows & nobody cares & I least of all. ...

I know Francie thinks I shall 'be in the way' but Francie must come out here to see what women are after a Crimean winter. – I am not now (or very seldom, sometimes I am) gentlewomanly & quiet as if butter wouldn't melt in my mouth, but come to <u>work</u>. I am delighted that I engrossed the conversation at Lord Fortescues and Lady Elingtons & oh morebili dictum! At a City feast!! whilst I most probably was fishing for sprats out of my cabin window, or larking over fences with some of the wildest hands in England. This pen will do nothing D– the pen! The weather for two days has been so hot! It has quite overpowered us, wrapped up as we are in winter clothing. ... The country is yellow with crocuses & white with snowdrops, sweet anthems of hope.

Heath is coming up directly, not as Harbor Master but as Principal Agent of Transports in room of Captain Christie who is recalled to everyone's regret...

On reading over the first part of this letter, I think I have perhaps expressed myself too strongly. Oh <u>do</u> believe that I am most truly grateful to you & Francie & all who have kindly offered me a home in England. I am deeply sensible of the kindness and affection which proffers it. You see I am in my own hut, or shall be in a day or two, and then I am as well off as if I was at home. I shall be quite free from all the vulgarity of Balaclava transports &c. and you must understand that <u>Never</u> from any men connected with the army have I met with any thing except the greatest consideration & kindness. I was very foolish to write the letter but

was distressed & cold and hungry. After
Henry had read your letter he said: 'Pussy,
if you go away from me I think I should
die' – so he got his ears boxed for supposing
I was going to leave him – but as to my
being ordered home as Francie suggests –

Mrs Finnegan (the soldier's widow) is all right and making
lots of money by washing. She has got over Finnegan wondrously
& talks of him now much as I should do about an old shoe, but is
a very good woman nevertheless.]

Wednesday, 14th – The warm sun drew me out of the
cheerless cabin, and tempted me to try and walk on deck,
though so weak as to be unable to do so without help.

[*The mail of the 23rd has just arrived but the letters are not yet*
given out but I hear from Lord Raglan's that Sidney Herbert,
Gladstone & Sir J. Graham have resigned. I hope to find such is
the case & may Palmerston soon follow them. The French General
Canrobert has received two telegraphic [messages] confirming the
death of the Tsar. Is there any chance of his two sons fighting for
the crown – I trust there may be as that would help us much to put
down Russia. One I believe is for peace, the other for war. [46]]

Thursday, 15th – A brilliant day for our Second Meeting.
The horses are improving wonderfully; and in the hurdle
race for English horses which had wintered in the Crimea,
they went at the fences as if they liked the fun. Men of every
regiment, English and French, were on the course. Amongst
the latter, a Comte Bertrand, who amused me by the
eloquence with which he descanted on his own powers of
equitation, his 'hotel' in the country, his ten English horses,
and English coachman called 'Johnson'. He spent the
evening on board the *Star of the South*, and showed us that,
whatever his equestrianism might be, he could play at écarté.

[*We are sweating & sweltering in the winter clothing beneath the*
already very powerful rays of the sun. We had such jolly races and
hurdle races last Tuesday (sic), *The* Illustrated *artist was sketching*

them. ... I have taken to riding parties and find them delightful after the dullness of that awful winter. ... Next week we go over to Kamiesh to buy hens, to lay in the camp. Major Peel, Poulett Somerset, Capt Agar (Lord Normanton's son) & Lord Burgersh. I mean to load them all and bring back as many chickens, bottles of Bordeaux, fresh woodcocks, & potted partridge as they can carry. Then on Monday we go up to camp ... And now we are looking out for peace – tho' we don't perhaps believe in it but it's a great fluke having Alexander, the peaceful party, on the throne.]

Sunday, 18th – Walked up to camp with Colonel Somerset and Mr Foster; found the house so far advanced that we settled to come into it on Tuesday.

Nothing reaches us from the front, except reports that the French attack, and fail nightly in taking, the rifle-pits of the Russians. The French can beat us in their commissariat and general management, but the Englishman retains his wondrous power of fighting that nothing can rob him of but death.

CHAPTER 6

The Camp

*News of the death of Tsar Nicholas (on 2 March)
reached the Crimea in mid-March, prompting hopes
for an end to hostilities; these were crushed when his
successor Alexander II declared that he 'would rather
perish than surrender'. Nicholas was widely believed
to have died of chagrin soon after learning that
the formidable mid-February Russian assault on
Eupatoria, led by Menshikov, had been repulsed by
the newly arrived Turkish commander-in-chief, Omar
Pasha. (Allied control of Eupatoria threatened the
Russian supply route to Sebastopol via the Sea of Azov
and Simpheropol; see map, p. 328.) Leaving Turkish
troops to garrison the port, Omar Pasha and a combined
Turkish-Egyptian force of some 20,000 men moved
south to Balaclava in preparation for the Allied spring
offensive. This began on 9 April with a massive assault
by 501 guns, of which only 101 were British. Although
there were numerous casualties within Sebastopol, it
once again proved impossible to breach the Russian
fortifications permanently. Shortage of ammunition
meant the Allies were forced to curtail the bombardment
and within fifteen days it had petered out with no
attempt to storm the city. Meanwhile Menshikov
had been replaced by Gorchakov, who immediately
complained to his Minister of War that he feared he
could be 'cut off, and perhaps broken, if the enemy had a
little good sense and decision'.*

*On 16 April Simpson wrote privately in equally
depressed tones to Panmure, the new Secretary of State
for War: 'The result of my observations since coming here*

*is that we are in a regular fix! It is impossible, my Lord,
that any military man of experience could have
recommended the descent of this Army in the Crimea,
and whoever has ordered this expedition has much to
answer for.'* Many of the British naval and military
officers agreed. This was a siege in name only. With the
Allies concentrated to the south the garrison continued to
receive regular supplies of food and men from the north.
Moreover, the Russian field army remained a threat.
And the divergent aims of the Allies were now apparent.
The French required a heroic victory to bolster their new
Emperor's prestige; they wanted a dramatic storming
and capture of Sebastopol, after extending the siege all
around the city if necessary. The British, primarily a
maritime power, wanted to ensure that the Russian navy
was no longer a threat to their naval supremacy.
Provided they could destroy the Sebastopol dockyards
they were prepared to force the city to surrender by less
drastic means. Looking beyond the immediate field of
action they planned to capture Kertch, which controlled
the Sea of Azov, and so starve the Russians of essential
supplies.

'Good sense and decision' appeared to have won the
day when a combined Anglo-French expedition sailed
for Kertch on 3 May. However, it was recalled while
en route when Canrobert, who personally disliked the
plan, received a telegram from the Emperor forbidding
French participation. Canrobert resigned a few days
later and was replaced by the more forceful Pelissier,
who immediately defied the Emperor and authorised a
second, successful expedition (see pp. 294 and 296, notes
15, 30 and 32).

The Russian force was cut off and, eventually, broken
by this action, but meanwhile they fought on. Although
they lost control of their fortifications at the Mamelon

*and the Quarries, to the French and British respectively,
in the successful Allied attacks on 7 June, they held on to
the Malakoff and the Great Redan during the bungled
and bloody Allied joint assault of 18 June (see p. 298,
note 41).*

*The death of Lord Raglan on 28 June from cholera,
exhaustion and (some said), a broken heart, after the
disaster of 18 June, shocked the armies. A profound
silence descended on the camps. Although wanting in
energy and initiative, his diplomacy and determination
to cooperate with the French had ensured the survival of
a difficult alliance (see Biographies: Raglan).*

———◆———

Tuesday, March 20th – Left the *Star of the South*, and once
more resumed our life in camp. A gleaming day, with lovely
lights and shadows. Thanks to the kindness of Captain
Buckley, of the Scots' Fusilier Guards, and Colonel Somerset,
who lent us means of conveyance for our impedimenta, I was
able to move up in one day. Major Peel and Captain Cook, of
the 11th Hussars, saved us from starving by most hospitably
inviting us to dine. The dinner was enlivened by a perfect
storm of musketry, which made us fancy something unusual
was going on in front; but perhaps my being unaccustomed to
be disturbed by musketry at night makes me fancy it worse
than it is. I am writing at one o'clock, and am, oh, so tired!

Wednesday, 21st – In our saddles by half-past-ten, riding
towards Kamiesh. We were to have been joined by Colonel
Somerset, who kindly undertook to be our guide; but by
some fatality we missed him, and reached Kamiesh at last by
a very circuitous route. Here we made purchases of
chickens, carrots, *petits pois verts*, and various other necessaries of life; all of which we packed upon our saddles, and
then cantered home. Henry decorated the pommel of his
saddle with six fowls, slung three on each side, and Bob, who

had never been turned into a market-horse before, was alike frightened at their screams, and disgusted at the way they scratched him with their claws; so he wisely took the shortest and quickest way home, hardly breaking from his hand gallop the whole way. Poor chickens!

Thursday, 22nd – The chickens are all walking about as if nothing had happened, except that one or two go a little stiff.

Colonel Shewell, Lord Killeen, Colonel Doherty, Major Peel, and Captain Cook called on me today. The French took, *and held,* four rifle-pits last night, which accounts for the tremendous firing that shook the hut. We hear that the loss was very great: they report here, 300 French, and eight English officers, names at present unknown.

Friday, 23rd – Our 93rd battery firing this morning, we ran to see what was the cause. A shell burst just at the foot of Canrobert's Hill; and with our glasses we saw two deserters running in, while three or four of our men went to meet them. Lord George Paget and Colonel Douglas called on us today. The former has promised to give me a little smooth terrier. The establishment only wants a dog to be complete; and I, who have never before been without a dog, look forward with great pleasure to having this little terrier to make a pet of.

Saturday, 24th – Can this be a journal of a campaign? I think I must change its name to a new edition of the Racing Calendar.[1]

The French races today were very amusing. The course was crowded, the sun shone, and French officers were riding at full gallop everywhere, and making their horses go through all the tricks of the *manège*. The 'steeplechase' course, 'avec huit obstacles', was delightful: the hurdles were not sufficiently high to puzzle an intelligent and active poodle; the ditches were like the trenches in a celery bed; and the wall about two feet and a half high. [*Mr Vansittart and I rode over the course – two ditches each about a foot wide, two tolerable hurdles and a stone wall about 2 foot and a half.*]

But it was a very merry meeting. We rode up with Captain Lushington, Colonel Douglas, Colonel Somerset, Mr Vansittart, and Major Peel, and afterwards lunched with le Comte Bertrand, on game pie and champagne.

Sunday, 25th – A day reminding one of the great heats in Bulgaria. The men fell out in all directions from church parade. Late in the afternoon Henry and I rode up to the band of the 27*ième de la ligne*.

Monday, 26th – Races at the Fourth Division; chiefly remarkable for the difference between the Englishman's and Frenchman's idea of a fence. Today we had a formidable wall of four foot, built as firmly as possible, while the ground on either side was hard enough to make it anything but a tempting jump.

[*We are supposed to open fire on Monday – the French say they will – but I don't believe it – in fact it's too hot to trouble about anything. I wish you could see my hut. It is full of provis[ions] & liqueur. We gave our first dinner party on Tuesday and had excellent soup, fish, hashed venison (from the Duke of Newcastle's fund)² & a roast chicken & a brace of woodcocks – (given me by Comte Bertrand). We dine on Saturday with Major Peel to meet the Brigadier (Ld. G. Paget) & 'the staff' (Raggles' staff).*]

Wednesday, 28th – More races. Count Bertrand, Mr Foster, Captain Lushington, Colonel Somerset, and Mr Vansittart came to luncheon, and we rode afterwards to the course. Goodboy, ridden by Captain Thomas, came in an easy winner. The day was most lovely, but too hot for enjoyment. We fancied that summer was come, and that we had done with the cold weather. [*You will see a picture in the* Illustrated, *& I hear I am included in the sketch.*³

Friday, 30th March – *Thank you for sending us the papers about Lord Lucan – he certainly has got into a hole, and if Master Cardigan comes out here as commanding the Division, he'll get himself into another if he don't look out.*⁴ *Lord Raglan*

*has come out better in this business of Lucan's than I expected, –
but after all he is a good old soul, and now the sun shines he has
come out & airs himself in the warmth like an old butterfly. He
comes to our races & goes to our trenches and seems disposed to
interest himself in everything now. He is very kind to me, I have
no personal ill will towards him and get everything I want out of
the Staff, who are most civil and kind. The last reports quite
overthrow our hopes of peace. They seem to think it will be war to
the knife. ... Horses are picking up wonderfully, men the same.
Very little sickness.*

*I have a garden round my house full of flowers. ... A Zouave
tailor is coming to make me a new riding body of light blue cloth,
embroidered in black. I have a lovely drab hat & feather that
Capt Agar brought me from Constantinople. ... Please send me
Tennyson's Ode.[5] It is not 'Half a League, Half a League, Half a
League onward!' as I have that, and rotten trash it is. ... the want
of money is like a perpetual grindstone, not but that we do well
enough out here. . . .*

*I talked sometime yesterday to a Polish deserter who came in
while I was calling on M. Tauski (the chief of the spies),[6] his dress
was exactly the same as a private's, only his epaulette was
embroidered instead of plain. – I also met some Russian women
who would shake hands with me with their sweaty puddy hands.
However of course I was all delighted graciousness...*

*I went to the trenches, there was a flag of truce to bury the
dead.*]

Saturday, 31st – Winter has returned. The very hills are
blue with cold. A hard, frozen-looking haze covers the
landscape, whilst a cruel north-east wind searches one
throughout, filling the bones with rheumatism, and the
lungs with cold. I did not move from my stove till evening,
when we were engaged to dine with Major Peel. We did not
return until rather late, which was fortunate, as, hearing
groans coming from the stable as we passed, Henry went to
see what was the matter, and found that my chestnut horse

had had a kicking fit on him, and had kicked away at the principal post till he brought the whole roof, rafters and all, down about his ears. The weight fell on all the horses' backs, but chiefly on the poor pony, Whisker, who was supporting all the heaviest rafters, and groaning with disgust. Luckily, none of the horses were hurt.

Tuesday, April 3rd – Went over with a large party to Kamiesh. We hear it is the general opinion that the fire on Sebastopol will recommence in a few days. The number of guns that it is supposed will be at work on that day, English, French, and Russian, are computed at between 1,600 and 1,700. Meanwhile our hut is shaken every night by the explosions of the heavy guns, and we ourselves are roused by the incessant rain of musketry. Some few are sanguine as to the result of this bombardment. I heard one person assert that in his opinion the place could not stand twenty-four hours against such a fire. The ships are to make a demonstration, as though they were going to attack the forts on the north side, but it is doubtful whether they will attack. War, horrid war! Why can we not ride in peace over this lovely country, abounding in flowers and coloured with tints, which, by their freshness and beauty, remind me perpetually of Copley Fielding's pictures.[7] It is strange that, to express my admiration for *nature*, I am obliged to compare it with *art*; but I never saw elsewhere scenery so clear, so wondrously coloured, looking so warm, yet actually so cold. It impresses me as a picture would. I admire it, but it does not affect me. Perhaps the absence of trees takes away from the 'home' feeling; and, by making the landscape appear like a picture, fails to excite any sympathetic feelings of admiration. The scenery and I may get on better when these cruel cold winds have passed, and the glorious sun throws some of his magnificent heat into it.

Saturday, 7th – Light Division races. The day was perfect; the races well attended; and, had it not been for an accident,

the sight of which seemed to stun me, and stop every pulse
in my body, we should have had an enjoyable day. In the
steeplechase course they had built a wall, over four foot, and
as firm as it could be built, turfed over at the top, and as solid
as an alderman's wit. Captain Thomas, R.H.A., and Captain
Shiffner, two of our best riders, were in the race. The crowd
collected round the wall to see the jump, and I shoved my
horse in as close as I could. After a moment's suspense, they
are off – three noble horses, all well ridden. Mr Wilkins's
horse takes the wall easily, and rushes on; Captain Shiffner's
horse strikes it with his chest, and, after one effort, rolls over
headlong, falling on his rider; Captain Thomas's horse clears
the wall, but lands on the man and horse already down.

At first, neither was supposed to have survived; but at last
Captain Thomas moved, and presently they found that poor
Captain Shiffner was not dead; but the doctors pronounced
him so much injured internally as to leave no hope of his
surviving the night. They were both carried from the ground.
About an hour after we rode to inquire for Captain Thomas,
who was lying in a hut close by, and found that he was
conscious. His first words were, 'Who won the race?' Of poor
Captain Shiffner we hear there is no hope. I think this has
rather made me lose my liking for steeplechasing.

Sunday, 8th – I heard this morning poor Captain Shiffner
died during the night. What little comfort for the mourners
at home to reflect that his life was lost in such a way! – with
neither glory nor honour to assuage the bitterness of death.
Such an accident, coming in the midst of strong excitement,
seems to make a pause, a stillness in one's own life. I am so
shocked, so nervous by what I have seen, that I am fit for
nothing; and yet, if he had been shot in the trenches, he
would have had, most probably, no other requiem than,
'Poor Shiffner was killed last night.' 'Dear me! was he? Poor
fellow!' instead of forming the subject for thought and
conversation to all.

Six o'clock – Colonel Somerset has just called, and tells me the report of Shiffner's death is false; that he lives, and they have hopes of him.

[*Bob, & I, & Henry were photographed yesterday. I on Bob & Henry at his head – a very good picture.*[8] *I am going to have one done of the hut and Whisker. It rains piteously and I am very tired today & disinclined to write but was afraid you would wonder if I did not. It is Easter Sunday – this time last year I was at church hearing the glorious Festival Anthems in Exeter Cathedral. I left next day for Plymouth and the torrents of sweet sounds followed me far over the sea. Ah! how I do crave for music!*[9] *Then I go to the Zouaves, who play their magnificent martial music till one catches the infection & frets like a horse for the roar of the guns & the thunder of a cavalry charge – but somehow the clatter & din is very wearying and I think after all my place will be eventually in a convent or a seclusion as stern.*

Poulett Somerset bought a trench cap the other day & I had to embroider it in gold lace – you cannot think how willingly one's fingers betook themselves to the fancy work. I am going to ride his horse Goodboy next week, he [has] always won both at Newm[arket] and here & never been beaten – oh he is such a stately, thoroughbred, gentlemanly horse – so clean – so gentle & with such a stride. You see I write more of the <u>horses</u> than of the <u>riders</u> – I like them best (I mean the horses).

The railway rope has broken and the carts all ran down hill into a working party of the 71st killing one and smashing several. We expected an attack on Balaclava & Kadikoi last night but it did not come off, which I was glad of having been 8 hours in the saddle. ...

We opened fire this morning. It rains in torrents – the guns hardly sound at all though they are incessant.]

Monday, 9th – Torrents of rain; incessant, soaking, unrelenting rain, in the midst of which the roar of the sullen guns came down to us with a sort of muffled sound; and no wonder, coming through so dense and sodden an atmosphere. Of course, everybody who was not absolutely on duty in the trenches staid at home, except, I believe, one or two soldiers, too red hot to be affected by the rain. We hear that our opening fire took the Russians so much by surprise, that each of our guns fired seven rounds before they returned a single shot.

The report is (as usual) that our fire is doing great damage to the enemy's works; but we hear that always, as a matter of course.

Tuesday, 10th – Rode up ourselves to the front to watch the firing. We saw it to great advantage (it being a very clear day) from a point opposite to Sir Richard England's division. I have not been to the front for some time; not, at least, far enough to observe the works before the town; they therefore strike me as being about twice as extended as when I saw them last, in, I think, December. The Mamelon and Malakoff batteries, both new, have opened a most formidable fire; while the Redan appears, to my eyes, much better furnished with guns in and about it than before. We did not remain long in the Quarry, but went to the Mortar Battery, on our right, to watch the practice of the Sea-service mortars.[10] Somehow I never felt less interested in any transaction of the war. I cannot believe that this bombardment will be productive of the slightest effect on a position which we have allowed to become so strong.

When Sir Richard England asked me, whilst we were watching from the Quarries, whether I was interested, I gave him two answers, equally truthful – 'Yes,' and 'No'. If we could see any point on which to build a hope – any gun dismounted – any embrasure knocked in, we could find something upon which to fasten and feed an interest; but it seems to me very like a bombardment in a picture – blue sky overhead, a town, and innumerable puffs of smoke all round it.

[*But it is nothing but battery versus battery and they may hammer away as they are now doing till the end of time. The*

Russians are the most magnificent fellows under fire – they will have the muzzle of a gun blown off – and half a dozen men killed – & will run that gun out, & run another in – and fire away ten seconds after with a will.]

Wednesday, 11th – Rode up again, but this time to the French left attack, and took up our position near the Maison d'Eau. I was much pleased by obtaining a better view of the town than I had hitherto been able to discover. We were almost over the harbour. We saw steamers and little boats pulling between the forts. We saw people moving in the town. The sea and the sky, all God's part of the picture, looked so blue and calm; while all man's part of the picture was noise, smoke, and confusion. I could not but reflect, though perhaps such thoughts are inappropriate here, upon the vastness of that Rest, which enwraps, as with an infinite mantle, all the fretfulness and vain effort of this world; and I must confess, that instead of attending to the statistics of my companions, I lost myself in a wondrous reverie, inspired by the contrasts of the scene before me, on that most blessed of all theories – 'There remaineth, therefore, a rest.'

[*April 14th … no box has turned up and I don't believe ever will, & I am in terrible distress for many things in it – not having a gown that is decent or any bandoline,*[11] *or gloves … and if I'm obliged to walk about in a jacket & trowsers – it will be because I've no clothes. …*

… You'll be glad to hear that I have been riding with Shiffner this afternoon and we went to enquire for poor Thomas who is all right – and I verily believe they will both ride in tomorrow's races, if tomorrow's races come off.

I send you a photograph of <u>*Bob.*</u> *In his picture he has only three legs – which is a libel on the old ruffian, for he has four – but he was taken unknown and we were none of us prepared. I was obliged to be taken on his back – to hide the mange spots about the saddle with my habit skirt. There have been an incredible number of copies struck off and sold, as I hear – at least every man I meet* *seems to have one – and Fenton would not charge us anything for it, I being the only Lady. If it appears at Ackerman's, I hope he will send another print – shewing that old villain's other foreleg. He is getting as cross and vicious as possible now that he is <u>stabled</u> and has lots to eat but you see by his picture how rough and worn he has got. The VIII on his quarters is the number of the regt. All are so marked. ... Henry's beard too will astonish you – the old brute knew he was going to have his picture taken – & stood all no how on purpose to spite me. ...*

All letters sent undercover to Lord Raglan's bag are delivered one – if not two days sooner, now adieu ...]

Sunday, 15th – Captain Lushington called, and seemed in despair.

It appears that his battery (that of the Naval Brigade) had knocked a breach in some particular spot at which they had been hammering with that wonderful energy and inconceivably careless courage which has characterised them so especially throughout the war, and had made an opening sufficiently wide for troops to storm, but 'the French were not ready.' Captain Lushington's brigade has suffered severely during this last bombardment, both in guns and men; above a hundred of the latter are killed and wounded.

We endeavoured to 'administer to the mind diseased' a little of the tonic wherewith we have often refreshed ourselves during the last twelvemonth, and which we have found serviceable. It is composed chiefly of one ingredient – namely, the contents of an old proverb: 'Blessed are they who expect nothing, for they will not be disappointed.' Leaving Captain Lushington to try the efficacy of my cure, Henry and I rode up to the French band playing on the hill.

Tuesday, 17th – Put up a large Turkish tent outside the hut, to serve as a drawing-room, and later as a dining-room; for we find it inconvenient to have only a room of twelve foot square in which to eat, sleep, and receive company.[12]

This tent, large, hexagonal, double-lined with dark blue, and open at both ends, is a great addition to one's comfort. We have it matted, carpeted, and furnished with a table and an armchair – luxuries which were to us, when in Bulgaria, but a dream of our youth. There is a great stir in Balaklava, owing to the arrival and disembarkation of the 10th Hussars, who have come from India, and are reported to be 680 strong, and mounted on the finest Arabs in the world (at least, so says Colonel Parlby, who commands them). Every one is anxious to see this new regiment; and it is most amusing to hear the various speculations regarding these same horses – some declaring that there is nothing like an Arab horse; he is up to any weight, can endure any fatigue, live without food, and never sleeps; whereas others remember the mud of last winter, and how the vast thews and sinews of the most powerful English horses were only strong enough to pull them *into* it – and then leave them there to die.

Wednesday, 18th – We rode up – Henry, Colonel Somerset, Mr Calvert, and I – to look at such of these 'wondrous winged steeds with manes of gold' as had landed. We found them perfect in shape, so purely bred that each horse might have been a crowned king; clothed in coats of sheeny satin, that seemed defiant even of the rays of the blessed sun himself when he looked at them; their small heads never resting, and their eyes like outlets for the burning fire within. But I will write down my first impression, and then see if time proves it correct. These horses are not in one respect suited for their work here, and they will fail at the commencement of winter – too small, too light, too excitable. This is merely what strikes me, and I merely write it as a speculation, knowing of this country what I do.

Thursday, 19th – A strong reconnaissance went out this morning, commanded by Omar Pasha, to Kamara, to inspect the Russian force, and with the intention of ultimately pushing forward, and allowing the Turks to occupy their old position in the plain from which they ran with such a cheerful alacrity at 'Balaklava'. Omar Pasha is very anxious to impress us favourably with the Turkish force that he has brought with him from Eupatoria, and which is composed of the same men who fought so well at Silistria. We hear, also, that the soldiers themselves are most anxious to give proof of their courage and steadiness under fire. They assert that the Turks who formed part of our force in the winter were only militia, and all those poor creatures had died of the plague.

I had arranged to accompany the reconnaissance, but Henry was unfortunately so far from well as to be unable to go, and of course I remained also.

I seldom like writing from report; and as I was not present, am unwilling to say anything about this reconnaissance, save that the Russian force appears to be by no means numerous.

[*It resulted in nothing but a beautiful ride, a few rockets fired and two gazing, gaping English Amateurs, who went looking about by themselves being made prisoner. Henry being ill I could not go out. He is now much better. Tomorrow I lunch with Omar Pasha – who is anxious to 'shew his Turkish troops to the English Lady who rode at Balaclava.' He has them all turned out for the occasion I believe, but of this in my next. The box has never turned up ... I have no gowns, no bandoline, no nothing – however it's lucky the warm weather is coming as I shall gradually appear in less & less raiment.*]

Saturday, 21st – Rode with Henry and Colonel Poulett Somerset to the headquarters of the Turkish force, as Omar Pasha had done us the honour to ask us to luncheon. We found him sitting in a small but very light and convenient tent, which opened to Sebastopol; and being on high ground, we had a very good bird's-eye view of the position of the English and French armies. The band, a remarkably good one, was soon after sent for, and played for some time with a great deal of precision. They played, amongst other *morceaux*, *Il Rigoletto*, and some marches composed by Madame, the wife of Omar Pasha, for His Highness's band.

Madame is, I believe, either German or Wallachian, and evidently possesses a knowledge both of the science and *esprit de la musique*. The pieces played by the band, and written by her, evinced both taste and power.

Luncheon, consisting of champagne and sweetmeats, was going on at the same time as the music; and when both were finished, His Highness ordered his horse, and we accompanied him to General Bosquet's, and afterwards to the brow of a hill opposite the Russian camp, where one of the mountain guns used in the Turkish army was placed and fired, to show General Bosquet its enormous range.

These guns are small – made precisely like the barrel of a Minié rifle, about five feet in length, and firing a conical leaden ball of four and a half pounds' weight. It is mounted on a very small carriage, and drawn by a single mule. Omar Pasha said it would carry 4000 yards. This fact, however, I am unable to vouch for from personal observation, as I never saw the ball after it was put in at the muzzle of the gun – I mean to say, my eyes were too much unaccustomed to follow the shot, nor did we see it strike. But, like true believers, we admitted that it struck wherever we were told it had done so; and, as far as I was concerned, I was quite satisfied. We then re-mounted, and returned to General Bosquet's tent. Our order of march was somewhat as follows:

Omar Pasha, on a chestnut Arab, which he made go through every evolution that a horse's brain was capable of remembering, or his legs of executing; a group of attendant pashas and effendis, amongst whom we were mixed up; Lieutenant-Colonel Simmonds, English engineer, attached to the Turkish staff; General Bosquet, and one or two French officers belonging to his staff; and an escort of Turkish lancers on small horses, very dirty, very slovenly, and diffusing a fragrance of onions which made one's eyes fill with tears.

We took leave of our host at General Bosquet's camp, and rode slowly home in the dusk.

Omar Pasha impressed us as being shrewd, decided, energetic, as well as an amusing companion, and a man capable of appreciating more of the refinements of life than I should have thought he would have found amongst the Turks; though he tells me he hopes, after the war is over, to be made Minister of War at Constantinople, and, – very probably, be bowstrung![13]

[*April 24th – The luncheon with Omar P. was highly successful (you must forgive my bad writing but it is after dinner after innumerable goes of brandy & water so I can't see very well being sleepy & half blinded with cigar smoke) … [we] arrived about 2 o'clock found him sitting up in a beautiful tent full of arm chairs & surrounded by Pashas. I was riding good Bob, the best bred & handsomest horse out here – so we alighted in front of the tent – & the Pashas salaamed & I salaamed and O.P. made me a deep bow & handed me in & put me in the biggest & softest chair. – A silence – 'Madame – votre man doit être bien heureuse d'avoir un si joli femme'! – Well this was a stunner to begin upon so I took up my parts of French speech and began to talk 'Altesse – vous me faite trop d'honneur &c &c' then came the band – playing as if for their lives & playing very well. Then came – 'Madame – puis-je vous offrier un frot de champagne?' I began to think things looked a little less fishy then – & more like a good business, so the champagne & the sweatmeats came. Zephir Pasha sitting X legged and Col. Simmonds the ADC looking after the distribution of the feast. After the wine our tongues got freer and OP & I had a long and most delightful talk, he spoke with dignity, sense, philosophy and the nonchalance of a man who has lived in danger & become accustomed to it. Then we rode – he & I first, then Zehir [sic] Pasha, Henry & Poulett, then the inferior Pashas – and a long escort of Turkish lancers. Full tilt we went over rocks*

and holes – up hill, down hill – a regular case of sitting back &
hardening your heart. Finally we arrived all right at General
Bosquet's who we picked up with his staff and galloped on to the
rocks overlooking the Tchernaya & the Russian camp – here we
planted a small Turkish rifle mountain gun we had brought with
us & amused ourselves by potting at the Russians at 4,000 yards,
while I sat on a high stone & Omar sat at my feet – and we talked
of all his wondrous warfare – of 'great old houses & of deeds done
so long ago' mingled with so much pleasant wit, so much kindness
of manner, so much chivalrous politeness that I quite mourned
that I could not always be with a man so brave, so dignified, so
calm I forgave him afterwards the feelings, which made him urge
his horse into every imaginable shew of action & of temper – till it
got ill temper – & the fine Arab horse became really farouche.
Now, I said, I will shew the difference between a hot-headed Arab
enragé and that most perfect of all gentlemen a thoroughbred
English horse. Goodboy quiet as a forest pool in midsummer mid-
noon. One touch with spur & curb and springing on his hind legs
he flung himself in air – and then with one powerful disdainful
kick – settled down into his calm walk. No fretting, no fighting, no
squabble, he received his insult – resented & forgave it. Omar P is
now gone to Eupatoria – went last night but I trust will soon come
back as he ought to dine with us next week if the Russians do not
chew him up. Meanwhile Lord Raglan had a conference
yesterday – & was good tempered today which he has not been
some time. ...

The box has not turned up, nor will I fancy ... in fact so hard
up am I that I have sent to the Zouave tailor to desire to come to
me next week and make me a body, which will soon be followed by
breeches. I have had a delightful ride & came back with my hat
covered with flowers.]

May 1st – Captain Christie died this day at Kamiesh,
where he was awaiting court martial,[14] to consider his
conduct with reference to the ships left outside Balaklava
Harbour on the 14th November. The decision of trying him

by court-martial, the worry and grief consequent upon so cruel an interpretation having been put upon the conduct of a man distinguished for gentleness, kindly feeling, and a desire to act rightly towards all parties, doubtless caused his illness and his death.

Captain Christie was beloved and regretted by all over whom he had control. The masters of transports, I think eighty-three in number, had subscribed for the purpose of presenting him with a testimonial of their affectionate esteem. I hear many of them have determined on going over to Kamiesh, to show a last mark of their respect for him by attending his funeral.

May 3rd – Expedition started to Kertch – 7,000 French, and about 2,600 English, with a few Cavalry; the object being to take and destroy Kertch, and to intercept the conveyance of provisions and stores into Sebastopol. We had ridden over to Kamiesh in the morning, and when we returned, we saw from over the hills the ships silently stretching out from Kamiesh and Kasatch to sea. We all hope much from this expedition.[15]

May 6th – The expedition to Kertch is returned, and, at the moment that I write, it is off to Balaklava harbour. It was recalled by an express messenger. I suppose we shall hear more about this tomorrow, – at present, the simple fact is as much as we can digest. [... *when George Paget came up to attend Church Parade the first words he rung out right across the brigade were 'I say Douglas – the* expedition's come back! *It's outside Balaclava now.'*]

The sun is come to visit us once more in all his magnificence; and we should be able to give ourselves up to perfect enjoyment of the, to me, delicious warmth, were it not for the violent gusts of wind, which deprive us of all comfort and all satisfaction in our otherwise delightful Turkish tent, which is always, except when the wind blows hard, a charming place of refuge from the sun.

Yesterday, Henry and I rode into the plain as far as the Woronzov Road, the extreme limit that prudence would allow. We let our horses graze for an hour on the thick, rich grass, which covers these most marvellously fertile valleys and plains, and then covered the dear old horse's head with branches of white May and dog roses, with a wreath of mignonette and larkspur. The mignonette grows in these plains in far finer specimens than are usually found in English gardens.

[*I did not write by last mail as I really had nothing to say and my mind was busy taking a rest. I required repose – and for the last week I have been attempting no exertion whatever, of the mind, at any rate. I have been reading* Heartsease *or the Brother's Wife* [16] *... the book has it merits. Mrs Portal sent it out to her son Bob. ... Lord & Lady Stratford* [17] *have been up here with their daughter & Lord Raglan has been Bo-ing them all about the parish – they quite brought him out! They are gone now back to Constantinople.*

Omar Pasha is also gone, I am sorry to say, but I trust he will return as suddenly some day. ... The moment he arrived – instead of holding a Council of War – and writing 50 letters and then sitting down in indifference – he got on horseback & scoured the country for miles – that's the man! I only wish we could serve as a contingent to the Turkish force, and he made P.P. [18] *I've heard many a man wish it. ... I got a most elaborate bow from Canrobert which didn't please me a bit – for he is a terrible humbug – & lies, as only a Frenchman can. ...*

How they are firing now! What a tremendous gun! & in the valley too – close to us – Whizz – Whizz – I suppose there's something up – Henry is gone to see. Lady Geo. Paget [19] *is here – she came up with Lady Stratford & is staying on board a ship in harbour for the present. But George is such a bore – and she is not in love with him – so I think she won't stay long.*

General Estcourt asked for you a day or two ago. ... I like General Estcourt, he is such a nice ladylike old woman. [20] *General*

Roger Fenton: *Cooking House of the 8th Hussars*. The side of Fenton's photographic wagon can be just seen on the left.

Roger Fenton: *Officers and Men of the 8th Hussars.*
(From left to right) Regtl.-Serjt.-Major Harding;
Quartermaster Lane; Paymaster Duberly; Serjt.-Major Harrison;
Capt. Lord Killeen (mounted); Serjt-Major Clarke; Doctor Anderson;
Lieut. Phillips; Serjt.-Major Williams; Cornet Mussenden;
Lieut. Heneage; Capt. Tomkinson; Serjt. O'Meara.

Roger Fenton: *Camp of the 4th Dragoons, convivial party, French and English*

Roger Fenton: *Cavalry camp, looking towards Kadikoi.*

Airey and I are great friends, he was an old friend of Henry's and he has a beautiful thoroughbred horse which he lends me – he is such a nice man – it is a pity they are all so effete as far as <u>work</u> goes, for personally there is not a man on the whole staff who is not very nice. Sir Richard England has put me in the way of getting my medal[21] – and I believe I am to have one with the Balaclava clasp – I am <u>fully</u> entitled to it – and shall be buried in it – if I do not die before it comes.]

Monday, 7th – Stretched out again into the plain; this time, underneath the hill occupied by our Rifles. We crept up the green ravine between the Rifle hill and the hill in occupation of the enemy. But the Rifles were amusing themselves with target practice far over our heads; and the whistle of the balls, as they flew over us, made us remember that we were very much in the position of a brace of partridges on the 1st of September; so we turned, and reached home just in time to change horses, and canter over to the Guards' encampment, where we dined with Lord Adolphus Vane.[22]

[… a feast for a sybarite – Flowers without end – Mayonnaise with fresh lettuce, at about 10/6 a piece, Dindon aux truffles, Croquet de Saumon, Ducks & olives.

The arrival of the emperor [23] here is looked forward to with great pleasure and anxiety. Canrobert has proved himself so utterly effete (I know no better word) that even Lord Raglan is disgusted and between the two the mess they make of every thing is as you say enough to make one grieve at being born an Englishwoman. And if we women feel it so heavily & bitterly what must not many a brave man out here do who has distinguished himself. … Every night the bottles and glasses in our hut shake as if they were coming down – with the reverberations of the heavy guns – but nothing ever comes of it.

Son Altesse Omar P. is not yet returned from Eupatoria. I fancy he is not in much of a hurry to be entourné with these <u>pair auld bodies</u>. That's a man if you like. I'd give something to have that man's mouth & chin, grisly beard, moustaches and all! But

he has five wives already, though to us Xtians he only
acknowledges to one. Clever old dog – he was wide awake when he
made himself half Christian & half Turk.]

> *Tuesday*
> *Wednesday*   Three days of incessant rain.
> *Thursday*

Oh, how miserable everybody was! the ground ankle-deep
in swamp, – a slippery, sticky sort of wet clay, which sends
you sliding as though you walked on ice; while, at every step,
it closes over your horse's fetlock-joint. Added to this,
towards nightfall came occasional gleams of rheumatism
glancing through the bones.

I feel myself like St Simeon of the Pillar as Tennyson
describes him –

> While I spake then
> A pang of shrewdest pain ran shrivelling thro' me.[24]

And all this cold, damp, rain, wind, and sleet have come to
make memorable this tenth day of May 1855.

Saturday, 12th – Rode up the hill to see how the 10th and
12th had prospered during the wet weather. Poor little
brilliant Arab horses, they looked like rats that had been
drawn through wet mud and hung up in the sun to dry. They
were living cakes of mud; their long tails reminded us of
ropes of sea sand. Poor little gay creatures, all draggled and
besmirched! Vicious to a degree beyond words are these
fairy horses; and if they once get loose, they fly at, fasten on
to, and tear each other with a tenacity and venom that I
should have supposed only to have existed amongst women.

[*The Hut, May 18th – You know we've got the Cholera at*
Constantinople and a case or two in camp.

Florence Nightingale is here. I rode into that stink hole
Balaclava yesterday to call on her, but found she was ill with fever,
or rather recovering from it and in one of the huts for the
convalescents on the hill by the Genoese fort so I did not see her. It

*was the first time I had been into Balaclava for a month &
despite the Sanitary Committee <u>how</u> it did stink! The crowd there
is unbelievable – but old Boxer is doing good. ...*

*By the way, I had an offer the other day of £1,000 for my
Journal, this was from a Mr Walter, one of the editors of* The
Times. *I don't know if Routledge would give me more. I mean, by
the first private hand I can trust – going home – to send you the <u>first</u>
year. You must not however let out that you have it – or let anybody
see it but you and Francie – you may read it (it's awful bosh) and
see what you think it is worth.*[25] *You must not estimate its price by
<u>its worth </u>but by its fashion; for rot sells better than the proverbs of
Solomon often enough. ....*

*The Zouave tailor has not finished my jacket. Imbecile! He has
been ever so long at work on it, but it is to be embroidered in all
directions and will be what Yates would call 'a stunner'. ...*

*This campaigning life don't suit Henry, he gets absolutely
peevish, but it must be a bore to be a man fond of comforts. Lady
G. Paget seems imprisoned in her ship. I have never seen her on
horseback once, I believe she is nervous on horseback. She has
such pretty eyes. How she has remained so long in the stink of
Balaclava I can't think. There. I can't write any more. Henry is
getting troublesome and I must attend to him. So goodbye dear
Selina, ever yr affect sis. F.I.D.*]

Saturday, 19th – The first arrival of the Sardinian troops in
Balaklava harbour.[26]

Sunday, 20th – Omar Pasha, who has returned from
Eupatoria, whither he took flight the day after the one I have
previously described, in consequence of a reported augmentation of the Russian force before that town, called on me
this morning. He gave us a very pressing invitation to
accompany him to Eupatoria, where he intends to go on
Tuesday, and offered us accommodation on board the
Valorous.

Monday, 21st – A match for 50l., between Colonel Poulett
Somerset's chestnut, Goodboy, and General Barnard's

brown horse, Coxcomb – Goodboy ridden by Captain Townley, who had the reputation of being the best race-rider in India (he came over with the 10th Hussars, to which regiment he belongs), and who certainly rides like a professional jockey, and looks like a gentleman rider; and Coxcomb ridden by Mr Morgan, of the Rifle Brigade, son of Sir Charles Morgan, of Tredegar. Coxcomb was an easy winner – at least, so I was told; for the match I was not destined to see, as General Airey had very kindly lent me a very pretty horse of his own to ride; and which horse, never having been accustomed to a habit, fancied that by dint of galloping he could run away from it. This he found was a fallacy; but I could not bring him to the course until after the race had been run.

[*I had a near [chance] of going to glory or elsewhere the other day – riding a horse, who got away with me & ran off to the edge of a 300 feet precipice, however luckily I made him rear & so swung him round. I was much less frightened than anybody else. Henry got quite sick.*]

Tuesday, 22nd – Leave refused to Henry to go to Eupatoria. 500 Cavalry horses went over from our camp to Kamiesh, to bring back convalescents, who had arrived there from Scutari.

The Sardinians were disembarked in great numbers today; and, as we rode towards Kadikoi in the evening, we met two or three regiments marching up. Omar Pasha took a considerable Turkish force away with him today to Eupatoria; and those who were left behind, near Kadikoi, were changing their ground, and marching, with their frightful and discordant music, at the same time that the Sardinian troops were coming up the road. The dust, noise, confusion, and heat may be imagined, but I cannot describe it. The appearance of the Sardinian troops gives general satisfaction. The Rifle corps, which we met today, is most picturesque. They are dressed in a dark tunic and trowsers, with

a broad-brimmed glazed hat, with a bugle stamped in gold
on the front, and long massive plumes of black and green
cock's hackle flowing over the left side of the hat, reaching to
the shoulder. Their baggage transport is also well arranged.
They are large covered carts, on two wheels, made entirely of
wood, and painted light-blue, drawn by one, or sometimes
two or three, magnificent mules.

Wednesday, 23rd – A day entirely occupied with receiving
morning visitors. Whilst we were at dinner, we heard some of
the heaviest firing that we have listened to for months.
Captain Lushington, who was with us, was at first anxious to
go to his own battery, being alarmed lest the firing should be
on the English, but after listening some time, we found that
it came entirely from the French on the left.

Thursday, 24th – The morning, till five o'clock, spent in the
same busy idleness; but at five o'clock we ordered the horses,
and rode down to our old grazing ground, near the
Woronzov Road. As we were sauntering home, flower-laden,
we met a second regiment of Sardinian Rifles, and rode by
the side of the regiment until we reached our camp. As soon
as they came in sight of the Cavalry camp the men began to
cheer them; and as they passed, regiment after regiment
took it up, and such a storm of shouts filled the air as must
have frightened the pale young crescent moon looking shyly
down from the serene, calm, evening sky – such cheers as
only Englishmen know how to give.

I have been much amused today by hearing of the theatre
which the Zouaves have established at the front, and where
they perform, greatly to their own satisfaction, '*Les Anglais
pour rire.*'

[*That is hardly fair tho'* – *for they caricature the English
soldier* – *in a red coat a perfect web of rags* – *and a* tremendous
stock[27] – *who struts in with his head stuck up in the air with
'Now I'll show you b........ Frenchmen the way into Sebastopol'
whereupon he walks straight on till a shot takes his head off just*

above the stock which remains firm, & he falls en règle *on the flat
of his back, whereupon after he is dead a very fat Jean Bull in
topboots & a huge waistcoat comes running in with a new coat,
and sundry comforts from the Crimean Fund.*[28]]

This morning brought us news. Twelve hundred French
were killed and wounded, besides many officers. One company went in 100 men, and came back 3. They had attempted to storm and take the Flagstaff Battery, and had failed.
General Pelissier, who has succeeded to General Canrobert
in the command of the French army, will doubtless fight it
out again, as his chief characteristic seems to be most
resolute determination, and disregard of all that interferes
between him and his object.[29] I think that General
Canrobert's resignation of his post as commander-in-chief
has given rise to many an expression of respect and kindly
feeling, which would most necessarily have been withheld
from him so long as he continued to hold a position for
which it was obvious to himself and others that he was
incompetent.[30] [*I admire Canrobert for resigning and made him
a lower bow today than I ever did to him as Commander in
Chief.*]

This evening we made up a party, and rode to Karani, to
hear the band of the Sardinian Guards. There was a crowd of
Englishmen and Frenchmen already assembled. Perhaps it
was because one fancies that every Italian must necessarily
be a musician; but I certainly waited for the commencement
of the music with an impatient interest with which no
military band ever inspired me before. But today at least I
was disappointed. Beautifully they played, each instrument
weaving its own peculiar harmony, with a truth and
expression, such as could only be produced by genuine
artists; but for today they contented themselves by looking
round at their audience, and playing to them Valse and
Polka, Galop and Quadrille. I fancied, as I watched the
handsome swarthy faces of the band, that there was a proud

look of concealed scorn as they regarded the waggling heads and beating hands of the admiring crowd. To me it seemed a derision, a mockery of music. We left early.

While we were listening to the Sardinian music, the French were repairing their last night's work: they succeeded tonight in driving back the Russians, and there is nothing now between them and the town. [*The new broom Pelissier seems inclined to go ahead, ... (the French) had une parade Victoire – they took the Flagstaff battery & now there is nothing between them and Sebastopol.*]

Today has been kept as the Queen's birthday, with a Cavalry review, at which Lord Raglan, General Pelissier, and Omar Pasha were present, with a very brilliant staff. [*10th Hussars band playing till the very drums melted & sweated – Turks playing 'God Save the Queen' and myself – dying of thirst & heat – and a fidgety horse of 16 hands riding between My Lord & Omar P. the admired (of course) & bitterly envied, of all beholders.*]

Omar Pasha's dress was to my idea perfection. His dark-blue frock-coat, magnificently embroidered in gold, was fastened at the waist by a sword belt, the buckle of which, as well as the hilt of his sword, blazed with diamonds; a crimson ribbon across the shoulder bore the French order of Napoleon, while his crimson fez, instead of the usual tassel, was embroidered in front with diamonds and gold. The review was satisfactory enough. It was very hot, and rather dusty. The Staff in scarlet must have paid dearly in discomfort for the brilliancy they gave to the *tout ensemble*. The 10th Hussars and 12th Lancers made a numerous, but I cannot think an imposing show. The remains of our Heavy Cavalry looked to my eyes far more soldierlike, more English, more solid.

Declining an invitation from Omar Pasha to take luncheon in his tent, we rode straight to headquarters, where Henry saw, tried, and purchased a horse; and then we went to the plain below Kamara, where the Guards had games and footraces, and Lord Adolphus Vane an illumination in the evening, in honour of the day. We remained until about eleven o'clock; and then, to quote the words of the famous Mr Pepys, 'with great content, but much weariness, home to bed.'

Friday, 25th – In our saddles by five, ready to accompany the Sardinian and Turkish armies, together with a strong force of French and some English Cavalry, who were to take Tchergoum, a village on the banks of the Tchernaya, and to establish themselves in the plain lately occupied by the Russians.

The troops began to march at midnight; and consequently, when we reached the foot of Canrobert's Hill, we found the French Cavalry returning from Tchergoum, from which, after some sharp firing, the Russians had fled. The French destroyed some of the houses, and plundered others, and then left the village. Seeing that it was useless to go to Tchergoum until later in the day, we followed some French Artillery until we came to a very handsome stone bridge over the Tchernaya. Here the Russians opened fire on us from a battery on the Inkerman heights; but though they fired several shots, it was at long range, and they did no damage. One or two passed over our heads as we were watering our horses in the clear stream of the Tchernaya; and several more annoyed the French, who were destroying an earthwork from which the Russians had removed their guns. We ascended the hill, and had a good view of the valley and ruins of Inkerman; and soon after, finding the heat on the hillside becoming intolerable, we turned our horses, and proceeded, a party of five, along the winding banks of the Tchernaya.

To us, who had not seen a river, and scarcely a tree, since our arrival in the Crimea, the shady windings of the Tchernaya appeared to possess greater beauty than, perhaps, actually belonged to them; though none but ourselves can know the wondrous luxury of rising through the tall and flowering grass, under the shade of oak and ash, creeping clematis, and climbing vine. We crossed the ford, and let our horses graze, while we sat underneath a spreading tree. Some more adventurous members of the party found two fish-traps, full of fish, which we carefully put into a haversack, and then rode over the hill and along a lane, until we came to the height overlooking Tchergoum. Here we found various parties of English officers, all exploring, like ourselves.[31] We descended into the valley, but were presently warned that the Cossacks were behind us, and we must lose no time in getting away, which we did in as dignified a manner as we could. A few shots followed us, but not sufficiently near to excite any apprehension; and, clambering up a perpendicular hill, through thick masses of underwood, we got once more into our own country, and rode home in peace.

[*We came to a great wide brook & very deep – I was on the pony – however there was no time to lose as the Cossacks were advancing on us – Henry dragged the pony through – I scuttled across over a fallen tree, and then mounted again & took snookers at them. Afterwards we had a lovely ride home by the renowned Baider valley.*]

Saturday, 26th – This evening must always keep its place in my memory. We rode to hear the Sardinian band. Owing to a large number of their army having arrived, their audience was mostly composed of their own people. Then they played!

Amongst other pieces selected for our enjoyment, was one with solos on the cornet-à-piston which the maestro played himself. I listened with closed eyes, to shut out all this outer world of camps and trumpet-calls, roundshot, dust, and noise, that I might be alone with the clear voice now speaking to my heart. The music was so sad! it rose and fell like the sighs and aspirations of a soul shut from Paradise, yet striving to enter in. Now there was an agony of wild, impassioned anguish; now the notes fell soft, low, clear, and calm, as though angels had come to minister to the distracted soul. Each tone spoke, – not to my ears, or to my heart, but to the innermost depths of my soul – those depths that lie far down, as much out of human knowledge as the depths of the deep, deep sea!

Sunday, 27th – Rode this evening all over the valley of the Balaklava charge – 'the valley of death', as Tennyson calls it; but it reminded me more of another expression of his, 'Oh, death in life!' The ground lay gaudy with flowers, and warm and golden in the rays of the setting sun. It was literally covered with flowers; there was hardly any grass, – in places, none, – nothing but dwarf-roses, mignonette, larkspur, and forget-me-nots.

Here and there we passed the carcass of a horse; we saw five with 8.H.[Eighth Hussars] on the hoof. Six-pound shot lay strewn about thickly enough, and pieces of shell. I did not see it, but was told that a skull had been found quite blanched and clean, with most wonderfully beautiful and regular teeth. We saw today no traces of unburied human bodies – the horses had all been lightly covered over, but many of them were half-exposed.

We gathered handsful of flowers, and thought, – oh, how sadly! – of the flowers of English chivalry that had there been reaped and mown away!

News came this morning of the expedition to Kertch.[32] It was put into general orders, and read to the troops. Kertch was taken, without difficulty, the moment the allies appeared before it, as the Russians blew up their forts and retired. We also became possessed of sixty guns of large calibre, and many ships of transport, laden with grain and stores. The Russian steam gunboats attempted some resistance, but the *Snake* went at them in the most gallant manner, and very soon drove them back. General orders went on to say, that the Russians had sunk several steam-ships, and that our fleet is in possession of the Sea of Azov. The plunder, we hear, has been enormous. No casualty up to this time had occurred in the allied force.

We hear most distressing reports of the sickness among the Russians. Fifteen thousand are supposed to have been sent from Sebastopol to Kertch, Yenicali, &c. These, of course, are now (such as were not blown up with the forts at Kertch) distributed amongst the various villages, to be abandoned again as we advance.

Sunday, June 3rd – Chiefly remarkable for a proposed ride to the Baidar Valley, which did not come off, and for a delightful *diner à la belle étoile*, which did. We sat on the summit of a rock, so perpendicular that one dreaded looking down its giddy height upon the quiet sea below. At length the glimmering twilight died away, and, one by one, the stars came out. As far as nature was concerned in it, never was a fitter evening to conclude a Sabbath day.

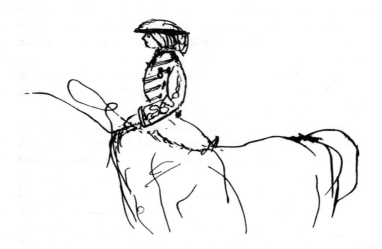

'This is the Chasseur d'Afrique habit.'

[*Light Cavalry Camp, June 4th – I send you some flowers from the plain where the flower of our chivalry were mown & reaped away. There has been the devil's delight here – in consequence of an application made by our Col. for the Balaclava clasp for me.* [33] *There is no doubt as to my being entitled to it, as I was driven from my tent by Cossacks and was under fire repeatedly during the day. There appears to be some difficulty about my getting it <u>officially</u> – I being a woman – but Colonel Poulett Somerset has written to Colonel Phipps – and to the Duchess of Gloucester – to beg them to lay it before the Queen. I was for so long the only woman out here (except for my maid) that there is no doubt about the medal – but now that so many woman are out here – it is thought that if I get the medal they will all be clamouring for one too … However there seems such determination about it on the part of Genl. Airey, Sir R. England, Poulett Somerset, Sir George Foley &c, all men of influence and good connection in England that I have no fear of getting it.*

This is the Chasseur d'Afrique habit (& medal & clasp as they <u>will</u> be). Sky blue galonne with black braid, precisely like the French uniform. It is (as you may imagine), <u>stunning!</u> With a white (drab) jean skirt. Michael our Maltese disappeared this morning … so you may fancy the state of helpless confusion we are in. If it was not for Lord Adolphus Vane we should be quite done for – but he has kindly lent us his French cook till we can get one from Kamiesh. The Cholera is <u>dreadful</u>. … Ah! what a life this is! I wonder first that I am alive – 2nd that I have kept my own good name & my mother's memory free from stain.]

Wednesday, 6th – I was extremely unwell; overpowered with the terrible heat, and weak and languid to a degree that compelled me, as I thought, to remain perfectly quiet

Sebastopol defences

and still. We intended to give our saddles a rest-day, when suddenly, at three o'clock, the guns pealed out from the front, and announced, with their tremendous voices, that the third bombardment had begun.

We knew that *this* time the guns would not play an overture for another farce; so we ordered our horses, Bob and the pony, for I was unequal to riding any other horse than my 'sweet pony,' and we galloped to the front. The first point of observation was opposite Sir George Cathcart's grave; our second at the quarries, further on. At neither of these places could we see the least what was doing, owing to the dense smoke which hung over town and battery. Lady George Paget was sitting on the rock-work of the quarry, vainly endeavouring, as were many more, to trace the operations through the fog. We, who came up at so much cost to ourselves, were determined to see if possible, and rode along the front until we came to a post of observation opposite the Maison d'Eau. Here we saw very well, as the breeze had risen, and left the French attack clear from smoke. Altogether, our observations today were very unsatisfactory, as the principal firing was on the Mamelon vert, which stands to the right of the Redan and Malakoff batteries. We were told that the storming of the Mamelon vert would take place tomorrow; and as we were determined to see as much as possible of the working of the guns on that battery before the assault, we left the Maison d'Eau at seven o'clock, and, dining about eight, went to sleep earlier than usual.

Thursday, 7th – Rose at three. Started at four for the front, where we established ourselves in the piquet-house, exactly opposite the Mamelon vert. The firing at that time was tremendous. Gun after gun, shell after shell, pitched into, on, or near the fated battery. Most of the embrasures were knocked in, nearly every gun dismounted. The Russians, who had already begun to fire very wild, only replied with two guns, one at each corner of the battery. These guns worked till the last.

Presently a shot came bobbing up the hill, like a hare, to where we stood, though we were not in the line of any of our batteries; but it seems that, whenever the Russians saw a group of people, they fired into them.

The heat, for we had watched (I confess to having fallen asleep in the middle – but then I was very tired and weak) from half-past four till ten o'clock, was getting intolerable, so we mounted and rode home by the Fourth Division. On our way home we met a French officer, who told us on no account to omit being at the front by four o'clock this afternoon.

[*We crawled home like lizards in the burning sun. Got some lunch & laid down to sleep. God only knows how powerful was the Will that mounted me on my sweet pony. ... But who – in the presence of such sights as I was to see – could have remembered pain or even death?*]

By three o'clock we ordered fresh horses and started once more. As we approached the French lines of General Bosquet's division we saw the storming party forming up – five-and-twenty thousand French. They stood a dense and silent mass, looking, in their dark blue coats, grim and sombre enough. Presently we heard the clatter of horses behind us, and General Bosquet and staff galloped up. General Bosquet addressed them in companies; and as he finished each speech, he was responded to by cheers, shouts, and bursts of song. The men had more the air and animation of a party invited to a marriage than to a party going to fight for life or death. To me how sad a sight it seemed! The divisions begin to move and to file down the ravine, past the French battery, opposite the Mamelon.

[... *having on my French Chasseur jacket in honor of the French, I was cheered by the whole French regts & frightened out of my senses. ... [Bosquet] again took off his cap & cheered them like a pack of hounds towards the Mamelon – lying straight before them about 2,000 yards – then they began to move – & then the*

*English voices spoke, & sent them on with a cheer that shook the
earth. My eyes were raining. Many an Englishman's eyes were
wet. ... It was everybody's impression that the Forts were mined
& so they might all be blown up at once.*]

General Bosquet turns to me, his eyes full of tears – my
own I cannot restrain, as he says, 'Madame, à Paris on a
toujours l'Exposition, les bals, les fêtes; et – dans une heure
et demie la moitié de ces braves seront morts!' But let us ride
up the hill to the piquet-house and watch from thence for
the third rocket – the signal of assault. Our stay at the
piquet-house is short, for shots are coming up there fast. A
navvy just below us has had his head taken off; and, besides,
there is a place a little further back commanding a much
better view. Here we can seat on the grass, and let our horses
graze.

What a vehement fire! and all directed on the one spot.
Two rockets in quick succession are gone up, and a moment
after comes the third. Presently the slope of the Mamelon is
covered with men, ascending separately and rapidly; not
marching up in line, as our Infantry would have done, but
scattered like a flock of sheep. Two guns, hitherto masked, in
the Mamelon open quickly upon them; but they rush up,
and form when they reach the entrenchment.

[*I can never forget the sight. Would that I could get it out of my
eyes a moment – five & twenty thousand men – the forlorn hope*[34]
*running up the hill like sheep – all scattered as gun after gun ...
opened upon them. Forward & upward they ran, and then
forming into line charged with their muskets. One officer raising
his sword arm falls backwards dead, several wounded are seen
hobbling to the rear.*]

For a time we can see nothing but clouds of smoke. The
guns are all silent now, – nothing but the volley and file firing
of musketry.[35] The Russians, standing on the fort, fire down
on the advancing French; but presently some men are seen
leaving the Mamelon and rushing towards the Malakoff.

They are Russians, and the Mamelon vert is now in possession of the French. A momentary silence which succeeds
enable us to distinguish musketry on our left. It is the
English, who are attacking the quarries in front of the
Redan; and an Artilleryman, who comes up soon after,
informs us that the English have taken the quarries with but
little loss, and, if let, will take the Redan.

But the noise in front commences again, and I see men in
hundreds rushing from the Mamelon to the Malakoff. *Per
Dio!* they are not satisfied with what they have gained, but
are going to try for the Malakoff, with all its bristling guns.
Under what a storm of fire they advance, supported by that
impenetrable red line, which marks our own infantry! The
fire from the Malakoff is tremendous – terrible; but all admit
that the steadiness of the French under it is magnificent. On
our left the sun is setting in all his glory, but looking lurid
and angry through the smoky atmosphere, that is becoming
dense and oppressive from perpetual firing. Presently the
twilight deepens, and the light of rocket, mortar, and shell
falls over the beleaguered town.

We cannot hope to hear any accurate report of what has
been done tonight; and as it is now ten o'clock, and too dark
to see anything, we catch our horses and ride slowly away.

[*During which process I fainted in my saddle, & had it not
been for dear, good old John Buckley, I should have tumbled off.
At last in agonies of pain from over fatigue, illness & excitement I
was tumbled from my saddle & tumbled into bed where I've
remained until now. – But go up to the Front again in an hour's
time. – Oh that I were a man to take part in such magnificent
deeds of wondrous courage & glorious self sacrifice.*]

Meantime cholera is come among us, and at Balaklava has
asserted itself by stopping a career of much energy and
usefulness. Admiral Boxer has fallen a victim to its remorse-
less gripe, and is buried at the head of the harbour, where
he worked so hard, early and late, to endeavour to rescue

Balaklava from the plague-stricken wretchedness in which he found it a few months before.

Friday, 8th – The French are in the Mamelon, where they found seven big guns. They have thrown up an 18lb. battery, from which I saw them throw the first shot at the Malakoff. We should have taken the Malakoff but for a deep trench twenty feet wide and eighteen deep; and there was no reserve with trusses of hay to throw in, so the French could not cross it. We have nearly silenced the Malakoff guns with our fire to-day. They were burying in all directions. We lost thirty-three officers killed and wounded. I have not heard of any one I know being killed. No words can do justice to the gallant conduct of the 49th Regiment; and all are full of admiration of the French, and the way they rushed at the forts. A strong sortie is expected tonight.

Saturday, 9th – Was again at the front, though the fire has considerably slackened, and there was nothing doing.

But who could keep away from a place where so many interests were at stake? Not I.

Monday, 11th – Took such a lovely, quiet ride to the Sardinian outposts, through a country of massive foliage, green hedges, and deep mountain gorges, to where a little village peeped out at us from beneath its heavy crown of verdure. The little village looked gay and smiling enough at a distance; nearer, it was all deserted and desolate. The houses had been plundered, and terribly knocked about. I found a deer's foot, which I carried away as a memento of our pleasant ride, and which I shall have mounted as a riding-whip if I ever live to return.

Thursday, 14th – The Kertch expedition has returned, and is in Balaklava Harbour.

The destruction of Anapa appears to afford the principal topic of camp conversation. We hear that the 'Kertch heroes' have brought home lots of plunder, and we are rather curious for their disembarkation. The success attendant on the expedition seems to have put everybody in good spirits; and 'We must have a try for Sebastopol now' is the cry from the General to the newly-arrived Ensign.

I was occupied principally with a private grievance of my own, which, although to me a cause of very great annoyance and inconvenience, put me much in mind of the Old Lady in Albert Smith's ascent of Mont Blanc, who lost her favourite black box.[36] This box (of mine) has been coming out to me ever since the latter end of February, and it is now the 14th of June! Disgusted by the delay which at first attended the delivery of goods via Hayter and Howell,[37] this immortal box was sent out to me by what was to have been a shorter route; and after an expensive correspondence, an incalculable quantity of ill temper on my part, and a most vexatious delay, we heard this day that the ship in which this *bête noire* left England had arrived in Balaklava and had discharged her cargo. We sent down a man and pack horse to the agents of the ship, but received a message in reply denying all knowledge of the box. Next morning the same man and horse went down to Balaklava to the Parcels' Office. No box. Immediately on their return we sent them down a third time; this time desiring the servant to see the ship-master, and to go on board the *Odin* himself. He did so, and returned with a note saying that, in consequence of a stupid mistake on the address of the box, it had been left at Scutari, where it had been delivered on the 7th of May!! It contains my summer clothing.

Friday, 15th – Breakfasted with Général Feray, who commands the Light Brigade (Chasseurs d' Afrique), and afterwards rode, accompanied by his staff[38] and an escort of Chasseurs, to the Château Periouski, a Russian hunting-box about a mile from Baidar. The ride was through a country absolutely lovely – a country of hills and valleys, green trees; and fountains bright, clear, and cold. The château is evidently only just completed. It consists of a large dining room, with a beautiful parquet, and several smaller rooms on the ground floor, and a turret and gallery. Except near the stables, where were two large rooms, there seemed no accommodation for servants. There was a granary, a coach-house, a four-stalled stable – such narrow stalls! – and a cow-house, carefully floored with boards, but looking clean and comfortable nevertheless. A garden all run to waste, and a perfect wilderness of trees, completed the inventory of the place. After we had thoroughly explored it, we returned to the camp of French Heavy Cavalry, at a village about two miles in the rear (Vernutka), where le Marquis de Forton, the General commanding the Heavy Brigade of French Cavalry, gave us a most hospitable invitation to a *déjeuner à la fourchette*, arranged under large spreading trees, the branches of which had been interlaced to form an arbour, and ornamented with masses of flowers.

In this delicious shade we remained chatting as gaily as if we had all been old friends, until the sun went down behind the cliffs on the sea shore, when Général Forton and some of his officers accompanied our party back to the tent of le Général Feray, which we did not leave until near midnight, after having passed one of the most agreeable days of our Crimean experience.

Saturday, 16th – The Brigade of Guards marched up to the front, to be in readiness for the storming, taking, and destruction of Sebastopol, which is announced to come off on Monday next.

Sunday, 17th – The guns opened fire in their usual rattling style, and had a magnificent burst of about half an hour without a check. They then slackened for a little while, but soon recovered speed, and went on at best pace till the afternoon, when they got very slack. But people seemed everywhere in the highest spirits about tomorrow.

We remained at home till late in the evening, as several friends came down to see us, to say and to hear kind words, and to be wished good luck for tomorrow.

About six o'clock Henry and I rode up to the front, not so much to see the fire as to shake hands with many who we knew were going in tomorrow morning. A few amongst these were, Captain Agar, Colonel Windham, Major Hamilton, Captain Hume, Lord Adolphus Vane. It was eleven o'clock before we reached home, and at that hour we found le Capitaine Léon Müel awaiting us in the tent. We sent our horses to have a double feed of corn. I am sorry to say we have two horses out of four useless; Bob having hurt his heel, and the other, Chestnut, his back. Ordered some tea for ourselves, and then, having listened as long as my weariness would permit to an elaborate account of the wonders about to be performed by the French Cavalry and Chasseurs d'Afrique tomorrow, I crawled into the hut, and lay down for two hours without taking off my habit.

Monday, 18th – At two a.m., we were drinking some coffee, and at three o'clock we were at the front, seated on the ground as far forward as the Light Cavalry (who have been made into special constables!)[39] would permit. We were a few minutes late for the opening fire, but in time for such a storm of shot, grape, shell, and musketry[40] as had never before annoyed the ears of Heaven. We could see no troops. The Malakoff is firing gun after gun, though as many as five of our shells burst in it at one moment. The answering fire of the Malakoff is tremendous, and they have run up an enormous flag. The heavy guns of the Redan play away like so much file firing: the whole western horizon is dense with their smoke. So long as these guns fire, it is evident these forts are in possession of the Russians. But the French sent down 25,000 men, and what with all our men told off for the storming party, such pertinacious resistance cannot last long; and if once we get in, the Russians will pay dearly for their obstinacy. The firing, however, grows less: there are no guns from the Malakoff now. The great flag which they hoisted there is hauled down; and the Mamelon has been silent for some time. They fire a stray gun or two from the Redan; and we, who are looking on and wondering, inquire, 'What next?' Alas! we are soon told. The supports are seen moving. We fancy they are going down to the quarries to strengthen the force already there, for they disappear for a moment in a ravine – but no, they are advancing towards us: they are coming away. The firing is over; ambulance mules are going down. So, then, we have been beaten back.

The Brigade of Guards and Highlanders who have been waiting on our right are forming in column, and marching back to camp. We too turn away – blind with watching, and stupefied with the intense heat of the sun. We meet countless wounded coming down. Sir John Campbell is dead, Colonel Yea dead, and Colonel Shadforth; while many that we know are cruelly wounded: there seems no end to the ghastly train. Colonel Mundy, of the 33rd, shot through the thigh with a Minié rifle ball, walked into the mess hut of the 23rd, where we were sitting, as gaily as though he were untouched. Many soldiers, shot through arms and legs, walked up from the trenches, self-supported and alone; nor would any one have perceived their wounds but for the small hole in the coat or trousers.

How magnificent is such defiant courage!

[*June 18th – Such a day! & on the anniversary of Waterloo.*[41] *The storming Army was told off that night to go in at 2 a.m. ... The French to take the Malakoff, the English the Redan and then to rush into the Town. Fire opened yesterday – all very surprised. I had a very trying day, so many of my friends came down to say goodbye, & give me instructions for their friends in case of their being killed. Afterwards we rode up to the Front, saw several more and got home at eleven – did not undress but laid down booted & spurred, and at 2 were up again but afterwards watching till 9 we saw the French driven back from the Malakoff, the English driven back from the Redan!!! Poor Col. Yea is dead – and the Russians sprang over the parapet & plundered him before*

*he almost ceased to breathe. ... I never saw such horrible wounds
as they seemed to have – some were quite blown to pieces – legs &
arms off. ... Oh those poor French they came up load after load.
Thus the Russians have done just what they liked with us & have
scarcely lost any. It is clear now the town cannot be stormed. We
who expected to have razed it by this time are now anticipating
another year's campaign. Pelissier is frantic. My Lord I have not
seen to speak to – he rode home as if to a funeral. There was some
mistake about the scaling ladders, they wouldn't fit into each other
& were too short. – I am too tired to write more.*]

Tuesday evening – We heard that poor Captain Agar is also
dead! He was mortally wounded, and expired from exhaustion soon after he was carried back to camp. Poor Shiffner,
who so nearly lost his life some time ago, is also killed.

[*Captain Lushington was with us . . . he says that on the
evening of the 17th he received orders to open a rapid fire on the
Malakoff as soon as the day had sufficiently dawned to enable his
men to take aim – and he was to fire incessantly till about 9 or 10
o'clock when the storming party would advance. Lushington went
down into his battery about 2 o'clock a.m. and gave the orders
and neither he nor his men entertained a doubt that in two hours
they would have battered the Embrasures in & dismounted all the
guns. . . . about 25 minutes to 3 – he called to his men to stand to
their guns – they did so, & were just going to give 'a noble salvo
shot' – when Lushington heard* <u>Musketry</u> *just where they were
aiming and looking through a glass saw the French advancing to
storm [the] Malakoff – with all its guns firing into them & ready
to play on them!!! – Before he had recovered his aghast amazement, a shower of grape & canister was pouring all over & wounded him. 'Where on earth does this come from?' – 'Oh from the
Redan, the English are gone up to it' – 'But it hasn't been bombarded any more than the Malakoff!' – Lushington ran to the
Eight gun battery, where he found Lord Raglan & staff sitting
quite cool amid a very heavy Fire, but giving no orders, & doing
nothing. Dickson (Commandant 8 gun battery) ran up to Ld*

Raglan – 'My Lord you <u>must</u> give me orders to open fire, every man there will be butchered if you don't! – and you must get out of my battery directly for I <u>must</u> fire – and this is no place for you.' – At last Ld Raglan gave him permission to open on the Redan. Lushington implored the same permission for himself, which was granted – & in <u>one hour</u> after the Naval battery had opened – the Malakoff had not a gun fit to use! – <u>Fancy this.</u> – This is of a piece with what I told you about General Eyre.[42] *–Why we should have walked in there – with great loss certainly, but comparatively as easy as going upstairs if they had only not acted like insane people.*

The feeling about <u>the Staff</u> on the 18th is this: that they sat under fire as coolly as if eating their dinners at home – but that they did nothing – they sat waiting for orders – from a general who had no orders to give – and that their insouciance, and indifference was distressing to see. ...

Our officers universally behaved wonderfully well. But Lord West had to draw his sword & drive the 21st out of the trenches, up to the Redan, & they say the 33rd would not stir! At last the officers, instead of going round by the covered way, sprang over the trenches calling out – 'Who'll follow me?' & in some instances were followed by five or six men volunteers – in one place a sergeant & 20 men were seen going out alone to storm the Redan! – Oh you can't imagine the confusion, the butchery, the absurdities, the courage, the self-sacrifice of that day. Poor Agar, you know, had wandered away with his company far to the left & got quite cut off. General Eyre's division were in the cemetery in the town all day, & could not get out till after dark & then with a very heavy loss.

Mr & Mrs Howe Browne are here with poor Georgy. I've not seen them yet. Lushington tells me he saw Georgy's arm fly clean over the parapet of the trench!!]

Thursday, 21st – The 10th Hussars are moved out into the plain with the Turkish and Sardinian force. The French talk of storming the Malakoff again in about twelve days;

meantime, they are making regular approaches to it as to a town.[43]

Friday, 22nd – General Estcourt is taken ill with cholera. What a suppressed feeling of disgust and discontent runs through this army! It is no part of my business to enter on such a discussion, and I have hitherto carefully avoided doing so; but I cannot help sharing in the general interest and anticipation of a great and speedy change: men feel that their lives have been trifled with too long.

[*Such a feeling as is now afloat. You have read about the 18th June? Do you know that Lord Raglan never sent a single support to those poor 1,700 who went in? – or indeed to any of our men. 'Tis even said that Lord Raglan himself gave the signal for the assault, having taken up his position in the only place where he could not possibly see how matters were going at the Malakoff. ... Lord Raglan's recall is now as universally expected as it is universally desired. They say he has neither spoken nor smiled since the 18th. Generals Pennefather & Codrington are gone home under excuse of illness, but really from disgust. We have orders to prepare for Winter quarters.*]

Saturday, 23rd – General Estcourt is still alive, and the account today is more hopeful.

We rode to the monastery, and returned in one of the most tremendous thunderstorms I ever remember. The lightning was continuous and dazzlingly vivid, while the rain poured down in such torrents as to detach pieces of rock of half-a-ton weight from the cliff, and send them headlong into the road. The waters too rose so rapidly that tents, saddles, and kits were all washed away; while near Balaklava eight Turks were this morning found drowned.

Sunday, 24th – Poor General Estcourt died this morning. It strikes us that Death has taken the recall of those in authority into his own stern hands.

[*My Lord (Raglan) is ill in bed. Col. Steele the Military Secretary is better. Poor Estcourt, I told you his wife went to the funeral. Instead of his being buried as the Adjutant General should have been – they merely dug a nice little hole in his garden & put him in all bagged – just as you'd bury a pet dog.*]

Thursday, June 28th – We had heard that Lord Raglan was prevented by indisposition from attending General Estcourt's funeral, which was a strictly private one; and we heard yesterday that Lord Raglan's health was improving, and that nothing serious was apprehended. Our consternation was great, when one of his staff, who was with us at the monastery, received a hasty message that Lord Raglan was rapidly becoming worse. I can hardly imagine a greater misfortune to the army than his death at such a moment as the present. Now, when we may be about to lose them, we remember how valuable and necessary are his diplomatic powers in an army composed of so many nations. We are almost tempted to lose sight of the inefficient General, in the recollection of the kind-hearted, gentlemanly man, who had so hard a task, which he fulfilled so well, of keeping together and in check the heads of so many armies.

Friday morning, June 29th – Lord Raglan died last night!

It seems as though some pulse in this vast body had ceased to beat, the army is so quiet. Men speak in low voices words of regret. The body is to be conveyed to England for burial. There is a report that Baraguay D'Hilliers is coming out with *40,000* men to land at Eupatoria, and invest the north side of Sebastopol. A day or two ago, this might have caused some interest; now, for today at least, the thoughts of all meet in one darkened room, where lies he who a few hours ago was commander-in-chief. [*Poor Lord Raglan died last night! We fancy it must have been some sudden shock, as I saw Poulett Somerset at 6 o'clock & he said he was much better. There is a report that Sir Harry Smith is now in Balaclava harbour having come out to supersede him.*[44] *As a man, poor Lord Raglan is everywhere regretted and at present we are too much occupied with regretting the gentleman & the diplomat to remember his faults as a general. Sir H. Smith is old, & v. delicate – both bad qualities for the Crimea!!*]

Saturday, 30th – The Russians, always aware of our movements almost before we are so ourselves, having heard of our loss, made an attack on our trenches last night, and were driven back with some loss on our side. I hear that thirteen of the Naval Brigade were killed, and sixteen of the Guards.

General Scarlett and Colonel Lawrenson arrived in Balaklava yesterday; the former takes command of the Cavalry Division, and Colonel Lawrenson of the Light Brigade. We are all glad to have General Scarlett in command of the Division, instead of the senior colonel, himself commanding a regiment, which is always objectionable, and indeed in the French service is not permitted.

I have been ill for some days, as, indeed, who has not? and would gladly avail myself of Captain King's kind offer of his cabins on board the *Rodney*, in Kamiesh Bay; but Henry dares not apply for leave, as the troops have no money. The officers' field allowances are all due today, and for the last *ten days* there has not been *any* money in the Commissariat chest!

The report in camp is that Commissary General Filder has signified his inability to provide forage for the number of horses now in the Crimea.

[*The fat pony & I go out almost daily ... [he] kicks up no end of a row from morning till night. Henry won't ride him & Jennings said the other day – that he was the greatest man out here for Mrs D. bullies everybody & the pony bullies her.*[45] *I think I have stuck a French General with the Chestnut & if he don't give him some merry rides, I'm mistaken.*]

Sunday, July 1st – As we were riding yesterday along the banks of the Tchernaya, we could not but remark the vast herds of cattle grazing by the stream, and we compared them with our own starved, over-driven, cruelly used beasts, with broken tails, and bleeding from hard knocks and blows. The

Transport Corps some days ago reported that they would not be in an efficient state until they had *22,000* baggage animals. At present they have between *8,000* and *9,000*. If Commissary General Filder's report is correct, the poor horses already here, and the hundreds that are coming out, may look forward to a cheerful winter ! The very idea of such another winter fills me with pain and dread.

[*We've got Cholera in the regiment now. Oh that this fearful malady would cease. Balaclava is <u>full</u> of ladies, I don't know <u>any</u> of them, having called on no one but poor Mrs Estcourt. ... I've not been well for some days, with this vile diarrhoea – but try not to think about it. Today tho' I have tasted milk for the first time since August – except for the 18th when Major Herbert of the 23rd gave me some goat's milk. ... I know nothing about my medal – I suppose I shan't get it.*]

July 2nd – It is in orders this morning that the Cavalry Division moves out to the plain, in the direction of Baidar, on Wednesday next, to strengthen the position at the out-posts held by the Sardinians, as two divisions of the Russian army have marched down within the last few days to the Crimea. This will disarrange us all very much, we have become so settled in our old camp. As for me, when I look at the number of things with which I have become surrounded in hut and tent, I confess I can only sit down and shrug my shoulders, for it is absurd to think of *packing* in this tremendous heat.

Lord Raglan's body is, I understand, to be escorted by ten squadrons of cavalry tomorrow to Kamiesh, where it will be put on board the *Caradoc*, and so taken to England. Meanwhile General Simpson reigns in his stead.

CHAPTER 7

The Fall of Sebastopol

After the failed attack of 18 June and the death of Raglan, Pelissier dominated the Allied forces. Not only was the French fighting strength greatly superior, allowing him the final word in every council of war, but Simpson, Raglan's reluctant successor as British commander, was too timid to defy him. The Allies returned to the long-term French strategy: bombarding Sebastopol with mortars and guns to drive the Russians from the south of the city before launching a further attack on the Malakoff, the key to their defences. As before, they inflicted little damage on the fortifications but within the city casualties mounted and hundreds died daily, their sufferings increased by the shortage of medicine and food after the break in the supply lines.

Determined to end this, and alarmed by the build-up of Allied forces, the Tsar intervened, insisting on an immediate all-out assault on the Allies before the Russian field army, already suffering from lack of ammunition and forage, finally disintegrated. Additional French and British troops had arrived throughout the summer months, augmented by a contingent of 15,000 Sardinians (see p. 295, note 26). Against the advice of all his commanders, the Tsar demanded an attack on the well-fortified French and Sardinian positions on the Fedoukine heights. The battle at the Tchernaya river on 16 August was a massacre and destroyed the Russian army (see p. 301, note 20). At once, plans were made to evacuate the south of Sebastopol and work commenced on a bridge of boats across the harbour (see p. 225, Monday 20th).

Freed from any fear of attack on their flank the Allies now prepared for the final storming of Sebastopol. The following day, 17 August, they began a massive four-day bombardment (killing four or five thousand citizens), but this did not, as previously, herald an attack. The noise disguised the activities of the French sappers edging ever closer to the Malakoff. The British fared less well. The rocky terrain before their objective, the Great Redan, prevented them from reaching any closer than 400 yards, with disastrous consequences. The final assault took place on 8 September, after a huge three-day bombardment. The French almost immediately seized the Malakoff but then had to drive back five counter-attacks. The British failed to capture the Redan and suffered over 2,500 casualties in their repeated attempts (see p. 303, notes 31 and 32 and Biographies: Windham). Without control of the Malakoff the Russian position was untenable; that night they blew up the magazines and laid mines before retreating across the bridge of boats to the northern side of the city. Sebastopol, it seemed, had fallen.

But this was an illusion. The city remained under constant fire from the forts on the northern shore and was never truly occupied by the Allies. The engineers destroying the docks were shot at and no Allied ships ever anchored in the harbour. On 1 October Fanny wrote: 'Windham has been shelled out of Sebastopol from the earthworks on the North side, of which I maintain the Fleet might have prevented the construction' and a few days later added that the Russian mortars 'shake my hut & table as I write' (see p. 306, note 44). The Russians were keen to improve their position at the impending peace negotiations by inflicting damage on the Allies whenever possible. (See Introduction, pp. xxxiv–xliii for the final months of the war.) On 28 February an

Armistice was signed in Paris and the next day Russian and Allied officers met to celebrate peace. A month later the British commander invited Russian officers to a race meeting near the Tchernaya river.

The Treaty of Paris, signed on 30 March, was finally ratified on 27 April. The Allies agreed to withdraw from the Crimea and give up both Kertch and Kinburn; the Danube was to be an open waterway; and the principalities were to be free from interference in their internal affairs. Finally, the Black Sea was partially neutralised; it was closed to large warships of every nationality and there were to be no naval bases on its shores. (This condition was renounced by Russia only fourteen years later.) It was not a total victory; the Russians could still operate their Baltic fleet and their naval ambitions were only briefly checked. The demilitarisation of the Black Sea was unilaterally abrogated in 1870. For the British, the major benefit of the Crimean War was the long overdue reform of the army.

Lord Raglan's funeral procession from headquarters to Kasatch, where the body was embarked on board the *Caradoc*, to be conveyed to England, took place on Tuesday, the 3rd of July. It was escorted by several squadrons of English Cavalry, and the melancholy procession left headquarters after a salute of nineteen guns. Vast bodies of French troops, with Sardinian Cavalry, lined the road the whole length of the journey, whilst the mournful notes of the Dead March in *Saul*[1] were taken up at intervals.

I describe this from hearsay, as all those who were not actually engaged in the ceremony were confined to camp; in consequence of which order we were unable to witness a sight which I have since been told was 'too fine to be described;' and also, that 'the Duke of Wellington's funeral was nothing in comparison.' From headquarters to Kasatch Bay is between seven and eight miles, and such a distance lined with the armies of three nations must in itself have been a magnificent sight.

July 6th – Anniversary of my mother's death. For some days past I have been very far from well, and am now reduced to such a state of weakness that I am desired to procure change of air, if possible, and without delay. To this innumerable difficulties oppose themselves. There is the difficulty of Henry's obtaining leave, the difficulty of my getting over to Kamiesh, for I fear it will be many days before I can ride so far. I have written to Captain King, of the *Rodney*, to ask his permission to go on board for a week; but, with an ill-luck peculiarly mine, he is on the point of leaving that ship for the *St Jean D'Acre*; and of course, in the confusion consequent on such a change, I should only be in the way. Meantime I must endure the mighty heat of this breathless valley as best I may, knowing that if I *am* to live, I shall do so in spite of everything; and if I am to die, so it has been ordered by One who cannot err. I cannot understand that inordinate fear of death, which possesses the souls of many. He who sees not as man seeth, and who can do no evil, will surely do with us what is best.

July 7th – A draught of men and horses came out yesterday for the 5th Dragoon Guards. We had a great deal of thunder in the air, and one or two heavy showers, followed by bright hot sunshine. Several people, hearing that I was ill, kindly came to inquire for me today, as well as yesterday. How many friends has this break-up at headquarters caused us to lose![2] I shall feel, as I ride about the camp in future, almost as though I were in a land of strangers. Poor deserted headquarters! – the ravens always used to croak up there: they will croak twice as much now.

The chestnut pony, sole survivor of the aides-de-camp, came down to us yesterday, and like another sleek and well-conditioned pony that he knows, he bears the name of 'Poulett Pasha'. Poor pony! I think he had a presentiment that headquarters, and its comfortable stable and litter, was lost to him for ever – for he tried his utmost to conciliate us, his new masters, by licking our hands, and cramming his nose into all the pockets he could see, in search of bread.

July 10th – The chances of my being able to get away, at any rate for some time, are getting less and less. Everybody seems to be going home. I sent the first part of my journal to England by an officer going home sick; another, who has been out here about a fortnight, returns immediately from the same cause. Colonel Steele merely remains to wind up his affairs, and then he too sets sail for England. General Airey and Colonel Blane are alone left at headquarters of all my old friends. Mr Calvert and Vico are there still, I believe. In fact, who would not get away if they could from the flaming sword of the pestilence?

[*I couldn't write the last two mails because I have been very ill, and am still very weak and unable to get out of the tent. I wouldn't let Henry write as I thought it might frighten you and in this country if one is going to die – one is normally off the books before there is time to think about it. ... I am going to try to ride down to the sea this evening on a very quiet pony lent me. I have not been out of my tent for ten days. ... Bob Portal has been very ill but is better now.*]

Omar Pasha has withdrawn himself and 20,000 men from Baidar, much to the dissatisfaction of the French, who reckoned on his remaining there until they had cut the magnificent grass of the valley and made it – oh, English memories! – into fragrant hay.

[*The French and Omar P. have nearly had a row already as Omar has withdrawn ... thus leaving all the French hay at the disposition of the Cossacks. One French officer who came to enquire for me yesterday told me – 'I would like to recall Omar Pasha – to cut his throat.'*]

Canrobert and 10,000 men have left the plain, and are gone up to the front before Sebastopol. From this it is augured that we shall, before long, have another try for the Malakoff. In Canrobert's division are included the *Premier* Zouaves, one of whom I overheard saying to a comrade the other day, when they were both sitting fishing on the banks of the Tchernaya – 'Ah, mon enfant, mais, quand il n'y aura plus de Zouaves, l'armée Française sera finie!'

Thanks to the kindness of Mr Vansittart, who lent me a very quiet pony, I was able this afternoon to leave the shadow of my tent, with which I was getting sorely discontented, and to reach once more the cliffs overlooking the sea. I know of hardly any more lovely spot than the one we chose as our resting-place this afternoon. Before us lay the sea, blue, serene, and quiet, 'like beauty newly dead.' [3]

To our right and left rose the magnificent outlines of a coast naturally stern and terrible, but now bathed in a flood of rose-coloured light, with which the setting sun soothed the landscape, all flushed and scorched before from the power of his great heat; while round us, and underneath our feet, grass, leaves, and flowers looked up with pale, exhausted faces, thirsting for the evening dew.

July 11th – Spent the morning in bewailing the hard fate which bereft us of our cook – a Maltese, who for some time had officiated in that capacity, having gone out one morning, and left us, as a legacy, the delightful intimation, that 'he was gone away, and warn't coming back any more!'

We soon fell in with a *real* Samaritan in Captain King, then commanding the *Rodney*, who lent us his own invaluable servant; but Captain King's subsequent removal to the *St Jean D'Acre* obliged him to take his cook with him, and we are once more left servantless, helpless, and dinnerless.

Feeling that we were doing no good by sitting at home, we ordered the horses, and rode to hear the Sardinian band. I had heard no sound of music for nearly two months, and when I pulled up in the crowd round the band I was in a state of mind that jarred with everything save annoyance, impatience, and disgust. (Bob had refused to jump a gutter, and eventually dropped his hind legs into it, though all the Sardinians were looking at him – Bob, who is the best water jumper out of Ireland.) In fact, I was as much out of temper as out of health; but presently a voice, to which no one not utterly devoid of soul could listen unmoved, speaks to me in low and trembling tones. Ah, where is the petty gall that 'wrung my withers' not a moment ago? It is down below me, in the mire and mud of my daily life; while I am carried away far beyond this material world of trial and annoyance, and am walking side by side with angels – dreaming that I have caught the commencement of a harmony such as 'ear hath not heard, neither hath it entered into the heart of man to conceive.'[4]

Returned at half-past eight, or rather, I should say, fell crashing down from the top of Mount Olympus, where I had been conversing with the gods, into a soup tureen, and dish of fried fish more disgusting than anything ever produced in the annals of cookery.

July 12th – I think I have a cook! We rode up first of all to General Bosquet, and afterwards to General Féray. We found him at dinner with le Colonel Polles, who commands a regiment of Zouaves, and who took pity on my distress.

The French made a reconnaissance beyond Baidar yesterday – met a few Cossacks, and saw a body of regular troops in the distance. A large Russian force is supposed to be hovering about somewhere in the neighbourhood.

Lord Ward's sale took place today, as he is returning to England immediately. I was shocked to hear of the death, by cholera, of Mr Calvert, who at headquarters filled the office of Chief of the Secret Intelligence Department. He had been consul at Kertch for some years, and was a man of great information, as well as a universal favourite with all who knew him. A few hours later we heard that Vico was also

dead.[5] How the plague festers at headquarters! The perpetual presence of death is enough to make the strongest of
us quail.

July 14th – News reached the camp that a new
Commander-in-Chief is to be appointed in place of General
Simpson. Vico's sale at the English headquarters.

Tuesday, 19th – A heavy cannonade was opened tonight by
the Russians on the French left attack. General Luders is
supposed to be in Sebastopol now; and we imagine that he
ordered a sortie, as nearly at the same moment the Russians
made an attempt on our quarries. But they could not bring
their men on; and as we opened our heavy guns on them,
they soon retreated, with loss. For some time after this they
kept up a cannonade, apparently for the purpose of making a
noise, as they fired very wild, and did not aim at any special
point. They succeeded in disturbing everybody. We fancied
that it was the opening of another fire. They kept it up from
seven p.m. on Tuesday, to about the same hour on Wednesday morning, and since then there has been hardly a gun
fired by anybody.

July 20th – Sat once more by the seashore in the quiet
evening, saying over to myself the last words of Spenser's
Faerie Queene, at which the poet himself paused, and was
silent evermore:

> Then gin I thinke on that which Nature said,
>   Of that same time when no more change shall be,
> But stedfast rest of all things, firmly stay'd
>   Upon the Pillars of Eternity,
> That is contraire to mutability:
>   For all that moveth doth in change delight;
> But thenceforth all shall rest eternally
>   With him that is 'The God of Sabaoth' hight –
> Oh, Thou great Sabaoth God, grant me that Sabbaoth's sight ![6]

July 22nd – I have had today the pain of bidding adieu to
nearly the last of my kind old friends in the Crimea. Captain
Lushington, now Rear Admiral Sir Stephen Lushington,

K.C.B., who was promoted a few days ago, returns to-morrow, laden with honours, to England. And well deserved honours they are, and must be, for this reason, that not one man out in the campaign has made an observation implying that his distinctions were cheaply earned, or that he had been rewarded above his merit; and as such observations are very rife in the camp on like occasions, I think that their absence now is the surest sign that 'his honours do become him well.'

[*The command of the Naval Brigade falls on Captain Keppel of the* St Jean D'Acre *and I lose another influential and* most *kind friend (in Captain Lushington). In fact when General Airey goes I shall be completely 'cleaned out', there will be not a single man whom I know, and this after knowing them all! Last winter Col. Somerset could get us coals, General Airey planks, Capt. Lushington built the hut, Capt. Christie let me go & do just where & what I like – and now that Odious Heath reigns in Balaclava.*

... will you please send me out a tail comb in the box and the last volume of Household Words *or* The Newcomes *or anything clever with a lot of reading in it or I shall cut my throat this winter.*[7] *You may add a pair of warm gloves for me. That terrible Mrs Finnegan has hid your last letter & I can't find it anywhere. She is going to get married, I believe, and is more inexorably stupid than the head of man can conceive – & as deaf as a post.*]

I am writing late at night, amid a storm of heavy musketry. Occasionally a huge gun flings forth its volume of death, shaking our hut and the table, at which I write. All the Guards, and Sir Colin Campbell, are in the trenches to-night; Sir Colin going down as a volunteer, to give a little novelty and spirit to men who – God help them! – after being shot at every third night for ten months, like rabbits in a warren, require a little stimulus, not to give them courage, but to keep them from the heavy sleep induced by the overwhelming heat and the monotonous voices of the guns. The heavy guns are silent now, but the musketry is pouring

on, making ghastly 'music in the ear of night.' I heard today
of two atrocities committed in the army, and I think it
strange we should have so few to record. One was a tragedy
which took place two nights ago. Some Greeks – two men
and two women – live in a hut near the railroad, and also
within a couple of hundred yards of a troop of artillery. The
people were honest and quiet enough, taking in washing,
and earning money by various kinds of work. Two nights
since, some Turkish soldiers went down to the hut,
murdered the two men, after a vehement struggle, and clove
the head of one of the women open to her throat; the other
woman they stabbed in three places, and left for dead. They
then ransacked the house, and found 100l. in money – what
enormous sums are made by the hangers-on of the camp! –
and escaped. All next day the mutilated woman lay, the only
living thing amid such ghastly death, and the day after it
occurred to her neighbours to inquire why none of them had
been seen on the previous day. The survivor is now in
hospital, and has intimated that the murderers were Turkish
soldiers, and that she could identify them. Only a week ago
Henry and I took shelter under the eaves of that very house
during a thunderstorm.

The second story is shorter and occurred some little time
since. A man attached in some way to the army, Commissariat or otherwise, was walking late from Balaklava to
the front, having about him 120l. Some Greeks, who knew
that he had money with him, had tracked and followed him
until he reached a sequestered spot in the road, when they
fell upon him. He called out lustily, 'Au secours! au secours!'
Whereupon a French soldier of Artillery ran to his aid; but
the Frenchman's eye detected the glitter of the coin, and,
with a presence of mind truly admirable, he rapped the
howling wretch over the head with the butt end of his
carbine, seized the money-bag, and sped away before the
astonished Greeks could at all recover their wits, either to

cry out or to give chase. So the Frenchman got the money, and escaped, while the Greeks were discovered standing, open-mouthed, beside the corpse, and were carried off forthwith.

Four squadrons of Light Cavalry – one of the 8th Hussars, one of the 11th Hussars, one of the 4th Light Dragoons, and one of the 19th Lancers – went out this morning to Baidar, ostensibly to collect forage, but really to keep the peace between the Frenchmen and the Turks.

July 24th – On the 12th of this month I was credulous enough to believe the asseverations of a French General, and a Colonel of Zouaves, who, with many protestations, promised me a cook. I might as well, at any rate, have saved myself the trouble of believing them, for no cook, or servant of any description, has made his appearance, and the consequent discomfort of our lives must be felt to be appreciated.

[*... we have <u>suffered,</u> I do not use the wrong word – from the want of someone to supply us with actual food. The doctor attributed my illness to insufficient and unwholesome food. I hope to induce Henry to write to London for a servant – we would gladly pay £8 or £10 a month. ... I hear they are going to increase the soldiers' pay, but how clumsily! Fancy not giving the man the money into his hand when he has worked so hard for it, and it would purchase him some trifling alleviation. It's all very well saying that the army is well fed & all that – but our men get salt rations five days a week, and fresh meat 2 & then the fresh meat is not fit for anything but making soup of. ... In fact it is a very disheartening life and I for one don't care how soon we cut it and come home. The French say the war will last ten years ... However I mustn't take to grumbling.*]

The cause of the heavy firing on the night of the 22nd was a smart attack made by the Russians on the French, and on our left attack. We hear the Russians were not repulsed until they had suffered severe loss.

A messenger came over to me this evening from the squadrons at Baidar, telling me that they would start for a reconnaissance tomorrow morning, about fifteen miles further up country. They kindly offered us the accommodation of a tent if we wished to ride up overnight and join them; but the letter found us smitten down beneath the fierce strokes of the mighty sun, far too weak and oppressed to think of undertaking so long and fatiguing a ride.

The report is that 300,000 Russians just arrived in the Crimea; and as they are perfectly aware that they cannot be provisioned, they intend to seize on our stores, and drive us into the sea! This report is balanced by a fact that I happen to know – namely, that the Quartermaster-General has telegraphed for enormous supplies of wood, boards, and huts, to quarter us and our horses for the winter months.

[*28th July, Light Cavalry Camp. A terrible thing happened yesterday. We have only 2 married women – except my little widow (who is going to console herself), and one of these women's husbands, a fine healthy strong man, was taken with cholera & died in about six hours. The woman's frantic frenzy of grief I cannot describe. I never had to deal with anything so frightfully extravagant before. He was buried the same evening. I have been and still am very far from well – liver & diarrhoea, and all this coming yesterday, when I could hardly sit up, upset me terribly. I dread to let Henry out of my sight. Fancy, alive in the morning & buried at night!! Oh God only can support one under such sickening anxiety. Indeed both H & I feel that our health has been completely undermined by this pestiferous summer, our energy is so tired that we feel at present that at <u>any sacrifice</u> we <u>must</u> escape before the heat of next summer commences – Oh when will that poor woman cease screaming & wailing. ...*

Mrs Finnegan has shown the greatest kindness, good-feeling and common sense with the raving widow who was much older than her husband & who (I fancy) makes more noise than – but I oughtn't to say so. Mrs F. sat up with her all day and night, nursed the man – for his wife screamed at him & shook him, so that the doctor says that she hurried his end...

So, there are various things in the first box for which I shall be truly thankful, the tent lining, the bear's grease & bandoline ... If this reaches you in time just put into the box 2 very thick flannel petticoats and a warm dark gown, for Mrs Finnegan, 2 or three pairs of warm stockings for her and a knitted worsted jacket or something warm. ... Don't send the Newcomes *as I have just had it lent me.*

I heard from Tremenheere[8] this day. It is his letters that the Queen sees & says 'she has never read any letters so interesting & curious, & returned them to Mr Tremenheere with many thanks.' She heard of them thro' Col. Lake who is a great friend of mine and who told Miss Matilda Paget.

I must add one line more. After all this flourish – you will be delighted to hear that there is a Mrs Forrest out here, wife of a man in the Heavies,[9] who as she is near me, & did not appear to know a soul out here I called on one fine day, out of charity. She is a very dowdy sort of a woman & it was really only kindness that made me call. Her immaculate virtue has not allowed her to return my call!!! Very possibly if she has an opera glass she sees all sorts of swell people in my tent half the day & thinks I keep too good company for my station.

My dear Selina, if I am stronger by next mail I will write again, I am to be taken out today on my sweet pony. The Doctor insists on getting me out of this foul air – isn't it hard that we can't get away for a day or two!! Oh this vile country & war.]

July 30th – A stronger will than my own, one which the most resolute and powerful among us are obliged to obey, has kept me silent these few days. I have been ill: and to be ill in the Crimea is no light matter, as many beside me can testify. Poor Lord Killeen, too, is gone away to Therapia. In my distress I wrote to Captain Moorsom, of the Naval Brigade, to implore him to make arrangements so that I also might go on board ship. My position here is unfortunate. If my husband were ill – which God forbid! – he could obtain leave to go at once; whereas I am wholly dependent on the kindness of such as have not had all human feelings knocked out of their hearts. My appeal to the Naval Brigade was answered in a way that I must ever remember with gratitude. Captain Moorsom and Captain Keppel, who now commands the Naval Brigade, rode down to our camp, although the latter was quite unknown to us, and with the former we had but a very slight acquaintance; and in minutes they had arranged everything for going either on board the *Rodney* or the *St Jean D'Acre*, as soon as I am able to be moved. It seems as though I could never speak gratefully enough of the kind hospitality of these two sailors. Now, the only difficulty is, whether the *soldiers* will have humanity enough to permit Henry to accompany me. If they do not, I must go quite alone.

The dearth of any active proceedings at the front gives me time to remark on a little circumstance which rather edified me the other day, as I was riding home from an afternoon spent among the cliffs on the sea-shore.

At a little distance from us were riding three officers belonging to the English Cavalry, when we suddenly heard shouts and cries, and saw a Tartar running with all speed towards the three, holding up his hands, and apparently appealing for protection. The three rode on, until at last the Tartar, by dint of running, overtook them and tried to speak. With frantic gestures he endeavoured to induce them to listen, and with what success? Two endeavoured to ride over him, and I believe I am right in saying that one of the two struck him with his hunting-whip; at any rate, the arm was raised. As we rode homewards, I reflected on the vast superiority that exists in the civilised over the uncivilised part of the world: the latter, true to the old world instincts implanted by nature, appeals from the weak to the strong for protection – from ignorance to education and Christianity; civilisation (perhaps because he has not been introduced) rides over the man who is defenceless and wronged, or rids himself of him with the thong of his hunting-whip. Let us sing 'Te Deum' for civilisation, Christianity, and the Golden Rule.[10]

[*I will write by next mail and as we are daily expecting another fight, I may have something to tell you. Will you please address the enclosed to any London ready-made-linen shop you know or deal with – as it is of importance I should have more of the articles without delay as Mrs Finnegan is* <u>*Going Home!!!*</u> *And I like Sir John Moore shall be left alone in my glory.*[11] *There has been a deal of very fishy business . . . and the upshot is that Sergeant Lynch refuses to* <u>*marry*</u> *the lady, as does also Corporal Hurst. I believe the lady is in a high state of indignant virtue & has been washing for everybody except us – & having select parties in our place while we were away & breaking the plates & all kinds of scandals – so when I can get these things out I shall not be obliged to wash much during the winter – but must turn to and do all the work as there is only* <u>*One*</u> *other woman in the regiment & she disgustingly disreputable & also going home. However I suppose the saying – Aide toi, Dieu t'aidera – will hold good in my case & if it pleases God only to let me keep my health I don't think I shall want for pluck . . .* [12]

I have seen Mrs Forrest, she is a stupid little ass. I had an invitation today to go to a ball given in a Merchant ship & as an inducement was told that Commissary Drake & his <u>*wife*</u> *&* <u>*daughter*</u> *with* <u>*ladies*</u> *from Kamiesh were to be there. Fancy a Locke of Rowdeford*[13] *dancing with a Commissary & talking to the Commissary's wife. It's too genteel for me after my monastic life in the Crimea. Write & tell me about Paris.*]

July 31st – Heavy mortar practice all last night, with what result I have not heard. My husband has succeeded in obtaining leave to accompany me to Kasatch, on condition that he returns twice a week to camp. This permission is kindly given him by Colonel Shewell, Acting Brigadier in the absence on leave of Lord George Paget, and by General Scarlett.

[*August 4th,* HMS Rodney – *No duchess who lords it in London felt a greater lady or inclined to give herself more unsufferable airs than I – I have been very ill, all last week, one day was in incessant pain from 4 a.m. till 8 p.m. and have had Congestion of the Liver – and a very narrow escape from Jaundice. Jaundice in this country is not like the trifling thing it is in England – but you have to swim thro' it for your life. Yesterday (as soon as I was able to be moved) I came over to Kamiesh and Henry and I are now occupying Captain Keppel's cabins in the* Rodney – *a fine old 90 gun ship. We dined & breakfasted & slept in what you might call only common comfort – but what is to us the luxury of royalty. Here I am to remain until I am quite strong – which at present I think will be never. For this climate is so enervating that one becomes too weak to stand up without support – and I had to ride over yesterday, ten miles.*

Poor Chetwode is very ill with fever, I left him delirious yesterday. They hope to be able to move him away soon – today I believe. If you see the Deanes tell them, as he is a relative of theirs. Poor Bob Portal has had a very severe attack of Jaundice and had a squeak for it – but he is now gone to Scutari or Eupatoria. ... Poor little Lord Killeen of ours is also gone away very sick with Liver like mine – too weak to walk – & Puget of ours goes away today also very ill. We have hardly had a single officer sick until now – &. now they all go at once. How kind the sailors are! I never saw Captain Keppel yet half an hour after he heard I was ill, he was down in our camp & arranged everything for us to come here.... I can never speak too gratefully of the Sailors. Captain Hillyar of the Gladiator sent me over milk & cream for breakfast. Poor old Sir Edmund is very shaky[14] *– his son's death and the worry of his present life & old age coming on – have made it go hard with the old man & I shouldn't wonder if he tumbled off his perch with his old brother in arms Raglan.*

I cannot tell you how kind & good a nurse Henry has been to me....

The widow whom I mentioned last time is gone home – after sticking me with a <u>cow</u> for £10 – not worth £2. All that howling was the Irish expression of grief & the <u>lies</u> she told before she went were something awful.

Oh – Mrs Forrest <u>has</u> returned my call.]

Monday, August 6th – We have now been since Thursday on board the *Rodney*, in Kasatch Bay. The first evening that we arrived Captain Charles Hillyar came on board, but only to say good-bye, as he left the next morning in the *Gladiator* for Corfu, where he was sent to fetch up troops and guns. It is reported here that General Simpson intends opening fire this autumn, and with 400 fresh mortars! [*This is the most energetic thing that has been done for some time, or indeed at all. They are sending round the Mediterranean for more troops.*]

> Ah! what a sound will rise, how wild and dreary,
>   When the death-angel touches those swift keys!
> What loud lament and dismal miserere
>   Will mingle with their awful symphonies!
>
> I hear even now the infinite fierce chorus,
>   The cries of agony, the endless groan,
> Which thro' the ages that have gone before us,
>   In long reverberations, reach our own.
>
> The tumult of each sack'd and burning village,
>   The shout that every prayer for mercy drowns;
> The soldier's revel in the midst of pillage;
>   The wail of famine in beleaguer'd towns.
>
> The bursting shell, the gateway wrench'd asunder;
>   The rattling musketry, the clashing blade,
> And ever and anon, in tones of thunder,
>   The diapason of the cannonade.[15]

One would fancy Longfellow had been himself an actor in the weary tragedy that is dragging on around us, so faithful are his descriptive lines.

During the cool evenings we sit in the stern walk of the ship, and watch the shells bursting over the 'beleaguered'

town. Last night there was a very extensive fire in Sebastopol, which shot its fitful gleams far up into the sky. The
French must have made it doubly hazardous to extinguish,
as they poured in rockets and shells as fast as possible,
producing to us lookers-on a beautiful effect – a large sheet
of light in the background radiating on all sides with
exploding fireworks. The *Terrible* steamed away yesterday
afternoon to Gibraltar for heavy guns and ammunition. We
envied her the trip, for she will catch the cool sea breezes;
while we, lying in harbour, surrounded by shipping, can with
difficulty induce a single wandering zephyr to waft himself
past our vessel. Captain Drummond, who is appointed to
the *Albion*, but is at present commanding the *Tribune* here,
called on us during the afternoon of yesterday, and rowed us
out as far as the *St Jean D'Acre* and the *Algiers*. Captain
King, of the *Acre*, called on me the day before yesterday and
has promised to send me a pianoforte which was taken from
Kertch, and which is now on board the *Princess Royal*.[16]
I think there must be something in the profession of a sailor
that makes him less selfish and more considerate for others
than men of any other class.

The Duke of Newcastle is on board the *Royal Albert* with
the admiral, who has changed his position, and moved out,
together with the *Hannibal*, the *Queen*, and one or two other
ships, off Sebastopol. The Duke is reported to be suffering
from the effects of the climate; and I have not heard anybody
say they were sorry to hear it. If Cinderella's good fairy
would but reappear and turn him into a private soldier in the
trenches, in the depth of winter, I still do not think that many
would be very sorry for him. Poor man! perhaps he was
misled by false information after all.

A large American transport came in yesterday filled with
French infantry. The French have constructed a series of
earthworks and redoubts, so as to fortify the harbours of
Kamiesh and Kasatch, and also to take up a position (and a

very strong one) on the rising ground inland, in case they should ever be driven back from their trenches.

A French steamer, with heavy guns, went today round Strelitzka Point, and occupied herself for some five hours in firing mortars at the enemy, with what success we in the harbour were unable to determine; but at seven o'clock she returned to Kamiesh, bringing with her a smaller steamer in tow.

About four days since Captain Baillie, Lord Rokeby's aide-de-camp, came on board the *Rodney*, suffering extremely from an attack of one of our prevalent diseases. Mr Layard, brother to the memberof Parliament (who, with a noble cause, and with half England at his back, contrived to ruin it)[17], has died within the last two days, also on board a man-of-war.

I was interested today in listening to anecdotes of the trenches. Amongst them was the following. The Guards have been engaged in trench work since the 17th of June, and have of course taken their fair share of the work. A few days ago Lord Rokeby was going the round of the hospitals of his division, to see that the men wanted for nothing, when he recognised among the recent admissions a young man who had distinguished himself for steadiness in the camp and gallantry in the trenches. On being asked what was the matter, the poor fellow said, 'I've lost a leg, my Lord. I and my two brothers came out with the old regiment: the first one died at the battle of the Alma; the second one had both his feet frozen off when we were up in the front, soon after Inkerman, and died in hospital; and now I've lost my leg. 'Tis not much to boast of – six legs came out, and only one goes home again.' Profoundly touched, Lord Rokeby asked him whether they three were the only sons. 'Oh no, my Lord, we are seven brothers in all; but we three preferred soldiering, and enlisted at the same time.'

The *Arrow* gunboat went away last night to Perekop, and the *Harpy* is under orders for the Sea of Azov tonight.

Our hopes of a servant are small indeed. We have written to Constantinople, Malta, and England; and today I hear that General V——, the greatest gourmet of the French army, is at his wits' end to find a cook.

[*August 10th,* HMS Rodney – *I don't get strong. … Chetwode is on board ship and having survived through so much will now I hope pull through. I can give you no idea of the <u>overwhelming</u> heat – it is truly the life of a salamander – & none but a salamander can bear it with impunity. Oh! How it debilitates. I wish you would come out here for a fortnight, instead of going to Paris – it would do you both a 'power of good' and interest you beyond measure. You can come in 9 days, via Marseille, only you must make up your minds to rough it – It wouldn't do for you – send Francie out. Mr Lane called on us from Constantinople – but we were over here. He left me* Grace Lee[18] *& two bottles of Eau de Cologne.*]

August 12th – Went on shore yesterday afternoon, and inspected the dockyard [at Kamiesh], which is rapidly approaching its completion. It consists of several huts, two of them very lofty and very large; one occupied as a foundry, the other containing machinery of every description, worked by a steam engine in a building adjoining; machinery for turning wood, cutting and finishing iron, and performing all the work required for the ships. The energy and resources displayed, the use that was found for every bit of old wood or iron, the ingenuity which turned every material to account, made the inspection doubly interesting. Here were three forges, built of stone work brought from Kertch, of fire-bricks taken from various of our own steam ships, a pair of bellows from somewhere on the coast of the Sea of Azov, and the anvils from the ships in harbour, or else supplied from England. A part of the machinery was of French manufacture, and taken from Kertch.

Saw-pits are being dug, pipes are laid down, bringing a constant supply of water from the sea, and the little row of store huts are each provided with a couple of buckets hung outside, and a large cask, half sunk in the earth, and filled with water, close to the door; that there need not be the delay of a moment in case of fire breaking out. From the dockyard we went on to examine the stables and horses. The stables are models of ingenuity and good workmanship. In some cases the walls are built of stone, with a wooden roof, the building divided into stalls, and the floor pitched with small stones, as neatly as we are accustomed to see our own stables in England. Where damaged hay or straw cannot be procured for litter, the stones are thickly covered with sand, so that the horse cannot injure the foot when stamping, as he does all day at countless hordes of flies. The Admiral's stud consists of six Arab and Turkish horses. One flea-bitten grey was a gift from Omar Pasha; but his favourite horse, and the one Sir Edmund usually rides, is a dark chestnut, very small, but well-bred, active, and clean limbed. I recognised in one of the stalls a dun-coloured pony, which formed one of Lord Raglan's stud some months ago. We were shown, too, a wonderful proof of the efficacy of a little kindness and care in the case of a mule, which came to Balaklava in the baggage train of the Sardinian army, and having been terribly knocked about, and very severely hurt on board ship, during a rough passage, was left by them for dead on the sea shore. The boatswain of HMS *Rodney* happened to pass where the wretched animal lay bleeding but still alive, and with the blessed instinct of humanity, he stopped to help the sufferer. He raised the dying head, and gave the parched throat some water, and by-and-by he brought some food. In a day or two the mule was able to crawl, and, to make a long story short, when I saw him yesterday he was fat, and strong, and sleek; still covered with sores, which are in a fair way to heal, and following his friend, Mr Collins, the boatswain, precisely like a dog. In and out into the huts, among the workmen, wherever his business on shore calls him, may be seen the boatswain and the attendant mule; and when he recovers from his scars, he will be one of the finest and handsomest mules that we have out here. Such instances as these of kind-heartedness and humanity on the one hand, and gratitude on the other, are doubly pleasing in the midst of a life where we must, necessarily I suppose, see so much that is distressing and painful of suffering and indifference.

Monday, 13th – We dined last night on board the *St Jean D'Acre* ; and amongst the guests was Lord Rokeby, who is staying on board the *Tribune*, to be near his aide-de-camp, who is still in a critical state on board the *Rodney*. Just before the party were thinking of dispersing, Captain Wellesley, also one of Lord Rokeby's aides-de-camp, came on board, and reported that the Russians were advancing on all sides, and that the whole of the allied army was turned out. The night, however, passed off quietly, and the enemy did not appear, and at daylight the forces were turned in once more. The reason assigned for the postponement of the attack by the Russians is, that a man of the 21st Fusiliers deserted early in the evening, and is supposed to have given such information to the Russians as would make them aware of our being in readiness for them at all points. I went this morning for a short cruise in the *Danube*, which, as tender to the flag ship, runs from Kasatch Bay to the *Royal Albert* some four or five times daily; and during the run homewards was extremely interested in conversing with an English officer, Captain Montague, of the Engineers, who has just returned from Russia, where he has been a prisoner since March.[19] He appeared to speak very fairly of the Russians, mentioned gratefully the kindness he had received from Osten Sacken, and the hospitality which he had met with generally. Soon after he was taken, he travelled for more than a month in the wretched post *Talega*, going only eleven or twelve versts a day. He was detained for three days at Fort St Nicholas, in Sebastopol, and one or two more in a house in the north side of the town. I was the more glad to have seen Captain Montague, as he had spent some time with Mr Clowes and Mr Chadwick, both taken prisoners in the disastrous Light Cavalry charge, the former belonging to our own regiment, the latter to our brigade. He was able to give us favourable news of them.

Thursday, 16th – A grand fête-day with the French army and navy. All the ships of the united fleets were decorated, and at noon a tremendous salute was fired. About three o'clock, three of our smallest mortar-boats left their anchorage, and took up a position before the harbour of Sebastopol, for the purpose of shelling the camp and barracks on the north side, and the town behind Fort Alexander on the south side. We went out in the *Danube*, and had an admirable view of the practice. The shells from the little mortar-vessels pitched with great precision, and must have caused no little consternation in the camp and barracks, as we saw many people running about in haste, and making for Fort Constantine. Presently a flag of truce was hoisted from the top of this fort. Our fire, however, continued, although it was principally directed on Fort Alexander. We remarked that, with a single exception, all the answering shots of the Russians fell short.

There was nothing but feasting and gaiety on board the French ships. Sir Edmund Lyons and Sir Houston Stewart both dined on board the *Montebello* with Admiral Bruat, and before sunset the French flagship fired a second salute.

The medical inspector of the fleet pronounced sentence on me yesterday – namely, that I retrograde instead of improve as far as my health goes, and I am to go, if possible, for ten days to Therapia, for further change of air.

Of sixty shots fired by the mortar-boats yesterday afternoon, twenty pitched into the Quarantine Fort, but those fired at Fort Alexander were at too long a range, and all fell short.

News has this moment come in as I write, of an engagement on the banks of the Tchernaya.[20] The Russians came down in force (I give merely the first reports as they have this instant reached me), and the French and Sardinians gave them a tremendous repulse, took their floating bridges, and drove them back, with a loss on the side of the Allies of 500 men. Up to this time I cannot hear that the English Cavalry were engaged.

Five o'clock – Henry has just ridden over from Balaklava, and tells me that the Cavalry turned out at daybreak. The Russian army amounted to about 50,000; and they attacked the exceedingly strong position of the French Zouaves and Sardinians in a most gallant manner. The French, by whom the attack was quite unexpected, were very weak, as to numbers, on this point; the position itself being so strong. The Sardinians, also, had to collect themselves after their outposts were driven in. The Russians crossed the river with determination and gallantry, and ascended the hill side of the French position. By this time French reinforcements had come down, and the Zouaves, leaving their camp, charged downhill upon the enemy with bayonets, repulsing them with fearful slaughter. They were also beaten back by the Sardinians on their left attack, materially assisted by our new heavy field battery (Captain Moubray's 32-pound howitzers), which ranged far beyond all others, and blew up nearly all the Russian ammunition waggons, dismounted their guns, and killed their artillery horses. The loss of the French and Sardinians was not heavy. It was a brilliant day for our Allies. The English Cavalry was not under fire, except the 12th Lancers, who crossed the river, but were recalled immediately by Lieut-General Morris, who observed that '*ces diables d'Anglais* were never satisfied unless they were trying to get annihilated.' The Russians were all gaunt and hungry men, who had evidently been driven to death by forced marches. *The enemy fired on the French* while they were charitably engaged in removing the wounded Russians.

[*August 17th* HMS Rodney – *We have had another fight yesterday but of course as I was a prisoner on board ship I can as yet tell you no more particulars than the following – At three a.m. the cavalry were turned out with horse artillery, Field batteries and the famous Grey Battery of the 18lb guns & 32lb howitzers. They formed up, at least the cavalry did, over the graves, where those were buried who fell in the Balaclava charge.* [21] *The Russian 50,000 came down from Mackenzie's Farm to the Traktir bridge over the Tchernaya – bringing with them pontoons &c for crossing the river. They were met by the Sardinians & French. ... Henry who was in camp rode over the field directly the Russians began to retreat – they were retreating for hours in great confusion. H. said he saw about a thousand dead, besides wounded. But as the whole business was over by ten or eleven there was plenty of time to fetch in the poor wounded. But the French were very short of stretchers. The Russians were all in great coats the same as at Inkerman in November with big boots. All looking horridly emaciated and thin – some were tall big men but all looked gaunt & ill. They had haversacks like ours, but filled with the* <u>blackest</u> *bread – Henry brought me a bayonet from a Russian who was blown to pieces. They had no cavalry with them. ... our 18lb [gun] dismounted all their guns & blew up their ammunition & the 32lb howitzers did great execution. ...*

[*The Russian Army*] *had only marched down from Warsaw the day before. Poor devils – they had none of them a drop of water in their canteens for of course there was none between the Belbec & the Tchernaya – but as they fought on the banks of the latter stream of course there was plenty at hand for the wounded as soon as the row was over. ... The Russians had no idea we had such heavy field (artillery) power ...*

It was quite an Inkerman for the French and they say no Englishman could have fought better. 1,400 against as many thousands until reinforcements came in. The Sardinians are also very proud. Had the Sardinians been driven in the French must have gone...

We are hammering away at the town today – as if we had begun another bombardment.[22] *... & certainly old Simpson was more discreet than my Lord for not a soul knew it until the telegraph came down to the Admiral after they had begun. It frets me terribly being shut up here – but as I decline to improve beyond a certain point in spite of some physic that would kill a horse, I believe I am to be sent out for a cruise down to Constantinople. I am going to see Sir Edmund Lyons about it today. I get a horse lent me whenever I like – one, an Arab, bought at a fabulous sum from the Sultan's stables – but in spite of riding & walking the liver keeps so torpid that I am fit for nothing.*]

Sunday, 19th – Went to church on board *The Royal Albert,* by invitation from Sir Edmund Lyons. We remained to dine; and as it came on to blow so hard that it would have been difficult for us to reach the *Rodney,* we stayed in our most hospitable quarters all night.

During the afternoon, Admiral Bruat came on board; and I had an opportunity of seeing, for the first time, the French Naval Commander-in-Chief. He struck me as being shrewd, and I was going to write *false,* but perhaps my meaning may hardly be understood; his manner was certainly polished enough. The two admirals sat in conversation, side by side, and the contrast struck me with such force, that I was obliged to lie awake at night to try and analyse it. [*Admiral Bruat has put his carriage & four horses at my disposition but the roads in Portland, Ireland are good to what they are round Kamiesh & so I declined.*]

Monday, 20th – The sea going down slightly, enabled us to leave for the *Rodney* in the *Danube* at ten o'clock, after we had listened to the band playing on board the *Royal Albert,* and gathered a more distinct acquaintance with the Russian works of defence than before. They are now busily employed in constructing a bridge across the harbour, so as to form a

retreat from the Malakoff and Redan when we take triumphant possession of those two forts. [*Our mortars on shore
cannot touch it. I believe it is supported on empty barrels.*]

The sunlight shone full on the face of the town, showing
us long lines of windowless houses riddled with shot; and
yet, standing in the centre of the town, one or two houses
still intact; one a fine house, with a light green roof (I fancied
it was only their sacred buildings that are green-roofed), and
another house, solid, handsome, and large.

Sir Richard Airey, who received an official notification of
his promotion to the rank of Lieutenant-General, is also on
board the Flagship, endeavouring to shake off an attack of
fever which, like every disease in this country, however
slight, leaves you weakened in a wonderful degree. There
were two explosions in the Russian batteries this morning,
but I fancy neither were of much importance.

[*21st August – I hope to return to camp on Thursday next the
30th inst. I am not much better, as far as strength goes having still
a good deal of pain & being weak. But I fancy the doctors are
treating me wrong – they have given me sufficient Calomel &
Mercury to induce another kind of symptom very weakening and
painful – so I shall throw up the drugs & take to pigskin [a
saddle] & the freshest air I can get. There's nothing like pigskin &
a gentlemanly horse who carries you tenderly when he feels you
weak. ... I must see what constant riding and resolution will do,
towards making me forget pain. I suppose I shall make new
friends – I know very nearly everybody worth knowing, French
& English, except Simpson & I fancy his reign will be short. His
staff are anything but prepossessing after the <u>gentlemen</u> of the last
dynasty.*[23] *.. Henry can't sell out now, he could only by resigning
– & so lose £1,400 at least & his pay. But he must risk even that
before next Summer heats come on.*]

Wednesday, 22nd – The *Gladiator* came up from Balaklava
yesterday, where she had discharged the products of her trip
to Corfu; she brought, in addition to eight mortars, *2,200*

shells and a couple of hundred artillerymen. I dined on board with Captain Hillyar, and there was a report that the French intended opening fire from their new work on the extreme left this afternoon, and that our little mortar boats were to go in, and throw mortars at the same time; but this did not take place. The mortar battery did not open, and although our pretty little boats got under weigh, they dropped anchor again almost as soon as they got outside. There was a telegraph made from the Flagship to Headquarters about twelve o'clock, to the effect that 'large bodies of troops were assembled outside the loopholed wall'; but they did nothing unusual this afternoon, although just before sunset a very heavy fire was opened all down the line of the right attack on the town. It was a lovely afternoon, and I walked along the shore towards the Lighthouse of Khersonese. Here, driven almost on to the beach, I found the remains of a French or Austrian brig, which had been cast ashore. She was mostly broken up, and so close in that I could easily climb about among her rotting timbers. She had been laden with bullocks; their bones lay white and glistening all around; polished skulls, white as plaster of Paris casts, many with a bleached rope still wound about the horns, and several with the rusty shoe and large-headed nails adhering to the shrivelled hoof. I brought away a bone or two, more than usually polished, and a few parts of the fittings of the ship; and then, feeling that the sea was shaking the driftwood on which I stood, I carefully collected my relics, and scrambled to the shore.

Friday, 24th – Went to stay on board the *St Jean D'Acre,* anchored off Sebastopol, and remained on board some days. During my stay I had frequent opportunities of inspecting, through powerful glasses, the works, guns, and actual movements of the inhabitants. The bridge across the harbour, in front of the men-of-war moored at the entrance, which they commenced a week or two ago, is now complete. The traffic over it is perpetual both of men and horses. For two days, as the stream set principally from the south to the north, we fancied that the Russians were removing their goods, previous to evacuating the south side; and this appeared more probable, as they were busily employed in erecting fresh earthworks on the north side; but lately opinion has changed on the subject. It is universally believed that the Russians in the town are suffering cruelly from short rations and over-work. All deserters agree in the same sad story of sickness, privation, and distress. Meantime the town looks outwardly fair enough. On Monday we heard that the Highland Division has been sent down to the Tchernaya, to strengthen the position of the Sardinians, as another attack is expected. The English Cavalry turns out every morning at four o'clock, and takes up a position in the plain, ready, in case of another attack from the hungry Russians. The reason of this daily turn out is obvious enough. There are only two outlets from Balaklava to the open plain, and a large force would necessarily be detained some time in filing through.

I could not but be struck on Tuesday evening, as I was watching the moon rise from the deck of the *St Jean D'Acre*, by the wonderful and glorious difference between God's work and man's. It was a picture composed by two artists. It might have been fitly called 'Peace and War.' Shining over the central forts of the town was the full moon, looking with calm and steadfast face out of the serene sky, in whose 'deep heaven of blue' star after star trembled into life and light; whilst down upon the placid waters gleamed the pale broad pathway reflected from her beams. The distant hills wrapped in light haze were visible to the eye; but, immediately before us, no object save the grim corner of a fort could be discerned from the heavy, heavy weight of smoke that clung to and covered the city like a shroud. Here and there across it shot the lurid glare of the guns, darting across the palpable atmosphere like a flying ball of fire. Who cannot see in this a representation of what has often filled his own mind? The wrathful stir of passion raging within, until calmed and softened by the blessed influence of the Holy Spirit of God.

Last night and this morning two explosions occurred. The one at half-past one a.m. I am sorry to say was in the Mamelon, where a shell blew up the magazine. This did, of course, immense damage; not so much to the battery, as to the soldiers. There were, I hear, above 200 killed and wounded.[24] The explosion about nine a.m. was in the Russian works, but was not nearly so extensive.

Lord Stratford de Redcliffe has been up here to invest the G.C.B.s and K.C.B.s. On his arrival and departure, he was saluted by the English and French ships. Being on board ship and away from the horses, I had no opportunity of going to witness the ceremony, which, I believe, was as imposing as uniforms, decorations, forms, and ceremonies, could make it.

[*25th August* HMS St Jean D'Acre – *I remind myself of the Fable of the Frog & the Bull, the longer I live the greater* swell *I become.* [25] *When I look back on the time when I lived at Wycombe, glad to get the companionship of Miss Saunders Nash and Miss Whytt, &c &c and find myself now very much in the position of a Queen – fêted by Admirals, asked to meet Ambassadors and Generals – how strange are the changes of a life – and yet how naturally one falls into acquaintances and societies, whether of Merchant sailors or of Commanding officers. ... We dine on board the Flagship tomorrow to meet Lord Stratford de Redcliffe ... & Admiral Bruat. ... Today all the ships are dressed & yards manned for Lord Stratford. Ah Hah! What a fuss for a cantankerous old cat-a-mountain like that.*]

I cannot refrain from mentioning a brilliant little work entitled *The Roving Englishman in Turkey*,[26] and from thanking the author for the pleasure he has afforded me in its perusal. It was put into my hands a short time ago, and since then it has sparkled on my table like a gem.

[*August 30th – I am come back to camp – returned today. Saw my dear old horse for the first time for a month and burst out crying on his neck to the astonishment of Sir Ed Lyons & Five Post Captains who escorted me to the beach. Simpson comes tomorrow to take his picture – I am to be stuck in too, I believe. ...* [27]

I ain't very fond of kissing any body, luckily for me. What fools women are to be sure – I don't think I could live among 'em again for the world. ... I am informed she (Mrs Finnegan) is in the family way, which is delightful for all concerned, especially me. ... at all events she is going on in no way that I approve – & I am going to have it out with her presently. We have a new cook, a Maltese, [28] *& such an overpowering swell that I am quite afraid of him, & so I think is Henry. I believe Poulett Somerset has also dispatched us a servant from England by this time so we shall do for the winter.*]

September 5th – For the last three mornings in succession we have been kept on the *qui vive*, turning out the whole Cavalry at two a.m., and marching them down beneath the hill which hides the Traktir bridge, as, from information received from spies and deserters, the Russians have been meditating a second effort for the repossession of the Balaklava plains.

They have been augmented by a large reinforcement of Imperial Guards and other soldiers, it is said, to the amount of 90,000 men. The attack, for which we have now been waiting patiently for three days, was to have been made by the whole of this force; 50,000 were to endeavour to take the Traktir bridge by storm, while the other 40,000 were to attack the French and Sardinians on the right and left.

Rumours relative to the non-appearance of this army are rife. Some say that in marching down they met the wounded from the Tchernaya going to Bachsi-serai, and were so horrified at their number and their ghastly wounds, that they refused to advance, and more than 100 of these wretched soldiers were shot forthwith. Now, it appears that the whole force are either sent into Sebastopol, or dispersed on the plain of the Belbec, where they can get water. Meanwhile, we have opened a very heavy cannonade upon the town. The traffic over the bridge is incessant, and the Russians appear to be carrying all their valuables, goods, furniture, and pianofortes over to the north side, as we suppose previous to evacuating the south side entirely.

Last night we dined with General Féray, (who commands three regiments of Chasseurs D'Afriques) and when we arrived we found him just returning from the front, where he had been inspecting the works of the Mamelon Vert and the Ouvrages Blancs.[29] During dinner, he told me that a Tartar deserter had come into General Bosquet's division during the day, and had told them of the agonies of thirst suffered by the army which fought at the Tchernaya on their march. Some little distance before they reached the Belbec, they passed some wells. Order of march was at an end; the foremost threw themselves down headlong; the rest, struggling to get at the water, and impatient of those before them, drew their bayonets, and presently the wells were filled with upwards of 150 dead and dying bodies!

I remember our own sufferings while marching, for short distances, in the hot weather in Turkey, and especially the frantic horses at Jeni-bazar, so that I can, in some slight degree, understand the torments of the Russians. As we rode home from General Féray's our way was absolutely illumined by the light of a fire which seemed to set all heaven in a blaze. We could not see the fire itself for the hills which intervened; but, from the brilliancy of its light, we fancied the whole of the south side must be in a blaze. Not that Sebastopol would ever burn; the houses are too detached, and built so much of stone, that they would never keep alight for any length of time.

The cannonade was densely heavy, and the light of the guns radiated off from the brilliant centre of the vast fire, and seemed like perpetual lightning.

The French are supposed to have opened their new battery, by which they are to reach the ships. I am now on the point of mounting, to ride up and ascertain for myself what the light of the fire meant.

Ten o'clock – The blaze of last night was caused by the firing of a two-decker, one of the ships in the harbour. Captain Keppel, to whom I went for information, tells me he fancies it was set on fire by a French rocket. However that may be, she burned away famously; the outline of mast, spar, and rigging showing with terrible distinctness in the lurid light.

We reached Cathcart's Hill this afternoon in time to see a perfect explosion of guns from the French line of attack. Every gun and mortar appeared to fire at once; those that did not go off at the precise moment following with the rapidity of file firing. It was, indeed, 'a noble salvo shot', and was loudly cheered by the English soldiers who were looking on. Presently we met the brigade of Guards marching down into the trenches. The whole brigade goes down now every third night.

We were fortunate enough to see General Markham just starting for a ride, as we passed his quarters. His reputation as the most rising man in the army, and likely to succeed to General Simpson's command, made me very anxious to see him. General Markham was formerly colonel of the 32nd, to which regiment Henry belonged. He is slight and wiry, with long grey beard, and eyes which, though ambushed behind a frightful pair of spectacles, I could tell were piercing and keen beyond most others in this vast camp. Having an engagement at the moment, he was prevented saying more than a few courteous words, and left us, with a promise to call upon us at his earliest leisure. The fire from the French lines still continues fast and heavy.

September 8th – We rode up to the front again yesterday afternoon, although the northeast wind was blowing a hurricane; and for half the distance I trotted with my hat in my lap, and my left hand gathering up my habit to prevent its acting like a mainsail, and blowing me completely off my balance. We passed General Bosquet's division, and struck out the shortest track to Cathcart's Hill. A party of Fusilier Guards were marching slowly towards us, and close behind them followed a chestnut horse I knew but too well. Poor Captain Buckley, who yesterday was so full of strength and life, is being borne to the resting-place of many brave hearts, and will sleep on Cathcart's Hill. I begin to grow super-stitious. I fancy that every man to whom I speak just before any great danger, is sure to fall a victim to it. Last night, on his way to the trenches, I met Captain Buckley, and he stayed a few moments to talk to me. Within two hours after I saw the last of him, spurring his pony round a corner of the ravine to overtake his men, he was lying on his face, shot through the heart! I cannot watch that sad procession. I cannot picture to myself the frame so full of life and vigour yesterday, now a mouldering heap of dust. I show him what respect I can, although a black habit, and handkerchief, and a strip of crape round my arm, is all. He said he would 'live and die a soldier', and right well he kept his word.

[*My heart and eyes are so full of tears, I can hardly write to you. Poor Buckley was killed last night in the trenches – shot as he was posting sentries beyond the advanced sap. Shot through the heart. I for one have lost a real friend, who showed me many a kindness and sad enough I was the last person to whom he spoke before going down last night to the trenches. I was up at the Fourth Division calling on Col. Windham, who commands a brigade, and while there poor Buckley and young Scarlett came in as the Brigade of Guards was filing past us to go down to the trenches. There was some alteration in the plan of posting the sentries and poor Buckley and Scarlett called on Windham to have it explained. Scarlett went in but 'John' which was the name he always went by, staid outside to talk to me. He seemed in good spirits. I said laughing – 'I wish you would let me go down in your place – & you ride home with Henry' – he said 'No that's to (sic) dangerous even for you Madame. But I suppose I shall come out alright.' – 'Well', I said 'Goodbye & good luck to you, you are such an old soldier now that Destiny must pull you through altogether now.' – 'Ah, I don't know, but I am not afraid, still no man can say his life is his own till he comes out.' He rode away, spurring down hill his pony stumbled – he called back to me – 'One escape already you see' – and then cantered after his men. He was as thorough a soldier, as sterling-hearted a fellow – and as full of gentleness & kindness as any man out here. I have known him of course ever since I was a child & he lent me a horse all last winter & was often with us. Really sometimes this war seems to me too terrible. He was about 23. . . . I lose one of my very few friends, who always fought my battles & always shewed me kindness. He was severely wounded at the Alma – returned the day before Inkerman – and has been working like a slave in those trenches ever since the 18th. If I had a bit of mourning I would wear it for his sake. – I have taken up all my letter with this, I feel it so much.*

There will be more fearful work today as I have just had word from Henry to be on horseback in an hour as all the 5 Divisions & the French & Sardinians are to parade at the Front to take either the Malakoff or the south side.

Young Deane called on me two days ago – he is very well – went down last night to the trenches for the first time – I was pleased at his calling immediately on his arrival. I am getting an old woman – & like little attentions from little boys – tell his mother he looked well – and was in famous spirits & likes his regiment.]

But I must turn away from the melancholy funeral on my right, and look forward at the siege. There is a huge blaze in the centre of the harbour, and Colonel Norcott, of the Rifles, tells me it is a frigate set on fire by French shells. How bravely it burns! bright and clear as a wood fire in the vast home-grates at Christmas time. Presently General Markham rides up, and says, 'Mrs Duberly, we shall have a fight tomorrow. You must be up here on Cathcart's Hill by twelve o'clock.' And then we ride briskly home, for the evenings are chilly, and the horses' coats begin to stare. As we lay our horses into their long, striding gallop, we talk of the prospects of tomorrow, and the chances of our friends – how much their number is reduced! Of Major Daubeny; of the boy Deane, who only joined last week, and will make his first entry into the trenches tomorrow; of Mr Glyn, who exchanged only a day or two ago from the 8th Hussars to the Rifle Brigade; of Colonel Handcock, whose wife is with him at the front; of Lord Adolphus Vane; of General Markham, and many others.

September 9th – Last night I was overcome with the shock of poor Buckley's death, and felt so unhinged that I did not start for the front until eleven this morning. The cannonade was terrific, exceeding anything that had previously occurred during the siege. After some difficulty in 'dodging' the sentries, which General Simpson, with his most unpopular and unnecessary policy, insists on placing everywhere, we reached the Fourth Division just as the Guards were marching down to their places in reserve. The Highlanders were the first reserve, and then the Guards. [… *& as I wanted much to see Lord Adolphus Vane, we joined in their ranks & so passed the sentries.*] Here, I am glad to say, we overtook Lord A. Vane, and he promised to come down to us the first moment that he could get away, after the fight was over. I remembered poor Captain Agar's like promise, and my heart grew still as I listened; but we were advancing on the batteries, so we turned our horses' heads across the ravine, and rode up to the front of Cathcart's Hill, where we found the Cavalry at their usual ungracious work of special constables, to prevent amateurs from getting within shot. Now, in the first place, amateurs have no business within range; and in the next place, their heads are their own; and if they like to get them shot off, it is clearly nobody's business but theirs.

[. . . *the Russians seeing a large body of Cavalry up there . . . fired at us heavily with shell. None however did any damage though some burst almost immediately over our heads. Meantime cannon & musketry raged as I throughout this long siege never heard them rage before, it was miraculous. A heavy smoke obscured the town.*]

The cold of today has been intense. Two days ago I was riding in a linen habit; and today, with a flannel wrapper, a cloth habit body, and an extra jacket, I was chilled to my very bones. If hospitable Mr Russell, the *Times* correspondent, had not kindly sent me down to his hut, and told me where I should find the key of the tap of the sherry cask, I think I must have collapsed with cold. [*Russell gave me the key & orders to his servant to make me a boiling glass of sherry & water, kind, hospitable Russell!*]

Meanwhile in the front nothing was to be heard or seen but incessant firing and masses of smoke. The perpetual roll of musketry and the heavy voices of the guns continued without intermission, and the anxious faces of all were strained towards the Malakoff and Redan. By-and-by wounded soldiers come up from the trenches, but their stories differ, and we can place in them no faith. 'I was in the Redan when I was wounded', said the first, 'and our fellows are in there now.' 'We have been three times driven out of the Redan,' said a second; so we found that we could depend on nothing that we heard, and must wait in faith and patience. We left at about half-past six o'clock, thoroughly tired, and chilled to our very hearts. Since then, within the last half hour, I have heard that Colonel Handcock is dead.

[*Wounded came up perpetually. ... Presently came a mule, bearing the dead body of Col. Handcock, whose wife has been living in camp for the last month. He headed the storming party, so his fate was certain before he started. After he had been gone down about a couple of hours, she got nervous & went to the Picket House, she had scarcely got there, when the mule arrived. He was just able to recognize her before he expired. The day drew on and the firing & the bitter cold increased. We rode down to the 3rd division who were in reserve (the first reserve) & much nearer in, here we talked to Major Plunkett but got no satisfactory news. The French had been in the Malakoff for hours and were now advancing on the Little Redan – through glasses we could see the trench in front of the Redan, covered with red coats. Still we could learn nothing, & still the musketry poured on. At seven we left, I almost insensible from cold. Then the Highlanders & Guards had not gone in.*]

And poor Deane, the young boy, just entering into life and hope, lies in the hospital of his regiment, laid out ready for burial. As he was standing on the parapet of the Redan, waving his sword and urging his men to follow him, a bullet struck him in the eye, and taking an upward direction, passed through the brain. His fearless courage, although for the first time under fire, has been several times remarked. I fear this is but too authentic, as our assistant-surgeon, who was working in the hospital of the 30th, assures me that he saw him brought in dead. [*He came to our tent at 9.30 & reported a young man of the 30th, handsome, well-built, name Deane, quite a lad, shot through the brain while springing on the parapet of the Redan & waving his sword to his men – the ball entered at the eye & took an upward direction. I have written to his mother. I asked for a lock of hair to enclose but they said it was so clotted & bloody it was better not sent so (I) am to send his epaulettes & buttons. ... The boy was most plucky – not content with having been right through the Redan & come out unhurt, after he had remained some time in the trench he said: it was very*

poor fun & he would go & rally the fellows again – so he must
needs scramble a second time on the parapet whence he fell directly
headlong.]³⁰

The firing is just as continuous, – just as rapid, – just as
heavy. I am told the Guards are not yet gone down. Oh! who
can tell, save those who are on the spot, in whose ears the
guns roar incessantly, what it is to see friends one hour in
youth, and health, and strength, and the next hour to hear of
them, not as ill, or dying, but as dead, – absolutely dead? Ah!
these are things that make life terrible.

Colonel Norcott, of the Rifles, is a prisoner, and I hear
unwounded. He sprang first into the Redan with his usual
courage and recklessness; and the two men who followed
immediately behind him were instantly shot, and he was
taken prisoner before he had time to turn round to look for
fresh supports. He will soon be exchanged we hope. Meantime who will buy and keep that pretty, prancing, chestnut
pony he was riding last night when he took his way with his
battalion to the trenches?

[*September 11th – 'Sebastopol est prise' – the cry was echoed in*
Paris months ago. Now it rings through every ravine and valley of
the camp – 'Sebastopol est prise' – And yet, strange to say, there is
no elation, no cheers, no drunkenness, no bonfires, except the vast
bonfire of the smoking blazing city, which obscures the whole
horizon and which fills the air with a smoke as heavy & black, as
the hearts of the Russians themselves. … During the night I was
too exhausted not to sleep, but woke this morning by repeated &
violent explosions. I listened – no guns – no musketry. Presently
news came down. The Russians had evacuated the whole place –
and we were in possession of their forts, their town, their guns.
Then I thought of my many friends: General Markham,
Windham, Norcott, Daubeny, Lord A. Vane, Lord Arthur Hay.
Poor Buckley fell asleep before, and my heart grew still. Henry
mounted & rode to the Front, he returned after five hours – he
had been though every English & Russian work – no soldiers were

allowed in the town, which was mined everywhere. An Engineer officer was sent in to cut the wires. All my friends are safe – thank God!]

Wednesday, 12th – Since writing the foregoing I have been three or four times to the front. On Monday we endeavoured to ride as far as the Redan and Malakoff, but were stopped by the Cavalry, who were posted as sentries just this side of the twenty-one gun battery. On Sunday Henry rode up at eleven a.m., and after making such inquiries after our friends as might tend to relieve our anxieties on their account, he went on to the Redan. He described it to me as a heap of ruins, with wonderfully constructed defences, and with bomb-proof niches and corners, where the Russian officers on duty in the battery lived, and where were found pictures, books, cards, and glass and china for dinner services.

Le Capitaine Müel called on me on Sunday, and told me the French loss was 17 general officers killed and wounded, and about 22,000 men. This I have since heard reduced, I think correctly, to 10,000 .

On Sunday evening as it grew dusk I ordered the pony Charley, and rode up to the Turkish heights. From thence I could see distinctly the south side in flames. I counted ten separate fires. It was a magnificent sight, and one which afforded me, in common I fancy with many more, greater satisfaction than pain. I could not think at such a moment of the destruction and desolation of war. I could only remember that the long-coveted prize was ours at last, and I felt no more compunction for town or for Russian than the hound whose lips are red with blood does for the fox which he has chased through a hard run. It was a lawful prize, purchased, God knows! dearly enough, and I felt glad that we had got it.

[... *the whole place is ablaze – Forts Paul & Alexander, & Quarantine are blown up, the shipping is mostly destroyed, not a Russian in the place – tho' I see their lights gleaming on the plateau by Mackenzie's Farm. An attack on the Tchernaya is*

universally expected – & we expect to move in a day or two up to
Simpheropol or somewhere. Meantime I am getting chilled again
– and it is getting dark – so I give Master Whiskers a touch with
the spur – and he never stops till he reaches his Stable when I find
dinner ready & Henry & I drink the 'taking of Sebastopol & a
speedy end to the War' in Crockford's champagne – & then go to
bed to try and get rid of the scorching, disgusting wind. The army
must rest for two days or more. Meantime Major & Mrs Forrest
dine with us on Tuesday, also Col. Peel & Col. Lawrenson and I
rayther flatter myself our new Maltese cook – who costs us £100 a
year – will turn out quite as good a dinner as any in the Crimea.
This is a wonderful letter, & not a bad picture of our life here –
beginning with a fight & ending with a dinner. I am delighted to
hear that my box is on the way out as now, unless it arrives soon,
I may miss it & I do not think I can get thru' the winter without
it. Mrs Finnegan goes home as soon as the last linen I wrote for
arrives. Ever yr very sleepy & affect. Sister F I Duberly.

   Henry was present when the funeral service was read over 700 of
our fellows buried in the trench of the Redan. He says the dead were
awful. The 23rd behaved infamously – but they are all recruits and
young boys & got frightened, left their officers & ran! – & left the
old soldiers. Consequently the officers & old soldiers are much cut
up.]

On Monday I rode to see Major Daubeny, 62nd Regiment,
Colonel Windham, and General Markham. Whilst calling on
Colonel Windham, I heard of poor Colonel Eman's mortal
wound. Our loss in officers has been heavy enough, I believe
149. In the 62nd Regiment 180 men went into attack, and 105
were killed or wounded. There can be no doubt that the
assault was unexpected, and the Malakoff taken by surprise.
The Malakoff was the key to the whole fortress; the Malakoff
once taken and held by the French, the Redan became
untenable by the Russians. We assaulted it after a curiously ill-
managed fashion, and we were driven back. About that there
exists no doubt. Nor should we ever have forced the Redan,

unless the plan of attack had been entirely reorganised. Two hundred, a hundred and fifty, or three hundred men out of every regiment in the division formed the storming party. Men who had been fighting behind batteries and gabions for nearly a twelvemonth could not be brought to march steadily under fire from which they could get no cover. As Colonel Windham said, in speaking of the assault, 'The men, the moment they saw a gabion, ran to it as they would to their wives, and would not leave its shelter.' Why not have taken all this into consideration, and ordered the newly-arrived regiments to lead the assault? – the 13th Light Infantry and the 56th.[31]

By daybreak on Sunday morning, just as we were preparing to 'go at' the Redan again, it was discovered to have been evacuated during the night. Malakoff gone – all was gone; and by night on Sunday all that remained in Sebastopol were burning houses, mines, and some wounded men, prisoners. The English until today have been denied admission to the town, except with a pass provided by Sir R. Airey. The French, on the contrary, have been plundering and destroying everything they saw. The town was mined, and these mines, going off perpetually, made it very unsafe for amateurs.[32] Nothing, however, deters the French. Five officers were blown up today; and a Zouave came out driving a pig, carrying a dead sheep, a cloak, and a samovar, and wearing a helmet, like those which were taken at Alma, and brought on board the *Danube*.

It is exceedingly difficult to gain admission into the Redan and the town. Until today orders were only procured through the quartermaster-general; but I see it is in general orders now, that any general officer can give a pass; and Colonel Windham, who commanded the storming party, and distinguished himself by his magnificent conduct, and his frantic efforts to rally and lead on the men, while standing himself *inside the Redan, and on the parapet*, is made governor of that quarter of the south side appropriated to the English.[33] I need scarcely say, the English quarter is the worst, containing all the public buildings round the dockyard, the custom-house, hospital, &c., but no dwelling-houses that are not reduced to the merest heap of ruins.

[*Charley Windham, Brigadier General of the 2nd division is appointed governor of Sebastopol and is trying to clean out and mend up the magnificent public buildings for winter barracks. ...*

Our dinner when Mrs Forrest dined went off wonderfully. It poured all day – so the mud *was up to your ankles & over. She came in bronze slippers & little galoshes – an opera cloak – a silk gown all over flounces & six bracelets. Her poor feet and legs and petticoat a (blot) draggle of mud so I gave her stockings & then it went off all right. The men had to ask her leave to smoke – but she bore that better than I expected.*]

Thursday, 13th – A memorable day of my life, for on it I rode into the English batteries, into the Redan, the Malakoff, the Little Redan, and all over our quarter of Sebastopol. Such a day merits a detailed description.

Eight consecutive hours spent in sightseeing under a blazing sun is no light and ladylike délassement at any time, but when the absorbing interest, the horrible associations and excitement of the whole, is added to the account, I cannot wonder at my fatigue of last night, or my headache of today.

[*Descriptions of the various works you will see much better in the papers than I can tell you. But you may be interested to hear of my knowledge of the place. Henry was in there about five hours after it was evacuated but as a woman stalking about sight-seeing among the dead & dying is very like a vulture or any other unclean bird of prey* [34] *I remained at home having in truth no strength or heart to move being exhausted with the fatigue & anxieties of the previous day.*]

So many descriptions, pictorial and otherwise, have gone home of our own batteries, that I need not stop to describe them in their present half-dismantled state; so, clambering down (how wonderfully the Turkish ponies can climb!) the stony front of our advanced parallel, we canter across the open space, and ride at a gallop over the steep parapet of the salient angle of the Redan. [*Well we rode on, & on, past our first, second, third, fourth parallels till we came into the open place, across which our men charged the salient angle of the Redan – the parapet was perpendicular enough only to be taken at a gallop, a spring, a rush & a scramble & we stood on the parapet of the Redan.*] 'Look down,' said Henry, 'into the trench immediately beneath you; there, where it is partly filled up, our men are buried. I stood by Mr Wright, on Sunday morning, when he read the funeral service over 700 at once.' [*The newly turned earth in the half-filled trench was their only grave, and the frowning battery their grand & solemn monument.*]

What wonderful engineering! What ingenuity in the thick rope-work which is woven before the guns, leaving only a little hole through which the man laying the gun can take his aim, and which is thoroughly impervious to rifle shot! The Redan is a succession of little batteries, each containing two or three guns, with traverses behind each division; and hidden away under gabions, sand-bags, and earth, are little huts in which the officers and men used to live. Walking down amongst these (for we were obliged to dismount) we found that tradesmen had lived in some of them. Henry picked up a pair of lady's lasts the precise size of my own foot. Coats, caps, bayonets lay about, with black bread and broken guns. The centre, the open space between the Redan and the second line of defence, was completely ploughed by our thirteen-inch shells, fragments of which, together with round shot, quite paved the ground. We collected a few relics, such as I could stow away in my habit and saddle-pockets, and then rode down into the town.

Actually in Sebastopol! No longer looking at it through a glass, or even going down to it, but riding amongst its ruins and its streets. We had fancied the town was almost uninjured – so calm, and white, and fair did it look from a distance; but the ruined walls, the riddled roofs, the green cupola of the church, split and splintered to ribands, told a very different tale. Here were wide streets leading past one or two large handsome detached houses built of stone; a little further on, standing in a handsome open space, are the barracks, with large windows, a fine stone façade of great length, several of the lower windows having carronades[35] run out of them, pointing their grim muzzles towards our batteries. Whilst I am gazing at these, a sudden exclamation from Henry, and a violent shy from the pony, nearly start me from my saddle. It is two dead Russians lying, almost in a state of decomposition, at an angle of the building; while in the corner a man is sitting up, with his hands in his lap, and eyes open looking at us. We turn to see if he is only wounded, so life-like are his attitude and face; no, he has been dead for days.

A little further on we came to the harbour, and by the many mast-heads we count the number of ships. Here, too, are fragments of the bridge which I had watched the Russians building, and across which I had seen them so often pass and repass. There is a kind of terrace, with a strong wooden railing, overlooking the sea, and underneath us is a level grass-plat, going down with handsome stone steps to the water's edge. Following the wooden railing, we overlooked what had evidently been a foundry, and a work-shop for the dockyard; Russian jackets, tools and wheel-barrows, were lying about, and hunting among the ruins was a solitary dog.

But all this time we are trying to find our way to Brigadier General Windham's office near the custom house. To get there we must ride round to the head of the dry docks, as the bridges are either broken or unsafe. What is it that makes the air so pestilential at the head of the dry docks? Anything so putrid, so nauseating, so terrible, never assailed us before.

There is nothing but three or four land transport carts, covered with tarpaulin, and waiting at the corner. For Heaven's sake, ride faster, for the stench is intolerable. We go on towards the custom house, still followed by this atmosphere: there must be decaying cattle and horses behind the houses; and yet they do not smell like this! Admiral Sir Edmund Lyons and Admiral Bruat are riding by, so we stop in a tolerably sweet place to congratulate each other on meeting in Sebastopol. We then continue our road to the custom house. What is it? It cannot surely be – oh, horror! – a heap, a piled-up heap of human bodies in every stage of putrid decomposition, flung out into the street, and being carted away for burial.[36] As soon as we gained possession of the town, a hospital was discovered in the barracks, to which the attention of our men was first attracted by screams and cries. Entering, they found a large number of wounded and dying; but underneath a heap of dead men, who, as he lay on the floor, fell over him and died, was an English officer of the 90th Regiment, who being badly wounded, and taken prisoner, was put into this foul place, and left, as in the case of the hospital near the custom house, to perish at his leisure of hunger and pain. He had had no food for three days, and the fever of his wound, together with the ghastly horrors round him, had driven this poor Englishman to raving madness; and so he was found, yelling and naked. I think the impression made upon me by the sight of that foul heap of green and black, glazed and shrivelled flesh I never shall be able to throw entirely away.[37] To think that each individual portion of that corruption was once perhaps the life and world of some loving woman's heart – that human living hands had touched, and living lips had pressed with clinging and tenderest affection, forms which in a week could become, oh, so loathsome, so putrescent!

At the moment, however, and I think it a wise ordinance, no sight such as war produces strikes deeply on the mind. We turned quickly back from this terrible sight, and soon after left the town. Riding up towards the Little Redan, we saw where the slaughter of the Russians had principally been. The ground was covered with patches and half-dried pools of blood, caps soaked in blood and brains, broken bayonets, and shot and shell; four or five dead horses, shot as they brought up ammunition for the last defence of the Malakoff. Here we met Colonel Norcott, of the Rifles, who had been reported a prisoner, riding the same chestnut pony which has had honourable mention before. Our congratulations on his escape, when we fancied him marching with the retreating Russians, were neither few nor insincere. The Malakoff lay just before us. I am told that it is, and it struck me as being, one of the most wonderful examples of engineering work possible. It is so constructed, that unless a shot fell precisely on the right spot, it could do no harm. What with gabions, sand-bags, traverses, counter-traverses, and various other means of defence, it seemed to me that a residence in the Malakoff was far safer and more desirable than a residence in the town. Buried underground were officers' huts, men's huts, and a place used as a sort of mess room, with glass lamps, and packs of cards. We are not allowed to carry any outward and visible signs of plunder, but I filled my habit pockets and saddle pockets with various small items, as reliques of these famous batteries and the famous town – lasts, buttons, and grape shot from the Redan; cards, a glass salt-cellar, an English fuzee [a kind of match], and the screw of a gun from the Malakoff; a broken bayonet from the Little Redan; and rifle bullets from the workshop in the town. Then, as it was growing late, we rode back to camp by the Woronzov Road, and down the French heights on to the Balaklava plain. On these heights are still retained a few guns in position, which are, and have been ever since the 25th of October, worked by Turkish Artillery-men. They are famous for their Artillery practice; and when the heights were reinforced after the Balaklava charge, they were placed at these guns, with a French regiment close behind them in case they should run. With these Turks I have made quite a pleasant little speaking acquaintance, as we are constantly scrambling either up or down their heights. 'Bono Jeanna,' 'Bono atla,' 'Bono, bono,' being the extent of our conversation, varied sometimes by 'Bono Cavallo,' according to the province from which 'Johnny' comes.

September 17th – I went again last Saturday, provided with a permit from the French Head Quarters, to see that part of Sebastopol, and the French works which lie to the left – the French parallels running to almost within a stone's throw of the opposing battery, the Bastion du Mât, the Garden Battery, and the fortifications of the town itself. The French have by far the most extensive quarter, but I begin to doubt whether they have the best. We have such fine ranges of buildings for barracks; while they have streets of ruined dwelling houses, with the addition, however, of the Court of Justice, a very handsome building, and two churches. I was not much interested with what we saw in our expedition; indeed, we could not well be, for we were scarcely permitted to enter any of the houses without producing our pass, and making more fuss and chatter than it was worth. Many French and English soldiers had evidently been drinking 'success to the war,' for they lay about in all directions hopelessly drunk. One French *sous-officier* professed himself so astonished and delighted at seeing an English lady in Sebastopol, that he induced us to turn back half a street's length, in order to present me with some 'loot.' I fancied, of course, it was something that I could carry in my saddle-pockets; fancy, then, our dismay, when he approached with the solid leg of a large worktable, with a handsome claw, about three feet high, and proportionably heavy. He tried to fasten it to my saddle, but Bob would none of it, and snorted and backed. We all, with many protestations of gratitude, declined the leg, and accepted a piece of Russian black bread instead – more portable and more valuable.

We heard last night that the Artillery are under orders to be inspected tomorrow morning; and we also hear a rumour that all the Cavalry are to march up towards Simpheropol. It has been much commented on, that no movement was made by the army immediately on the evacuation of the town; and, on discussing the matter with one of the authorities, I was told that at one time we were under orders for Eupatoria, but next day they were countermanded. The Cavalry have done nothing since the 25th of October.[38] We are now nearly 4,000 strong, with an enormous amount of Artillery. Our horses are in good condition, our men are fairly healthy; and if they do not keep us out too long, and the Commissariat can be urged into acquitting itself with anything like decency for once, we may have a very brilliant little campaign of about three weeks in comparative comfort. At the end of three weeks the weather will become such that we must pack up, and be off to winter quarters. These are to be upon the Bosphorus. Oh! how we had hoped they would have been in sunny Egypt instead of on the shores of the draughty, miry Bosphorus, with its 'Devil's Currents' both of sea and wind!

[*We certainly go to winter quarters, perhaps to the Bosphorus, perhaps to Egypt, perhaps home. The Duke of Newcastle said something of our going home the other day – but I dare not allow myself to think of it. … all sailing ships being ordered home.*]

The Naval Brigade, now that there is no longer need for the Sailors' Battery, are all ordered on board their respective ships. I think there are very few but are sorry to leave their comparatively free life on shore for the imprisonment and strict discipline of a man-of-war. They would be (if we were to remain the winter) a very serious loss to us, as there were no workmen, carpenters, joiners, builders, half so handy or so willing to assist as those in the Naval Brigade. There certainly was no camp in which more kind consideration for others, more real active help, has been afforded to all than in that of the sailors; and their cheerfulness and willingness to labour encouraged and comforted all through the difficulties and sufferings of last winter.

I rode down to Balaklava a day or two since; and while the memory of the miseries of that terrible time are fresh in my mind, I may as well say how much, in common with everything else, Balaklava has changed. It is no longer a heap of dirty lazar houses, infested with vermin, and reeking with every kind of filth. Its principal street is no longer crowded with ragged, starving soldiers, hauling along dying horses by the head, and making the houses echo back their curses and blows until one's very heart grew cold. Balaklava was then filthy, naked, and starved. Balaklava is now washed, and dressed, and fed. Balaklava was ugly and loathsome to see; Balaklava now is fresh, healthy, and even pretty. Neat rows of store huts have replaced the wretched houses of the Russians. The navvies have their stable at the entrance, and in the midst of the town is an open space; walls are pulled down, the road is raised, and a strong railing runs along its outer side; rows of trees are planted, and down the centre street the railway runs, giving dignity and importance to the place. Admiral Boxer did wonders towards facilitating the arrangements for embarkation and disembarkation, by the construction of his admirable quays, as well as by reclaiming the shallow water and marshy ground at the head of the harbour, which was generally covered last winter with the half-imbedded carcases of bullocks, and was always emitting a malaria most foul and deleterious. I think the thanks of the army, or a handsome national testimonial, ought to be presented to Mr Russell, the eloquent and truthful correspondent of *The Times*, as being the mainspring of all this happy change. That it was effected through the agency of the Press there can be no doubt; and the principal informant of the Press was 'Our own Correspondent,' whose letters produced the leaders in *The Times*, the perusal of which, in many a sodden and snow-covered tent, cheered the hearts that were well nigh failing, and gave animation, hope, and courage to all. More than once, when I have been fireless and shivering, the arrival of the then often delayed mail would bring me a copy of *The Times*; and its hot indignation, its hearty sympathy, and the mutterings of its wrathful anger have warmed me, and revived me, and made me feel for the moment almost like my former self.[*]

We are still in a state of uncertainty whether we move or not.

September 18th – Nearly opposite the loopholed walls of Sebastopol, and about half a mile distant from it, lies a ravine with a church and graveyard, behind the French advanced works, and within easy range of the Russian shot. The tall spire of the church is covered, in common with all their sacred buildings that I have seen, with lead painted green; and it is only when you are close to the church that you discern the ravages of shot and shell. We turned our horses' heads down the precipitous side of the hill, and tied them to the churchyard gate. Trees of various growths filled the enclosure, and flowering shrubs, laburnums, and acacias, with clumps of lilac. Struck by the shots of their own

---

[*]The evil done by the *Times* to the Crimean army predominated greatly over the good. The *Times* spread the news that Sebastopol had fallen, and when this turned out to be untrue, continued to predict its immediate capture, thus preventing private speculators from carrying supplies to the Crimea. The *Times* had previously softened the horrors and blunders of Devna and Varna and it again for weeks concealed the sufferings and wants of the army before Sebastopol, and suppressed the accounts given by Mr Russell of the mismanagement and inefficiency which prevailed in almost all departments. It was by means of private letters, handed from man to man and read with the greatest eagerness, that the true state of the case became known; and it was only when starvation and cold had done their work, and concealment wàs no longer possible, that the *Times* broke silence, and endeavoured to gain credit as the mouthpiece of public indignation. – 1855 Editor.

people, the monuments and gravestones lay scattered and broken all around, while the sun, glancing through the thick green leaves, played upon broken pillar and shattered cross. How I lingered under the shadow of the trees! How the repose of the place and scene diffused itself over my heart, which never felt so travel-stained with the dusty road of life as now! My life seemed to stand still, and be wrapped for the moment in a repose as deep as that of the slumberers around me, whom shot or shell could not waken, nor bugle-call arouse. At last I heard myself repeating those exquisite lines by some author whose name I cannot remember –

> Give me the soft green turf, the fresh wild flowers,
>   A quiet grave in some lone churchyard's shade,
> With the free winds to breathe a requiem, where,
>   Imploring rest, the restless heart is laid.

'Why Mrs Duberly, you are a living representation of Hervey's "Meditations amongst the Tombs!"[39] For heaven's sake come away from the churchyard, or you will not be amusing any more all day.' So I mounted, and we speedily got into the hard clattering road again.

[*In my life among the soldiers I have few opportunities, nay, I would <u>scorn</u> & <u>dread</u> to let them know such thoughts were ever in my mind. Half of them know me as the never omitted guest, where a dinner is wanted to be amusing & brilliant & half as the rider of their troublesome horses. I wish I was a man.*[40]]

Returning home from this long ride, we were sensible of a sudden and keen change in the atmosphere of this always variable climate. The wind veered to the north, a cold deep purple haze covered the distant hills, clouds from the sea came up full of promise, not of a good hard soaking rain, but of that penetrating cold mist than which nothing is so chilling and depressing. We lost no time in hurrying through the gathering darkness, back to the camp; and, having arrived there, lighted our stove for the first time this autumn. How comfortable and pleasant the hut looked in the warm fire-light! Thanks to the kindness of many contributors, I have been supplied with sufficient copies of the *Illustrated London News* to paper the walls entirely. This has afforded employment to my ingenuity. But the walls when covered looked too black and white for my fastidious ideas; they wanted warmth, colour, and effect. I delight in colours. They give me almost as much pleasure as music. I like gorgeous music and gorgeous colour. I would have all my surroundings formed for the gratification of this taste if I could. I have therefore tried to colour those pictures which appeared most to require it, and the effect on the walls of our hut is now, I flatter myself, good; at any rate they look home-like and soigné, which is a great point. We both confess to an incipient affection for this little wooden room, where we have lived so many months; and we shall be quite sorry to leave it, never to see it any more, when we go down to the Bosphorus for our winter quarters in November.

The facility of attaching oneself is a great misfortune. If it adds a little to the enjoyment of life at times, it increases the pain of it, I think, in a double proportion. My anxieties, for instance, when my dear friend and companion the chestnut horse embarks for the Bosphorus, will be positively painful to myself, and very probably a nuisance to my husband.

September 23rd – After some days of cold and wet, mud and discomfort, the sun blazed out again in all his strength. Nature, washed and refreshed, looked red, green, and golden, in the warm autumn tints. We came out like the lizards; and although there were still heavy thunder-clouds about, we disregarded them, and at three o'clock on the 20th started to join a party of twelve who were to meet at Kamiesh, and dine at the *Luxembourg*. We were unpunctual, and started late; but made up for it on the road, or rather along the track of the ravine from Karani to Kamiesh. It was well we lost no time, as a thunder-shower came pouring down just as we reached the shelter of the stables. The dinner really deserves a place amongst the annals of the war, and is worthy of description by an abler pen than mine. But I most enjoyed the exciting ride home by moonlight, galloping along the narrow track, by furze and bush, past carcases of French bullocks left unburied, and lying ghastly in the moonlight, a terror to all ponies, and a horror to our own noses. Every now and then a clink underneath an iron shoe tells of fragments of a broken bottle, but it is too dark to see; and a Turkish pony never stumbles or puts his foot down in a wrong place by any accident: and so on we go, our ponies leaning on the bit, till they reach the watering troughs of Karani, where they plunge their heads in to their eyes, and then walk steadily along the slippery slope of the hill side down into the hollow where the Cavalry is encamped.

The certainty that we are to leave the Crimea for winter quarters makes us anxious to revisit every part of its known world once more before we go; and yesterday we rode to the Sardinian observatory, a building erected on the summit of their highest hill, and from which a wonderful view is obtained of all the surrounding English, French, and Russian camps. We left this observatory behind us, passing to the right of it, and soon after came upon the tents which form the French depôt for General D'Allonville's Cavalry at Baidar. Beyond these again, on the extreme outpost, were Turkish Cavalry, and Turkish guns in position, overlooking a deep and precipitous hollow closed in with rocks. This was the neutral ground, across which Russian and Turks could glare at each other to their hearts' content. A dignified wave of the hand from the Turkish sentry warned us that we could not pass; so we rounded the base of the hill, and, by a judicious turn into a vineyard, came up with the *avante poste*, also Turkish, and were able to look down the dizzy height into the deep hollow.

On every side the rocks rose perpendicular, stern, and bare, while far down beneath our feet lay the valley, clothed with trees and shrubs, appearing such a mass of verdure that the Tchernaya, which ran swiftly through it, foaming like a mountain torrent, looked but a silver thread wound in and out amongst the overhanging trees. A mill and a lane, scarcely perceptible through the trees, but running – the lane I mean, not the mill – close alongside the river, were all that occupied this profound valley. The only music to which that mill-wheel ever could have turned – the only song the miller ever could have sung – must have been the *De profundis clamavi*.[41]

The Turkish sentry close to us suddenly began to jabber away with a face of unmistakable delight. He had evidently discovered something, for his picket soon joined him, and, after some little conversation, turned to us, and said, pointing with his finger to the side of the opposite rock, 'Russes.' We could not find them, even with our glasses, though we saw Cossack horsemen further on. The 'Russes' whom he saw were probably tending a large herd of cattle, which was grazing on the opposite hill-top, not 1,000 yards from us. He took the glasses, and appeared much pleased with them. He then pointed out the Turkish Cavalry picket; and having remarked on the number of fires which blazed last night on all the Russian hills, we exchanged bows, and rode away; for the sun was set, and the moon looking at us over the shoulder of the hill. Nor could we stay to listen to the Sardinian band, which was playing on the plateau near Kamara, but had to make the best of our road to reach the camp.

Thunder-showers have not failed us these last three days. Yesterday morning the Highlanders at Kamara were deluged, and the watering places at Kadikoi were fetlock deep in mud – a faint foreshadowing of what the roads would have been after two or three months' rain, had not the siege been stopped, and all the army turned into road-makers. Beautiful roads are now being constructed: one runs by the side of the railroad from Kadikoi, joining that made by the French last year, and lately put in thorough repair by the Army Works' Corps; another runs from the Woronzow road to the French position on the heights; while one railway is to be constructed from Balaklava to Kamara to bring provisions for the Sardinian army, and another to Kamiesh to transport food and forage for the French.

The little stream which runs from Kadikoi into the sea at Balaklava, instead of being in a shallow bed, and deluging the plain after every two hours' rain, flows now between two high banks, so that it cannot easily overflow. It is really a pity – except, of course, on account of the trenches – that the siege is over; for if we remained here another year or two, we should be as comfortably established as if we were at home.

September 25th – Yesterday, to everybody's infinite surprise and pleasure, Mr Clowes, who was wounded and taken prisoner at Balaklava, walked up into camp in a shooting coat and wide-awake[42], looking precisely as if he had never been absent, and answering everyone's greetings with much the same sort of dignified composure that a very big dog exhibits in noticing a little one.

I had taken an opportunity afforded by a flag of truce, to send him in a letter about a month ago; but he was then travelling down to Odessa, and did not receive it. He gives a most painful account of his adventures on the 25th of October, and afterwards in his march up the country. He was wounded in the back by a grape shot, which took him across both shoulders; but he rode on until his horse was shot, when he, of course, fell to the ground. Seeing our brigade returning from the charge, he tried to run after them, but soon fell down from loss of blood. His first thought was to lie quiet, and pretend to be dead, so that he might have a chance of escaping after dark; but he very soon saw parties of Cossacks coming down, who ran their lances into everyone of the English lying on the ground. Perceiving that the really dead were stabbed as well as those who pretended to be so, he rose, as well as his wound would allow, and throwing down his sword, gave himself up to a Russian officer of Lancers. He took him and Mr Chadwick, of the 17th Lancers, before the General, who asked them several questions, all of which they declined to answer. They were then sent to Simpheropol, and soon after they began their march to Perekop. They marched on foot in company with prisoners and convicts, and at night were locked up with them. They remonstrated, but were told that there were no horses or means of conveyance to be had, and that there was no other way of transporting them. Their sufferings during this severe march were very great; aggravated, of course, by the utter want of consideration shown them. The last part of the time during which Mr Clowes was a prisoner appears to have passed pleasantly enough. He went into society, and travelled post. I think his case is a hard one, as he cannot get a month's leave to return to England, if only to provide himself with clothes. He has no uniforms, no kit, and has been obliged to buy back his own horse.[43]

Yesterday we rode up the heights till we overlooked Vernutka, and then returned by the good and even road made by Sir Colin Campbell along the summit of the heights, through his own camp down to Balaklava. After all, Englishmen are not so helpless, so hopeless, and so foolish, as they tried hard last year to make themselves out to be. I think they rested so entirely on the prestige that attached itself to the name of a British soldier, that they thought the very stars would come out of their courses to sustain the lustre of their name. Alas! their name was very literally dragged through the mud, during the miry winter months.

Upon the strength of the evacuation of the south side of Sebastopol, the Fleet made a demonstration in their turn. They all got up their steam and their anchors, and sailed away, some to Balaklava, some towards Eupatoria. One of the first-rates crowded her forecastle with marines, dressed in their uniforms, and made as if for Eupatoria. This was merely a ruse, to persuade the Russians that she was transporting regular troops.

The Tchernaya outposts are still vigorously watched. The French have it that 125,000 men are encamped on the plateau and about the Belbec, with the intention of making a rush upon our position should we weaken it by sending any considerable force to harass the retreating garrison. The Russians in that case aim at burning Balaklava and Kamiesh; but their murderous designs do not prevent our sleeping just as soundly in the neighbourhood of Balaklava, or enjoying the triumphs of art in the shape of the Luxembourg dinners at Kamiesh.

The Indian summer is come to us, and we are again almost complaining of heat at mid-day; whilst the clear sky and brilliant moonlight show us how enjoyable autumn would be in this climate, if we had all the advantages of the fertile soil, and could live in peace and plenty. The Russians, however, appear determined that we shall not have much peace. They have begun to throw shot and shell into the town from the earthworks on the north. One of these round shot came through the roof of Brigadier General Windham's house, and fortunately struck without doing any injury to the inmates.[44]

Could not the fleet have so annoyed the Russians with their mortar boats as to prevent the construction of these works? And if so, why did they not do so?

A Frenchwoman, riding in the French quarter of the town yesterday, is reported to have had her horse struck by a shell. For the truth of this I cannot vouch; but it is not improbable, as on the day I was last in the town, the firing was very heavy, and the riding consequently dangerous. It has also been said by General Morris that none of the French Cavalry will move into winter quarters, as the object of the large Russian force on the plateau, and by the Belbec, is to make a rush upon Balaklava, as soon as they find the army sufficiently weakened to admit of their doing so with a chance of success. We called today upon General Bosquet, who was very severely wounded at the assault on the Malakoff, and to our surprise and pleasure, he was sufficiently recovered to be able to admit us. We were shown into his room, which forms one of the compartments of a large wooden hut, and found him reclining in an armchair, having been able to sit up only within the last two days. He was struck by a piece of a 13-inch shell under the right arm and on the right side; it had completely smashed all the muscles and sinews, and his arm is as yet powerless above the elbow-joint. He showed us the piece of shell by which he was struck; it could not weigh less than four pounds. It is astonishing how he escaped with life, from a wound inflicted by so terrible an implement of war. He appeared cheerful enough, and glad to 'causer un peu'; said he was ordered away for change of air, but did not wish to leave his post here, and fully coincided in my quotation, pointing to his wounded side, 'On ne marche pas à la gloire par le bonheur.' In his room was a *fauteuil* taken from Sebastopol, and which he had very appropriately covered with the green turbans worn by the Zouaves of his division.

[I see the Emperor [Napoleon] has been shot at again. I have just read a well-written little 1/- book 'The life of Napoleon III'. What a life his has been – I should like mine to resemble it as far as the adventure, the excitement & gratified ambition go. Talk of vultures, gnawing at your heart, there's no vulture whose beak is half as sharp as that of an ambition that Will *be gratified – and has no means for being so.* They say *we are to be quartered 20 miles from Scutari, away from Pera. I* hope *so – I dread Constantinople, its dirt, its expense & its mixed society. I wish with all my heart & soul I could get home, at least I mean* we *– for you know how impossible it is for me to leave Henry. He has now got his medal and three clasps – has been through the Crimean campaign – & seen the end of Sebastopol – it does seem hard that*

we must continue out here after all ... I fear I shall never again be 'the man I was' – in two or three ways my health is breaking up. ... Never was anything like the distribution of medals. Men have got medals & clasps who were never on the ground even. ... In fact they are flung away. I think the medals and clasps are rather an insult than a reward, but perhaps my notions are old-fashioned. When I saw Henry get his medal I grew as nervous as possible – & drowned his jacket in tears as I sewed it on, but nobody else seemed to think anything of it. Tis a wonderful world. A brilliant little affair at Kertch.][45]

September 27th – News reached us today of two *affaires de Cavalerie*: one with General D'Allonville's division, at Eupatoria; the other with the 10th Hussars, at Kertch. These reports require, of course, official confirmation; but, as the engagement at Eupatoria appears to receive credence from one or two French generals whom I have seen today, it must be tolerably authentic. We rode this afternoon to the Sardinian observatory, and, after admiring, as all must do, the neatness of the fortification as well as its strength, we ascended to the telescope, which is placed at the summit of a high *tour d'observation*. By its aid we could discern huts in the course of erection, and the plateau by the Spur Battery, and could even see the Russians sending their horses down to water – one man riding and leading a horse. The Russian huts are wooden and like ours; while the Sardinians are digging out and covering with earth huts, that will not only be waterproof, but absolutely warm, from the solidity and closeness with which they are built. There never was such a pretty little army sent into the field as that of the Sardinians. Had they not established their reputation by repulsing the Russians on the 16th of August, they would be still considered in the light of the prettiest 'toy army' that ever was sent to fight, each department is so pretty and so perfect – their Artillery, their Cavalry, their Guards, and, above all, their band.

[*I went all round the Sardinian fortifications the other day –
they are beautifully made, well engineered & very strong, in
commanding positions – their neatness, & finish are beyond all
praise, as contrasted with our slovenly, coarse work or with the
French. … The Sardinian heights were blazing with beacon lights
– an hour ago, the Russians have 120,000 men between us & the
Balbec, it may not mean anything after all; don't you remember –
how the red blaze on Skiddar roused the burghers of Carlisle.* [46]*

We have two dinner parties this week & to my terror on Friday
the Marquis de Forte and le General Féray with an ADC & Col.
Foley attaché to Pellissier. On Saturday – Michaelmas Day – we
have a party of the 'heroes of the Redan' to eat roast goose.*]

Today is my birthday, and in consideration of it, I was
allowed to choose my own horse to ride, and my own
country to ride over. I chose the celebrated Café au lait, that
prince of pretty Indian horses, and rode him to the observatory, and back by the Sardinian band. Here we met several
officers of the Highland Brigade, and heard that General
Markham, on whom we had all built such magnificent hopes
of British achievement under British generalship, was going
on board ship ill; I am sorry to say, very ill, and it is said he
must return to England. Coming out with all the prestige
which surrounded his name, I think this sudden sinking into
ill-health, and the abandonment of the army, will have its
bad effect. We want good generals; we want men who are in a
position to lead, not brigades, for we have good brigadiers
enough, but divisions or even the whole army; we want men
with youth, energy, and courage to fight against and pull
through any adverse fortune that may assail them. Our best
general, our most unflinching leader, has been the Press. To
the columns of *The Times* the army owes a 'National Debt';
and so long as every incident of this war is laid before the
public at home, so long as every man is familiarised, as it
were, with the life of the soldier, so long will this war be a
popular war, and so long will the sympathies of all England

be enlisted on our side. We suppose that the campaign for this year is over. The Cavalry, we understand, are to go into winter quarters on the Bosphorus. It is now becoming late in autumn, and the nights, and even days, are chilly enough. No orders have been issued, nothing official is known. Should it be *at last* decided that we really embark for the Bosphorus, I trust we may find ourselves transferred to proper accommodation for man and horse; but, if not moved before many days, to say nothing of weeks, are over, we shall be much worse off on the Bosphorus than we should have been, had we been allowed to remain on our old ground and permitted to prepare ourselves, from our own resources, for a second winter in the Crimea.

THE END

'We take wonderful rides sometimes with Lord Cardigan, but not often as I detest him. Then we dine about seven and go into one of the officers' tents, generally Capt. Tomkinson's, till bedtime. There we sit on the ground just like the interior of a tent in the *Illustrated* [*London News*] and they smoke while I surreptitiously drink their rum and water and coffee.'

NOTES AND COMMENTARY

Chapter 1: The Voyage

Previously unpublished letters or parts of letters are printed in italic within square brackets. The source in this chapter is British Library MSS Add. 47218 A f.47. Unless otherwise stated, all letters are to Selina or Francis Marx.

1. She means small, like the little chamber made by the Shunamite woman on the wall of her house for the prophet Elisha. 2 Kings 4. 9-11.

2. British Army officers were provided with one soldier servant from their regiment to clean their kit, cook their meals, pitch their tents, empty slops and look after their horses etc. In addition they could pay for extra help from other soldiers or employ civilian servants. Fanny complained that the French officers were better treated. 'In the French army a Captain has <u>three</u> servants & three horses. We have 4 horses and are only allowed <u>one</u> servant from the regiment' (21 July 1855).
   Private Timothy Connell was born at Kingstown (now Dun Laoghaire), Ireland, and was a groom prior to his enlistment on 4 July 1845. He died on board the *Himalaya* on 13 September 1854.

3. S. is Selina, Fanny's eldest sister, favourite sibling and chief correspondent. W. is Wadham, Fanny's eldest brother; her letters to him do not appear to have survived. Mrs F. may have been Fanny's sister-in-law. Her second brother, Francis, had married Katherine, the daughter of Admiral Fellowes, and they took over Rowdeford House. Katherine would have been called Mrs Francis by servants within the family circle to differentiate her from Wadham's wife who, as the wife of the senior brother, was Mrs Locke. From comments in her surviving letters it is clear that Fanny corresponded regularly with Katherine and Francis, although these letters do not appear to have survived.

4. The steep, stepped streets of Valletta were haunted by beggars. Their cry *nix mangiare* (nothing to eat) was a mixture of Italian and German (*nichts*).

5. The Chasseurs d'Afrique were a light cavalry brigade from Algeria, created in 1831.

6. The Royal Naval Fleet was gradually changing from sail to steam, so that the British Army was conveyed to Turkey, and later to the Crimea, in a variety of steamer transports and sailing ships. In fact it would probably have taken no longer for the steamers, ferrying back and forth, to transport the entire Army. The conditions on board the slower sailing ships were so appalling that many horses died or sickened during the voyage.

7. From 'A Wet Sheet and a Flowing Sea', a sea-song by Allan Cunningham (1784-1842).

8. *Singleton Fontenoy RN, A Naval Novel*, 1850, by James Hannay (1827-73). The eponymous hero is sent to sea and has many adventures in the Mediterranean.

9. 'Et in Arcadia ego': the tomb inscription in the painting *The Arcadian Shepherds* by Nicolas Poussin (1594-1665).

10. Queen Adelaide, wife of William IV (Queen Victoria's uncle), had died in 1849.

11. Some sailing transports remained becalmed for up to a fortnight in the Dardanelles if they failed to secure a tow from a passing steamer.

12. The barracks at Scutari were later used as Army and Royal Navy hospitals for the sick and wounded transported from the Crimea and, until the arrival of Florence Nightingale in November 1854, became notorious for lack of hygiene and the general neglect of patients (p. 315).

13. Bob (*c.*1840-58) – Fanny's affection for Bob is such that it is occasionally difficult to tell whether she is referring to him or to Henry but her determination to protect both of them was at times the only thing that gave her the will to survive the campaign. Although mocked in some reviews for her constant references to him – 'There are almost as many Ohs! & Ahs! in her diary as "Bobs & cobs" which is saying a great deal' (*The Examiner*, December 1855) – Bob became a hero in his own right. On the return voyage in April 1856 she described his welcome to Selina. 'I must tell you that the arrival of Bob on board has made a great commotion. All the officers of the ship requested to have him pointed out and I hear they have each got some of his mane or tail'. He had suffered too much to accompany the Duberlys to India in 1857 and remained with Selina where he died suddenly a year later. 'We are

almost as sorry for his death as you will be;' wrote Selina, 'he led an easy life while in our care. "The Squire" very seldom worked him, & he ranged about in his large loose box more a show horse than anything: for everyone who came to the house was taken to see him.' Fanny replied with her gratitude for everyone's 'bounteous kindness to one of my dearest friends, and also my thankfulness for the peaceful manner of his death. Now all I can hope is, that I may be spared many letters of condolence.'

14. A gig was a small four-oared boat, about 14ft in length, with a man to each oar and a coxswain.

15. A caïque is a light skiff propelled by one or more rowers, used on the Bosphorus (*OED*).

16. On 12 May the Royal Navy 16-gunned steamer *Tiger* had run aground off Odessa in thick fog, three weeks after taking part in the joint British-French naval action (the first of the war) against Odessa in which most of the port's fortifications had been destroyed. The crew surrendered after a fierce bombardment from the surviving Russian guns.

17. Only six women per regiment were allowed to accompany their soldier husbands on overseas assignments. These were chosen by lot, and they earned their keep by washing and cooking for the regiment, or by taking jobs as maids to the officers' wives. Officers' wives had to get permission from the commanding officer of the regiment and the Admiralty and then travelled at their own expense.

Mrs Emily Louisa Williams was the wife of Regimental Sergeant Major Samuel Williams. She seems to have left Fanny's employment once they arrived at Varna (Fanny comments then that one of her few expenses was £4 for Mrs Williams's food during the voyage on the *Shooting Star*). Emily Williams may be the woman in Roger Fenton's photograph of the 'Cooking house of the 8th Hussars'.

18. Lucan: see Biographical Notes.

19. Raglan: see Biographical Notes.

20. Chibouque, or chibouk – a long-stemmed Turkish tobacco pipe.

21. The British and French forces were to sail for the Bulgarian port of Varna, about 130 miles from Constantinople, to provide a

show of strength and support for the Turks who were besieged in the fortified town of Silistria.

22. Charles II was born on 29 May 1630.

23. A hard-wearing trunk used by Europeans abroad, especially in India.

24. Sherbet: 'a cooling drink of the East, made of fruit juice and water sweetened, often cooled with snow' (*OED*).

25. Fanny's great fear, until she finally arrived in Balaclava, was that she might be packed off to join the women at the Hôtel d'Angleterre at Therapia (modern Tarabya) on the north-western European shore of the Bosphorus. Therapia, so called because of its wonderful climate, was the most fashionable Turkish watering place, where the rich spent the summer to escape the heat of Constantinople, and where all the embassies had their summer palaces. The hotel was the centre for wives visiting their husbands, or mothers coming out to be near their young sons. Not only did Fanny dislike the thought of being surrounded by women, but it was expensive: '[Lord George Paget] & my Lady lived for a fortnight at the Hotel at Therapia & their bill was £60 tho' they had nothing out of the way. I should think some of the Army Captains & Navy Lieutenants who have their wives there must wish them safe at home!' (17 August 1855).

Chapter 2: Embarkation and Encampment at Varna

MS source in this chapter British Library MSS Add. 47218 A ff. 9-36.

1. Varna and the countryside around was a notoriously unhealthy area. Devna, where the Light Brigade camped, was known to locals as the Valley of Death. During the Turko-Russian War of 1828-9, when General Diebitsch won concessions from the Turks, the greater part of the Russian army had died of malaria and cholera.

2. Cardigan: see Biographical Notes.

3. At this date the term 'cocktail' was applied to someone of doubtful background trying to pass himself off as a gentleman; it had originally referred to a racehorse which was not a thoroughbred because it had a cock-tailed horse (i.e. a working horse with a

docked tail) in its pedigree. This could hardly apply to Lady Erroll, who was the eldest daughter of General the Hon. Charles Gore, the second son of the 2nd Earl of Arran, an Irish peer. Moreover her husband was the 18th Earl of Erroll and the hereditary Lord High Constable of Scotland, the first subject in Scotland after the blood royal. Fanny may have thought that Lady Erroll, as the daughter of a general and the sister of three soldiers, was showing off by masquerading as a soldier, but once they had met she became an admirer.

4. A narghile is a hookah, an oriental pipe with the smoke drawn through water. *Junk* here is a nautical term for hard, salt meat.

5. Fanny was afraid that she might have offended Lady Erroll by the words 'under arrest' and changed them in the second edition to 'detained in camp'. In the event, Fanny need not have worried. Lord Erroll, who was known for getting into 'scrapes', had been a 'positive nuisance to the Regiment for years' and had now insulted his long-suffering commanding officer – 'when at all excited [Erroll] becomes stark, staring mad, & is unsafe to live with ... & but for the constant vigilance of Lady Erroll who follows him everywhere, he must have been compelled to quit the scene long ago ...' (Brown to Raglan, 3 June 1854; see Massie, p.19). The pistols Lady Erroll was wearing may have been her husband's, to keep them out of harm's way. 'I am glad Lady Erroll wrote kindly to you about me – I shall always remember her with pleasure though I daresay we shall never meet again' (Fanny to Selina, 13 April 1856).

6. Bashi-Basouks – the most famous of the irregular forces fighting within the Turkish army. Muslim volunteer horsemen, who supported and equipped themselves through plunder, they refused regular pay because it would compromise their heavenly reward if they were martyred during a *jihad* against an infidel army such as the Russians. They flouted conventional military discipline. Their treatment of the Bulgarians so appalled Raglan that he refused the British government's request that he take them to the Crimea as a part of his force. The French tried, and failed, to organize them into a regular cavalry unit and they were not involved in the Crimean fighting.

7. Lord Cardigan did not camp with the brigade but took a room in a mill a little distance away, possibly the one in Fanny's drawing (see p. vi).

8. Lack of transport and baggage ponies remained a constant problem. The army mule trains, which had successfully supplied

Wellington's army, were expensive to maintain and were disbanded soon after the end of the Napoleonic wars on the assumption that during future campaigns the Commissariat Department would buy horses and mules as they were needed. Unfortunately they were not easy to find in Bulgaria or the Crimea. In addition, it was assumed that the 1854 campaign would be over before the winter began so that insufficient carts and supplies, including ambulance carts, were taken out at the start.

9. S is Fanny's sister Selina. F is Francis Marx, Selina's husband, and editor of the Journal. E is Fanny's sister Elizabeth.

10. Brown: see Biographical Notes.

11. Cardigan and Lucan, who were brothers-in-law, had been rivals and enemies for many years (for a full account see Cecil Woodham-Smith, *The Reason Why*) and the decision to place Cardigan under the command of Lucan was to have disastrous consequences since they barely spoke to one another and could not communicate calmly in moments of crisis. Raglan had not planned this combination. When war seemed imminent, Lucan had applied to Lord Hardinge, Commander-in-Chief of the army, for a post and consequently was appointed commander of the Cavalry Division; meanwhile Cardigan wrote to his old friend Raglan, who had just become Commander-in-Chief of the British Expeditionary Army to the East, and was rewarded with the command of the Light Brigade of Cavalry. From the start Lucan was determined to have full control over Cardigan, while the latter was equally determined to be independent. Cardigan convinced himself that since Raglan had appointed him, he was to answer directly to him and not to Lucan. Raglan, rather than confronting Cardigan with the necessity of obeying his commanding officer, avoided the issue by keeping them apart for as long as possible by sending Cardigan to Devna and keeping Lucan first in Scutari and then at Varna. But once they arrived in the Crimea such a strategy was no longer viable.

12. Edwin Lawrence Godkin (1831-1902) was Crimean War correspondent for the *London Daily News*. In 1856 he emigrated to the United States, settled in New York, working as war correspondent again, covering the Civil War for the *London Daily News*. In 1865 he founded *The Nation*, an influential independent weekly journal which became known for its support of free trade and liberal reforms and its attacks on political corruption.

13. St Arnaud: see Biographical Notes.

14. Omar Pasha: see Biographical Notes.

15. The Rifle Brigade and the Light Division had already been supplied with, and trained to use, the new Minié rifles, which were as quick to load as muskets but were more accurate over almost six times the distance – between 500-600 yards. The remaining regiments were gradually provided with the new weapons but many did not receive them until after they arrived at Balaclava and those that did have them were often without sufficient supplies of suitable bullets. The French army was already fully equipped with Miniés. By the end of the war the Minié was being replaced by lighter, longer rifles (easier to use with a bayonet), made in a factory at Enfield; this initiative had been prompted by Raglan when Master-General of the Ordnance.

16. 'That cunning old dodger Aberdeen': George Hamilton Gordon, 4th Earl of Aberdeen (1784-1860), was Prime Minister from 1852 until February 1855.

17. A sutler is one who follows an army, selling provisions to the troops.

18. The greater part of the letter from which this extract is taken, minus the reference to the old dodger, was published in the *Observer* of 16 July 1854 under the title: 'Camp Life at Devna. The following is an extract from the letter of a soldier of the light division.' See p. 47.

19. Round shot were the traditional solid iron cannon balls, particularly effective in a siege for breaching walls or against troops fighting in close formation. After hurtling through the air, they bounced across the ground and could kill or maim several men or horses in succession. Young, agile soldiers describe jumping out of their path during the battle of the Alma.

20. The 1855 editor, Francis Marx, is right to correct Fanny's comment. Fanny has confused the Turkish army regular troops with the Bashi-Bazouks; see note 6 above.

21. If the British and French armies remained in the area, they would have control over the passage of shipping on the Danube, Austria's outlet to the Black Sea. In the event, Austria remained in a state of armed neutrality and, by agreement with the allies, her troops occupied the Danubian principalities and so tied down forces of the Russian army.

22. The *Europa*, a small sailing ship carrying the headquarters of the 6th Inniskilling Dragoons, caught fire 200 miles out of Plymouth and had to be abandoned. The tragedy was greater even than Fanny suggests. Not only were the commanding officer, Lieutenant Colonel Willoughby Moore, and the veterinary surgeon dead, but another 16 men and two women also died. All the horses, equipment and baggage were lost. The tragedy was blamed on the sailors, who immediately took to the boats rather than staying to fight the fire. Willoughby's widow later went out to Scutari and organised the nursing of the officers there until her death in November 1855.

23. 'The sore-back reconnaissance', as it became known, was soon notorious throughout the army because of Cardigan's martinet approach to discipline and lack of consideration for both men and horses. The men were in complete marching order, which meant they weighed about twenty stone, and in addition carried another five or six stone in food, fodder and ammunition, so that each horse carried about twenty-seven stone. Their three-pint kegs of water were soon drunk but as there were few springs or fountains in the area the daily marches in the relentless heat were often prolonged in the search for water. Despite the cold nights and the heavy dew, they had no tents, except for Cardigan, and for seventeen days none of them took off their clothes except for Cardigan, once.

24. Glanders is a contagious disease of horses, mules, etc., characterized by swellings below the jaw and mucous discharge from the nostrils.

25. Cholera was brought to Varna by French troops who had embarked in Marseilles, where there was an epidemic. It spread rapidly through the crowded town and into the camps, where men already weakened by dysentery and fever succumbed in great numbers. Cholera was believed to be carried through a miasma in the air, rather than polluted water, so little effort was made at even the most basic hygiene The appalling sanitary conditions, with little proper supervision of latrines, and troops drinking water from the streams and lakes in which they washed themselves and their clothes, only increased the problem.

26. When in Dublin as Colonel of the 11th Hussars Lord Cardigan enjoyed staging reviews in Phoenix Park to show off his regiment's smart uniforms and skilful drill.

27. The fire, which broke out on the night of August 10th, lasted for ten hours and destroyed more than a quarter of the town (the

houses were mainly built of wood). Thousands of pounds' worth of equipment and food were also destroyed, including much-needed boots and rifles, all of which should have been passed on to the troops earlier if there had not been such a shortage of baggage ponies. The Greeks were blamed, and five were immediately bayoneted by French soldiers.

28. Mary Anne Duberly, Henry's half-sister, died on 22 July 1854. 'Last evening's mail brought ... news of poor Anne Duberly I would have dispensed with. She was poor, & deformed, but as gallant a woman as ever lived up to her principles and defended the right. Henry feels her loss and I regret her as a good friend, though I cannot grudge her her rest. For what with James D. [her brother] & a few more she endured to the end' (Fanny to Selina, 17 August 1854).

29. *Galignani*, i.e. *Galignani's Messenger*, an English-language newspaper published in Paris. George Mead Butt, Q.C., was Conservative MP for Weymouth from 1852 to 1857.

30. Wadham, the six-year-old son of Fanny's brother Francis and his wife Katherine, died on 30 July 1854.

31. 'What a day it was that day!' From Elizabeth Barrett Browning's 'Bertha in the Lane', stanza xi.

32. 'A ragout of partly roasted game, stewed with wine, bread, condiments etc' (*OED*).

33. Cornet Riversdale Richard Glyn was one of the youngest officers in the 8th Hussars; he was promoted to lieutenant on 26 October 1854, the day after the charge of the Light Brigade, but transferred to the Rifle Brigade, with the rank of captain, in August 1855.

34. So many women, both officers' and soldiers' wives, had followed the army that Lord Raglan had decided to limit the numbers of those travelling on to the Crimea. Special permission was required in each case.

Chapter 3: The Expedition to the Crimea

MS source in this chapter British Library MSS Add. 47218 A ff. 36-49.

1. When she was launched, the *Himalaya*, one of the earliest screw-propelled steamships owned by the P&O Line, was the biggest steamer in the world, but she ran at a loss and was sold to the Admiralty at the start of the Crimean campaign to use as a troopship; she ended her days as a hulk in Portland harbour and was sunk by German bombers in the Second World War.

2. *Sent in their papers to sell*, i.e. attempted to sell their commissions and leave the army before hostilities began, a sign of the general unease affecting the army's morale. These officers enjoyed the social life of the army but had no intention of suffering the discomforts and dangers of real campaigning, even though it might bring promotion without purchase; they were ready to lose money on their commissions (the official prices were enforced during time of war and most would have paid much more in peacetime), to avoid active service. See Introduction, p. xiv.

3. *Book of Common Prayer* 1662, Litany.

4. Adapted from *King Lear*, act V.

5. Each steamer towed up to three sailing vessels throughout the voyage to Kalamita Bay.

6. The British Baltic Fleet and the French Army had captured the strategically-important Russian fortress of Bomarsund in the Aland Islands, midway between Sweden and Russian Finland, commanding the entrance to the Gulf of Bothnia. It was the first Anglo-French victory of the war.

7. Duke of Cambridge: see Biographical Notes.

8. 'We got papers of the 5th August yesterday. I see many ladies are mentioned, they make mistakes in the numbers as well as the names, ours is spelt Jubilee' (Henry to Francis Marx, 25 August 1854). The nickname 'Mrs Jubilee' for Fanny seems to be a twentieth century invention, possibly introduced by Tisdall (see Further Reading) and based on this misprint. But see p. 304 note 37.

9. The Crimean peninsula had been annexed by Russia seventy years earlier, seized from the Ottoman Empire, and the local population still consisted mainly of Tartars and Turks, many of whom disliked the Russians. The port of Eupatoria surrendered without a fight on 13 September, most of the wealthy Russian inhabitants fleeing when they saw the Allied fleet; it was occupied by a small Allied garrison throughout the war.

The troops landed at Kalamita Bay, south of Eupatoria and some thirty miles north of Sebastopol.

10. The guns Fanny heard were the exchange of fire between the Russian and British Cavalry in the hilly Bulganek valley. Although only a brief skirmish, it increased the tensions already existing between three cavalry officers – Cardigan, Lucan, and Nolan – and confirmed many of the cavalry in their contemptuous view of Lucan.

The troops had marched across the sweltering plain towards Sebastopol, their cheerful singing replaced by a desolate silence as men began to collapse from cholera, dysentery and thirst (many had been unable to fill their canteens at the only fountain at Kalamita Bay). Lady Erroll, who had procured mules for herself and her French maid, rode with the army and before long their mounts were festooned with the rifles of men too weak to carry them. This exhausted, thirsty army finally reached the Bulganek river. While men and horses drank, Raglan noticed a group of Cossack scouts disappearing on the far side of the valley and sent Cardigan with four squadrons to reconnoitre. Cresting the first ridge, Cardigan saw a detachment of about 2,000 Russian cavalry drawn up on the next ridge. Despite being under long-range fire from the Russians, he was calmly forming his enthusiastic men in line, ready to charge, when he was joined by Lucan, determined to take control, who began immediately to criticise and alter the arrangement. This fractious delay saved the British cavalry; Raglan and Airey, the Quarter-Master General, standing on higher ground, saw that beyond the line of Russian cavalry there was an army of more than 60,000 troops, hidden behind the second ridge, and realised that they were about to be ambushed. Desperate to extricate his precious cavalry and avoid a battle while his troops were exhausted, Raglan ordered up strong reinforcements to cover their retreat and sent Airey and his aide-de-camp, Captain Nolan, with orders to Lucan to withdraw. Followed by the jeers of the Cossack cavalry, the humiliated and furious British cavalry drew back, squadron by squadron, with the discipline of the parade ground. Knowing nothing of the hidden army, the cavalry blamed Lucan for the failure of their first engagement. Captain Nolan, the author of two books on the effective use of cavalry, was frustrated by the unimaginative role Raglan forced on them and this fiasco increased his growing intolerance of both Lucan and Cardigan.

11. Thomas Chenery in his report of 25 September from Scutari to the *Times* described the arrival of the *Kangaroo*. 'The horrible episode of the *Kangaroo* may have created some alarm in the minds

of the English public ... nearly 1,500 sick and invalids were put on board ... the captain ... remained at anchor from sheer inability to go to sea with his decks encumbered with dying and dead. At last the *Dunbar* sailing transport was sent to his assistance, and took off nearly half of what was left of his miserable freight. They arrived on the morning of the 22nd, the *Kangaroo* towing the sailing vessel. The *Kangaroo* brought 600, the *Dunbar* 500 sick, who were at once placed in hospital ... About 300 more arrived in another vessel the next day. The numbers in hospital were originally about 1,000, which were raised to 2,200 by this new influx – a number of course having expired during the voyage, or soon after landing.'

None of these were wounded men; no battle had yet been fought.

12. Prince Woronzov: see Biographical Notes.

13. 'My maid' – Mrs Letitia Finnegan, wife of Private Francis Finnegan, 8th Hussars, who had enlisted in December 1831 and embarked for the Crimea on board the *Echinga* on 15 May 1854. He was killed during the Charge of the Light Brigade; his name is shown as Andrew Finnegan on the casualty list.

Fanny took having a maid for granted, so doesn't always mention her presence. During her erratic voyage from Eupatoria to Balaclava she never mentions Mrs Finnegan, who was with her before and after the journey. There is more information on Bob's travels than on Mrs Finnegan's.

14. A letter from Henry Duberly to his brother-in-law Francis Marx:

> *Battlefield of Bhurlak*
> *September 21st 1854*
>
> *My dear Marx, I have just time to write here on the ground where we are bivouacked & get this off with the dispatches. Troops never behaved as ours did yesterday the first shot was fired at half past one and by half past 4 we had crossed the river Alma & carried the extraordinary entrenchments on these heights. We have hors de combat I fear 2,000. Some of the Russian generals that have been taken prisoner say they thought no army to have done what the French & ourselves did yesterday in less than 21 days by which time they expected reinforcements, they were 60,000 strong & their best troops. They had heavy guns in position 32 pounders & we had only Field Guns 9 pounders so the Infantry went at them & drove them to a disgraceful flight. It is said they never stopped till they got safe into Sebastopol 14 miles off. I believe we land the siege guns & move on as soon as we can bury the awful quantities of dead & get the wounded properly attended to. We have nothing with us but a change just what our one horse can carry besides*

*ourselves so I am fortunate in getting this bad pen & bit of paper to write
upon. My dearest Fan is comfortable on board a transport & no doubt
with a good glass could see the action & I trust before long she will join
me in Sebastopol. I am happy to say <u>we</u> have no loss as the cavalry
although under fire of the great guns were not required in front but in a
skirmish on the day before we lost two horses. Going over the battle field
cannot be described, such a seen [sic] of horror I could scarcely believe.
The 23rd have lost many officers Col. Chester & poor Evans but you will
know more by the* Times *than I can tell you as Russell the correspond/t
is here. Love to Selina, your affc brother H Duberly.*

*I have to write to my mother so I write as fast as I can put pen to
paper.*

Henry Duberly's terse letter gives a good summary of the battle
of the Alma. This magnificent, though costly, allied victory was not
fully exploited. Prince Menshikov had expected to hold the heights
of Alma for some three weeks, giving him time to strengthen the
fortifications at Sebastopol which were negligible as he had not
taken seriously the earlier reports of a proposed invasion. As the
remnants of his disorganized and demoralised army fled back to
Sebastopol, the French and British commanders disagreed as to
their next move and finally remained on the battlefield for a further
two days. Raglan, who had landed his men with the minimum of
equipment, expecting a quick raid and grand storming of Sebastopol, wanted to pursue the enemy and then attack Sebastopol from
the heights overlooking the north side, destroying the city and
dockyard with heavy guns. But hampered by insufficient cavalry
(the Heavy Brigade had remained at Varna), and the exhaustion of
his men, who had borne the brunt of the fighting, he needed the
backing of the French troops. St Arnaud, the French commander,
weary and dying of cancer, refused to move, claiming that his men
needed rest and their rucksacks, which they had left in the valley
behind them. Raglan, anxious as ever to avoid confrontation with
friend or ally, finally sent Sir John Burgoyne, his adviser on strategy,
to discuss the matter with him. Burgoyne had always believed that
the city could only be taken by siege after a prolonged bombardment while St Arnaud was reluctant to commit his troops to the
storming of the Star Fort, the weakly defended earthworks to the
north of Sebastopol, so it was decided to make a flank march
around the city to the south, where the two armies could camp on
the uplands and use the natural harbours of Balaclava and
Kamiesch as their supply ports.

The British cavalry were particularly demoralised by the
aftermath of the battle, in which they had played no active part.
Anxious though they were to harass the fleeing enemy, they were
ordered instead to escort the artillery and Lucan had to be ordered

back three times to this duty when he had, on his own initiative, pursued the enemy and taken prisoners. Nolan complained, in strong language, to Russell that they were being 'kept in a band box' as decoration. Russell later described the three generals: 'The French General was dying. The English General . . . in order to take Sebastopol was marching round it! The Russian General, anxious to save Sebastopol, was marching away from it! Neither of them had the least notion what the other was doing.' At one point during their march the forward section of the British army, including Raglan and his aides, ran into the stragglers of Menshikov's army, to the astonishment of both.

During the two days respite, Menshikov had ordered a massive reconstruction of the Sebastopol defences, including strengthening the Star Fort, and the sinking of warships across the harbour mouth, to prevent Allied ships entering Sebastopol, before marching the greater part of his army out of Sebastopol and on to the heights beyond the Tchernaya river to the east, leaving Sebastopol with a small garrison augmented by sailors from the sunken ships. From this advantageous position he could receive reinforcements of men and supplies from the north and east and threaten the invaders, so that they too at times felt besieged.

15. 'Let us not inquire too deeply into the future:/It is today in which we have our pleasure.' From Donizetti's opera *Lucrezia Borgia* (1833), act 2, sc. 5.

16. Dundas: see Biographical Notes.

17. Elizabeth Barrett Browning, 'Rime of the Duchess May', last stanza.

18. Captain Creswell died of cholera on Tuesday 19 September during the march from Kalamita Bay and was buried the next day.

19. From the sonnet 'Art thou already weary of the way' by Frances A. Kemble (1809-93).

20. From the Book of Job, chapter 6.

21. 'Lord G. Paulet is in the Bay. He is proud of his band. The bandmaster has composed a piece called the "Entrance to the Black Sea" which takes 3 hours to play' (1 September 1854). George Paulet, Commander of the *Bellerophon*, had entertained friends to dinner a few days earlier while they listened to this piece. When finally they rose to go it was said that he tried to persuade

them to stay and listen to a companion piece, 'Exit from the Black Sea', also three hours long.

Chapter 4: Balaklava, October–November 1854

MS source in this chapter British Library MSS Add. 47218 A ff. 49-74.

1. The British had marched on the left of the forces from the start of the invasion and should therefore have wheeled around Sebastopol, through 180 degrees, and held the most westerly part of the land to the south of the city. They would then have been protected by the sea on their left and the French on their right. The French offered Raglan the choice of this position, with the two shallow harbours of Kamiesh and Kazatch, or the more vulnerable place on the right with the apparent advantage of the protected, deep water harbour of Balaclava to use as their supply base.

Raglan, still expecting a swift end to the siege after a brief bombardment, chose Balaclava on the advice of Rear-Admiral Sir Edmund Lyons (second in command of the British Black Sea Fleet and an old friend), because it was the more secure harbour. At that stage the difficulties of supplying the army via Balaclava and the single steep road up from the harbour to the plains did not seem a problem. With the coming of winter, mud, snow and ice, it was to prove a disastrous choice. It also left the British army with their right flank exposed to attack by Menshikov's army, while the French held the more protected position to the east.

Lyons may have been influenced by reading Demidov's *Russia* (note 9 below) which contains a clear account of the village of Balaclava and the harbour. 'Yonder was Balaclava, with its Genoese ruin, based upon a rock, and overlooking a narrow creek into which ships and fishing boats enter as in a port. At this place a basin, concealed from view, offers a safe and secret harbour; no mast would be high enough to betray the presence of any vessel behind that screen of rocks. ... Here stands the port of Balaclava, capable of being used as a safe anchorage for a great number of vessels, to which it would afford an admirable shelter. Seen from the middle, this basin might be taken for a lake, so completely is the entrance masked by the position of the mountains' (Vol I, p. 328 and Vol II, p. 69).

2. Lancaster guns were new, experimental guns with elliptical bores designed to fire oval-shaped shells which spun through the air, increasing their efficiency in range and accuracy. As a more

effective weapon, hollow shells (filled with gunpowder and lit by a time fuse) were gradually replacing round shot.

3. Russian troops became notorious for bayoneting and killing wounded Allied soldiers and for attacking those who came to their aid when they were wounded; there are numerous eyewitness accounts in letters and diaries. The *Times* report dated 29 October 1854, but published on 18 November, provided one explanation for this behaviour: 'The Russians stripped our dead. Their Lancers were seen killing the wounded as they lay on the field. This is credibly affirmed by many witnesses of the horrible deed. ... There is too much reason to believe that the gay jackets and rich trappings of our Light Brigade – privates and officers – excited the cupidity of the Cossacks, who did not scruple to kill the wounded as they lay on the ground for the sake of their uniforms. They know that they would not be allowed to take the clothes of the men who were alive and so, *more Tartarico*, they made short work of it.' And according to information given to the correspondent of the *Morning Herald* by Russian prisoners, published in his report of 25 October 1854, their commanding officers had told them that if captured they would be treated with barbarous cruelty. As a result many of the Russian wounded attacked, and often killed, the Allied soldiers who came to their aid.

4. The description given by those within Sebastopol was very different, with men, women and children working like ants night and day to save their city. The defence was organised by the brilliant young army engineer Lieutenant-Colonel Eduard Totleben (1818-84) whose advice had earlier been ignored by Menshikov. Totleben abandoned the idea of the fortress as a static position and introduced the concept of a flexible defence system, capable of alteration and addition as circumstances changed. He made extensive use of gabions – wicker-work cylinders filled with earth – as protective walls in gun-emplacements. These were easily replaced when damaged so that the Allies were continually astonished at the speed with which the Russians repaired breaches in their defences. Totleben began by strengthening the Star Fort realising, as Raglan had done, that Sebastopol could be taken by an immediate attack to the north of the city. Then, as the Allies marched around the city, he built a series of earthwork defences to the south, including six redoubts, manned by guns taken from the sunken ships. Within thirty-six hours 100 naval guns were in position. The key defence point, the Malakoff tower, was defended by a complicated trench system connecting it to the Little Redan and Great Redan on either side.

5. *Morning Advertiser*, 28 and 29 August: to Fanny's embarrassment, her sister Louisa had circulated her correspondence. The *Advertiser*'s reports, closely similar in content to pp. 42-43 above, are strongly critical of Cardigan. One pro-Cardigan riposte appeared on 31 August.

6. With the ships of the Russian Black Sea fleet either scuttled as a defensive barrier across the entrance to Sebastopol harbour, or blockaded behind this, it had become clear that there would be little naval action. 1,000 British marines with field guns and a Naval Brigade of similar size, armed with heavier cannon and mortars, had come ashore to strengthen the land bombardment.

7. Lyons: see Biographical Notes.

8. Layard: see Biographical Notes.

9. *Travels in southern Russia and the Crimea; through Hungary, Wallachia and Moldavia during the year 1837* by Prince Anatolii Nikolaevich Demidov. (English edition, two vols., 1853). The book describes the author's six-month trip, with a party of geologists and naturalists, studying the geography, history and 'vanishing' original populations of the New Russia.

10. Lucan's failure to follow up this attack led to the invention of his nickname. 'I cannot tell you the dissatisfaction given by Lord Lucan as commander of the Cavalry. ... Some witty brain has changed Lord Lucan's name to Lord Look on' (13-19 October 1854).

11. Captain Robert Portal (1820-88), ADC to Lord George Paget, had served in Canada before joining the 4th Light Dragoons and obtaining his captaincy in 1846. He took part in the Charge of the Light Brigade. He was one of Fanny's favourite companions. 'I like him. I think he is honest, sterling, and possessed of appreciation where few soldiers are' (8 March 1856).

12. 'It is better to wear out to than to rust out.' Saying attributed to Bishop Richard Cumberland (1631-1718).

13. 'Poor young Thynne' was a nephew of Lord Raglan.

14. At this date only officers were awarded medals, and campaign medals were often distributed *en masse* to senior officers and the general staff simply for being present, regardless of their individual contribution. Non-commissioned men might be mentioned in

dispatches, but their acts of courage were otherwise ignored. Fanny was not alone in thinking that there should be a decoration in recognition of individual bravery, regardless of rank. After stories of heroic conduct in the Crimea reached England via private letters and newspaper reports the idea was raised in the House of Commons in December 1854 and was taken up with enthusiasm by the Queen and Prince Albert. The Victoria Cross, to be awarded to military and naval men of all ranks for 'some signal act of valour or devotion to their country', was designed by Prince Albert, with some modifications by Victoria, and was instituted by Royal Warrant in January 1856. Simply inscribed 'For Valour', the medals were cast in metal taken from guns captured at Sebastopol (as is still the case), and hung on plain ribbon, red for the army, blue for the navy. In all, 111 were awarded during the Crimean War, of which six were for conspicuous acts of bravery during the charge of the Light Brigade. Of these six, only one was awarded to an officer.

15. Nolan: see Biographical Notes.

16. Admiral Dundas was supposed to have carried out a simultaneous naval bombardment at dawn but delayed the start until 1.30 p.m. and even then kept the ships too far out for their fire to have any effect.

17. The *Times* of Monday, 2 October 1854 reported that Sebastopol had surrendered on 25 September and followed this up two days later with a long triumphant leader, to the fury of many camped outside Sebastopol.

18. Cathcart: see Biographical Notes.

19. For the Battle of Balaklava and the Charge of the Light Brigade, see Appendix 2.

20. Similar comments about the Turks' immediate capitulation and cowardice were made in almost every contemporary letter and report. These were not revised until some time later when it was realised that the Turks had, in fact, held off superior numbers of Russians for over two hours. But this immediate perception meant that the Turks were treated with contempt by all ranks of the army until the arrival of Omar Pasha and his troops the following spring.

21. Sir Colin Campbell: see Biographical Notes.
   'Sir Colin did not even form them into a square' – only the most disciplined and experienced troops could hold their ground

standing two deep rather than in the more usual square formation. William Howard Russell's famous description of 'the thin red streak', later amended to 'the thin red line', made the Highlanders' stand one of the most famous incidents of the war.

22. Colonel Shewell rallied the survivors of the 8th Hussars and the 17th Lancers after they had overrun the Russian guns. When he realized Cardigan was not present, he turned and, with about 70 men, charged back through the 300 Russian lancers who had formed up behind them, scattering them to either side and creating a gap through which others escaped, thus saving many lives. Shewell had been lying ill in Balaklava but hearing of the attack got up from his sick bed and hurried to join his regiment, arriving just in time to lead them in the charge.

23. Captain Lockwood survived the original charge but returned to the 'valley of death' in search of Lord Cardigan, whose ADC he was, in case he was in need of assistance. He was unaware that Cardigan had been the first out of the charge and had ridden back to the camp without waiting to see how many of his men survived. Lockwood's body was never found.

24. Admiral Dundas had resigned as Commander-in-Chief of the fleet in the Black Sea; he felt unequal to the task, in part because his authority had been compromised by the close friendship between Lyons and Raglan.

25. Fanny neatly hints at the news spreading through the camp, that Cardigan, having reached the Russian guns, felt that his duty was done and returned without fighting the Russian soldiers, or rallying his troops and bringing back as many as possible. This was left to three Colonels: Shewell, Douglas, and Paget.

26. 'The prices were fabulous.' But Fanny appears to have paid them. The next day Captain Bob Portal wrote to his sister: 'Mrs Duberly has just sent me from one of the ships a warm pea jacket, which is very kind of her. It is impossible to get them anywhere for any money.' Portal, p. 55.

27. General Baron Osten-Sacken had organised the defence of Odessa against the allied bombardment in April and now commanded the Russian 4th Corps in Sebastopol. He took command of Sebastopol in February 1855.

28. Sir Walter Scott, *Marmion*, canto 6.

29. The fierce and bloody but inconclusive battle of Inkerman, fought for most of the time in thick mist, became known as 'the soldier's battle' because of the fragmentary nature of the conflict, isolated skirmishes and lack of central command. Menshikov's army attacked the British along their strung out, ill-defended eastern flank and the line was only held through the discipline and extraordinary acts of bravery of individual men and companies as the fighting moved up and down the steep slopes. The French, whose offer of help was at first refused, arrived just as it seemed the line would break. The casualties, those killed or wounded, were horrific: almost 11,000 Russian troops, 1,800 French and 2,400 British. The French lost 25 officers, the British 39, including two generals. Although described by the Allies as a victory since they had held their position on Inkerman ridge, it was a Pyrrhic victory: they were so weakened that it was obvious they were now incapable of storming Sebastopol until they received reinforcements.

'I was myself almost under fire about ten o'clock & watched everything that was done as attentively as possible all day ... The regiments & I may say companies acted in most cases independently, they acting from the orders of their own officers who did their best at cutting down & killing all before them. Russell's account of the action is very good & true' (Henry Duberly to Francis Marx, 12 December 1854).

30. There had been constant complaints and representations to Headquarters about the lack of fortifications along the Inkerman ridge. The Sandbag Battery, the scene of some of the fiercest fighting and where many of the Guards lost their lives, in fact contained no guns.

31. Amateur – a civilian who had come out to view the war. By the following summer special tours, £5 for the round trip, were organised for visitors, stopping at Malta, Athens and Constantinople en route. Fanny was not alone in finding amateurs very irritating.

32. Captain Leopold Heath RN who, as Harbour Master, decided which ships were moored inside the harbour and which remained outside, was held responsible by many for the huge loss of shipping on November 14. The 1855 Editor refers to Heath's promotion to the senior post of Superintendent of the Transport Service in March 1855. See also p. 287, note 24.

Huge quantities of stores were lost. The food, clothing and medical supplies which should have been distributed to the troops had been kept on board ship because there was no means of conveying them up to the front, and nowhere to store them in

Balaclava. If transferred to the quayside they rotted in the mud. The shortage of baggage ponies and mules meant that priority was given to transporting ammunition; other supplies had to be collected by the regiments on an individual basis.

33. Nightingale: see Biographical Notes. Florence Nightingale is now so well known as the Lady with the Lamp that it is hard to recapture a time when someone might not have heard of her.

34. The sinking of the magnificent new steam-ship the *Prince*, with all the stores she was carrying, was to result in chaos and suffering throughout the winter. The *Times* reported that the loss was in part due to the negligence of her officers. On arriving in Balaclava she lost both her anchors because the cables were incorrectly fastened, so once moored outside the harbour she was held only by a small anchor, not strong enough to ride out the storm, and was smashed against the rocks. 'The whole of the winter clothing for the men has gone down – 40,000 suits of clothes, and boots, undergarments, socks, gloves ... vast quantities of shots and shell, and ... the medical stores sent out in consequence of the deficiencies which formerly existed. The latter were, with not uncommon negligence, stowed away under the shot and shell, and could not be landed at Scutari.' On shore, in Balaclava and on the plains above, were men who had not changed their clothes since landing at Kalamita Bay two months earlier.

35. Raglan's failure to attack Sebastopol immediately from the north still rankled with many, their feelings aggravated by the slow progress of the siege and information received from Russian prisoners about the initial weakness of the defences.

36. The map sent to Selina never reached her (the letter containing it was probably lost in the storm of 14 November) and was replaced by a later copy (see endpaper & p.x), but the Queen did receive hers: 'The same mail that brought your letter brought one from Major General Gray, Equerry in Waiting, thanking me in the Queen & Prince's name for the map which they had perused with much interest. So that's satisfactory so far' (4 January 1855). It would seem that this was the first step in Fanny's plan to persuade the Queen to accept the dedication of her Journal.

37. One of the most colourful French regiments, originally Berber soldiers from Algeria commanded by French officers. By 1854 most Zouaves were French but they kept their exotic uniforms and were known for their audacity.

38. Paget: see Biographical Notes. Lord George had a genuine reason to return home, his father having recently died, but the obvious hardships of the coming winter persuaded many officers that 'Urgent Private Affairs', as they became ironically nicknamed, required their immediate presence in England.

39. This sums up the widespread feeling of a lack of leadership, both during the fighting at Inkerman and in the day to day organisation of the army.

40. Lady Rodney was the wife of Sir Robert-Dennett Rodney, baron of Rodney-Stoke, near Cheddar, Somerset.

41. Fanny reflects the generally held view of the time that nursing was not a suitable occupation for 'fine young ladies', a view that Florence Nightingale fought hard to change.

42. Canrobert: see Biographical Notes.

43. The French used *cacolets*, mules with long couches fixed on each side, to carry their wounded in relative comfort over the rough ground.

44. The *Times* of Monday 13 November 1854 quotes Raglan's official dispatch to Lord Newcastle describing the events of the battle of Balaclava. Fanny may have been told that she was included in this but there is no reference to her either on the 13th or during the two weeks before and after.

45. The French and British had taken over nearly all the large public buildings, barracks, schools (naval, military, and medical) and hospitals in and around Constantinople to use for their sick and wounded, leaving very little space for the Turkish sick so that many were left in Balaklava, to die where they fell. Although there are contemporary estimates of the numbers of British and French sick and wounded and of those who died (both in battle and in hospital) there seems to have been no attempt to do the same for the Turkish army.

Chapter 5: Balaklava, December 1854–March 1855

MS sources in this chapter British Library MSS Add. 47218 A ff. 79-137.

1. It was a constant complaint by those writing home that letters, apart from those from Headquarters, were being held up, some-

times by as long as ten days. 'I know the last two mails were made up late so that only Lord Raglan's bag went, I suppose he does it on purpose, so that the news sent home by officers may be stale & the papers not care to insert any parts of them' (Henry Duberly to Francis Marx, 19 January 1855).

2. *Illustrated London News*, 11 November 1854, p. 490:
'A STOUT-HEARTED LADY
Oct. 17, two p.m. – The most awful thunder of cannon is now in my ears. The fleet has entered, and the forts, shipping, redoubts, and musketry are all engaged. ... We have one lady in our camp – the wife of the Paymaster of the 8th Hussars. I saw her quietly looking on while the place was being bombarded from the land.'

3. This was Dr Lawson, the principal medical officer at Balaclava. On 2 December Raglan set up a Court of Enquiry to report on the horrific treatment of the sick and wounded on board the *Avon;* it commented on the lack of equipment and the insufficient number of medical staff to care for the patients and found that 'this deficiency was known to Dr Lawson but that he took no steps to have it supplied.' After he had read the report, it was stated that 'Lord Raglan has seen with pain and sorrow the apathy and want of interest which Dr Lawson exhibited ... for the comfort and well-being of the suffering men ... and he is compelled to visit such conduct with the severest censure. The Inspector-General of Hospitals will take immediate steps to relieve Dr Lawson from his present charge.'

4. *Bât* ponies – ponies used for officers' baggage on campaign.

5. 'Mr Hupton [*sic*], the skilful engineer, who designed and directs the useful and important works of the port. His active and intelligent sons assist their father in conducting the immense undertakings executed with the aid of an army of military labourers' (Demidov, 1837, Vol. II, p. 64). When captured the younger Mr Upton refused to give Lord Raglan any information about the structure and layout of the docks because Sebastopol was now his home.

6. Thomas Chenery (1826-84) was the *Times* correspondent in Constantinople, from time to time relieving the Crimea correspondent William Howard Russell. In 1877 he became editor of the *Times*.

7. 'l'Allegro' – Fanny's light-hearted way of saying the Light [Brigade].

8. 'Mr Rochfort an amateur who is out here, a most agreeable and intelligent man of the world. Mr Anderson of the *Sanspareil* who supplies the beauty of the party & is the handsomest man I ever saw. Mr Aspinall the owner of the ship and H & I' (Sunday 17 December 1854).

9. Mr Willis probably originally went to Sebastopol with Upton, the engineer (note 5 above). He had owned houses in and around the town but was ruined by the war and he and his family were now dependent on Raglan for food.

10. Bosquet: see Biographical Notes.

11. Lyons replaced Dundas. See 26 October 1854, note 23.

12. 'A transport captain has just given me a Turkey to make my Xmas dinner' (22 December 1854).

13. In her letters Fanny always spells Homeopathy as she would have pronounced it. The saga of the non-appearance of Fanny's boxes, sent from England with essential supplies, runs like a leit–motiv throughout her letters.

14. 'I must tell you the sick come down principally on the cavalry troop horses ... & they make those that <u>possibly</u> can & many that <u>can't</u>, ride down on our cavalry saddle. ... I myself saw many of the poor fellows. One in particular I rode beside, he was dead in his chair with his feet a few inches off the ground, upon his feet he had <u>neither shoes or stockings</u>, the poor fellow had died on the road – his leg at the calf was about the thickness of my wrist. I believe six died in transit that day, when is it to end? We have embarked more than 2,000 in the last eight days' (Henry Duberly to Francis Marx, 19 January 1855).

15. Airey: see Biographical Notes.

16. Liprandi: see Biographical Notes.

17. See p. 284, note 38. 'It is said here, that the Queen asked to speak to Lord George Paget & recommended him to return to his regiment! Is this true? He certainly left for no reason' (28 December). This was a 'shave' – Paget had been invited to describe his experiences during the Charge of the Light Brigade to the Queen, but he was cut in his Club by acquaintances who were unaware of his reasons for returning to London.

18. 'You would not put a cow or a pig into the shed that I almost cried for joy at securing for Bob' (17 December 1854).

19. Mary Seacole (1805-81) stayed on the *Medora* when she arrived in Balaklava in March. She describes a similar fire, with considerably less panache then Fanny, in her *Wonderful Adventures of Mrs Seacole in Many Lands*, published in 1857. See Biographical Notes.

20. During the December session of Parliament Layard, newly returned from the Crimea (p. 313), joined other Radical MPs and Lord Derby, the Tory leader of the opposition, in attacking Lord Aberdeen's handling of the war. Disraeli joined them, complaining that the government had only provided for a small war though they had embarked on a major one. If the papers had 'purposely miscarried', it was because of the growing criticism, in officers' letters, correspondents' reports and leading articles, of the suffering of the troops caused by the mismanagement of the general staff. These attacks widened to include the government, as it was realised that the malaise went deeper than individual military incompetence, and were summed up dramatically in the leading article of the *Times* of 23 December 1854: 'We echo the opinion of almost every experienced soldier or well-informed gentleman, when we say that the noblest army England ever sent from these shores has been sacrificed to the grossest mismanagement. Incompetence, lethargy, aristocratic hauteur, official indifference, favour, routine, perverseness and stupidity, revel and riot in the camp before Sebastopol, in the harbour of Balaclava, in the hospitals of Scutari, and how much nearer to home we do not venture to say. We say it with extreme reluctance – no one sees or hears anything of the Commander-in-Chief.'

21. A large cake used for Twelfth Night celebrations.

22. Wordsworth, *Peter Bell*, p. 1. 'Capt. Chetwode when he read the quotation. "The primrose etc ... to him" &c, asked me what I meant, what more it was? Which thing delighted my weak mind.' (January 1856, after publication of the Journal).

23. It would appear from her next letter that it was Fanny who wrote to Lord Raglan about the fire hazard.

24. Much of the chaos in Balaklava was due to the lack of firm, overall command. The shore was subject to military authority while the shipping and harbour were divided between two naval officers. Captain Heath RN, the Harbour Master, was responsible

for allocating the position of ships and for the maintenance of the harbour (the dumping of rubbish, etc.) but Captain John Christie RN, as Superintendent of the Transport Service (overseeing the carrying of men and supplies), was his senior and thus took final responsibility. Christie was an amiable man, incapable of enforcing his wishes on the masters of the merchant transport ships, whom he complained would not attend to him. Unused to naval authority, and lacking the discipline of the Royal Navy ships, the merchant marine accepted it grudgingly if at all. Heath, aware that Christie and he were being blamed for the loss of the shipping moored outside the harbour on 14 November, realised that a scapegoat would be required and protected himself by canvassing Testimonials (as to the orderly state of Balaklava harbour), from the masters of the transports; he received more than thirty. After the arrival of Simpson, Christie was dismissed and Heath was appointed in his stead. This was not a popular move. Russell, perhaps anticipating who was going to win this skirmish, failed to maul Heath as strongly as Fanny had wished.

25. Russell: see Biographical Notes.

26. Henry's comments on the transportation of the sick and the delays to the post are quoted above, notes 1 and 14. He ends: 'No soldier was ever treated so badly by England before & I trust & hope they may never be so again. The Crimean Expedition will be a black page in England's history' (19 January).

27. The following day's letter shows she still hoped to get a house.

28. Letter of 5 February 1855 to her sister, Mrs Colquhoun, of Clashick, Crieff, Perthshire. Lord Raglan had requested that nurses be sent from Scutari to the General Hospital at Balaclava and Florence Nightingale reluctantly agreed. The hospital was known to be filthy and inefficient and the orderlies undisciplined, making life even harder for respectable women than it had been at Scutari, but several nurses wished to escape the discipline Florence imposed and eventually eleven volunteers were sent to Balaclava with the Superior of the Sellonite sisters, known as the 'Mother Eldress', as Superintendent. Miss Sellon's Anglican sisterhood was a Devonport religious order, dressed in black habits, who were founded to provide nursing care for the poor; the eight Sellonite nurses who had travelled to Scutari with Florence were among the most efficient in the group, with practical nursing experience learnt during the Plymouth cholera epidemic of 1853, although Florence complained that they did nothing but complain at the

'fatigue & privation.' Miss Jane Shaw Stewart, sometimes given the courtesy title 'Mrs', was almost the only 'fine lady' among those at Scutari to have done any real nursing. The sister of an MP, she had trained in Germany and worked in a London hospital. She later supervised the nurses in the new Castle Hospital, a collection of huts built on the heights above Balaclava harbour.

Madame Roland, one of the leaders of the Girondins during the French Revolution, was guillotined in 1793, steadfastly encouraging others and proclaiming on the scaffold 'Oh Liberty! How many crimes are committed in thy name!' Becky Sharpe is the heroine of Thackeray's *Vanity Fair* – ambitious, sharp, independent but penniless, who has to make her own way in the world.

29. Captain Stephen Lushington commanded the Naval Brigade until July 1855 when he returned to England on leave after being promoted to Rear-Admiral and awarded a K.C.B. He was probably Fanny's favourite among her many admirers. 'I like him because he is clever, energetic & resolute and I am not afraid of him when he chooses to say disagreeable personalities which he some times likes to do to shew off his sharpness.' He teased Fanny, describing her as 'wilful & wayward', but clearly enjoyed her company and without his help in providing a hut she could never have lived on shore.

30. The arrival of the Grand Dukes was usually a sign that an attack was imminent.

31. *Courtship & Wedlock; or Lovers and Husbands* by Harriet Maria Gordon Smythies, London 1850. A romantic three-decker novel based on 'soundness of principles and purity of faith.'

32. Sir Tatton Sykes, 4th baronet, a wealthy Yorkshire landowner, may have been a family friend.

33. Each French regiment had an integrated group of paid women auxiliaries to provide food and drink for the soldiers, organize the laundry and nurse the sick and wounded. The *vivandières* wore smart uniforms and marched with the regiment. The food they provided was the envy of the British troops who had to cook their own.

34. Both killed during the charge of the Light Brigade.

35. Boxer: see Biographical Notes.

36. 'I am on board the *Herefordshire* and as she is an E Indiaman she has all lattice work instead of blinds & the doors are all lattice

work – precious airy – however ... the Steward on board here is such a nice man. Goes half crazy trying with efforts to warm our cabin with red hot shot &c &c' (23 February).

37. On 16th or 17th February Captain Fred Dallas wrote: 'A day or two ago, Wombell and I rode over to a "Monastery" called St Georges about 4 miles from here ... We walked up the cliff afterwards behind Mrs Duberly & Party, & very nice black Trousers she had' (Dallas, pp. 87-88). See note 39 below.

38. Francis Marx's 'ripping letter' in *The Spectator* of 13 January 1855 was a strong attack on Lord Palmerston and the detrimental effect his actions had had on Britain's foreign policy, and her relationship with Austria in particular, over the past twenty-five years. The tensions in parliament came to a head on the first day of the January 1855 session when the barrister and backbench MP John Arthur Roebuck called for the setting up of a select committee to investigate the conduct of the war. The motion, which was in effect a vote of no confidence, was carried by 305 votes to 148 and Lord Aberdeen's ministry resigned. On 4 February, after several others had refused, the Queen reluctantly invited Lord Palmerston, whom she disliked, to form a government so that by the time Fanny was writing this letter Francis Marx was already 'in a stew.' Palmerston made several ministerial changes, the most important being the appointment of Lord Panmure to the combined positions of Secretary for War and Secretary of War, thus ending a foolish division of responsibilities.

39. 'The identical inexpressibles' were the 'trowsers' Fanny was wearing instead of petticoats, given to her by Mr Lane, master of the *Himalaya*. 'I saw on shore the lady of Balaclava, Mrs Duberly, wife of the Paymaster of the 8th Hussars. She is an extraordinary person – wears a very long gown, which she does not mind holding up pretty high, & discloses a regular pair of trousers lined with leather' (Kelly, on 19 January 1855, his first day at Balaklava).

40. Fanny's letter, dated 1 January 1855, was published in the *Devizes Gazette* of 25 January 1855 and signed 'One who has shared the Fortunes of War.' It refutes suggestions that all is well with the British Army, repeats the criticisms made in her private letters on the misadministration of resources and comments on the suffering of the soldiers through the lack of huts. Fanny regularly wrote letters to be published in the press, either sending them direct or via Marx, but as they were written under pseudonyms it has not

been possible to identify them all. 'I also send you a letter which if you approve of it you can forward to the Editor of the *Times*. If not – put it in the fire' (19 October 1855). One of her lists home included '10 or 12 quires of large writing paper like what you use in writing to me, Envelopes not <u>very</u> thin (300), Five quire packets of note paper – good.'

41. Simpson: see Biographical Notes.

42. To make or raise hob is old North American slang for making mischief, hence hobbery means mischief. Colonel Reynell Pack in his memoir *Sebastopol Trenches and Five Months in them*, describes his arrival at Balaklava in February 1855: 'with some difficulty we found a suitable landing place, as the harbour was choked with shipping. An elderly gentleman in the garb of a naval officer, busily pulling about the harbour in his gig, observed and put us ashore, his kindly act belying the reputation he had unfortunately acquired for roughness and incivility. It was the late Admiral Boxer, one of the many now no more.'

43. 'Pray don't suppose that I hunt dogs – not only have I set my face against it – but I have stopped several men from joining in so unsportsmanlike an amusement' (14 April). However, on 6 March the *Morning Herald* stated: 'The dog hunts are now fixed for every Tuesday and Thursday.'

44. Psalm 57.

45. Henry would be unable to leave until he had sold his commission, so that if Fanny was to leave immediately he would have been left behind.

46. Herbert, Gladstone and Graham had resigned because they opposed the acceptance of the committee of inquiry proposed by Roebuck (see note 38 above).
  'We heard the day before yesterday that the Tsar is dead, the news came from Lord John Russell to Lord Raglan by Telegraph from Vienna where it was believed to be true. I fear it is too good news to be true. I fancy it must be the Emperor [of France] that is dead' (Henry Duberly to Francis Marx, Friday 9 March 1855). Tsar Nicholas I had died on 2 March 1855, but his death was kept secret from the Russian troops for some time. 'Lord Raglan at Sebastopol, and Omar Pasha at Eupatoria, have notified the death of the Emperor Nicholas to the Russians. They refused to credit the report' (*The Spectator*, 24 March 1855).

Chapter 6: The Camp

MS sources in this chapter British Library MSS Add. 47218 A ff. 104-90.

1. Fanny was an enthusiastic spectator of the regular race meetings that took place throughout the summer and autumn; courses were laid out on the high ground between Karani and Kamiesh and, a little later, to the north-east near the Tchernaya river. These favourite activities of the peacetime army, races and hunting (of wild dogs for lack of foxes), broke the monotony of camp life. Fanny's attendance did not always excite admiration: 'On the impromptu course might be seen admirals, generals, Turks, Sardinians, and French, whilst but few ladies graced the spectacle. There was one, however, the wife of a hussar paymaster, who could hardly be called a stranger or visitor, for at all times and seasons, in pleasure or depression, amidst the tumult of bombardment or on the field of carnage, attended by an escort of beaux, she might be found' (Pack, pp. 112-3).

2. The Duke of Newcastle had been Secretary for War until January 1855, when he was replaced by Lord Panmure. Fanny is probably referring to the Crimean War Fund (see note 28 below). Henry Duberly wrote to Francis Marx: 'I can buy plenty of the best [wine] now Crockford's ship is out' (9 March 1855).

3. The sketch is on pp. 516-7, Vol. XXVI of the *Illustrated London News* of 26 May 1855. Fanny is seated on Bob, surrounded by her 'Escourt of beaux'. Many officers sent sketches back to be printed in newspapers and journals.

4. Lord Lucan, angry that he was being made a scapegoat (alongside Nolan) for the disaster of the Light Brigade Charge, demanded the right to a court martial, which he believed would clear his name. This was refused. On 19 March he made a long and detailed speech in the House of Lords claiming he had been maligned by Lord Raglan's official reports, and complaining that he had been unfairly recalled to England in disgrace. His speech antagonised many of his peers who felt he had abused his privileged position.

5. Possibly *Ode on the death of the Duke of Wellington*, 1852.

6. M. Tauski (the chief of the spies) has not been identified further and this may be a pseudonym. Raglan disliked making use of spies and had ignored the information (which proved to be correct) brought by a Turkish spy on the eve of the battle of Balaclava.

Information about the conditions within Sebastopol, and future Russian plans, came mainly from deserters, most of whom were Polish. The Russian officers, many of whom spoke both English and French, seemed to enjoy the challenge of infiltrating the British and French trenches, dressed in captured French uniforms when visiting the British lines and vice versa. Amusing anecdotes about their daredevil behaviour are included in letters home.

7. Anthony Vandyke Copley Fielding (1787-1855) – water-colour painter known for his atmospheric landscapes, particularly downland paintings and marine scenes.

8. Fenton: see Biographical Notes.

9. Fanny's taste in music was eclectic, ranging from opera to the music-hall. In February 1856 she wrote to Selina, 'Jullien publishes my song – I don't think I have published more than one – with my dear Jackey's Polka – But when I get home, I will have the polka that the 97ieme de la ligne wrote for me. "L'Amazone" with such a woman, on such a horse, with a poodle dog – and such a stirrup foot – written for and dedicee a Madame Duberly.' Unfortunately there is no trace of *Jackey's Polka* among the hundreds of pieces of surviving sheet-music published by Louis Jullien, the French conductor and flamboyant entrepreneur, who produced promenade concerts of light music in London. Fanny's manuscript may have been burnt in the fire which destroyed Jullien's office in the spring of 1856. The sheet-music for *L'Amazone, Air Chevaleresque*, [A Knightly Air] with words by A. Han and music by Luigi Bordese, survives. The many compliments in the song include:- 'I jump into the saddle and everyone says "What an Amazon! Look! What a horsewoman!" A general chorus of Bravos "To the Englishwoman!" And hop, here I go, bowing in the French manner, I hurry away and fly like the wind! But how miraculous! in the chase, I go faster than lightning, clearing walls and obstacles with no fear.' The tempo is, appropriately, Allegro. (See illustration, p.346).

10. Mortars, which looked like giant cauldrons swinging on hinges, were used more often than guns because they had a longer range; they were the most effective of the weapons used against the Russian defences. The sea-mortars were later taken back on board and used in the attack on Kinburn in October.

11. Bandoline – a gummy preparation for keeping hair in place. It was always top of Fanny's list of necessities to be sent out from England.

12. Portal, who described Fanny as someone who 'goes everywhere and does everything' wrote to his sister on 7 May 1855 'Omar Pasha is here again, and paid a visit this afternoon to Mrs Duberly, with whom I dined last night. Mrs D. is now living in a hut in the 8th Camp, and having two or three little tents attached to the hut, they manage to make plenty of rooms, and to be fairly comfortable. I should, all the same, be very sorry to see my wife, if I had one, out in the Crimea in a camp! We are visited often now by snakes, but I don't believe they are poisonous, though of a great size' (Portal, p. 179).

Fanny's requests in her letter of 29th January include: '25 yards of some thin dark blue or green calico stuff to make a lining for my tent. The pretty marquee we had is lost on the Himalaya so we must have a bell tent which <u>unlined</u> is <u>intolerable</u> & too exposed for me on account of the shadows being seen through. ... You can stop it from my dibs' [her own income].

13. Bowstrung, i.e. strangled with string, the Turkish method of execution.

14. 'Of course you have heard ere this of poor Christie's death, they bullied him to death poor man, nothing could have suited the Admiralty better as his evidence before the committee would have been terribly against them' (Henry Duberly to Francis Marx, 14 May 1855). On 9 March, writing to Marx, Henry had mentioned the testimonial Fanny refers to in the next paragraph: 'they have put their hands deeply into their pockets to present him with a handsome piece of plate, many have given as much as £5.' More than £100 was raised, together with a Testimonial to his good management.

15. The British command realised that the only way for the siege to be successful was to deprive the Russians of food and munitions. A joint British-French expedition to capture Kertch, under the command of General Brown, set off on 3 May. Unfortunately, just one week earlier, the electric telegraph from Varna had been completed which enabled the French Emperor, Napoleon III, to interfere directly with the actions of the French forces. The French ships were recalled on the Emperor's orders when only two hours away from Kertch and the whole plan had to be aborted since the British could not continue alone.

16. *Heartsease or the Brother's Wife*, by Charlotte M. Yonge (1823–1901). This was her second novel, influenced by the Tractarian views of Keble (whom she knew from the age of fifteen), and published in 1854.

17. Stratford : see Biographical Notes.

18. P.P possibly stands for Premier Pasha, to take precedence over Commander-in-Chief.

19. Lady Agnes Paget, described as 'the Belle of the Crimea' by Roger Fenton, was much admired and entertained by Lord Raglan and the only woman in the small group present at his deathbed. In 1807, as a young man, Raglan had briefly accompanied her father, Lord Arthur Paget, on a diplomatic mission to Turkey.

20. Estcourt: see Biographical Notes.

21. It is unlikely that there was ever any realistic chance that Fanny would receive a medal for being present at Balaclava; she was not a member of the army and it would have set a most awkward precedent. Even so, she seems to have seriously expected to be awarded one. See note 33 below.

22. Vane: see Biographical Notes.

23. The arrival of the emperor was dreaded by both the French & British High Command; he already interfered with their decisions via a daily stream of telegrams. But Fanny's information was out of date. Napoleon had been deflected from coming to the Crimea after the lure of a State visit to London in mid-April which soothed his vanity. His acceptance as royalty was signalled by his investiture with the Order of the Garter, and he no longer felt the need to lead a victorious army in the field.

24. Tennyson, 'St Simeon Stylites.'

25. Fanny's worries about the editing of her Journal and choice of publisher are discussed in the Introduction, p. xxviii–xxxiv.

26. 15,000 Sardinian infantry had arrived under the command of General Alfonso La Marmora. The kingdom of Piedmont (which included Sardinia), had joined the alliance against Russia on 7 January 1855, under the leadership of the Prime Minister, Count Camillo Cavour. Although they had no interest in the immediate conflict, this was a part of Cavour's long-term plan to win the good will of the allies, particularly the French, and gain their help in expelling Austria from the Italian peninsula which would, he hoped, lead to the unification of the separate Italian states. In 1859 Napoleon III joined Piedmont in the war which seized the

province of Lombardy from Austria – the first step towards the eventual unity of Italy.

27. At the start of the campaign General Brown had made himself very unpopular by insisting that the troops continue to wear their stiff, high, leather stocks even when marching in the summer. Many men collapsed, unable to breathe properly. Now that conditions were improving, Brown attempted to reintroduce the wearing of stocks. This was strongly resisted.

28. The Crimean Fund was set up to bring extra food and supplies to the army but was at first badly mismanaged: 'to get things from it is very difficult. ... They have lots of things that officers would give any money for now, but they won't sell them yet ... They have iron stoves & matting which would be useful now but in a month or so when the hot weather comes they no doubt will try & sell them when nobody will buy them. ... Don't show up the Crimean Fund yet, until I write further' (Henry Duberly to Francis Marx, 9 March 1855).

29. Pelissier: see Biographical Notes.

30. General Canrobert had resigned (and taken command of his old division), on the 16 May. He was exhausted by the responsibility of command and overwhelmed by the daily stream of instructions from the Emperor.

31. Not every English officer present welcomed Fanny's presence; once again Reynell Pack was critical: 'On the high ground where the Woronzov Road descends through the gorge, close to where the mutilated and wounded might be expected to pass after the recent reconnaissance, amongst a host of men, was Mrs D—. She had evidently ridden out in haste, and her graceful person figured in a scene where she could boast, if it were a subject worthy of boasting, that she was the sole representative of her sex' (Pack, p. 131).

32. Within a week of taking command of the French forces Pelissier defied the Emperor's orders and joined forces with the British to send a second, successful expedition to Kertch. Although a large foundry, a flour mill and a bullet factory were all deliberately blown up, the rest of the town was at first protected by allied sentries. But this triumph was marred by the subsequent shocking news of a two-week orgy of looting and violence, rape and murder. Much of the town was burnt and the unique collection of Greek art in the Kertch museum was seized or destroyed, the floors covered inches deep with shards of pottery, broken glass and marble. At

first the Turks were blamed, but it became apparent that the looters included French and British soldiers.

33. 'I have just been informed that a regular official application has been this day sent in by Mrs Duberly of the 8th, signed by Colonel Shewell, applying for the Crimean Medal and clasps for Balaclava and Inkerman. I rather think that Parlby refuses to forward it, but if she gets it, I will apply for one for Mrs Rogers who deserves it ten times more than half the men who will get it' (Hodge, p. 84). Hodge viewed Fanny and her admirers with some suspicion; in his diary entry for 9 May he commented: 'The grass in the plain is beautiful. Mr and Mrs Duberly and Paulet (sic) Somerset out grazing. The publicity of all this is very disgusting.' But he was full of praise for Mrs Rogers: 'We have one or two excellent women here. One who washes for me is a hardworking good person. She cooks for the Captain of her Troop' (31 January); he had given her one of his flannel shirts when she was without warm clothing (Hodge, pp. 104, 110). Both Mrs Rogers and Hodge appear in Fenton's photograph 'Hut of Captain Webb, 4th Dragoon Guards'; and Mrs Rogers can also be seen in the photograph 'Camp of the 4th Dragoons, convivial party'. William Parlby was Lieutenant-Colonel of the 10th Hussars.

34. 'The forlorn hope' – a name given to the first group of infantry running across open ground towards an enemy's defensive position, initially used to describe Wellington's men attacking French siege fortifications during the Peninsula War. The French had learnt from this; by attacking 'scattered like sheep' they were more difficult to hit than by advancing in a solid line.

35. 'Volley and file firing' – troops advancing in two lines, each alternately firing and reloading, so that there is continual fire.

36. Albert Smith (1816-60), alpinist, novelist, miscellaneous writer, humourist and lecturer climbed Mont Blanc in 1851. In the following year he presented at the Egyptian Hall in London an entertainment he called *The Ascent of Mont Blanc*. It was a considerable success. Smith made a second ascent of Mont Blanc in September 1853 accompanied by, among others, Lord Killeen of the 8th Hussars and William Howard Russell.

37. 'Hayter and Howell, army packers, Mark Lane, London, who are empowered by the Government to forward parcels for officers and men in the Crimea by any steamer or transport free of expense, and that will be your best way of sending anything' (Kelly, p. 151).

38. Anatole de Berthois, one of Général Féray's aides de camp, who had been eager to meet the 'young and pretty Mistress Diuberlay[*sic*]' called her 'a true Clorinde, for she charged with her husband at Balaklava'. He described their delightful day: 'you can imagine all the follies we said and did, all in due propriety as her husband was present who, by the way, seems a good sort'; finally, with 'the belle and her husband, [we] rode for another merry gallop to have dinner . . . and spend a joyful evening laced with champagne'. 'Letters de Crimée du Capitaine de Berthois' (p. 113).

39. Lord Paget was commanding the brigade and disliked the task because of the 'very unruly people we had to deal with, from the general officer . . . down to the captains of transports, to say nothing of a whole army of travelling gents, with an occasional yeomanry officer in full canonicals' (Paget, *The Light Cavalry Brigade in the Crimea,* London 1881).

40. 'Grape' were small, loose, iron balls held within an artillery shell, which burst open once fired, scattering the contents with lethal effect. 'Musketry' – smooth-bored muskets, which had largely been replaced by the Minié rifle in the French and British armies, were still used by most of the Russian forces.

41. 18 June was the fortieth anniversary of the victory at Waterloo and had been deliberately chosen for the attack, which made the ensuing failure all the more humiliating for the British. The original plan was for the bombardment, intended to breach the enemy's defences, to resume at 3 a.m., followed by infantry attacks three hours later. At the last moment, and without advance warning to Raglan, Pelissier decided to attack at 3 a.m. without preliminary fire. Confusion and mismanagement followed. The French attacked at different times, one division mistook a Russian shell for the signal, others waited for the agreed signal, so that they met fierce resistance and suffered appalling casualties. Raglan, knowing a British attack would result in similar carnage, still felt it would be dishonourable to leave the French unaided and ordered in two divisions. They advanced across a quarter of a mile of open ground between the British lines and the strongly fortified Great Redan. The result of this noble gesture was 1,505 British casualties. The French incurred 3,500 casualties, the Russians 5,500. The Great Redan and the Malakoff remained in Russian hands. 'Poor Agar is dead!! And I have had to write to Lady Nelson' – his sister Mary who had married the third Lord Nelson in 1845.

42. Russell had repeated to Fanny the complaint made to him by General Eyre – that the French troops Raglan had assured him were

available to back him during the assault were in fact camped in the Tchernaya valley. They refused to assist him without orders from French headquarters, which were not forthcoming.

43. The French were advancing the trenches and tunnels from which they made their final assault. They got so close they could hear the Russians laughing and swearing.

44. Sir Harry Smith had been an effective, dashing and courageous young officer in the Peninsular War, some fifty years earlier.

45. 'Georgy [his sister] has asked in her letters what I think of Mrs Duberly. Her husband is the paymaster (lieutenant-colonel) [*sic*] of the 8th Hussars, consequently a non-combatant; and as to the humbug of her coming out here from light principles or a wish to take care of her husband, it is all moonshine and may be believed 3,000 miles off, but the Crimea is a place of dry, unpleasant facts and words: no nonsense, all is seen through. She has no connection with the hospital that I ever heard of but is constantly *à cheval*, a pushing, vulgar woman, and treats her husband more as a servant than what he is: in fact, wears the ———— and the boots too, as I see in the *Hue and Cry* of the Army: "*Lost:* A lady's spur without a rowel. Please return it to Camp, 8th"' (Captain Robert Beaufoy Hawley to his father, 1 June 1855, *The Hawley Letters*. He was too modest to mention the 'inexpressibles', her trousers).

Chapter 7: The Fall of Sebastopol

MS source in this chapter British Library MSS Add. 47218 B ff. 1-73.

1. Oratorio (1738) by Handel. The Dead March was regularly used for army funerals.

2. Lord Raglan's aides-de-camp, because they were his personal appointments, were not kept on by Simpson but returned to England.

3. From Robert Pollok, *The Course of Time*, 1827.

4. Adapted from Bottom's speech when he awakens in *A Midsummer Night's Dream*, IV, i.

5. Lieutenant Colonel Vico was the French commissioner at the British Headquarters, acting as principal liaison officer between the French and British armies.

6. Spenser, *Faerie Queene*, last stanza of the Mutability cantos.

7. *Household Words* – a weekly periodical started in 1850 by Dickens. In addition to serialisations of his novels and those of others, among them Mrs Gaskell and Wilkie Collins, it included poems and a wide variety of entertaining articles as well as attacks on abuses of the day. *The Newcomes*, by Thackeray (1811-63), was published in instalments 1853-55.

8. Tremenheere: see Biographical Notes. Miss Matilda Paget was a cousin of Lord George Paget.

9. Annie Forrest, the wife of Major William Forrest of the 4th Dragoon Guards, had joined her husband in camp early in June. The son of an officer in the East India Company, Forrest had originally joined the 11th Light Dragoons as a Cornet, aged 16, in India in 1836 and attained the rank of Captain in 1841. He was one of the few officers to stand up to Cardigan's bullying despite being continually picked on, as an 'Indian' officer, for trivial or non-existent offences. Finally, in 1843, he was refused extended leave by Cardigan when Annie was seriously ill just before the birth of her first child and he wished to escort her to friends for her confinement. He remained with Annie, rousing Cardigan's fury, but refused to apologise or admit any fault. In the furious row that ensued he was supported by the Duke of Wellington, the Commander-in-Chief, who strongly reprimanded Cardigan, declaring that Forrest's behaviour was 'fair and proper' and that he had never known the Army's time to be wasted 'in so useless a manner as in the present instance.' Forrest transferred to the 4th Dragoon Guards a year later and in 1848 became a major. Fanny's dislike of Annie may have been aggravated by the realisation that her husband was a stronger personality than Henry, who could not have stood up to Cardigan, and was destined for high rank. In 1877 he was promoted to Lieutenant-General and he became Colonel of the 8th Hussars in 1880, the year before Henry retired. It is impossible to tell whether this influenced Henry and Fanny's decision to leave the regiment.

10. For the Golden Rule of reciprocity, see 3 December 1854.

11. Referring to 'The Burial of Sir John Moore at Corunna', a poem by Charles Wolfe (1791-1823): 'We carved not a line, and we raised not a stone/But we left him alone in his glory.'

12. Fanny enclosed a long list of clothing she required for the winter months. And she did turn to and do the work. In mid-

February she wrote to Selina from Ismid: 'Could you tell me how to get up collars, either I cannot make the starch right – how is it made? – or something, but, after a morning's labor, they look villainous which is a bore to say the least' (19 February 1856).

13. Fanny is nervous, and is reflecting the contemporary snobbery – the Lockes of Rowdeford are included in *Burke's Landed Gentry*, whereas the Commissary and his wife are trade, her social inferiors. As wife of a Paymaster, Fanny feared some would consider them her social equals.

14. Captain Edmund Lyons RN, son of Admiral Lyons, died at Therapia on 23 June of wounds received in action off Sebastopol on 17 June.

15. From Henry Wadsworth Longfellow, 'The Arsenal at Springfield'.

16. 'He [Captain King] dined with us a few nights ago & as he had sent me a piano Forte on board I sang to him' (17 August 1855).

17. Layard's attacks on Lord Aberdeen and his conduct of the war had been so outspoken that Queen Victoria refused to accept Palmerston's proposal to include him in his cabinet.

18. *Grace Lee, A Tale* by Julia Kavanagh (1824-77), two volumes 1855. Grace, an orphan, inherits a fortune, loses both it and her lover, suffers poverty, calumny and sickness but survives all to be reunited with her lover. 'Have you read a newish novel called *Grace Lee*, if not I recommend it – it has been as good as a friend to me' (10 August 1855).

19. Captain Montague's release was negotiated earlier than that of his fellow prisoners because the British Army was short of engineeers (p. 305, note 43 below).

20. The battle of Tchernaya was fought against the advice of both Totleben and Prince Mikhail Gorchakov, who in February 1855 had succeeded Prince Menshikov as commander of the Russian forces. The Russians, suffering 250 casualties a day in Sebastopol, were faced with three options: to continue the siege despite the lack of new supplies; to abandon the south of the city and withdraw to the northern shore; or to attack the heavily fortified French and Sardinian positions on the Fedoukine Heights, on the extreme right of the Allied defence. Gorhachov came under increasing pressure from Tsar Alexander II, who wanted one final, decisive attack on the Allies before their expected reinforcements arrived,

to carry out the latter plan. Although this had no strategic justification, Alexander hoped that a dramatic victory would persuade
the Allies to negotiate for peace. Totleben and Gorchakov's fears
were fully realised; it was a massacre. The Tchernaya river ran red
with Russian blood; they lost nearly 2,300 dead and their total
casualties were an estimated 8,000 men. There were about 1,800
French casualties, some shot, as Fanny reports, as they helped the
Russian wounded, and 28 Sardinians were killed. The Russian
army in the Crimea was virtually destroyed.

21. Among these was Nolan, said to be buried in a shallow grave in
the ditch of No. 5 redoubt.

22. This bombardment of Sebastopol by 704 allied guns lasted four
days but was not, as at first expected, followed by a renewed assault
on the Malakoff and the Redans. It was a ruse to disguise the
activities of the French who were extending their trenches near the
Malakoff.

23. All four of Raglan's ADCs were his nephews or great-nephews.
On 10 July, soon after Simpson was appointed, Fanny wrote: 'They
say old Simpson is very vulgar'. Fanny was probably sulking at the
loss of all her favourites. There is no other indication that Simpson
was vulgar, or that his aides-de-camp were not gentlemen.

24. The French had taken the Mamelon in the joint allied attack of
8 June 1855, so the wounded and dead were French.

25. The frog puffs himself up to show that he's as big as the bull,
and bursts.

26. *The Roving Englishman in Turkey* by Eustace Clare Grenville
Murray, London, 1855. A chatty, discursive guidebook, with plenty
of anecdotes. It includes sharp observations on the 'cousinocracy of
England', the faults of the British army interpreters in
Constantinople, and the failure to prepare army officers to
understand Muslim culture and religious traditions.

27. Not General Sir James Simpson, but the Crimean War artist
William Simpson (1823-99), who in the event had taken on so
many assignments that he never turned up.

28. Not to be confused with the earlier Maltese cook Michael, 'that
inf-rn-l scoundrel Michael.'

29. Originally constructed by the Russians in the spring of 1855 as
additional defences to the Malakoff and the Little Redan, the

batteries known as the Mamelon Vert (often simply called the Mamelon and situated some 600 yards in front of the Malakoff), and the Ouvrages Blanc (so-called because of the exposed limestone and set on the most eastern point of the allies line), had been captured by the French in June – the first major blow to Totleben's defence system. The entrenched Green Hill (sometimes confused with the Mamelon Vert), on which stood Chapman's battery, lay further west within the British lines, south of the cemeteries and to the left of the Worontsov Ravine.

30. 'I hear the officers of the 30th have forwarded poor Deane's epaulets, pistol, buttons &c. . . Does Mrs Deane know that her son is buried on Cathcart's Hill?' (Fanny to Selina, 1 October 1855). The Deanes, who were family friends, have not otherwise been identified.

31. Many felt that the Highlanders and other surviving seasoned troops should have been employed. Simpson had put in those who had failed earlier so they could redeem themselves. Instead, the young recruits were terrified and refused to move even at the flat of the sword. 'After all – it was discovered that the Redan was untenable by [the] Russians after the French had got Malakoff – & so there was no occasion for us to have assaulted it at all! I think Simpson erred in not sending some of his cavalry to harass the retreating garrison – and I fancy the *Times* will say so too.'

32. A mine or fougasse is 'a square or oblong case, made of metal or stout timber bound with iron hoops ... filled with gunpowder, or gunpowder enclosed in bottles, grenades or shells ... the case itself is buried from an inch to a foot below the soil. Gutta-percha or other pipes, filled with gunpowder, spring from each end; these rise above the surface and are connected together' by glass tubing which contains a phosphoric preparation at one end and powerful acid at the other. The glass tube breaks when trodden on, the charge ignites 'and an unexpected mine is fired ... the actual explosion did not inflict such injury as the dread engendered amongst the men by these diabolical, hidden, machines; the very feeling which the enemy was naturally anxious to cause' (Pack, p. 154). The Redan was widely believed to be mined, which added to the panic among the soldiers fighting on 8 September.

33. Windham: see Biographical Notes.

34. Fanny may have been aware how some viewed her behaviour. 'You ask me if I know Mrs Duberly, I do by sight very well, and should like to see her book, though I would not give a pin for her opinions. She is known in the camp by the name of the Vulture,

from the pleasure she seemed to take in riding over fields of battle. I should think her feelings (if she has any) cannot be very fine, and she is certainly more fit to follow a camp than to live in an English drawing room' (Godman, *The Fields of War*).

35. A carronade was a 'short large-calibred ship's gun' (*OED*).

36. It took three days for the French and English to remove all the Russian dead from Sebastopol.

37. Fanny seems to have disguised her horror almost too well. Frank Currie, a young subaltern in the 79th Highlanders writing to his sister, was shocked at her behaviour. 'What disgusted me excessively was seeing Mrs Jubilee going about the town when all these horrors were still visible, surely that was no place for an English lady, as I believe she considers herself, however her husband is such a fool, he lets her do just what she likes, which is a thousand pities' (*Letters from the Crimea*, letter 32). Apart from the misprint in the newspaper a year earlier, this appears to be the only time that Fanny is called Mrs Jubilee by a contemporary. It seems to be the result of mishearing her name, rather than a nickname – in an earlier letter he calls her Mrs Jubile.

38. The Cavalry had taken no active military role since the battle of Balaclava.

39. James Hervey (1714-58), a rector in Northamptonshire prominent in the early Methodist movement. His prose poems were probably influenced by the vogue for 'Graveyard' poems with their themes of human mortality. Fanny sometimes found it hard to be amusing all day and felt oppressed by the men around her. 'How many of those men <u>understand me</u> do you think? Does Jack, who soaks beer, & sherry & gin & water & champagne all day & half the night, & who is scarcely perceptible thro' the fog of smoke always streaming from his mouth & nostrils? Does Tom, who is only not a groom or a Jockey because he wears a uniform & whose standard of a man's worth is his racing seat, or his hands? Does Harry, whose day is spent amongst the "ladies" of Kamiesh, & whose nights are passed till parade time, at high play?' (29 October 1855).

40. Fanny to her brother-in-law Francis Marx, advising him on his career and discussing their mutual need for worthwhile employment. She dreads the fact that her energies will 'droop & flag & wither… when I am suffocated into conventionality & worsted work once more.'

41. Psalm 130: 'out of the depths I have cried [to thee].'

42. A wide-awake was a soft-brimmed felt hat (*OED*). On 13 July 1855 Fanny wrote to Selina with a long list of requests which included: 'A black wide awake hat, or any other sort that will not crush in packing, low-crowned and pretty, also three yards Black ribbon velvet and a comb of cock's hackle or an ostrich feather, also black – these had better be packed separately so I can trim the hat when it arrives. Enclosed thread is the size of my head.' After her success with the Chasseur d'Afrique jacket it seems that Fanny now wanted to emulate the Sardinians with a cock's hackle in her hat.

43. Lieutenant Clowes travelled back from Russia with several other officers including Lieutenant-Colonel Richard Kelly, who had been taken in the advanced trenches by a Russian sortie on the night of 22 March. From Colonel Kelly's letters to his wife it appears that officers were treated more like gentlemen in exile than prisoners and enjoyed a comfortable captivity. On his first day in Sebastopol a flag of truce was sent to the British camp to arrange for his clothes to be collected and his horses sold to raise money. While he and Captain Montague of the Engineers, who had been taken in the same raid (see note 19 above), waited for their belongings to arrive, their wounds were dressed and they were fed from General Osten-Sacken's kitchen and entertained by his ADC. When they left Sebastopol for the interior the Russians paid them a daily allowance (one and a half roubles, about five shillings), for their keep, and gave them a captured English soldier as a servant. Provided with introductions to families of importance in the towns and estates they passed en route (Kelly sounded quite petulant after spending three dull days in Voronezh, where they made no acquaintances), they travelled under armed escort to Riasan, about eight hundred miles north. They were shocked by the roads which were 'mere tracks crossed by ruts in every direction' and the primitive Russian post-waggons (small open carts without springs), but there was no other means of travel for those without their own carriages. In late May they arrived at Riasan, about a hundred miles south-east of Moscow, and met six other British officers. Clowes seems to have joined them later. They rented a house opposite their compatriots and shared their meals when not invited elsewhere. At first there was not much society, 'most of the upper classes being in the country at present', but they dined with the Governor three times a week and were lent English and French books. By the time Kelly and Clowes left in mid August they were visiting all the local families of note, dining out regularly and taking part in musical evenings. As prisoners, they led a more

sophisticated, but not dissimilar, life to that experienced by Fanny and the 8th Hussars when they were quartered at Ismid in Turkey during the final months of the war. Their release was delayed because the Emperor hoped they would prefer to remain in Russia but once negotiated, they returned to the Crimea via Odessa. As a final courtesy, they were allowed to make a detour to visit Moscow, at their own expense. This privilege was not extended to the Transport or Commissariat prisoners.

The rank and file prisoners were not treated by their captors with the same easy camaraderie as that extended to the officers; they complained that the ordinary Russian soldiers, who were often unpaid, stole the money and clothes given to them by the Russian authorities. None, however, complained of ill-treatment. Their wounds were dressed and they were housed in barrack-like accommodation where they organised their own courts martial and floggings to maintain discipline when necessary.

44. 'The Russian Mortars, firing from the Forts on the North side shake my hut & table as I write. They are heavier than any yet employed. They do very little harm & kill very few because we have no men in the town. It would be a great lark if the Russians were to come across in boats now there is no moon & re-take the South side!! They might easily do it. We've got a subaltern's guard (100) men & I think not more than a sergeant's guard in the Redan' (13 October). The firing came from the very forts that Raglan might have taken the year before if he had not deferred to St Arnaud and Burgoyne.

45. The Crimean Medals were considered 'vulgar looking things, with clasps like gin labels' according to Hodge and were nick-named 'Port, Sherry and Claret'. He agreed with Fanny about their distribution: 'I wish they would make a *small* Maltese Cross out of the gun metal taken at Sebastopol, and give it to those who were *under fire* in the trenches and *to none other*. These medals given to all the world are of no value. They are too common' (19, 21 September 1855. Hodge, p. 130). He appears to have seen the designs for the Victoria Cross. See p. 279, note 14.

46. A misquote from the popular poem 'The Armada 19 July 1588' by Macaulay (1800-59). 'The red glare on Skiddaw' was one of the beacons lit as a warning of possible invasion by the Spanish, which in the event never occurred. The Armada was defeated by Drake and the remnants of the fleet scattered by the gales in the North Sea.

BIOGRAPHICAL NOTES

Airey. General Sir Richard Airey (1803-81), Quartermaster General, in charge of supplies and transport, was blamed by the press and parliament for the failures of the system during the winter of 1854-5. Although he struggled, unsuccessfully, against the bureaucratic lethargy in London and Balaclava he lacked the determination and energy to break free from the traditional form-filling and procrastination of the commissariat and the independence of mind to set up the emergency systems vital for the army's survival. His brusque manner made him unpopular and Fanny was not alone in thinking him 'a thorough humbug from his cap peak to his spurs'. Friends at first, they later quarreled (and he became 'so ashamed of himself when he sees me – in consequence of one or two little things we tried to transact and failed – that he will ride two miles round to get out of my way'). She expressed her sympathy for him, however, when he was criticised in the government commission of 1856 even while pin-pointing the trait that made him, and many of the general staff, so disliked: 'I cannot help saying I am sorry for Airey – for he is such an agreeable, gentlemanly well bred man – that I do believe he did not know what he had to do, as he was always immensely busy about something or other. And then you know, Society of a certain set, of the higher class, is not given to see the oi polloi except through bandaged eyelids. I think they regard them much as we do sheep or cows that we see out in the wet – we think it is their nature & they are used to it – & so it's all right.'

Bosquet. General Pierre François Joseph Bosquet was a distinguished battlefield commander whose attack on the Russian left wing at the Alma and timely intervention at Inkerman played major parts in both victories. The Chasseurs d'Afrique he had sent in support of the British cavalry at the battle of Balaclava played a decisive role in covering the retreat of the Light Brigade. During the siege he commanded the Corps of Observation, the 1st and 2nd Divisions, based on the Uplands to protect the rear of the French army from attack by Menshikov. His life-long rivalry with Pelissier, which had begun in Algeria, continued in the Crimea when he failed to pass on to Pelissier a plan of the Russian defences (found in a dead Russian's uniform), and he sent a continual stream of critical reports back to Paris. Matters came to a head on 16 June, when Bosquet criticised Pelissier's plan to attack the Malakoff, rightly fearing huge loss of life if they attacked before the trenches had been extended up to the outer defences. Pelissier sacked him, unsettling the troops two days before a major assault. Although Bosquet continued to send back despatches condemning the disaster of 18 June and the mishandling of the French forces, Pelissier realised his skills were vital and reinstated him in early July. Bosquet had a very different attitude to loss of life from Pelissier. Fanny and he watched the French storming of the Mamelon with tears in their eyes and he told Fenton that 'it was not possible for anyone to have a greater dislike of war than a soldier like him, whose life for the past twenty years had been spent in burying his friends'. But Bosquet is best remembered for his comment while watching the charge of the Light Brigade – 'C'est magnifique, mais ce n'est pas la guerre'.

Boxer. On 10 May 1854, Rear-Admiral Edward Boxer (1784-1855) received his warrant as Admiral Superintendent 'from the entrance to the Dardanelles to the east Entrance of the Bosphorus at the Black Sea'; this authorised him to oversee the provision of all transport-ships, for men and supplies, and to control the passage of all British shipping in this area. He was directly responsible to the Admiralty rather than to Raglan, as Commander-in-Chief of the military forces. Raglan and the general staff had to ask Boxer to provide extra transport for their men and equipment, first from Scutari to Varna in June 1854, and then on from Varna to the Crimea, and they were entirely dependent on his decision as to which ships they could use and when they would be available. There were continual disputes caused by the serious shortage of ships, which became worse after the storm of 14 November and the resultant disagreements over which cargo should have priority, the sick, the supplies, or the troops and their horses. Complaints were continually raised about the manner in which the stores were sent out from England; mixed cargoes were often loaded so that items needed at the initial port of call were put in first and could not be disembarked until the return journey; some items even went back to England and were not delivered until the following voyage. In addition, cargo books were not regularly kept until December 1854 so that the ships' masters were frequently unaware of what they had on board. As the weather deteriorated in the Crimea, and the army stripped the land of crops and firewood, the commissariat first requested, then demanded, extra transports to convey the necessary provisions. But none were to be had. It had been apparent from the start that the admiral was incapable of organising the complicated rotas needed to keep the ships working efficiently, and in the resulting chaos and disorganisation he was considered by many to have 'never done anything properly in his life.' With the change of government in March 1855 Boxer was posted to Balaclava to oversee the running of the harbour. He continued to cause chaos with his muddled organisation of the shipping, but once he concentrated on repairing and enlarging the quays and landing-wharfs he found his true métier, and his final legacy was an efficient harbour which contributed much to the improved conditions for the British army during the second year of the campaign.

Brown. Lieutenant-General Sir George Brown (1790-1865), Commander of the Light Division, had fought in the Peninsular War before holding a series of staff appointments. A brave soldier but strict disciplinarian, he rejected all attempts at army reform. He disapproved of wives accompanying the army, whatever their husband's rank, and did his best to get rid of them.

Cambridge. Lieutenant-General George Frederick Charles, Duke of Cambridge (1819-1904), Queen Victoria's cousin and the youngest general in the expeditionary force, had no practical military experience but was made commander of the 1st Infantry Division after he had lobbied the Queen who then requested a senior post for him from Aberdeen, the Prime Minister. He fought at the Alma and at Inkerman but appears to have had a nervous breakdown and returned to England in November, after first spending a terrible night, weeping as he anticipated drowning, on board ship in Balaclava harbour during the storm of 14 November.

Campbell. General Sir Colin Campbell (1792-1863), was commander of the Highland Brigade and fought with distinction at the Alma. The son of a Glasgow carpenter, he was an inspirational leader, a man of proven ability and courage, and the most experienced of the divisional commanders; he had served under Moore and Wellington in the Peninsular War before seeing action in China and India. With no family or contacts to speak for him he had achieved his seniority by merit. Many in the army were shocked when, in the autumn of 1855, he was passed over for Commander-in-Chief in favour of General Sir William Codrington, a more emollient character with all the right social connections. He was considered too rough in his manners, too hasty and hot-headed to avoid confrontation with the officers he would be commanding and too boastful about the exploits of his Scottish soldiers. As a sop he was later given command of the newly formed Highland Division in the Crimea. His talents were finally recognised when, in 1858, he was made a peer, taking the title Lord Clyde of Clydesdale, after his success as Commander-in-Chief of the British Army in India during the Mutiny.

Canrobert. General François Certain Canrobert (1809-95) succeeded St Arnaud as Commander-in-Chief of the French forces in September 1854 but resigned in favour of Pelissier in May 1855.

Cardigan. James Thomas Brudenell, seventh Earl of Cardigan (1797-1868) was notorious both for his vindictive and unreasonable behaviour as a commanding officer and for his scandalous private life. As the only son and heir, he was pampered and spoilt from his earliest years and grew up to be selfish and arrogant – unusually harsh and domineering toward his social inferiors – and subject to fits of extraordinary and uncontrollable rage. Apart from a brief time at Harrow he had been educated by tutors at home, where he was cosseted by his seven sisters; all his life he retained a fondness for female company. He did not join the army until he was 27, when he purchased a cornetcy in the 8th Hussars, but through the patronage of the Duke of York his promotions were swifter, and even more expensive, than those of his brother-in-law, Lucan. After only six years, in August 1830, he became a Major and by December the same year he was a Lieutenant-Colonel. Two years later he left the 8th Hussars and purchased the command of the 15th Hussars, an efficient and cheerful regiment. His time as commanding officer was remarkably brief. Within a year he had antagonised every officer with his excessive discipline (including floggings over minor misdemeanours), daily drills and his insistence that they buy new, extremely expensive, uniforms. He persecuted individuals over trivial matters and finally court-martialled Captain Wathen, an experienced soldier who had fought at Waterloo, because he protested at the changes. When the case was heard, early in 1834, Wathen was acquitted and Cardigan was afterwards publicly removed from command of the 15th Hussars. The proceedings of the private hearing were leaked to the *Times* and Cardigan's appalling behaviour became common knowledge. Unembarrassed by this public shaming, he employed his family's influence over the aging William IV to ensure his reinstatement (against the direct wishes of the army Commander-in-Chief), and two years later, after paying the reputed sum of £40,000 as purchase price, he became commanding officer of the 11th Hussars, who were stationed in India. Cardigan joined them there briefly but they returned to England in 1837. Once again, he treated his regiment as though it were his private fiefdom, initiating a similarly harsh regime and indulging in victimization. In particular, he attempted to remove the many 'Indian' officers whom he felt were too impecunious and insufficiently aristocratic in demeanour to add lustre to his troop. On his succession to the Earldom in 1837 he acquired an income of £40,000 a year, and spent almost a quarter of it annually on horses and uniform for the men of the regiment who, arrayed in tight-fitting pink overalls, were soon nicknamed the 'Cherry Bums'. During the next sixteen years further regimental scandals, duels and the subsequent court cases increased Cardigan's unpopularity – he was booed in the street and hissed and shouted at in the theatre and the opera. His private life was equally dramatic. He had eloped with a married woman in 1823; they married three years later after a very public divorce but the marriage was a disaster – she was promiscuous, extravagant and bad-tempered – and they separated about twelve years later. With his good looks and louche charm he was involved in a series of liaisons, one of which resulted in yet another salacious court case.

Fanny was shrewd enough to realise that Cardigan's friendship was essential for her survival but her letters show that she never at any time admired him. Indeed, she originally disliked him – his treatment of the regimental horses horrified her – but later felt 'sincerely sorry for him' even though she remained aware of his faults. As she explained to Selina, 'I have not abused old Chargeagain (Cardigan) since he has been in the Crimea as he has been very civil to me; & we have had more comprehensive abuses to complain of than are included in any single man. ... He was always called Chargeagain by our brigade because when he used to have field days in Bulgaria he always made the Turkish cavalry attend & used to make them charge till their horses were fit to drop.'

Cathcart. Major-General the Hon. Sir George Cathcart (1794-1854), commander of the 4th Division, had advocated an early attack on Sebastopol before the defences were strengthened. He believed that he and his men could run into it even in open daylight, risking only a few shots, and had written so to Raglan, who refused to allow any such attempt. As the holder of a 'dormant commission', by which he would assume command on the death of Raglan, he was insulted that he was not more frequently consulted by Raglan.

Dundas. Vice-Admiral Sir James Dundas (1785-1862). As Commander of the British fleet in the Black Sea he was independent of Raglan, who found him haughty and obstructive, but every joint action had to be agreed between them. Much of the day-to-day operational handling of the fleet was delegated to Rear-Admiral Sir Edmund Lyons, who liaised more easily with Raglan. Lyons and his circle regularly criticised the cautious Dundas for keeping his ships out of range of the Russian guns, ignoring his good sense. Dundas probably considered Fanny to be part of the Lyons circle.

Estcourt. Major-General James Bucknall Bucknall Estcourt (1802-55), Adjutant-General, in charge of army discipline, had little experience of practical army life and none of warfare. A friend of Raglan, he was considered too kind and forgiving: 'Poor old Estcourt you know was accustomed to be considered as utterly useless. Lord Raglan did not even, latterly, pay him the compliment of attempting to transact business with him. ... as an actor in H[ea]d of a department he did not exist.' Fenton photographed him – relaxing in a deck-chair.

Fenton. Roger Fenton (1819-69) had arrived in the Crimea on 9 March with his cameras, two assistants and a van (specially equipped as a dark room to develop collodion wet plates), under commission from the art publisher Thomas Agnew & Son to photograph scenes of camp life. Although this was a commercial venture, designed to profit from the popular interest in the war, it received royal and government backing. Fenton had a letter of introduction to Lord Raglan from Prince Albert (he had earlier photographed the royal family), and his passage was paid for by Lord Newcastle, the Secretary of State for War; the need to retain their patronage and ensure sales imposed some restraint on his choice of subjects. Although he wrote home describing the half-buried corpses still visible on the battlefields and the horrific condition of the wounded in the regimental hospitals, none of these appear in his photographs. Even so, many of his pictures have a dramatic impact. The desolation and waste of war is apparent without the physical presence of the dead.

The son of a wealthy Lancashire MP, he had studied painting in Paris and London, working on historical genre paintings (the influence is evident in his carefully composed pictures of camp life) but, failing to sell his pictures, he trained and worked as a lawyer before becoming interested in photography. A founder member of the Photographic Society and official photographer to the British Museum, he was one of the first to make a living by selling photographs to the general public.

Fenton had many acquaintances in the British army and his brother-in-law was with the Connaught Rangers. Living conditions had improved by the time he arrived and he was welcomed in both the French and British camps, even acquiring a pass to visit the trenches. As well as taking official photographs, he was besieged by requests for private photographs, even by the navvies, and had to turn many away. Fanny and Henry were more fortunate, and their picture sold so well that he took no payment from them. The extreme heat made his working conditions difficult and he suffered from cholera and the pain of broken ribs after a fall when unloading his equipment on his arrival at Balaclava. But he started early in the morning (later in the day, the glare of the sun forced everyone to squint), and worked at great speed before the wet plates dried out. Exposure took up to twenty seconds so the scene had to be staged in advance. Despite these problems, his photographs convey a vivid sense of camp life, the camaraderie and the boredom, and for the first time those at home could see the real conditions – soldiers in patched and shabby uniforms, their horses suffering the after-effects of the winter's starvation, ships crowded into the harbour and the chaos on the quayside. In all he took over 350 photographs, the first large-scale photographic documentation of a war. He is not a 'war-photographer' in the modern sense – there are no action shots – but the soldiers are no longer drawn as gross caricatures or portrayed as gilded heroes in immaculate uniforms. Their humanity is exposed for all to see.

Layard. Sir Austen Henry Layard (1817-94) English archaeologist and radical MP. In 1849 he had excavated the remains of four palaces at ancient Nineveh in Mesopotamia. He spent four months in the Crimea, returning to London to attack the conduct of the war as well as the system of bought commissions and incompetent aristocratic officers who lacked practical experience.

Liprandi. General Pavel Liprandi (1796-1864) fought against the French in 1813-14 and in the Russo-Turkish war of 1828-29. He commanded the Russian forces at the battle of Balaclava and was so moved by the heroism of the Light Brigade that he told the captured cavalry they were 'noble fellows', although at first he found it hard to believe that they had not been drunk. His force remained based round the village of Tchergoum, to the north east of Balaclava, and posed a constant threat to the harbour and to the lines of communication between it and the allied forces. He took part in the battles of Inkerman and led the attack on the Sardinians at the battle of the Tchernaya.

Lucan. George Charles Bingham, third Earl of Lucan (1800-88) became an ensign in the 6th Regiment of Foot at the age of sixteen. By judicious use of the purchase system (he appeared on the rolls of five different regiments), he advanced rapidly in seniority and by December 1825 was a Major in the 17th Lancers. A year later he purchased command of the regiment, as Lieutenant-Colonel, for £25,000. 'Bingham's Dandies', provided with new uniforms and thoroughbred horses, were soon among the smartest soldiers in the army but they suffered under their new commanding officer. A martinet and a workaholic, who immersed himself in the day-to-day minutiae of administration, unable to distinguish between trifles and matters of importance – a trait that was apparent all his life – he imposed excessive discipline and a heavy workload of drills, parades and inspections. Stubborn, bad-tempered and arrogant, he was unpopular with both men and officers. But he was also brave, ambitious and determined to experience campaign life. In 1828 he joined the staff of Prince Woronzov during the Russian invasion of the Balkans. Returning to his regiment a year later, covered with glory, he married Anne, the youngest daughter of the sixth earl of Cardigan, and set in train his rivalry with her brother, whom he considered a 'feather-bed soldier'. In 1837, bored with peacetime soldiering, he gave up command of the regiment and went onto half-pay in order to live on the neglected family estates at Castlebar in Mayo, the first non-absentee landlord there for several generations. On succeeding to the Earldom in 1839 he became one of the most notorious of the 'consolidating landlords', evicting thousands of his impoverished peasant tenants (even during the famine years), with no thought to their immediate fate, in order to replace their small holdings with larger, more productive farms. Detested and, to his mind, misunderstood by all around him, his naturally irritable temperament worsened. When Lady Lucan and he separated, Cardigan blamed him for treating her disgracefully by expecting her to live in Mayo, short of money and far from fashionable life, and their mutual enmity increased. Meanwhile, Lucan had automatically received promotion while on half-pay and by 1854 had reached the rank of Major-General. On the outbreak of war he was appointed commander of the Cavalry Division under Lord Raglan, and reverted to his harsh military regime of twenty-five years earlier, insisting on long field-days in Bulgaria despite the excessive heat. But the form of drill he used was obsolete and he was too obstinate to learn the new commands – expecting the officers to resurrect the old drill instead – so that the exhausted troops were in total confusion. Once again his unpredictable temper and his continual, nagging orders over trivial matters made him unpopular with all those around him even though, unlike Cardigan, he spent the whole of the campaign with his men, sharing their hardships, including suffering from lice. Even this modest way of life irritated some officers, who hoped for occasional treats from their commanding officers. 'Dined with Lord Lucan. A moderate feed, very', wrote Lieutenant-Colonel Hodge sourly. Yet, despite their dislike of him, when Lucan was recalled during the controversy with Raglan which arose after he refused to accept the blame for the loss of the Light Brigade, the cavalry sided with him and felt he had been hard done by.

Lyons. Rear-Admiral Sir Edmund Lyons (1790-1858), second in command of the British fleet and commander of the in-shore squadron, was a dashing and ambitious man who enjoyed his physical resemblance to his role model, Nelson. Due to his close friendship with Raglan, his influence over events was considerably greater than that of his superior officer Dundas.

Menshikov. Prince Alexander Sergeevitch (1781-1869), Commander-in-Chief of the Russian forces in the Crimea, was respected for his courage as a soldier but inflexible in military matters. He was chosen to conduct the delicate negotiations with the Porte in February 1853, but his arrogance towards the Sultan strengthened Turkish opposition to Russian demands. He commanded part of the naval force that attacked the Turkish fleet at Sinope, but was eventually dismissed in late February 1855 after his failure to capture Eupatoria.

Nightingale. Florence Nightingale (1820-1910) had trained as a nurse, studying in Paris and Kaiserwerth, after years of opposition from her wealthy parents who had hoped their well-educated daughter would make a suitable marriage. Nursing was not seen as a respectable alternative. By 1853, aged 33, she had become superintendent of a nursing home for gentlewomen in Harley Street. On 12 October 1854 a report in the *Times* by Thomas Chenery first alerted the British public to the appalling conditions in the British hospitals at Scutari, where the shortage of doctors and equipment meant that many of the wounded from the battle of the Alma still lay unattended in their filthy, bloodstained uniforms. The response was immediate. John Delane, the editor of the *Times*, initiated a fund to provide comforts for the men in the Crimea and Scutari. And Sidney Herbert, the Secretary at War with responsibility for the Army Medical Board, who was already trying to improve conditions for the troops, wrote to Florence Nightingale, a family friend, inviting her to become Superintendent of the Female Nursing Establishment in Turkey. His letter crossed with one from Florence to Herbert's wife, offering to create a nursing service to take to Scutari. On 4 November she arrived there with an initial group of 38 nurses, some from religious orders, to assist the overworked doctors and orderlies, many of whom strongly disapproved of allowing women into a hospital.

At this time the two hospitals already held over 8,000 sick and wounded but by the following February, after the hardships of the Crimean winter, the numbers had risen to about 14,000. During the campaign the British army lost approximately 19,500 officers and men. Only about a fifth, some 3,750, were killed, the rest died from disease or the infection of their wounds, brought on by the filth and squalor in the hospitals. Even the most basic hygiene was ignored while men remained covered with vermin and suffering from gangrene. Barred from attending the patients until she had won over the younger, more energetic doctors, Florence Nightingale and her nurses spent the first weeks scrubbing the wards, improving the supply of linen and bedding and equipping a kitchen to provide edible food – often working fifteen hours a day to create order from the chaos around them. All the supplies, from small lice combs, scrubbing brushes and soap, to the food, the operating tables and stump pillows had to be bought with money collected by the *Times* War Fund. The mismanagement of hospital resources by the Commissariat and the Purveyor's departments had caused as much hardship as the unsanitary conditions.

Although she became famous as the Lady with the Lamp (every night she walked for miles through the hospitals, checking the comfort of the patients), and was revered by the soldiers, Florence Nightingale's true achievement was her skill in cutting through the army medical bureaucracy and initiating much needed practical reforms in hospital administration. After managing the hospitals by day, she sat up late almost every night compiling statistics and reports to send to Sidney Herbert and his successors at the War Office. Acting on her suggestions, Herbert took steps to improve the Purveying and Commissariat departments and to recruit sympathetic doctors and younger orderlies; it may also have been at her suggestion that a Sanitary Commission was sent out to Scutari in March 1855. An earlier Hospitals Commission had 'inquired' only but the Sanitary Commission had a remit to act. Its members initiated the construction of a new drainage system at Scutari (the number of deaths from disease immediately dropped), before going on to Balaclava and overseeing the cleaning of the harbour and improvement of sanitary arrangements in the regimental camps.

Alongside her plans for major reforms of the military nursing establishment, Florence Nightingale cared deeply for the general well-being of the soldiers. Realising that they had little to do in convalescence but squander their money on drink, she arranged for the remittance home of their pay and used the resources of the *Times* Fund to provide educational facilities, reading rooms, and games rooms for the illiterate. When she first arrived at the Barracks she had found more than 250 soldiers' wives, left behind after the army had sailed from Varna, living in the most wretched conditions in the cellars. They were rescued from this plight by her friend Lady Alicia Blackwood, who not only set up a laundry for the hospital, where they could earn money, but also established a school for their children.

Nolan. Captain Edward Louis Nolan (1818-54) was a brilliant horseman and dedicated cavalry officer whose reputation is overshadowed by his part in the Charge of the Light Brigade. The son and grandson of British army officers, he was exceptionally well-educated, speaking five European languages and several Indian dialects. After joining the Hungarian Hussars (a part of the Austrian army) as a cadet at the age of fourteen, he attended the Engineering School near Vienna, famous for teaching military and equestrian skills. He served with distinction in Hungary and Poland before leaving the Austrian army in 1839 and buying a commission as a cornet in the 15th Light Dragoons. During the next fifteen years he was promoted, by purchase, to captain, served briefly in India and visited Sweden, Prussia and Russia to study cavalry manoeuvres. He trained as a riding master at the cavalry depot in Maidstone in 1842 and while there first outlined his theory that light cavalry charging at speed could take a battery. Irritated by the traditional view of the cavalry as little more than the eyes and ears of the army, he published two books outlining his radical views – *The Training of Cavalry Remount Horses* (1852) and *Cavalry: Its History and Tactics* (1853) – which provoked widespread debate and earned him as much opprobrium as praise. William Howard Russell, writing on the evening of Nolan's death, succinctly summed up his views : 'I had the pleasure of his acquaintance, and I know he entertained the most exalted opinions respecting the capabilities of the English horse soldier. Properly led, the British Hussar and Dragoon could in his mind break square, take batteries, ride over columns of infantry, and pierce any other cavalry in the world as if they were made of straw.' He had been sent on ahead of the Expeditionary Force to Turkey in the spring of 1854 to buy remounts (new horses) for the cavalry and was then appointed ADC to Airey and moved with him to Raglan's headquarters.

Later rumours suggested that Nolan was Fanny's lover but there is nothing in her letters to suggest this and she was not affected by his death as she was by those of other friends. But they did share a mutual passion in their love of horses. Even so, she was one of the many who, writing home in the days immediately after Balaklava, blamed Nolan for the disaster – 'such an impetuous charge! Nolan who galloped on cheering was the first to fall, he whose folly cost so many lives.'

Omar Pasha. General Omar Pasha (1806-71), Commander-in-Chief of the Ottoman Army, was born Michael Lotis or Lattas, the son of a Croatian army officer, but took a Turkish name after converting to Islam. On first arriving in Constantinople he became writing-master to the future Sultan Abd-el-Mejid and married a wealthy, well-connected heiress, but even without these advantages he would have been successful in the Ottoman army, which was open to men of talent whatever their origins. During the autumn and winter of 1853 he had successfully repulsed the Russian invading forces and defended Silistria (see Appendix 1). After the fall of Sebastopol he wanted to march the Turkish army to relieve the Armenian town of Kars (besieged by the Russians since mid-June), which controlled access to the East and was of vital interest to Britain and Turkey. But for the French and British governments the war in the Crimea came first and he was prevented from leaving until late September by which time it was too late – on 25 November, defeated by hunger, cold and disease, the garrison at Kars surrendered to the Russians.

Fanny was a great admirer of the handsome Omar Pasha – he had the ambition, vitality and practical energy that Henry lacked. Henry himself appears to have been jealous of Omar; he became 'far from well' when they were invited to join Omar and his force on a reconnaissance so that Fanny had to stay behind and nurse him. And when they were later invited to travel with him to Eupatoria, Henry was suddenly unable to get leave.

Paget. Lieutenant-Colonel Lord George Augustus Frederick Paget (1818-80), Colonel of the 4th Light Dragoons and sixth son of the 1st Marquess of Anglesey, was not a rich man; his patrimony was tied up in his commission. In February 1854, intending to sell this, he had married his beautiful cousin, Lady Agnes Paget, against the express wishes of his father – she too had no fortune of her own – but once war was declared felt it would have been dishonourable to resign. However, after the battle of Inkerman, he returned to England to sort out his affairs after the recent death of his father. Paget was at ease among the aristocratic general staff and Raglan's ADCs, most of whom he had known from boyhood. Second in command of the Light Brigade under Lord Cardigan, he described him as 'easily managed, with calmness and firmness, and when one is in the right – which it is not difficult to be with him.' He appears to have managed Lucan as adroitly as Cardigan, although during his frequent negotiations between the two he feared that they were 'like a pair of scissors, which go snip and snip and snip, without ever doing each other any harm, but God help the poor devil who ever gets between them!' Extracts from the letters and journal he wrote for his wife were later published as *The Light Cavalry Brigade in the Crimea* (1881).

Pelissier. Maréchal Aimable Jean-Jacques Pelissier (1794-1864) was one of the group of officers who had served in Algeria and subsequently supported Louis Napoleon's coup d'état. Fenton said of him: 'he cares nothing for the sacrifice of life, and does not seem troubled with scruples of any kind. His face has the expression of brutal boldness something like that of a wild boar'. After heavy French losses, at the Flagstaff Battery and the Malakoff, he frequently repeated, 'On ne peut pas faire des omelettes sans casser des oeufs', but he was as reckless with his own safety as he was with that of his troops. An energetic man with decided opinions and 'resolute determination', he dominated Raglan. After Raglan's death, Fanny complained 'he bullies old Simpson like bricks' and he was a major reason for the latter's resignation. Short and stout, with fat little legs, he found riding a horse difficult and was a familiar sight in the camps tearing around in a pony trap.

Raglan. Lord Fitzroy James Henry Somerset, 1st Baron Raglan (1788-1855), Commander-in-Chief of the British Expeditionary Army to the East, had never yet during his 50 years with the army led troops into battle. He had been in action, and in danger, during the Napoleonic Wars but always as a staff officer implementing the orders of others. The youngest son of the fifth Duke of Beaufort, he was bought a commission as a Cornet while still a pupil at Westminster School, when almost 16, and three years later, through his family's connections, became an ADC to Wellesley (the future Duke of Wellington). The two men became close friends (Raglan married Wellington's niece), and by the age of 23, in 1811, he was Wellington's military secretary, remaining in his service until the Duke's death in 1852. Wellington obtained his protégé's promotion to lieutenant-colonel in 1812, ensuring further promotion automatically by seniority, without purchase. (By 1854 he had risen to the rank of general without ever having held a command, even of a company.) He served with Wellington throughout the Peninsular Campaign and at Waterloo, during which he was wounded in the right arm. He behaved with great courage throughout the subsequent amputation, never crying out during the operation until the end – when he called to the surgeon to bring back his arm because, 'There's a ring my wife gave me on the finger'. He was always cool under fire, but lacked most other attributes, and the experience, necessary to command an army. He spoke excellent French and had worked alongside one of the greatest generals of his generation – observing him both in the field and as peacetime Commander-in-Chief of the army – but, at the age of 66, years of deskwork and administration as Military Secretary at the Horse Guards had sapped his initiative. Before making any decision he always asked himself what the Duke would have done. A natural second-in-command, his time spent acting as a conciliator between the harsh, autocratic Wellington and the rest of the world had honed his diplomatic skills but left him unprepared to stand up to the tough French generals he was to fight alongside; he was always too courteous to make his own wishes clear and too diffident to force anyone to act against their will. Although he was unjustly criticised for the maladministration of the Commissariat and the consequent lack of resources, he must bear some responsibility for the hardships borne by his troops. A more determined man, like his mentor the Duke, would have been more forceful from the start in ensuring that improvements were in hand. His staff shielded him from the desperate conditions endured during the winter months and he rarely visited his men to find out for himself how things were. Instead, much of his time was spent writing long reports that could well have been delegated. His manner and character were not suited to command or to inspire an army. The day after the battle of Balaclava, Paget described him riding through the Light Brigade camp – 'which caused some excitement among our fellows, rushing out to cheer him in their shirt-sleeves. But he did not say anything. How I longed for him to do so, as I walked by his horse's head! One little word, "Well, my boys, you have done well," or something of the sort, would have cheered us all up, but then it would have entailed on him more cheers, which would have been distasteful to him; more's the pity, though one cannot but admire such a nature.' Although naturally reserved and aloof, he was not always suitably independent for a commander-in-chief and could cause offence by his favouritism; his obvious preference for the company, and sometimes the advice, of Lyons to Dundas, Cardigan to Lucan, and Brown to Cathcart aggravated situations that were already difficult. But his worst fault was his inability to give clear orders, he was notorious for making suggestions rather than precise commands. During the skirmish at the Bulganek river, Airey had to reinterpret his message to Lucan and the next day, at the Alma, the Duke of Cambridge at first refused to move his troops because the initial order he received made no sense. A month later, at the start of the battle of Balaclava, Raglan's ADC interpreted his order to Cambridge as – 'There's a row going on down in the Balaclava plain, and you fellows are wanted.' Fortunately the Duke understood him this time.

Fanny repeated the gossip on the misdoings of Raglan as told her by her favourites and shared the widespread prejudice against him as Commander-in-Chief, blaming him not just for his moments of hesitancy but also, unfairly, for all the troubles that beset the organisation of the army. But even she frequently comments on his sweetness of manner and his gentle charm. Her obituary sums up the feelings of many of those around him – 'We are almost tempted to lose sight of the inefficient General, in the recollection of the kind-hearted, gentlemanly man, who had so hard a task, which he fulfilled so well, of keeping together and in check the heads of so many armies.'

Russell. William Howard Russell (1820-1907) was born in Ireland and educated at Trinity College, Dublin. He wrote occasionally for the *Times* and in 1843 the editor John Thadeus Delane (who was three years his senior), invited him to London as a regular contributor. The impact of his reports from Ireland during the Famine convinced Delane that Russell should accompany the British army during the war against Russia. This was an unusual move; until then newspapers had relied for war news on dispatches written by officers accompanying the forces. Other London newspapers – the *Daily News*, the *Morning Post* and the *Morning Advertiser* – soon copied this idea but the *Times* with a circulation of 51,000 (more than double all its rivals together), dominated public opinion. Newspapers were still a luxury item, the *Times* cost five pence (one penny of this was tax), and their readership consisted largely of the influential newly enfranchised middle-classes who had the time and the education to enjoy long, well-written articles. From 14 August to 12 December 1854, when Parliament was in recess, the reports in the *Times* remained largely unchallenged by official sources. Delane told Russell that he wanted 'the truth in all things' and his discursive, uncensored dispatches were unlike any previous war reports. Although some of the early articles took almost a fortnight to reach London (Inkerman was fought before the news of Balaclava reached the public), once the telegraph was extended from Varna to Balaclava in late April 1855 they arrived within forty-eight hours – giving a shocking immediacy to the horrors of June 18. Russell's vivid account of the battle of Balaclava made his name but his detailed descriptions of the muddles, mismanagement and ensuing hardship of day-to-day army life had an even greater effect. His private letters to Delane were still more outspoken and many of the *Times* editorials were based on these – including the accusation, avoided by Russell in his dispatch, of a 'blunder' after the charge of the Light Brigade, which caught Tennyson's eye. Later editorials were credited with bringing about the downfall of the Aberdeen Government (see p. 287, note 20). The order authorising Russell to travel with the Guards went astray and for most of the time he had to make his own arrangements – 'I was nobody's child on shore' – so that he was only too aware of the prevailing lack of resources and equipment. Raglan made clear his dislike of the press and considered Russell in particular as little better than a spy, whose reports were often read in Moscow and Sebastopol before they reached Balaclava. Information published in the *Times* – on the position of the regiments and the artillery and ammunition stores – was frequently followed up by accurate bombardments from the Russian guns. Russell claimed that his dispatches were out of date by the time the Russians read them and, moreover, it was his editor's decision to publish them, but this did not mollify those who were being shot at. However most of the navy and army, with the exception of those at Headquarters, praised his reports and were happy to pass on information when asked. Lack of official information meant that Russell had to rely on these private sources but as the situation deteriorated this was occasionally little more than a litany of ill-natured gossip and individual complaints – prompting the *Spectator* to describe him (in a review praising Fanny's 'truthful' Journal), as 'a collector and arranger of camp stories and after-dinner judgments.' Russell's chief fault was a too credulous acceptance of the widespread assumption that Raglan was personally to blame for the shortages and mismanagement. His criticisms of the latter were valid but he overestimated how much change any commander, however dynamic, could have effected. He was even more outspoken in his scorn of Simpson after he became Commander-in-Chief. Codrington, who succeeded Simpson in October 1855, was furious that Russell had pointed out his shortcomings as a commander during the assault on the Redan, and ordered the expulsion of any correspondent whose reports might provide information to the enemy. Russell realised that his life would be made impossible and left the Crimea in early December, returning briefly the following June to cover the final departure of the British army.

Fanny, who may have met Russell earlier through his friendship with Killeen, enjoyed the company of 'the eloquent and truthful correspondent of the *Times*' and concurred with his views on Raglan. But she, like many others, became alarmed when he attacked Simpson. 'The *Times* gets too scurrilous; it overshoots its mark ... After all Simpson is not to blame ... The *Times* did an amazing amount of good last year & has grown conceited on it & is altogether above its weight ... and I must say I think it unmanly to load an old man's shoulders with such sheer abuse' (see Simpson, below). There was a growing feeling that Russell had pursued a private vendetta against Raglan, treating him as a villain rather than an incompetent man enmeshed in a cumbersome system, and that this had contributed towards his death. Although both Raglan and Simpson were widely criticised, private grousing in letters took on a quite different force when elevated to diatribes in the *Times*. Despite this, Fanny spoke for many when she declared 'I was glad to be able to speak up for Russell and the *Times,* which paper however it may err politically has certainly been the soldier's friend' (28 September 1855).

St Arnaud. Maréchal General Leroy de St Arnaud, the French Commander-in-Chief (1801-54), had seen active service in Algeria and as Minister for War had backed Napoleon III in his coup d'état of 1851. Determined and ambitious, he attempted to take overall command of the Allied forces but by the time the armies arrived in the Crimea he was a sick man and resigned his command to Canrobert four days before his death on 29 September 1854.

Seacole. Mary Seacole (1805-81) was born in Kingston, Jamaica, the daughter of a Scottish soldier. Mrs Seacole had learnt her skills from her Jamaican mother, a doctress who kept a boarding-house where she nursed invalid Army and Navy officers and their wives. Widowed while still young, she became known as a skilled nurse and doctress after she had successfully applied her 'healing arts and simple remedies' during epidemics of cholera and yellow fever in Panama and Kingston. In 1854, hearing that the regiments she had nursed were now suffering in the Crimea for lack of medical care, she went to London and applied to work as a nurse. Turned down by both the Army and the committee recruiting nurses to join Florence Nightingale, she wondered whether they shrank 'from accepting my aid because my blood flowed beneath a somewhat duskier skin than theirs?' Undeterred, however, she travelled independently to the Crimea (stopping en route at Scutari to meet Florence Nightingale, who declared herself happy to do anything in her power to help her), and set up the British Hotel to provide 'a mess table and comfortable quarters for sick and convalescent officers' alongside a store which eventually sold everything 'from an anchor down to a needle'. With the profits from these ventures, she bought or prepared medicines which she provided free for the navvies and the soldiers, many of whom preferred her natural remedies to the rough and ready treatment of their regimental doctors. Nicknamed Mother Seacole, she became a familiar sight at the front, tending the wounded, and after the war was awarded the Crimean medal. She returned to England bankrupt but a committee of senior army officers and William Howard Russell, recognising her contribution, organised a military festival in an attempt to pay off her debts.

Simpson. General Sir James Simpson (1792-1868)) was sent out to the Crimea in February 1855 as Chief of Staff to the army by the new Secretary for War, Lord Panmure (a fellow Scot and old friend), in effect to spy on Raglan and his staff. He was placed in direct command over Airey, Quartermaster-General in charge of army supplies, and Estcourt, Adjutant-General in charge of army discipline, who had been overwhelmed by the problems facing them, many of which were not immediately solvable. However, they had often appeared dilatory and the public, which had lost confidence in them, was now censuring them by name. As the press began to include the government in its accusations of mismanagement, they were seen as useful scapegoats, and it was hoped that Simpson would find grounds to send them home. But although he admitted that he had gone out prejudiced against Raglan and the staff-officers, once there, perhaps realising the full extent of the problems and to the surprise and annoyance of Panmure and many in the Crimea, Simpson changed his mind and reported back in their favour. On the death of Raglan he reluctantly succeeded to the post of Commander-in-Chief. Although he saw himself as a caretaker appointment, he worked hard to improve conditions for his troops but after the fall of Sebastopol and the carnage in the Redan he lost heart. Unable to convince Panmure that it was impossible to assault northern Sebastopol without leaving Balaclava vulnerable to attack, he wilted under the strain of Panmure's increasingly critical daily telegrams. On Saturday 29 September the *Times*, which had just published Russell's detailed account of the events of 8 September, attacked Simpson for not revealing the full horror of the day in his official despatch. Branding him an 'incapable commander', it thundered: 'He deserves recall. ... The British army had been beaten, and beaten, it was reasonable to suppose, through the incapacity of the General ... It cannot be too often repeated that our army requires a younger man ... not [a man] of the age of the British Commander-in-chief who sits in a ditch muffled up in a cloak when a whole army rushes to the assault.' Worried by Panmure, bullied by Pelissier and continually attacked by the *Times*, a 'mortified and disgusted' Simpson resigned, although he was not replaced for several weeks.

Stratford. Lord Stratford de Redcliffe (1786-1880) was at the embassy in Constantinople in 1810-12 and twice became Ambassador to Turkey, in 1825-28 and then again in 1842-58. He and his wife were criticised for preferring to give parties rather than improving conditions for the sick and wounded soldiers in Constantinople. Fanny was not an admirer; 'What we think of Lord Stratford is merely that he is a pompous, bullyragging old man – in complexion very like a washed out cotton gown – and very fond of display – and being made a great man of. I never heard a single soul say a word in his favour & I think with the *Roving Englishman* [see p. 302, note 26] that he would try to bully the devil himself let alone the Sultan poor man'(1 October 1855). See Appendix 1.

Tremenheere. Hugh Seymour Tremenheere (1804-93) was called to the Bar in 1834. He served on numerous Royal Commissions and was instrumental in bringing about fourteen Acts of Parliament, all concerned with improving the working conditions of factory workers, particularly children. In the autumn of 1854 he visited the Crimea, which is probably when Fanny and he first met (he was not known to her family), and on his return journey conveyed despatches from Lord Stratford to the Foreign Office.

Vane. Lord Adolphus Vane Tempest (1825-64) was the second son of the third Lord Londonderry. He had joined the 3rd Regiment of Scots Fusilier Guards at the age of eighteen and served with them in Corfu and India. He became MP for Durham City in December 1852 but, after considerable controversy over vote-rigging and bribery, was unseated after six months. He was re-elected to the same seat in mid-1854, but in October obtained leave of absence as an MP to join his regiment on active service. His mother, the Dowager Marchioness of Londonderry, was so angered by his descriptions of the appalling conditions the army suffered that she wrote to Disraeli urging him to use his influence to alleviate them. She herself did what she could to help, giving Vane a hut for the use of the men of his company for reading and writing letters home (*Illustrated London News*, 19 May 1855). After his final return from the Crimea at the end of the war, Vane suffered a breakdown and retired from his regiment. In 1860 he married, but he suffered recurring bouts of madness, during which he was incarcerated, until his premature death in 1864.

Windham. Lt-Gen Sir Charles Ash Windham (1810-70) became known as 'Redan Windham' or the 'Hero of the Redan' because of his bravery on 8 September 1855. He had led assault after assault on the Russian defences in the Redan, desperately attempting to rally his terrified, dwindling forces against increasing numbers of Russian reinforcements, who were rushing from the town and pouring down from the Malakoff, which the French had just taken. The urgently needed reserves were held back by General Sir William Codrington, who was in overall command of that section of the attack; he was later condemned by other officers for lack of initiative and loss of nerve. Three times Windham sent junior officers to ask Codrington for more men, but at each attempt the messengers were wounded or killed before reaching the General.

Finally, after clearly stating his reasons for leaving his men, he went back himself to demand men from Codrington who, after some argument and strong words from Windham, grudgingly agreed. But it was too late. Thousands of Russian soldiers, in a last attempt to save their city, had pushed the British from the parapet into the ditch below and back into their own trenches, with appalling loss of life. The assault was abandoned. Windham was one of the few to defend the men, who were widely accused of cowardice, and his remarks obviously influenced Fanny's comments.

Woronzov. Prince Woronzov (1782-1856) was Governor-General of the Crimean Peninsula from 1823 to 1853 and still owned estates in the area, including the land on which the Allied armies camped outside Sebastopol. He discouraged the Russian practice of serfdom and was known for his liberalism. Born and educated in England, the son of the Russian Ambassador, his sister, Lady Pembroke, was the mother of the British Secretary-at-War, Sidney Herbert.

APPENDIX I

How the War Began

In 1854 the lands surrounding the Black Sea were dominated by the empires of Turkey and Russia. The Ottoman [Turkish] empire stretched from the Adriatic to the Persian Gulf, encompassing the southern shore of the Black Sea and extending on the west to the principalities north of the Danube. But the Turkish borders were fragile. Memorably described as 'the sick man of Europe' by the autocratic Tsar Nicholas I, Turkey was a constant temptation to Russian imperial ambitions. In 1828, the Russians had crossed the Danube into the Balkans and fought their way south. Nicholas, as champion of the Greek Orthodox religion, claimed he was guaranteeing the rights of the fourteen thousand Christians living under Turkish rule but it became clear that his aim was to seize Constantinople, which controlled entry to and from the Mediterranean. His armies were alarmingly close to their goal before intense international diplomatic pressure forced them to stop and withdraw.

However, if Russia was to survive as a world power, unimpeded entry to the Mediterranean was vital. Every winter her northern fleet was frozen into the Baltic ports, leaving her reliant on the ships based at the newly built warm water dockyards at Sebastopol. Control of the Bosphorus and the Dardanelles therefore remained of vital concern. In 1833 Turkey agreed to close the Straits to foreign warships at Russia's request. Nine years later her exclusive control was removed when it was agreed that the Straits would be closed to all warships in peacetime. Thus the Russian fleet remained locked into the Black Sea, separated from those of the other European powers by the Sea of Marmara.

But the threat remained. Even though Nicholas might protest to Prince Albert that he did not want an inch of Turkish soil, Russia's designs were clear and her growing naval power and the campaigns in Asia Minor (always a potential threat to the northwest frontier of India), alarmed Britain. The Eastern Question loomed large in political debates, fuelled by fears that the perhaps imminent seizure of Turkish territory by Russia would upset the fragile balance of power in Europe. In addition, liberal opinion was outraged when Nicholas gave military help to Franz-Josef, Emperor of Austria, in crushing the uprising by Hungarian nationalists in 1848-9.

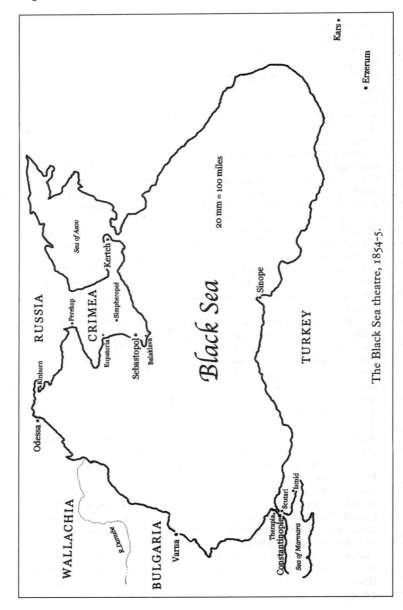

The Black Sea theatre, 1854-5.

In fact, Russia's apparent might was illusory. Although she could boast the largest army in Europe and a more numerous fleet than the peacetime Royal Navy, she lacked the industrial backbone to sustain such a show of strength. Her internal economy was undeveloped; an agricultural country reliant on serfs, with poor communications and transport, few railways and badly maintained roads, she proved unable to wage an extended conflict. But this was not apparent when, in 1852, France, rather than Britain, challenged her hegemony by meddling in Turkish affairs in Palestine and thus set in motion the events leading to war.

After the fall of the French monarchy following the 1848 revolution in Paris, Louis Napoleon had come to power as President of the Second Republic. Planning to declare himself Emperor, he was anxious to enhance the prestige of his new regime by reviving memories of his uncle's military triumphs. To this end he chose to interfere in a bitter feud that had been simmering for years between two rival groups of monks, the Catholics (traditionally supported by France), and the Greek Orthodox Christians (defended in their turn by Russia), over the guardianship of the Holy Places – the churches of the Nativity in Bethlehem, the Holy Sepulchre in Jerusalem and the Tomb of the Virgin at Gethsemane. This not only pleased the Catholics in France but also made plain his intention of curbing the Tsar's own imperial ambitions.

The French ambassador to the Porte in Constantinople (the court and centre of government for the Ottoman Empire), exploiting Turkey's obvious weakness, demanded, and received, the rights France wanted for the Catholic monks. The Russian ambassador countered by invoking earlier agreements, made in perpetuity, and regained the privileges for the Greek Orthodox church. Furious at this double-dealing, Napoleon sent a 90-gun steam-battleship through the Dardanelles to anchor off Constantinople, violating the international agreement but powerfully demonstrating his determination and the strength of his sea-power. Impressed, Sultan Abd-el-Mejid once more acceded to the French demands; the Catholic church was granted supreme authority over all the Holy Places and early in December they were given the keys to the Church of the Nativity. The scenes that ensued over the following months were both ridiculous and tragic with rival monks frequently coming to blows, and even beating each other with crucifixes and huge wax candles grabbed from the altars. When Muslim police failed to prevent the murder of Orthodox monks as they tried to stop the Catholics raising a silver star, bearing the arms of France, over the Holy Grotto of the Nativity, Nicholas had the excuse he needed. Claiming that the Sultan was incapable of protecting his Christian subjects, he sent Prince Alexander

Sergevitch Menshikov to lead a diplomatic mission to Constantinople with a list of demands.

The Tsar had three demands to make to the Turks, and he expected them to be accepted. If they were refused, Menshikov was to threaten the destruction of Constantinople and the occupation of the Dardanelles. The first two – the restoration of the Holy Places to the Orthodox church and a Russian-Turkish defensive alliance should France protest (which she surely would) – though intimidating were not new, but the final ultimatum – that all Christians within the Ottoman Empire should be placed under the immediate protection of the Tsar – could only lead to a critical undermining of Turkish sovereignty. In the Balkan states the greater part of the population were Christians and might call on the Tsar for help at any time, so providing him with the justification to invade Turkish territory.

Nicholas had assumed the Sultan would concede to his wishes and was horrified when, backed by both France and Britain, he refused. He had expected Britain to remain neutral but had miscalculated the extent to which her increased trade with Turkey and her fear of Russian expansion had changed her attitude towards his country. There was, too, a growing resentment against him personally; he was castigated as a despot, the ruler of a police-state who only five years before had been a major and active opponent of the liberal uprisings in Hungary and Poland. The British cabinet was divided but in the end decided that Admiral Sir James Dundas, the commander of the Royal Naval fleet in the Mediterranean, was to hold his squadron in readiness to intervene if Russia attacked Constantinople.

The Sultan and his advisers were supported in their negotiations with Menshikov by the British Ambassador, Lord Stratford de Redcliffe (formerly Sir Stratford Canning), whose experience of Turkish affairs and the workings of the Porte went back to 1810 when, at the age of twenty-four, he had unexpectedly found himself in charge of the Embassy there. Young though he was, he had vigorously furthered British interests by persuading Turkey to break her ties with France and then, in 1812, ally herself with Russia, thus freeing the Russian troops based on the Danube to join the fight against Napoleon. Although he left Constantinople the same year and, apart from a four year appointment there in 1825-8, was absent for thirty years his influence remained unchallenged. When he returned as ambassador in 1842 successive Sultans and their entourages sought his advice and approval and his shrewdness and firm authority gave Britain a dominant role in Turkish politics.

Under Stratford's guidance a compromise was suggested for the first of the Russian demands, the guardianship of the Holy Places, but the other two were rejected outright. This was far from satisfying Menshikov or his master. Diplomatic relations between Russia and Turkey were broken off and on 21 May 1853 Menshikov returned to St Petersburg. Angered by the Turks' intransigence, and blaming Stratford for their obstinacy, the Tsar let it be known that he would move troops into Wallachia and Moldavia, the principalities north of the Danube, and hold them hostage until Turkey gave way. Britain responded by ordering Dundas to sail his squadron to Besika Bay, close to the entrance to the Dardanelles. Four weeks later, on 2 July, Russian troops invaded the principalities but Turkey, now confident of British and French support, stood firm and mobilised troops in Bulgaria, south of the Danube. On 4 October she declared war, delivering an ultimatum to Russia to leave the principalities within two weeks. In mid-October the British and French Mediterranean fleets anchored in the Dardanelles and on 23 October Turkish troops crossed the Danube and advanced on the Russian army.

At this point, as diplomacy gave way to conflict, there was still a possibility that Russia and Turkey would fight it out alone. The Tsar had assumed Franz-Joseph of Austria would reciprocate the help given him in 1848 but Austria, alarmed by the presence of Russian troops along the Danube, her lifeline to the Black Sea and the Mediterranean, chose instead to defend her waterways by stationing troops in Hungary, over the border from Wallachia. Nicholas was said to be so angry at this lack of gratitude that he turned Franz-Joseph's portrait to the wall. Russia was left without an ally.

And the sick man of Europe turned out to possess unexpected strength. The Ottoman army beat back the Russians and then occupied a series of forts along the Danube, successfully defending them against Russian counter-attacks. Although usually referred to as Turks, the army included soldiers from all parts of the Ottoman empire, the different units varying widely in expertise. Most of those fighting along the Danube were from the mountains of Albania, Bosnia and Bulgaria, their regimental officers included English, Irish and Scottish mercenaries. Experienced soldiers, they had fought successfully against insurgents in the Balkans under their charismatic commander-in-chief, Omar Pasha. Born Michael Lotis or Lattas, the son of a Greek Orthodox Croatian army officer, Omar Pasha was a renegade from the Austrian army who had converted to Islam and taken his Turkish name when he joined the Ottoman forces. A skilful and courageous soldier, admired by the British soldiers, including Lord Raglan, he was an effective commander and subsequently defended Eupatoria against superior Russian forces. During the whole of November 1853 he held the Danube against increasingly desperate Russian attacks.

But the Russian fleet dominated the Black Sea. In late November a flotilla of twelve small ships from the Ottoman fleet, escorting transports laden with supplies, was spotted by a squadron of three Russian warships near Sinope, on the southern coast. Reinforcements were summoned from Sebastopol. Six Russian warships and three steam-powered frigates, the latter commanded by Menshikov, duly arrived on 30 November and attacked the Turkish ships, with devastating effect. For the first time in naval warfare, the Russians used explosive shells in place of cannon shot and within two hours the Turkish flotilla was destroyed and most of the transports were ablaze. The flames spread to the shore and soon the port and the batteries were on fire. Several thousand Turkish sailors were killed and hundreds taken prisoner. Only one steamer escaped, arriving in Constantinople two days later. News of the Russian victory reached London on 12 December.

Public opinion in Britain was outraged – the swift, well-executed and hard-fought naval action was a tactical success but a strategic blunder, transformed through numerous newspaper reports into a 'massacre'. Stories circulated of sailors shot in the water as they swam for the shore; the mortar shells were condemned as immoral; the Tsar was accused of duplicity for widening the localised conflict in the Danubian principalities and seizing control of the Black Sea – leading the *Times* to fear he was converting it 'into a Russian lake' – while the British and French fleets remained idle in the Bosphorus. Palmerston, the Home Secretary, demanded that something 'be done to wipe away the stain' of dishonour and the *Times* called for a 'sterner alternative' to diplomacy. In early January British and French naval squadrons entered the Black Sea. Lord Aberdeen, the Prime Minister, attempted to calm the growing war fever but it was too late, and a *Punch* cartoon summed up the growing mood by depicting him blacking the Tsar's boots. Britain's naval pride was deemed to be at stake and it was insisted that the independence and integrity of the Ottoman Empire must be protected against the Russian despot. Even without the public fervour and clamour for a 'poke at old Nicholas', the drive to war was becoming inexorable especially since the allied squadrons could not now be withdrawn from the Black Sea without leaving Russia in control and capable of seizing Constantinople. Although Britain and France did not sign a treaty of alliance until 10 April, in January and February they issued warnings to Russia – her warships must return to Sebastopol and her army must withdraw from the Danubian principalities. When these demands were ignored, war was declared on 28 March 1854.

A year earlier Sir James Graham, the First Lord of the Admiralty, alarmed by the implications of Menshikov's mission to Con-

stantinople, had begun planning a two-pronged naval attack on
Russia, designed to achieve a quick victory without a massive
mobilisation of troops. In the north, a fleet was to be sent to the
Baltic to destroy the outlying coastal and island fortresses
defending St Petersburg and to blockade any Russian ships not
captured or destroyed. In the Black Sea, a second fleet was to
destroy Sebastopol, with the aid of a swift amphibious attack if
necessary. Together these forays would end Russian naval
dominance. In the event, neither of these plans was implemented
as immediately or successfully as Graham had hoped, in part
because he had never discussed them in detail with his cabinet
colleagues. Indeed, no serious practical preparations were made in
advance of the war; the small mortar and gun boats, vital for
success in the shallow waters around the Baltic forts, were not built
until the autumn of 1854 while the logistical implications of an
attack on Sebastopol were never fully thought through.

In December 1853 Graham had spoken publicly of the need to
destroy Sebastopol and begun tentative discussions with the Duke
of Newcastle, the Secretary of State for War and the Colonies, on
the possibility of a combined naval and military assault, but it was
decided that the defence of Constantinople was to take priority.
However, when Lord Raglan, the Commander-in-Chief of the
expeditionary force, left for Turkey in April Newcastle warned him
that the taking of Sebastopol might become essential to settle the
conflict. Even so, it was not until late June, after the Russians had
withdrawn from Turkish soil, that the cabinet finally decided to
proceed with the assault. Raglan, without reliable information on
the strength or disposition of the Russian forces and knowing his
own to be weakened by their time in Bulgaria, reluctantly acceded
to the orders of his political masters. By the time the French and
the British armies landed in the Crimea they were decimated by
disease and the British Commissariat was already in chaos. Meanwhile, the Russians had had time to strengthen their defences. The
planned two week assault in March 1854 was prolonged to a year-
long siege.

The Battle of Balaklava

By concentrating on the siege of Sebastopol itself, Raglan had ignored the threat posed by Menschikov's field army and made inadequate provision for defence of Balaclava. Nearest the harbour, on the high ground to the north-east, were six batteries of naval guns. Next, overlooking the south valley and covering the entrance to the gorge that led down to the port, were the 93rd Highlanders (about 700 men), plus a Turkish battalion, under Sir Colin Campbell, who had overall command of the defence. The outer defensive line consisted of six redoubts – all hastily dug and still incomplete. Five of these were on the crest of the Causeway Heights, which divided the north and south valleys, and along which ran the metalled Woronzov road – the main route up to Sebastopol. Numbered from east to west, redoubts 2 to 4 were each defended by approximately 300 inexperienced Turkish soldiers, manning two British 12-pounder naval guns under the supervision of a British gunner. Redoubts 5 and 6 were unfinished and unmanned. Redoubt 1 stood alone on Canrobert's Hill occupied by a force of about 600 Turks, also inexperienced, with three British 12-pounder naval guns, again supervised by a British gunner.

Beneath redoubt 6, at the western end of the south valley, were camped the cavalry commanded by Lord Lucan, independent of Campbell, comprising the Heavy Brigade under Sir James Scarlett and the Light Brigade under Lord Cardigan. Cardigan, 'The Noble Yachtsman', was frequently absent, dining and sleeping on his yacht every night, leaving his duties to be carried out by Lord George Paget. In contrast, Lord Lucan shared the same dismal conditions as his men. Attached to the cavalry were Captain Maude's Royal Horse Artillery, with four 6-pounder guns and two howitzers. The Sapoune Heights rose at right angles to the western end of the two valleys and here General Bosquet was camped; beyond these lay the Khersonese Uplands with Lord Raglan's headquarters and, further off still, the camps of the 1st and 4th divisions.

On the evening of 24 October, Campbell and Lucan forwarded to Raglan the report from a Turkish spy, warning that a Russian army of about 20,000 infantry and 5,000 cavalry plus artillery, led by General Liprandi, was marching towards Balaclava, determined to cut the British off from their supply lines. Raglan brushed this report aside. But just before 6 a.m. the next day, while riding down the south valley, Lucan and Paget noticed two warning flags flying over redoubt 1, followed almost immediately by gunfire. The Russian attack had begun. Lucan's unpopular habit of making the cavalry stand to at 5 a.m. every morning finally proved its value; he was able to move his brigades at once, east along the south valley, ready to face the Russians if they overran the redoubts, and deploy Maude's horse artillery on the heights near redoubt 2. But neither of these forces was effective against the superior fire power of the Russians armed with seventy-eight 12- and 18-pounder guns. Maude was badly wounded early on and, since their supplies had been diverted to the bombardment of Sebastopol, the ammunition soon ran out. Lacking immediate infantry support Lucan could do little apart from providing a show of strength, although he recorded that the Turks made 'a very respectable resistance'. Pounded by devastating artillery fire and outnumbered by more than twenty to one, they stood firm for nearly two hours after which redoubt 1 was finally stormed and some 170 men slaughtered. (All the British gunners escaped, most first spiking the guns so that they could not be turned against their own troops.) Seeing their compatriots cut down by the Cossack cavalry, even as they raised their arms in surrender, the Turks in redoubts 2 to 4 fled soon after, taking with them their meagre possessions, so setting in train the canard (repeated in Raglan's official despatch, which was widely published in the British press), that they had fled without resisting the Russians at all.

Although Lucan had sent a message immediately the attack began, Raglan did not arrive on the Sapoune Heights until just before the collapse of redoubt number one. Now only the Highlanders, a few naval guns and the cavalry, stood between the Russians and Balaclava. The distances and the terrain were such that no reinforcements could be expected from the Uplands for at least two hours. When he arrived on the ridge, Raglan had sent for the 1st and 4th divisions but the two Generals, the Duke of Cambridge and Cathcart, were slow to respond; Cathcart had been called out unnecessarily on a previous occasion and was reluctant to mobilise his men, who were newly returned from the trenches. Both arrived too late to take any effective part in the subsequent events. There was, however, some support from the French; Bosquet sent a detachment of the Chasseurs d'Afrique to stand by at the western end of the south valley. And about this time Cardigan joined his brigade.

As the Russians poured along the north valley and onto the Causeway Heights, Lucan could only retreat towards the cavalry camp, frustrated and angry that Raglan had failed to mobilise the infantry the previous evening. Working in close cooperation with Campbell he made a stand just west of the Highlanders where, as he later stated, the cavalry were 'well placed to take in [the] flank any Russian forces marching against Balaklava when, to my great discomfiture, I received from Lord Raglan an order ... "Cavalry to take ground to left of second line of redoubts occupied by Turks.".' Raglan had decided that the cavalry were in danger. Leaving the hard-pressed Highlanders isolated, they were to withdraw even further west, beyond the cavalry camp, to a point between the hillock on which stood redoubt 6 and the base of the Sapoune ridge. Their purported new role was to keep watch down the north valley 'and take advantage of any movement on the part of the enemy'. In practice, their view was restricted by the hillock to a few hundred yards only. This confusion was a foretaste of later trouble. Ominously, it revealed that Raglan, 700 feet above on the Sapoune Heights and looking down at the flattened panorama below him, never realised how little was visible to those in the valleys beneath him. Suddenly he changed his mind, possibly realising the strategic value of Lucan's original position, and ordered eight squadrons (600 men) of the Heavy Brigade to move back towards Balaclava to support the Turkish battalion with Campbell. For Lucan this was a further insult, the independent command of the cavalry appeared to have been taken out of his hands.

Meanwhile some 2,500 Russian cavalry had appeared on the Causeway Heights and four squadrons (400 men) broke away to advance rapidly on Balaclava. The Highlanders, arranged in two lines, had taken cover from the Russian artillery, lying down behind a slight incline. They were joined by about a hundred invalids from Balaclava and some of the surviving Turks from the first redoubt. Campbell addressed them: 'Remember there is no retreat from here. You must die where you stand'. Then, as they stood up, and it looked as though in their enthusiasm they would charge (and lose the advantage of the slope): '93rd! 93rd! Damn all that eagerness.' So they stood, waiting. The Russians 'in one grand line dashed at the Highlanders. The ground flies beneath their horses' feet; gathering speed at every stride, they dash on towards that thin red streak topped with a line of steel' (W. H. Russell). The Highlanders fired, the Russians wheeled to the left and charged again, but the Highlanders had turned to face them and fired again. Once more the Russians wheeled to the left and once more the well-disciplined line turned to face them and fired. Dispirited, the Russians retreated into the north valley, followed by the shouts of the Highlanders.

Within minutes of this triumph, the eight squadrons of the Heavy Brigade marching towards Balaclava realised that the rest of the Russian cavalry (about 2,000 men) were descending on them from the Causeway Heights. Scarlett halted the advance, turned his men to face them and prepared for his first battle. The Heavies, picking their way through a vineyard and the remains of the Light Brigade camp (which had been over-run by the Cossacks), were in disarray. While their officers brought them back into line as calmly as though on the parade ground, the Russian commander inexplicably stopped, only about a hundred yards distant. He may have intended to realign his troops, he may have feared an ambush – either way, it gave Scarlett the advantage he needed. The trumpet sounded and the Heavies charged up the hill, at little more than a trot over rough ground, broke through the stationary Russian forces and sent them flying to the top of the ridge. Their officers tried to rally them there, but the Horse Artillery opened fire and they fled in confusion into the north valley, where they later reformed at the eastern end. From the Sapoune Heights French and British cheers rang out – the immediate danger to Balaclava was over.

But this success was squandered and the momentum toward victory lost. Lucan, seeing that the Russians were about to attack, had ridden off to warn the Heavy Brigade, leaving Cardigan with the Light Brigade. Lucan believed he had instructed Cardigan 'to attack anything and everything that shall come within your reach'. Cardigan recalled it differently; he had been placed in that position by his superior officer 'with orders on no account to leave it, and to defend it against any attack of the Russians; they did not however approach the position'. As the Russians fled, Captain Morris, commanding the 17th Lancers, repeatedly begged to be allowed to charge and complete their destruction. Enraged that a junior 'Indian' officer should instruct him in tactics in front of his brigade, Cardigan refused. Officers and men were shocked and angry at this lost opportunity – not just of routing the enemy but of sharing in the glory of the moment. They had been outshone by the Heavies. Lucan sent Cardigan a strongly worded reprimand that angered him further. Nolan too was furious that a chance of proving the cavalry's worth had once again been thrown away through lack of initiative; a friend who spoke to him at this time recalled how 'under the stress of some great excitement he had lost self-command'.

Raglan now needed to follow up his success with some decisive move; the Russians were demoralised and an immediate attack was imperative. But still his infantry had not arrived. In the ensuing lull the Russians placed troops and guns on the Fedukhine Heights, occupied the redoubts abandoned by the Turks and regrouped their cavalry, fronted by cannon, at the farther end of the north valley. Intending that the cavalry should immediately attempt to retake the redoubts, Raglan sent his third order to Lucan, which reached him just before ten o'clock: 'Cavalry to advance and take advantage of any opportunity to recover the heights. They will be supported by the infantry, which have been ordered. Advance on two fronts.' Lucan, not surprisingly, read this as meaning he should await the arrival of the infantry. The cavalry had been protected for so long that he could not conceive of risking them on so foolhardy a venture unsupported and he contented himself by moving the Light Brigade round to the end of the north valley, leaving the Heavy Brigade in the south valley, so that they could eventually advance on two fronts. With his staff around him, he took his place between the two brigades on the lower slopes of the Causeway Heights. From there he could see the whole of the north valley but nothing of the redoubts he was supposed to recapture and, foolishly, he neglected to remedy this by sending out scouts to keep him informed of the enemy's movements on the Heights, leaving him open to criticism later. Many of the cavalry now dismounted and relaxed as they waited. By 11 o'clock the 1st Division had arrived but the 4th were still making their way into the south valley; neither infantry commander had been ordered to provide support for the cavalry. A few minutes later Nolan came furiously galloping up with a further order.

Up on the Sapoune Heights Raglan had been watching with rising anger the leisurely advance of the infantry, the cavalry lolling idly in the sun, and the Russians strengthening their position. His empty sleeve was seen to twitch, a sure sign of his rage. Suddenly one of his staff shouted that the Russians were carrying off the guns from the redoubts. This was the greatest insult possible. To lose your guns was to lose the battle and Wellington, Raglan's great hero, had never lost a gun. Desperate to prevent such a calamity, Raglan dictated to Airey a further order for Lucan: 'Lord Raglan wishes the cavalry to advance rapidly to the front – follow the enemy and try to prevent the enemy carrying away the guns – Troop Horse Artillery may accompany – French Cavalry is on your left. R. Airey Immediate'. Raglan later claimed that this was to be read in conjunction with the previous order – sent almost an hour earlier – and needed no further elucidation as to which guns were meant. But nothing in the later order indicates this link.

Raglan chose Nolan, Airey's ADC, to deliver the order because he was the most accomplished rider present, capable of picking his way swiftly down the steep slope. It was a fatal choice, not least because Nolan was known to despise Lucan. And as he shot off, Raglan called after him, 'Tell Lord Lucan the cavalry is to attack immediately', the very words Nolan had longed to hear since the start of the campaign. Lucan received the note with amazement. The order seemed in direct contradiction to his reading of the previous one – was he now to advance without infantry support? Naturally he began to question Nolan, urging the dangers and uselessness of such an attack, but Nolan rudely interrupted him 'in a most authoritative tone', repeating Raglan's final words. Stung to anger, the always irascible Lucan peremptorily demanded more information – 'Attack, sir! Attack what? What guns?' Nolan, with an insolence that shocked all those present and 'in a most disrespectful but significant manner, pointing to the further end of the valley', replied: 'There my Lord, is your enemy; there are your guns!' The furious Lucan, accepting the convention that an ADC spoke with the authority of his general officer, questioned him no further but turned away and reluctantly gave the orders to prepare to advance down the valley. When Cardigan, still smarting from their former altercation, objected, pointing out the foolishness of such an attack with the battery ahead of them and the batteries and riflemen on ether flank, Lucan replied that they had no choice but to obey Raglan's order. Perhaps if they had been on better terms the brothers-in-law might have discussed the matter, but they had been too long estranged. Cardigan saluted and turned away, muttering as he went, 'Well, here goes the last of the Brudenells'. Within minutes the Light Brigade began their fatal charge.

Fanny's description clearly reveals the horror of those watching as they saw their friends and colleagues ride, not to attack the redoubts as they had expected, but straight at the enemy guns. As the charge began, Nolan, who had joined his friend Captain Morris in the first line some ten yards behind Cardigan, suddenly spurred forward and took the lead, shouting and waving his sword. Whether he was trying to change the direction of the charge to the right toward the redoubts (as suggested by Kinglake twelve years later and repeated frequently ever since), or to increase the pace so the troopers would break more efficiently through the Russian guns, will never be known – almost immediately he was killed by a splinter from an exploding shell. He was the first of 110 men to be killed, 130 more were wounded and 58 taken prisoner. In all 362 horses died or had to be shot. The Chasseurs d'Afrique also sustained casualties (10 dead and 28 wounded) as they came to their aid; they attacked a Russian battery of eight guns and drove them off the Fedukhine Heights. Lucan, leading the Heavy Brigade, revealed an unexpected initiative, when he halted them (at a point where they could protect the retreat of the light cavalry), as 'any further advance would have exposed them to destruction'; they had already lost more men than during their earlier charge. This later earned him censure from some of the Light Brigade who felt they had been abandoned to fight alone. Indeed, the major criticism of many of those taking part was not against the original confusion over the order but the lack of back-up. They had broken through the Russian cavalry, pursued them for some distance, trapping them with their backs to the Tchernaya river, and had even succeeded in capturing two guns. But all they had achieved was lost without additional help from the Heavies and the infantry. They had to turn and fight their way back up the valley.

After the survivors of the charge had struggled back it was five hours before they were allowed to return to the crushed remains of their camp, though little further action occurred during this time. The Russians withdrew from redoubts 4 and 5 (the latter was occupied by Turkish troops, 4 by a part of Cathcart's division), but they still held the more strategically important redoubts 1 to 3, and thus retained control of the Causeway Heights and the Woronzov road. Cathcart had no intention of attempting to take these, with his exhausted troops, unless specifically ordered to do so. Raglan wished to attack them but was dissuaded by the more cautious Canrobert who argued that if they were taken (possibly with many further casualties), they could only be held by diverting experienced troops from the siege work, which he saw as the core of the campaign. Raglan once again deferred to his French allies, against his better judgement, for the sake of harmony. Neither Commander seems to have appreciated that now, without access to the Woronzov road, all the equipment and supplies from Balaclava to the camps on the Uplands would have to be carried up the muddy, unmade road via the bottleneck of the Col, causing suffering and loss of life to men and animals throughout the winter months and, in addition, deflecting many men from the siege work.

There has been much discussion as to who bears the final responsibility for this disaster – Raglan who gave the original order; Airey who scribbled it down; Nolan who delivered it; Lucan who ordered the charge; or Cardigan who led the charge. Cardigan could probably have done little to change events even if he had not been feuding with Lucan, who was excessively obstinate. He swiftly deflected, onto Lucan, Raglan's initial accusation that he had lost the Light Brigade – he was, after all, obeying an order from his senior officer. His later troubles were of his own making, for, after leading the charge with impeccable courage, he abandoned his men (see p. 281, note 25). Paget, for one, never forgave him and he was publicly mocked, behind his back, by the 8th Hussars.

Lucan bore the brunt of Raglan's wrath and his furious rebuttals of Raglan's accusations finally led to his recall to England and the loss of his command. He, too, had been obeying an order from his senior officer, but Raglan was determined to prove that he had misinterpreted it. In fact the intended meaning of the order, to advance on the redoubts, uphill over rough ground against Russian infantry, artillery and cavalry without support, would probably have resulted in just as many casualties as the ensuing charge. It was a foolish order, and an imprecise and ambiguous order, which, when questioned, was open to re-interpretation. Nolan's actions, repeating the verbal order to attack immediately and then pointing toward the Russian guns, certainly indicated that Raglan's intended target was the Russian guns not the redoubts. Nolan's motives and meaning were not questioned at the time. It was assumed by all those present, including his friend Morris with whom he waited for the order to advance, that he knew the cavalry were to charge the Russian guns. He may have believed that this was Raglan's intention. He had not seen the previous order, but he had been briefed by Airey and Raglan before leaving the Sapoune Heights and it is possible that, in his over-excited state, he seized the opportunity provided by Lucan's confusion to prove his theory – that charging cavalrymen could break through a battery and capture the guns. Either way, he was largely responsible for the disastrous outcome. If he had been less angry and less contemptuous of Lucan, he could have explained the order with one simple sentence. And if Lucan had been a calmer man, he might have questioned Nolan further and then, if he had discovered that Nolan had deliberately changed the order, there might well have been a different outcome. But the written and the verbal orders both demanded immediate action, so Lucan carried out an order with which he disagreed without thoroughly checking its validity, and for that he must bear some blame.

But the major share of the blame belongs to Raglan. He was responsible for the flawed order that precipitated the tragedy. He dictated it to Airey and on hearing it read out made only one alteration – he added the word 'Immediate'. When choosing Nolan, rather than his own ADC, as the messenger he must have known of his antagonism toward Lucan and should have realised that he was overwrought and unfit for such a task. But he was angry with Lucan for ignoring his previous order and impatient for action, so he sent Nolan on his way with words that could only inflame him further. From the start he tried to shift the blame – first on to Cardigan and then to Lucan, telling the latter that as a Lieutenant-General he should have used his 'discretion, and not approving of the charge, should not have made it', an action that would itself have brought censure. His official despatch to Newcastle is more devious. Ignoring all mention of his spoken command, he wrote that from 'some misconception of the instruction to advance, the Lieutenant-General considered that he was bound to attack at all hazards', thus implying that Lucan was incapable of understanding or following orders. He elaborated further in a private letter in which he accused Lucan of making a fatal mistake by not linking the two orders, never mentioned his final instructions to Nolan and ignored the part that Nolan played in Lucan's decision. All this implied that he was well aware that his imprecise order, given to an impetuous messenger incapable of delivering it in a rational manner, was the true cause of the disaster.

Like many another military blunder, all this controversy might soon have been forgotten, discussed only by military historians and the families of the participants, if Russell had not written such a vivid and detailed account of the heroism of the day – concluding with the words 'our Light Brigade was annihilated by their own rashness'. This sparked Tennyson's imagination and his poem 'The Charge of the Light Brigade' – containing the much quoted phrase 'Someone had blunder'd' – was published in December. It was an immediate success and for over a century its dramatic narrative and easy rhythm made it a popular choice for children to learn by heart, ensuring that the 'glorious and fatal charge' is still remembered.

Books Referred to
and Further Reading

Adkin, Mark: *The Charge*. London 1996.

Cadogan, Sir George: *Cadogan's Crimea* (illustrations, with text by Somerset J. Gough Calthorpe). London 1979.

Chapman, Roger: *Echoes from the Crimea*. Green Howards Museum, 2004.

Currie, Frank: *Letters from the Crimea 1854-56*. London 1899.

Dallas, George: *Eyewitness in the Crimea: The Crimean War Letters (1854-56) of Lt Col George Frederick Dallas*, edited by Michael Hargreave Mawson. London 2001.

Demidov, Anatolii Nikolaevich: *Travels in Southern Russia and the Crimea; Through Hungary, Wallachia and Moldavia during the year 1837*. Eng. trans, 2 vols., London 1853.

Duberly, Frances Isabella: *Campaigning Experiences in Central India and Rajpootana during the Suppression of the Mutiny*. London 1859.

Fenton, Roger: [Photographs of the Crimean War]. 2 vols., Manchester 1856.

Gernsheim, Helmut and Alison: *Roger Fenton, his Photographs and Letters from the Crimea*. London 1954.

Godman, Temple: *The Fields of War: A Young Cavalryman's Crimea Campaign*. London c.1977.

Hawley, Robert Beaufoy: *The Hawley Letters: The Letters of Captain R. B. Hawley, 89th, from the Crimea, December 1954 to August 1856*. London 1970.

Hibbert, Christopher: *The Destruction of Lord Raglan: A Tragedy of the Crimean War 1854-5*. London 1961.

Hodge, Edward: *'Little Hodge', being Extracts from the Diaries and Letters of Colonel Edward Cooper Hodge written during the Crimean War*. London 1971.

Kelly, Richard Denis: *An Officer's Letters to his Wife during the Crimean War*. London 1902.

'Lettres de Crimée du Capitaine de Berthois' in *Carnet de la Sabretache N°414*, Juin 1956.

Kinglake, Alexander William: *The Invasion of the Crimea: Its Origins and an Account of its Progress down to the Death of Lord Raglan*. 8 vols., Edinburgh 1863-87.

Lambert, Andrew & Badsey, Stephen: *War Correspondents – The Crimean War*. London 1994.

Massie, Alastair: *The National Army Museum Book of the Crimean War - The Untold Stories*. London 2004.

Murray, Eustace Clare Grenville: *The Roving Englishman in Turkey*. London 1855.

Pack, Reynell: *Sebastopol Trenches and Five Months in them*. London 1878.

Paget, Lord George Augustus: *The Light Cavalry Brigade in the Crimea; Extracts from the Letters and Journal of Lord George Paget*. London.

Portal, Robert: *Letters from the Crimea, 1854-55*. Winchester 1900.

Rappaport, Helen: *'No Place for Ladies': The Untold Story of Women in the Crimean War*. Aurum Press, February 2007.

Rawlins, James: *One Hussar: His Journal 1853-1863*. Birmingham(?) 1985.

Russell, William Howard: *The Great War with Russia*. London 1895.

Seacole, Mary: *The Wonderful Adventures of Mrs Seacole in Many Lands*. London 1857.

Sweetman, John: *The Crimean War*. London 2001.

Tisdall, E. E. P.: *Mrs Duberly's Campaigns: An Englishwoman's Experiences in the Crimean War and Indian Mutiny*. London 1963.

Woodham-Smith, Cecil: *The Reason Why*. London 1953.

Acknowledgements

I am indebted to many friends and colleagues for their help while writing this book. First, I wish to thank the staff of the Bodleian Library for their assistance over many years; with particular thanks to Helen Rogers and Vera Ryhajlo in the Upper Reading Room, whose cheerful welcome always eased me into work, and to Sally Chestnutt in the Music Room, who patiently guided me through many catalogues. The staff in the Manuscript Room of the British Library were consistently helpful and the staff of the National Army Museum library answered my queries on military matters.

Major Patrick Timmons, Curator of The Queen's Royal Hussars' Collection, generously devoted time to showing me their archive and the regimental treasures. Catherine Morris followed up references to reviews of the 1855 edition of the *Journal* in the Colindale Newspaper Library.

I have enjoyed lively conversations and exchanges of information with Helen Rappaport; I'm particularly grateful to her for introducing me to the letters of Capitaine de Berthois. I also wish to thank other friends who have generously given their time, including Petra and Jeremy Lewis for help with the initial stages of the Introduction and Stella and Michael Irwin for a close reading of the final draft. Vicky Clouston provided continual support; she not only read successive drafts but produced excellent translations of the Berthois letters and the song, "L'Amazone".

I also thank my editor Matthew Cotton and the staff of Oxford University Press for so efficiently seeing the book through the final stages of production.

I owe special thanks to John Kelly for his unstinting generosity in commenting not only on the main text but also on the footnotes, even when submerged in his own. And I owe much to the enthusiastic support of my father, the late Michael Rahilly, R.N., who commented on the successive drafts and provided me with valuable information on ordnance and naval matters. I should point out, however, that any blunders, military or otherwise, are my own.

Above all I owe a great debt of gratitude to James Price who initiated this edition and has been closely involved in its development to the end. He was a constant friend and generous editor throughout our time working together. This book is dedicated to him.

ROSINE

L'AMAZONE

2 MÉLODIES

Pour Chant avec acc.' de PIANO

Nº1, Rosine.   Nº 2 L'Amazone.

Nº ___

PAR

LUIGI BORDÈSE

— k

Mayence, les fils de B. SCHOTT   Bruxelles, SCHOTT frères.
Londres, SCHOTT et Cⁱᵉ   82, Montagne de la Cour
Propriété des Editeurs   Déposé
Lith. H. Katto r d'Isabelle S Bruxⁱ

'When I get home, I will have the polka that the 97ieme de la ligne wrote for me. "L'Amazone" with *such* a woman, on *such* a horse, . . . written for and dedicee a Madame Duberly.' The chorus runs: 'Je saute en selle et je trone des que je reprend l'etrier chacun se dit quelle Amazone, voyez, voyez donc cet air cavalier! de bravos concert general pour la femme . . . A l'Anglaise'. (see p. 293)

Index

Figures in **bold** indicate biographical note

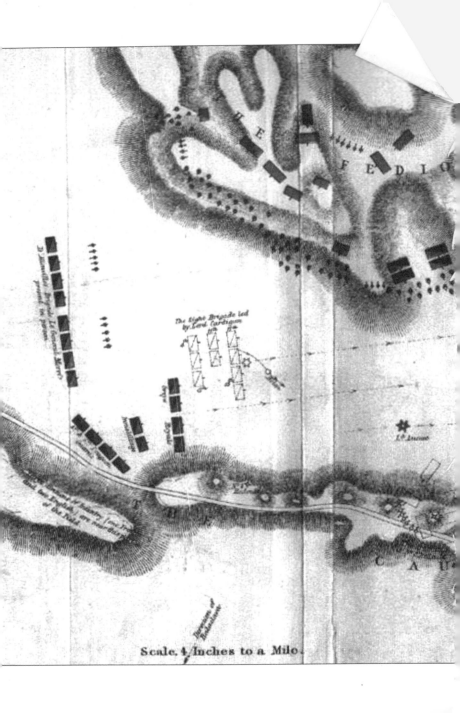

The Right Brigade led
by Lord Cardigan

1.st Avenue

Scale. 4 Inches to a Mile.